Islam and Asia

Chiara Formichi explores the ways in which Islam and Asia have shaped each other's histories, societies, and cultures from the seventh century to today. Challenging the assumed dominance of the Middle East in the development of Islam, Formichi argues for Asia's centrality in the development of global Islam as a religious, social, and political reality. Readers learn how and why Asia is central to the history of Islam, and vice versa, considering the impact of Asia's Muslims on Islam, how Islam became an integral part of Asia, and its influence on local conceptions of power, the sciences, arts, and bureaucracy. Grounding her argument in specific case studies, Formichi ultimately concludes that the existence of Islamized interactions across Asia have allowed for multidirectional influences on Islamic practices and interpretations throughout the Muslim world.

CHIARA FORMICHI is Associate Professor at Cornell University. Her publications include *Islam and the Making of the Nation: Kartosuwiryo and Political Islam in Twentieth-Century Indonesia* (2012).

New Approaches to Asian History

This dynamic new series publishes books on the milestones in Asian history, those that have come to define particular periods or to mark turning points in the political, cultural, and social evolution of the region. The books in this series are intended as introductions for students to be used in the classroom. They are written by scholars whose credentials are well-established in their particular fields and who have, in many cases, taught the subject across a number of years.

A list of books in the series can be found at the end of the volume.

Islam and Asia

A History

Chiara Formichi

Cornell University

CAMBRIDGE
UNIVERSITY PRESS

University Printing House, Cambridge CB2 8BS, United Kingdom

One Liberty Plaza, 20th Floor, New York, NY 10006, USA

477 Williamstown Road, Port Melbourne, VIC 3207, Australia

314–321, 3rd Floor, Plot 3, Splendor Forum, Jasola District Centre, New Delhi – 110025, India

79 Anson Road, #06–04/06, Singapore 079906

Cambridge University Press is part of the University of Cambridge.

It furthers the University's mission by disseminating knowledge in the pursuit of education, learning, and research at the highest international levels of excellence.

www.cambridge.org
Information on this title: www.cambridge.org/9781107106123
DOI: 10.1017/9781316226803

First published 2020

Printed in the United Kingdom by TJ International Ltd. Padstow Cornwall

A catalogue record for this publication is available from the British Library.

Library of Congress Cataloging-in-Publication Data
Names: Formichi, Chiara, 1982- author.
Title: Islam and Asia : a history / Chiara Formichi.
Description: New York, NY, USA : Cambridge University Press, 2020. |
    Series: New approaches to Asian history | Includes bibliographical
    references and index.
Identifiers: LCCN 2019040425 (print) | LCCN 2019040426 (ebook) |
    ISBN 9781107106123 (hardback) | ISBN 9781107513976 (paperback) |
    ISBN 9781316226803 (epub)
Subjects: LCSH: Islam–Asia–History.
Classification: LCC BP63.A1 F67 2020 (print) | LCC BP63.A1 (ebook) |
    DDC 297.095–dc23
LC record available at https://lccn.loc.gov/2019040425
LC ebook record available at https://lccn.loc.gov/2019040426

ISBN 978-1-107-10612-3 Hardback
ISBN 978-1-107-51397-6 Paperback

To my students

Contents

Figures

Maps

Boxes

Sources

Preface

This book offers a transregional approach to the intersection of Islam and developments in other spheres of the human experience across Asia. Here Asia is broadly conceptualized as the territorial expanse from the Mediterranean to the Pacific; and although I include recurrent references to the "greater Middle East region" as "West Asia," the main focus of this book lies with the lands beyond the Oxus/Amu Darya river – in cruder terms, all that lies east of contemporary Iran.

My primary interest is in offering the big picture of how and why Asia beyond the Oxus/Amu Darya river is central to the history of Islam, and vice versa. The materials presented cover a vast territory and a wide chronological span, during which these lands saw many social, religious, economic, and political transformations; any one reader is likely to think that something is missing, but I had no intention of achieving encyclopedic coverage. As I endeavored to capture the interplay of these changes across time and space, offering selected but rich and detailed examples, the main narrative threads are thematic, secondarily bounded by temporal considerations, with an evident bias toward the late modern and contemporary eras. In terms of geography, the "units" of reference necessarily fluctuate, depending on the historical period of analysis, ranging from transregional bird's-eye views of "Asia" to patchwork colonial possessions and clearly defined nation-states. Because the primary lens of each chapter is thematic, most chapters address a selection of locales, depending on what I saw as most illustrative of the matter at hand, and sometimes also to provide some degree of continuity across chapters. Hence, whereas I have attempted a balanced coverage of Asia's subregions – defined as Central, South, East, and Southeast – with relevant references to the Muslim Mediterranean, this book is by no means a complete survey of "Islam" in each and every polity/nation in "Asia." Similarly, not all themes could be addressed to the same depth. I have tended to favor political history, with a nod to intellectual and social phenomena, but – for example – issues of race and racialization of Islam are not addressed in a systematic fashion, and imperialism only takes a background role; much to my regret I was not able to include a fair elaboration of the impact of Islam (and Europe, in fact) on renegotiation of traditionally fluid sexual identities, but the role of women is integrated into the narrative through most chapters.

The theoretical contribution of this book is in its approach, in its endeavor to bring together two fields that have rarely (and only recently) spoken to each other – namely Islamic Studies and Asian Studies, as addressed in Chapter 9 – and to present an interwoven history that gives each of these two subjects due consideration. Hence, while this takes the form of a "history book," written by a historian for readers interested in understanding the historical trajectories of Islam across the Asian expanse from the seventh century onwards, the methodology deployed has more affinity with the field of "Area Studies," which I see as deeply rooted in and committed to multi-disciplinarity. The scholarship this book is grounded in, and the materials used throughout, hail from the "traditional" field of history as well as the fields of anthropology, archaeology, history of art and architecture, religious studies, political sciences, cultural studies, and more.

Beyond this theoretical intervention in the study of Islam and Asia, I intend for this volume to be accessible, useful to teachers and students at all levels, scholars of global history, and lay readers. Related to this intention was my choice not to delve too deeply into scholarly debates and theoretical approaches specific to any given subtopic addressed in the book. The "Further Reading" sections that conclude each chapter are curated lists of classic or recent scholarly works that can help readers further explore both the debates I tangentially touch upon and the details of the subject matter.

The book can be read from cover to cover, or one could pick sections through the book to follow the history of Islam in a specific subregion of Asia; individual chapters could be extracted from the book as inserts in a variety of syllabi, or a lecturer could offer any chapter's opening image and related text as a starting point for their own class. In whichever way you peruse this volume, I hope it will enhance your understanding of how and why Islam and Asia have been two intersecting subjects for the past 1,400 years.

Acknowledgments

As an undergraduate student majoring in Islamic Studies and with a keen interest in Southeast Asia, I often felt bounded by the structural limits of my department and by the discipline more broadly. Even in the most adventurous instances, a line seemed to exist coterminous with the usage of the Urdu language. But my professors encouraged me to follow that interest, to "cross" that line, and to explore what they saw as "the peripheries" of Islam.

Over the years I have incurred more debts than I could ever repay; this is only an attempt to acknowledge a few of them.

I am thankful to my earliest teachers at the Facolta' di Studi Orientali, Universita' di Roma La Sapienza, *Professore* Francesco Noci and *Professoressa* Biancamaria Scarcia Amoretti, who constantly reminded me with their own work that Islam stretched much further than the Arab lands. To *Professore* Gianmaria Piccinelli for supporting me in my desire to explore Indonesia for my *tesi di laurea*. To William-Gervase Clarence Smith, who at SOAS first gave me guidance in thinking about Indonesia as an integral and legitimate part of the "Muslim world" and who exposed me to global history as a field. And to Michael Feener, who since my postdoctoral fellowship in Singapore has pushed me to broaden my perspective, thinking regionally and comparatively.

A more specific intellectual debt rests with Ilyse Morgenstein Fuerst and Zahra Ayubi, who in April 2015 invited me to participate in the conference "Shifting Boundaries: The Study of Islam in the Humanities" at the University of Vermont, Burlington. This was the first opportunity I had to express my discomfort with the Arab-centric approach of Islamic Studies beyond the confines of my classroom. The conversations and collaborations that have since ensued have made this book and its larger framework much stronger than they would otherwise have been.

This book would not even have been conceived without Lucy Rhymer. Her work as Commissioning Editor at Cambridge University Press has been extraordinary. She first approached me when I was an Assistant Professor in Hong Kong, asking if I would be interested in writing a book based on my teaching of courses on "Islam in Asia." Since that day much has happened – a transcontinental move, a marriage, a child, and working toward tenure – but Lucy did not relent. Some of the final edits were dealt with at my grandmother's bedside. She never really understood what I was doing, and I had hoped that this book would help; alas, it came too late.

I am most grateful to those colleagues and friends who read the manuscript when it was still in draft form. From Eric Tagliacozzo (who got "first dibs," reading the very first semi-complete draft), to David Kloos (whose thoughts on Chapter 8 have been absolutely crucial), to the anonymous readers whose feedback was constructive and truly helped make this a better piece of scholarship, and to Michael Feener, Rian Thum, and David Atwill, who participated in a Manuscript Development Workshop I was able to host thanks to the financial support of Cornell University's College of Arts and Sciences. Their input and detailed feedback have been invaluable. Broader thanks go to all the colleagues whose amazing scholarly work has allowed me to rethink how we approach the study of Islam in Asia. Without the painstaking work of detail done in the field, broader "approach" endeavors would not be possible. All mistakes remain nonetheless mine.

The "big push" to fine-tune the conceptualization of the book and get a few core chapters written took place at the Asia Research Institute (National University of Singapore). I am most grateful to Kenneth Dean and Jonathan Rigg for facilitating my return to Singapore, hosting me as a visiting senior fellow during a semester of study leave from Cornell University.

The Production team at Cambridge was extremely patient and helpful, as we navigated the usual difficulties of getting a manuscript together, exacerbated by my desire to have many maps and to integrate illustrations in the narrative. Thanks go also to Getty Images, the Stiftung Bibliotheca Afghanica, the Collection Nationaal Museum van Wereldculturen, the Herbert F. Johnson Museum of Art at Cornell University, the Asian Civilization Museum of Singapore, and Kees Metselaar for providing the beautiful images that accompany this book.

For actually having the time and brain space for the necessary everyday thinking, reading, and writing, I owe more than I can say to my family. My husband, Eli, and daughter, Licia, got "shipped off" to Singapore for a semester, and then "sequestered" in Ithaca for a long summer and (even longer) winter, so that I could put the manuscript together. My mother and my in-laws were similarly displaced and "enlisted to help" when we needed it. I acknowledge that this is a privilege in an age when being an academic almost always entails moving and settling far away from our support networks. Thank you for allowing me to pursue my intellectual work while choosing to have a family.

I wrote these pages thinking about my students. The ideas and approaches presented in the following pages were shaped during the years I spent teaching courses on "Islam in Asia" in classrooms in Hong Kong and Ithaca. It was in that effort to make deep scholarly complexities digestible and understandable to my students that these thoughts developed and came together; it was in the everyday conversations that questions were formulated, and that answers were attempted; and it was in seminar discussions that scholarship was explored, dissected, challenged, and embraced. It is thus to my students that I dedicate this book.

Note on Transliteration and Foreign Terms

This book covers a wide geographical, linguistic, and historical span. In an attempt to bridge accuracy and accessibility, I have opted for a single (simplified) approach to the transliteration of "Islamic" terms. There are no diacritic marks. I have avoided placing an "h" at the end of words that in Arabic terminate with a *ta marbuta* (hence, *da'wa*, not *da'wah*), and I have not differentiated between '*ayn* and *hamza*, both being rendered with an apostrophe. I have compressed all regional variations into one consistent rendering (hence, the Indo-Malay term *dakwa* has become *da'wa*), making exceptions for quoted materials. Words that have entered the English language have been rendered in their English form, without italicization. All dates are indicated in the Common Era calendar.

Maps

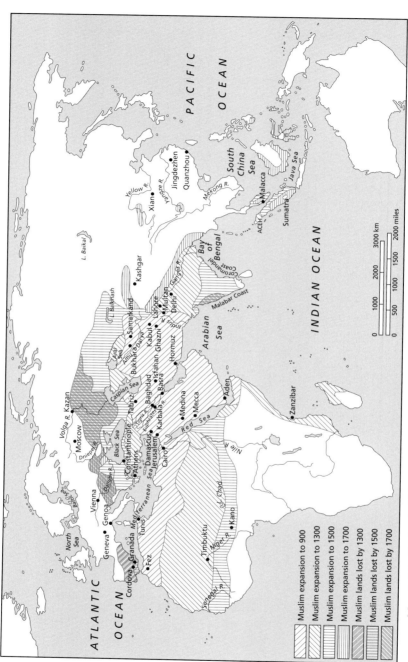

Map 1 Muslim lands 900–1700

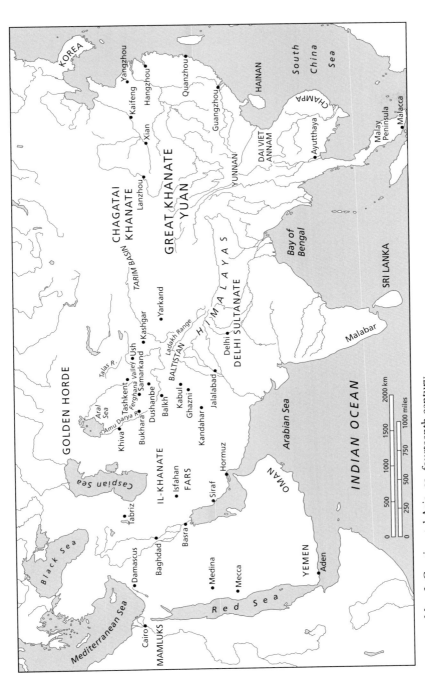

Map 2 Continental Asia, ca. fourteenth century

Map 3 Southeast Asia and coastal China

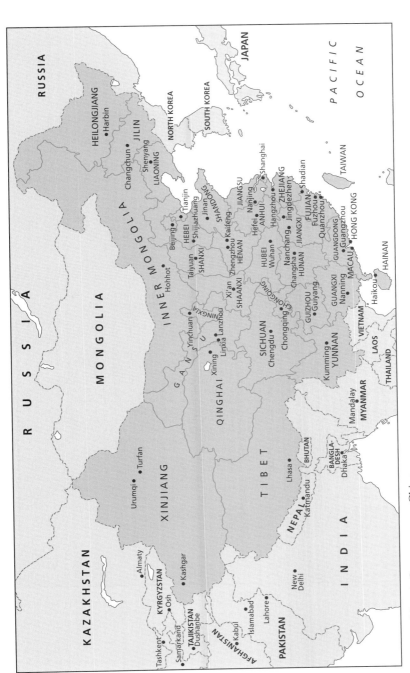

Map 4 Contemporary China

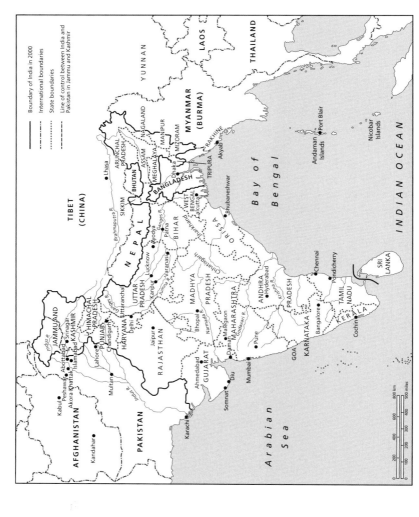

Map 5 Greater South Asia

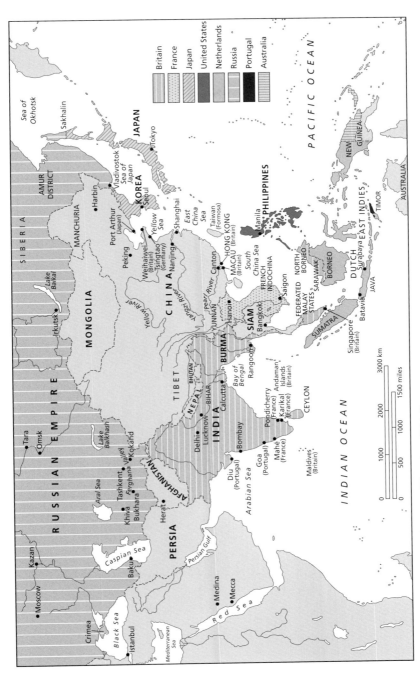

Map 6 Asia in the age of Empires (1914)

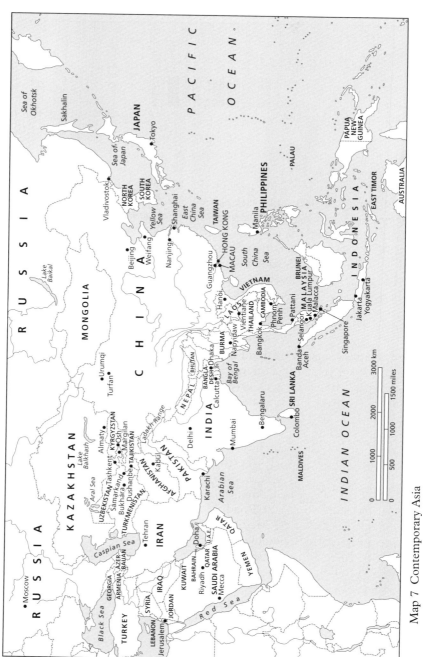

Map 7 Contemporary Asia

Introduction

"I'll never forgive myself," laments Professor Henry Jones Senior after hitting Junior with a large vase on the head. The subsequent scenes in *Indiana Jones and the Last Crusade* clarify that the Professor's concern was not directed at his son – who had, after all, come to save him from Nazi captivity – but at the damage inflicted on what appeared to be a fine exemplar of blue-and-white Chinese porcelain.

The underglaze porcelain with blue decorations on a white background, often reproducing floral patterns, has come to identify an aesthetic that is quintessentially Chinese (especially characteristic of the Ming dynasty, 1368–1644), but in fact Chinese ware functioned as a vehicle for assimilation and transmission of aesthetic choices across Asia and was highly prized abroad from the fifteenth century. Within a century, European manufacturers had learned how to imitate the Chinese technique, giving form to several regional variations, from Tuscany's Medici porcelain to England's Wedgwood *chinoiserie* and the Dutch Delftware. Such transformation further dissipated and obfuscated the genesis of this form; the origins of what are commonly held to be the archetypal Chinese aesthetics are in fact primarily rooted in the history of China's trade with West Asia (the term used in this book to refer to the Middle East), and in Asia as a space of Islamized connections.

Exchanges between China, Persia, and West Asia had occurred for centuries along the Silk Road, the informal network of routes and peoples connecting the Mediterranean to eastern Asia across the Eurasian continent, with notable hubs in Samarkand (Uzbekistan) and Xi'an (China); these links were further reinforced as the Muslim Abbasid dynasty (750–1258), based in Damascus and Baghdad, expanded so far east that it brushed against Tang China (618–907) (see Map 1). Hence, Chinese earthenware had been both common and a continuous source of fascination and admiration. An Arab merchant, Sulayman, wrote of his amazement at looking through a Chinese bottle: "[They] have the transparency of glass bottles; water in these vases is visible through them–and yet they are made of clay!"[1] In fact, while the Islamic Empire had achieved great refinement in courtly and literary cultures, West Asian ceramics were of unsophisticated quality, their kilns being unable to reach the high temperatures needed for glazing.

A primary motor was the desire to acquire beautiful ceramics, but wealthy Arab, Persian, and Turkic Muslims were also drawn to these foreign luxury goods by a commitment to Islamic propriety, as the traditions of Muhammad (*ahadith*, or sayings of the Prophet) warned Muslims against eating and drinking from silver and gold vessels.[2]

But if West Asian Muslims marveled at the sophisticated technique of Chinese ceramics, the somber monochromatic aesthetic embraced by the Song dynasty (960–1279) was of little interest to them, as they had inherited a tradition of color and decoration. This disjuncture between Eastern and Western Asian ideals of beauty became increasingly aggravating as in the twelfth to thirteenth centuries power shifts in West Asia had swollen the demand for luxury items and thus the volume of trade across Asia. Supported by the Mongol founding of the port city of Hormuz on the Persian Gulf, direct relations between West Asia and China were established via South and Southeast Asia, within maritime routes connecting through the Indian Ocean and now complementing the long-established Silk Road.

Among the several towns along the southern coast of China, it was the Fujian port city of Quanzhou (known to the Arabs as Zaytun) that would emerge as the most important site of exchange. Capitalizing on the presence of Muslim residents in the region – attested by the steles and gazetteers of mosques since at least the tenth century – at the turn of the millennium the Song elected Quanzhou as their trade tax collection office. This not only resulted in an increase in the general presence of Muslims, but it also encouraged further interaction between China and West Asia in terms of trade, religion, and aesthetics (see Source 1.3).

So it was that Muslim merchants in Quanzhou embarked on an innovative enterprise, sponsoring kilners in nearby Jingdezhen to experiment with new colors and motifs. The most successful of these customizations was the reproduction of patterns found on metalwork, carpets, and textiles purchased in West Asia by using an application of "Persian cobalt." It was particularly hard for Chinese kilners to get hold of cobalt, as the lapis lazuli rock from which it was extracted could only be found in Ghazni (Afghanistan) and Asia Minor (today's Turkey);[3] but its importance in meeting the desires of West Asian buyers made the effort compelling.

Already known as an important hub of international trade, Jingdezhen would eventually become the main center of "blue-and-white" ceramics in the Yuan dynasty (1271–1368), when these products were almost exclusively made for the export markets of West and Southeast Asia; archaeological evidence has in fact been found in Iraq, Egypt, Turkey, Iran, Indonesia, and the Southern Philippines. But by the early fifteenth century, the Xuande Ming emperor (r. 1426–1435) had himself abandoned the more somber Song monochromatic style and embraced this innovation, leading to "the Chinese adopt[ing] the traditional aesthetic values of the Middle East";[4] this came with a subtle but explicit acknowledgment of the impact of Islam on Chinese culture, as this specific shade of blue took the name of *sumawi qing* ("sky blue," from the Arabic) or *huihui qing*, i.e. "Muslim blue."

Let's take a few steps back and look at the bigger picture. The story of the origins of blue-and-white porcelain is not just one of intra-Asian connections, or of long-lasting Islamic influence on China. This is also a story of how Muslim merchants operating in East Asia, outside established networks of Islamic knowledge or authority, and even outside what is conventionally seen as the territorial purview of Islamic influence, intervened "as Muslims," solving a problem seemingly belonging to the "non-sacred" by applying their religious sensibility and identity.

It is this narrative that identifies and connects those historical moments when "Asia" came to be touched by Islam as a cultural phenomenon (not just as a religious system), and in which "Islam" came to be touched by peoples who originated from the *ma wara' an-nahr* – i.e. "that which is across the river," an Arabic figure of speech used to refer to the lands across the Oxus/Amu Darya, the river that today separates Turkmenistan from Uzbekistan – that constitutes the core of this book. Through these encounters, not only did Islam take root across Asia, manifesting contextualized orthodoxy and orthopraxy, but also the production of Islamic knowledge in Arabia received (and still receives) active and conscious contributions from the lands across the river.

Looking at Islam and Asia as two intersecting entities, the following chapters propose that the history of "Muslim Asia" is a narrative of how this continental and insular expanse emerged as an interconnected space, linking the Mediterranean to the Pacific; how the cultures and identities of its peoples became characterized, among other elements, by a shared sense of belonging to a community defined by religious commitment, an *umma* ("community"; see Box 0.1); and how Asia's Muslims did not passively practice "Islam" as a foreign religion, but actively contributed to its devotional practices and knowledge production.

Box 0.1   The *Umma* in the Qur'an

Our Lord, make us devoted to You; make our descendants into a community [*umma*] devoted to You. Show us how to worship and accept our repentance, for You are the Ever Relenting, the Most Merciful. (Q 2:128)

With these words the Qur'an sanctions the *umma* as a community of believers whose piety is directed toward Allah, "The God." Initially a very localized community (in Mecca first and Medina next), this *umma* eventually reached East and West after the death of Muhammad. And even in their movements, shaping each other's worldviews, Muslims consolidated that sense of a self-aware community united in a common devotion.

But in the Qur'an the boundaries of this "community of believers" move, ranging from including the entire humankind (Q 10:19) to exclusively marking Muslims as "the best community" (Q 3:110). In order to make sense of these transformations – which are not exclusive to the term *umma*, incidentally – we ought to think about the Qur'an beyond its current textual form and as an oral narration that occurred through time, while the sociopolitical status of Muhammad and his followers changed, and as an oral tradition that was only later codified in a written text.

It is narrated that Muhammad had retired on Mount Hira to meditate, when he heard a voice, "*iqra*": "[1]Read! In the name of your Lord who created: [2]He created man from a clinging form. [3]Read! Your Lord is the Most Bountiful One [4]who taught by [means of] the pen, [5]who taught man what he did not know" (Q 96: 1–5). This was the voice of the Archangel Gabriel, inviting Muhammad to read, or recite, God's message. It is thus that the revelation began in 610, only ending with Muhammad's death in 632.

These first words of the revelation are part of chapter (*sura*) 96, titled "The Clinging Form," showing how the Quranic text, as Muslims peruse it, is not arranged according to the chronology of the revelation. The official codex of the Qur'an was put together in the mid-seventh century, at the time of the third caliph, 'Uthman (r. 644–656), and the chapters were arranged by length, with the longest chapter at the beginning and the shortest one at the end. An exception was made for the "opening chapter," *sura al-fatiha*, which also includes the profession of faith (the *shahada*, see Box 1.2).

However, in the field of Quranic studies, much importance has been given to the chronological sequence of revelation, as newer verses are said to "abrogate" older ones on the same topic. Despite the "length" approach, then, each *sura* is also identified as either "Meccan" or "Medinan," referring to whether it was revealed during Muhammad's period in Mecca or after his migration (*hijra*, 622) to the oasis town of Yathrib (later known as Madina an-Nabi, i.e. City of the Prophet, and eventually just Medina). This change in location had a deep political and social undertone, as "Muslims" transitioned from being an oppressed minority in hiding to

Box 0.1   *(cont.)*

constituting themselves as a self-ruling community in which Muhammad operated as political leader, military commander, spiritual guide, and religious teacher.

Within this context, then, we see how *sura* 10 (the fifty-first chapter in chronological order, revealed in Mecca, and titled after the prophet Jonah), states: "[19]All people were originally one single community [*umma wahida*], but later they differed ... [47]Every community is sent a messenger, and when their messenger comes, they will be judged justly; they will not be wronged" suggesting that the initial community was later differentiated through multiple – albeit equally valid – revelations. This was a core principle in identifying other followers of Abrahamic (monotheistic) beliefs as "people of the Book" and thus as "protected minorities" (see Box 1.1).

But *sura* 2 ("The Cow," chronologically no. 87, revealed in Medina) says: "[143]We have made you [believers] into a just community [*umma wasat*], so that you may bear witness [to the truth] before others and so that the Messenger may bear witness [to it] before you." And *sura* 3 ("The Family of 'Imran," no. 89, Medinan), hails: "[110][Believers], you are the best community [*khaira umma*] singled out for people: you order what is right, forbid what is wrong, and believe in God. If the People of the Book had also believed, it would have been better for them. For although some of them do believe, most of them are lawbreakers." And ultimately, *sura* 5, "The Feast" (no. 112, Medinan) recognizes multiple different communities, asserting this fact as a deliberate choice of not leaving all humankind as one community (concepts introduced in *sura* 10) and sanctioning the scripture sent to Muhammad (i.e. the Qur'an) as "the truth" (Q 5:48).

★★★

The first lens deployed in this book, then, is one of intra-Asian connections, both in terms of physical unity and in terms of religious belonging. The philosophers of ancient Greece and Rome, as well as the early Arab geographers, thought of the continental and archipelagic expanse that reaches from the Mediterranean Sea to the Pacific Ocean as a space to be traversed and explored, as little was known of it. But by the tenth century, the Arab Muslim Abu Dulaf had traveled from Persia to Bukhara and (apparently) onwards to northwest China; from there, he supposedly returned to eastern Iran through the western coast of the Malay Peninsula and India. He might not actually have traveled as far as Southeast Asia, yet his acquaintances referred to him as a *jawwala*, "globe-trotter," and his itinerary connected places that had been known to Arab, Persian, Indian, and Chinese merchants for centuries.[5] This conception of physical unity was reinforced by the steady flow of peoples, goods, and ideas, as intra-Asian movements and exchanges were (and still are) fostered and facilitated by ever-evolving technologies of travel and communication (see especially Chapter 1, but see also Chapters 3, 4, 6, 7, and 8).

By the fifteenth century Islam had established itself across Asia. Islam had followed the movement of Muslim traders and conquerors, along both the continental Silk Road and the maritime trading networks of the Indian Ocean. Under Timur Lang (1336–1405), the Mongol empire favored intra-Muslim trade along the Silk Road for decades; Islam had become the primary referent across Bengal, and northern India was under the rule of the Islamized Delhi Sultanate (1206–1526); Ming China (1368–1644) relied on Muslims for scientific expertise and to assert legitimacy through its maritime expansion; and Islam was now prominent among littoral communities along the trading routes that connected Yemen to South Asia, the eastern ports of the Indo-Malay Archipelago, the Mekong River Delta, and the Fujian town of Quanzhou/ Zaytun (Chapter 1).

"Asia" was thus gradually transformed in a cohesive space of Islamized interaction, and Muslims across Asia expressed their identity as members of a historically defined "community of believers" (*umma*). But the emergence of an interconnected "Asia" did not happen in a cultural vacuum: while many traditions flowed across this space (including Buddhism, Christianity, and Shamanism), it ought to be recognized that Islam came to play a crucial role in the imagination of community and belonging.

The dish featured on the cover of this book, for example, brings to life the second theme of the book, which focuses on the influence of Islam as cultures intersected across Asia, beyond the transfer of techniques or materials or wholesale conversion to a new religion. In the center of the dish two peacocks stand beneath a blossoming flower: a classic Chinese trope, but one that could also be suitable for the Muslim taste. On the lip, four Chinese landscape vignettes (one can see the silhouette of a pagoda-like roof) alternate four medallions inscribed in simple, stylized Arabic calligraphy enunciating the Islamic profession of faith (*shahada*): "There is no God but God, and Muhammad is His Prophet." This object brings together an undisputable element of Islamic identity (the *shahada*), while deploying explicitly Chinese iconography, indicating that the two were not in contradiction with each other, but rather the outcome of processes of "transculturation" which retained a strong commitment to Islamic sensibilities.[6]

Objects, then, can fulfill Islamic paradigms of propriety while also incorporating non-Islamic elements. Such forms of negotiation between

Islamic and non-Islamic cultural elements can be found in the decorative arts, architecture, sciences, literature, and conceptions of power and bureaucracy, but also in elaborations of Islamic law and other religious texts (Chapter 2).

In the early centuries of Islam, then, Asia was transformed in an area in which conceptions of space and flows of peoples and ideas conflated in the emergence of local and foreign Muslim communities, giving life to imaginations of community congruent with a shared commitment to Islam. And despite the fact that "Islam in Asia" as an object of study has been constructed as syncretic and exotic, as a thin veneer on the pre-Islamic Hindu-Buddhist past of the region (see Chapter 9), these conceptions and imaginations that tied the Asian continent together as a Muslim space were also articulated within a commitment to normativistic forms of Islam.

Aspirations and commitment to orthodoxy – whether expressed through adherence to contextualized re-elaborations of "the right path" (Chapter 2) or purification of devotional practices (Chapter 3) – should not be seen as rejections of local identities. This had not been the case when Islam had first taken root in Asia, and it would not be the case in the nineteenth and twentieth centuries. In the late colonial period, during the emergence of independent nation-states, and again in the second half of the twentieth century when post-colonial nation-states failed their promises of development and "progress," Islam became an important element in the push back against established authority, but not at the expense of local priorities. Muslim nation-states emerged as independent entities (rather than as members of a transnational Caliphate, for example) (Chapter 4). Muslim populations made sense of "the nation" on their own terms (Chapter 5), and eventually developed "hyper-national" responses to the failure of post-colonial states, even though these processes of "re-imaginations of piety" had been inspired and stimulated by flourishing transnational networks (Chapter 6).

The third core theme of this book revolves around the contribution of Asia's Muslims to configurations of Islamic ideals of orthodoxy and orthopraxy. Mecca and Medina, where Muhammad received the message of Islam, continued to function as physical hubs for the *umma*, but most notably, the intellectual genealogies of some of the most influential scholars there connected them to Bukhara, Delhi, and other places across Asia.

Shaykhs and jurists from Java, Sumatra, and Patani (on the Malay Peninsula) led study circles in Mecca and Medina;[7] the vision of the Arab 'Abd al-Wahhab (1703–1792) was deeply informed by his studying with the South Asian scholar of *hadith* Muhammad Hayya al-Sindi

(d. 1750); in the late nineteenth century "the great majority of the students come [to Mecca] from abroad," including Java, Malaya, Malabar, and Dagestan;[8] and the Naqshbandi mystical order (*tariqa*) – one of the most far-reaching, penetrating, and popular spiritual movements calling for a closer alignment of devotional practices with the demands of legal thought – had its roots in Central Asia and its greenest branches in South Asia, before expanding further east (China) and west (Arabia and Turkey) (Chapter 3).

Awareness of Islamic orthopraxy, and concerns over keeping Muslims on "the right path" (the *al-sirat al-mustaqim* of the opening chapter of the Qur'an), continued to be widespread across Asia and to flow back to "the heartlands" of Islam: debates on how to rescue the fate of the Caliphate in the early twentieth century were most active in British India, Tsarist and Soviet Central Asia, and the Dutch East Indies (Chapter 4); Egypt's Muslim Brotherhood leader Sayyid Qutb (1906–1966) was deeply influenced by the writings of the South Asian Islamist ideologue Abu A'la Mawdudi (Chapter 5); the Afghan *jihad* against the 1979 Soviet invasion became a symbolic site of resistance for Muslims the world over in the latter part of the twentieth century (Chapter 7); and Southeast Asian reconfigurations of religious authority – whether in the realms of *halal* certification or feminist interpretations of the scriptures – are asserting themselves on the global scene today (Chapter 8).

This book, then, directly challenges the assumption of an Arab-centric paradigm of Islamic authenticity and authority, presenting an alternative narrative that delineates the impact (on Islam) of Muslims who inhabit(ed) the *ma wara' an-nahr*; it discusses how Islam became an integral part of Asia, influencing local conceptions of power as well as the sciences, the arts, and bureaucracy, converting individuals and influencing societies; and it ultimately concludes that the very existence of an intra-Asian space of interaction allowed for multidirectional influences on Islamic practices and understandings at the "center" as well as the "peripheries" of the "Muslim world."

Further Reading

Abdel Haleem, M. A. (2001) *Understanding the Qur'an: themes and style*, London: I. B. Tauris.

(2008) *The Qur'an: a new translation*, Oxford: Oxford University Press.

Adas, M. (1993) *Islamic and European expansion: the forging of a global order*, Philadelphia, PA: Temple University Press.

Ernst, C. W. (2010) *Following Muhammad: rethinking Islam in the contemporary world*, New South Wales: Accessible Publishing Systems.

Esposito, J. L., Abdel, H. M. A., Arberry, A. J., and Kassis, H. E. (2007) *Oxford Islamic studies online*, Oxford: Oxford University Press, www.oxfordislamicstudies.com/MainSearch.html.

Formichi, C. (2016) "Islamic Studies or Asian Studies? Islam in Southeast Asia," *Muslim World* 106(4): 696–718.

Hodgson, M. G. S. (1974) *The venture of Islam*, Chicago, IL: University of Chicago Press (Vol. 1, *The classical age of Islam*; Vol. 2, *The expansion of Islam in the Middle Periods*; Vol. 3, *The Gunpowder Empires and modern times*).

Lapidus, I. M. (2014) *A history of Islamic societies*, New York, NY: Cambridge University Press.

McLoughlin, S. (2007) "Islam(s) in context: orientalism and the anthropology of Muslim societies and cultures," *Journal of Beliefs & Values* 28(3): 273–296.

Ricci, R. (2011) *Islam translated: literature, conversion, and the Arabic cosmopolis of South and Southeast Asia*, Chicago, IL: University of Chicago Press.

Sells, M. A. (2007) *Approaching the Qur'an: the early revelations*, Ashland, OR: White Cloud Press.

1   Islam across the Oxus (Seventh to Seventeenth Centuries)

Figure 1.1 The mausoleum of Mahmood of Ghazni (Ghazna, Afghanistan).
Sammlung Werner Otto von Hentig © Stiftung Bibliotheca Afghanica, www.phototheca-afghanica.ch

No Muslim conqueror passed beyond the frontier of Kabul and the river Sindh until the days of the Turks, when they seized the power of Ghazna under the Samani[d] dynasty, and the supreme power fell to the lot of Nasir-addaula Sabuktagin [Sebuk Tegin]. The prince chose the holy war as his calling, and therefore called himself *al-ghazi* (i.e. *warring on the road of Allah*). In the interest of his successors he constructed, in order to weaken the Indian frontier, those roads on which afterwards his son Yamin-addaula Mahmud marched into India during a period of thirty years and more. God be merciful to both father and son! Mahmud utterly ruined the prosperity of the country, and performed there wonderful exploits, by which the Hindus became like atoms of dust scattered in all directions, and like a tale of old in the mouth of the people. Their scattered remains cherish, of course, the most inveterate aversion towards all Muslims.[1]

Al-Biruni (973–1025) was an Uzbek scholar known for his writings on geography, anthropology, astronomy, mathematics, and more. And it was to collect detailed knowledge of the ways of the Hindus that he had been sent to India by Mahmud (d. 1030), the ruler of Ghazni. He obviously had no words of praise for his patron, whom he thought would need God's mercy to redeem his actions. Mahmud, enshrined in the mausoleum pictured here (Figure 1.1), was the son of a slave soldier (*ghulam*) from Kyrgyzstan – the Sebuk Tegin of al-Biruni's text – whom, after rising in the ranks of the Samanid army, eventually settled in the Afghan town of Ghazna, at the time a minor commercial and agricultural center between Kabul and Kandahar. "Mahmud of Ghazni" would go on to establish a semi-independent Turkic dynasty, the Ghaznavids (977–1186).

Afghanistan was not a unique case: as the Abbasid Empire continued to expand, its central authority weakened, leading to a loose imperial structure and the emergence of local dynasties across Asia. Since the ninth and tenth centuries, local rulers paid tribute to the Abbasid Caliph by dedicating to him the Friday congregational prayer sermon (*khutba*), by minting the Empire's coins, and by sending to Baghdad slaves captured during raids on Turkic territories. These slaves were then (sometimes forcibly) converted to Islam and absorbed by the Abbasid army as soldiers; some succeeded in rising through the ranks and reached political-military power, as Mahmud's father did. While paying allegiance to the Abbasids, these new dynasties also sought to conquer as much territory as possible, in their own drive to obtain more resources. In the eleventh to thirteenth centuries, Islamized Turkic dynasties descended from slave soldiers ruled over the northern parts of the Indian subcontinent as well as much of Central Asia and "Western China" (i.e. the "Tarim Basin").

Under Mahmud I, the Ghaznavids gained control of Afghanistan, eastern Persia (Iran), and northern India, asserting Sunni Islam's hegemony *vis-à-vis* the growing influence of Shi'ism in Persia and Egypt. But in fact, the discourse on *jihad* as a theologically justified war against infidels and heretics had emerged as an expedient to further the political and territorial dominion of the 'Umayyad Empire, not to spread the faith (more on *jihad* in Chapter 7). Indeed, the Ghaznavids seemed less interested in converting the "heretics" than in ransacking their properties: the regular winter expeditions against the Shi'is (and Hindus) were as valuable for retaining prestige in the eyes of the Abbasid Caliph in

Baghdad as they were necessary to finance the Ghaznavids' own army, bureaucracy, and construction efforts.

The history of Mahmud's southern expansion is, then, until today often recalled in connection with violence and the destruction of Hindu traditions and heritage, as hinted in al-Biruni's account. In fact, as the Ghaznavids patronized the arts, they also built forts and garrisons, gradually asserting their presence in northern South Asia in a physical way that would constantly remind the local population of the new cultural matrix that had come to dominate in the area. At the time of Mahmud's death, the caliphal office in Baghdad formally recognized the Punjab as part of the Abbasid Empire, marking the widest expansion of its territory.

The mausoleum depicted here was decorated with "several pieces of Hindoo sculpture in white marble, some of them said to be fragments of the idol of Somnath, [which] lie scattered in the portico ... the doorway in which hang the gates, [is] said to be of Somnath,"[2] one of the most important temples in India, as it is considered to be one of Shiva's twelve traditional shrines. Other fragments of this idol were cast on the threshold of Ghazni's congregational mosque, and yet more were said to have been sent to Mecca and Medina. Reminding us of al-Biruni's "atoms of dust scattered in all directions," and as argued by Barry Flood, the looting, destruction and "reconfiguration" of India(n artifacts) mirrored the Islamic conquest of this Hindu area and its integration in the "land of Islam."[3]

★★★

At the time of Muhammad's death in 632, Islam had affirmed itself in Mecca, Medina, and some parts of the Arabian Peninsula. By the early eighth century it reached from Morocco to northern India. Known as the "rightly guided" caliphs (*al-khulafa' ar-rashidun*), the first four caliphs – Abu Bakr (573–634), 'Umar b. Al-Khattab (579–644), 'Uthman b. Affan (577–656) and 'Ali ibn Abu Talib (600–661) – led their armies westward conquering Egypt; north to gain control of Syria, Iraq, Turkey, and Armenia; and east toward Persia (651) and Khorasan, reaching the Oxus/Amu Darya river. It was under the 'Umayyads (661–750) – the first line of hereditary rulers in Islam – that the Empire eventually crossed the Oxus in 673, conquering the region known as Transoxiana or *ma wara' an-nahr*, in Arabic "that which is across the river" (roughly in today's Uzbekistan). In rapid succession the army also gained control of most of North Africa, Spain, Anatolia, and Sindh (the northwestern corner of the Indian subcontinent). By 711 the Arab Empire spread from Toledo (Spain) to Multan (Pakistan). The last push to the east took place as the 'Umayyads lost control of their Empire to the Abbasids (750–1258).

In 751 the Abbasid army engaged a small contingent of the Tang's Chinese army at Talas, north of the Ferghana Valley (not far from Samarkand, on the border of today's Kyrgyzstan and Kazakhstan), and won. The Tang Empire would shortly after shrink back. Nonetheless, this battle drew a symbolic line between the Muslim and Chinese empires, creating a buffer zone where two distinct cultural spheres – the Islamosphere to the west and the Sinosphere to the east – would continuously encounter, confront, and influence each other.

As pointed out by Richard W. Bulliet in the mid-1990s,

the view from the center leaves too many questions unanswered ...[4] portray[ing] Islamic history as an outgrowth from a single nucleus, a spreading inkblot labeled "the caliphate" ... [T]he view from the edge does the opposite. It starts with individuals and small communities scattered over a vast and poorly integrated realm, speaking over a dozen different languages, and steeped in religious and cultural traditions of great diversity.[5]

Hence, this chapter explores the territorial trajectory of Islam's expansion across Asia, from the time of Muhammad's revelation through the consolidation of Muslim polities in West, Central, South, East, and Southeast Asia in the sixteenth to seventeenth centuries. This narrative focuses on the military conquest of territories outside of Arabia as well as the movement of people (such as merchants, mystics, travelers, etc.) who connected the Mediterranean to China via maritime and continental routes (see Maps 2–5). This endeavor is pursued in order to lay the foundations for the exploration of "Islamization" as a broad set of processes that led cumulatively to the conversion of many societies across Asia.[6]

An Expanding Empire

In the very early days of Islam, the new faith had spread by word of mouth, and following kinship networks of allegiance. Within this framework, women had played a crucial role: Khadija (d. 620), Muhammad's first wife, was also the first convert. A powerful and wealthy businesswoman, she had been able to exert influence on many others from her own clan, the Quraysh, thus expanding the ranks of the converts. Many women had also participated in the migration (*hijra*) from Mecca to Medina in 622, in the early battles, and in religious congregations. 'A'isha (ca. 613–ca. 678) – Muhammad's youngest and favorite wife – was regularly consulted on Muhammad's practice, gave interpretative statements on Islamic laws and customs, addressed the believers in Mecca's mosque after Caliph 'Uthman's death (656), and led soldiers at the Battle of the Camel against 'Ali ibn Abu Talib (who would become the fourth Caliph; for more on him see Box 3.1). As argued by Leila Ahmed, Arab women enjoyed much freedom of movement and personal rights, and could choose their husbands and own property. This social reality was matched by the "stubbornly egalitarian" ethical vision of the Qur'an; however, she argues, this foundational aspect of Islam went unheard and left no trace in public discourse, as Islamic rule consolidated itself in the context of the conquest.

Arab women's participation in society was gradually curtailed, as practices detrimental to women were instead embraced by the male elite of the Abbasid era. As the empire expanded, it also incorporated elements of local culture, bureaucracy, and social norms. Alongside coin iconography and court protocol, the Abbasids assimilated to luxuries common in the urban Mediterranean (i.e. Byzantium and Sasanian Persia), such as ownership of slaves and concubines, refined foods and clothes, and sheer gathering of wealth. In this context, the ethical vision of the Qur'an was sidelined to privilege instead its legal and social visions, which established a political and legal sexual hierarchy centered around women's obligations as wives and mothers. Thus, Leila Ahmed affirms that "The weight Abbasid society gave to the androcentric teachings over the ethical teachings in Islam in matters concerning relations between the sexes was the outcome of collective interpretative acts reflecting the mores and attitudes of society."[7]

Interpretation and contextuality were thus key aspects of the Arab expansion. Alongside the position of women, it is worth addressing the position of non-Muslims and non-Arabs in this new (and constantly changing) socio-political environment. Territorial conquest at the hand of the Arab army did not directly translate in the religious conversion of newly subjected populations, especially in the early decades of the expansion. The Sasanian Empire of Persia (established in the third century) fell to the 'Umayyads in 651, but as Caliph 'Umar determined that Zoroastrianism – the predominant religion in Persia at that time – was to be recognized as a protected religion (with Zoroastrians considered *dhimmi*), Islam would take a long time to affirm itself there. Half a century later, the same would happen in northern India (Sindh), as the 'Umayyad general Muhammad Ibn al-Qasim (d. 715) determined Hindus and Buddhists to be protected *dhimmi*.[8] How, then, did the Arab Empire become a Muslim Empire?

Box 1.1 *Dhimmi*

A *dhimmi* is a non-Muslim who is under a pact of protection (*dhimma*) with the Muslim authority. In the scriptures this was a pact, or covenant, made exclusively with the "people of the book" (*ahl al-kitab*). This expression referred to other religious communities who were deemed to have a foundational "book." Jews, Christians, and Sabaeans are explicitly mentioned in the Qur'an, but in the early decades of the Arab Empire, Zoroastrians and Hindus were also assimilated as *dhimmi*. This status, offered in exchange for a land tax (*kharaj*) and a poll tax (*jizya*, calculated as a portion of each individual's income), guaranteed freedom of religious practice, a degree of communal self-government, and personal safety; but it also demanded respect of Muslims and Islam as well as refraining from proselytism.

The Islamic revelation called for a universal religion, yet its early practice reflected the Arab tribal ideal that Arabs were superior to other peoples, and that Islam was an "Arab" religion, as the Qur'an had been delivered through Muhammad to the Arabs, in Arabia, in Arabic language. Most new settlements were then built to retain the separation between the conquering Arab Muslims and the conquered non-Arab non-Muslim peoples.

Discrimination between Arabs and non-Arabs subsisted within the Muslim community, especially in the outer regions of the Empire. There, even though non-Arabs had succeeded in gaining some degree of power in military hierarchies, they were still governed by Arabs. Segregation soon led to tensions, and by the end of the seventh century non-Arabs who sought to improve their social status – whether in the military, administration, or commerce – attempted to do so by converting to Islam, even though they were required to commit most of their property to Islamic philanthropy (*waqf*). Real change only begun to occur after Caliph 'Umar II (r. 717–720) actively encouraged popular conversions and equality among Muslims, regardless of ethnicity. It was this shift in policy, demanded by the expanding geographical reach of the Empire, that allowed for its transition from being "Arab" to being "Muslim".

As Abbasid rule (750–1258) soon became characterized by a weakening of the caliphal authority and the increased autonomy of the provinces on the eastern and western edges alike, starting in the ninth century the history of Islam in Asia took on a life of its own, separate from developments at the Arab '"center" of the Empire.

Box 1.2   The Five Pillars

Islam, literally meaning "submission" (from the verb *aslama*), refers to a complex religious system that has manifested itself in multifarious ways through time and space, and it can be approached as a theological, political, ritual, social, or historical phenomenon. The question of what "constitutes" Islam has been posed by many scholars, leading to multiple answers. At its core, however, are some principles that are recognized by many Muslims as "pillars" (*arkan*) of the faith, and which most believers agree constitute Islam's theological and ritual backbone. That being said, these pillars should not be taken as a "checklist" by which to evaluate someone's belonging to the faith.

Each of these five pillars represent a different way in which individual Muslims stand as part of their community of believers, the *umma* (see Introduction, Box 0.1), yet they are never mentioned in the Qur'an as a "package." The five pillars are discussed as a whole only in the prophetic traditions (*hadith*) and later scholarly exegesis.

The first pillar is the profession of faith, or *shahada*, which affirms a Muslim's belief in the "One and only God" – hence, a declaration of monotheism – and in Muhammad as the Prophet of God. Muhammad also stands as the "seal of the Prophets" in a sequence that encompasses Abraham, Moses, and Jesus, among others.

The testimony of faith is followed by *salat*, understood as the ritual prayer owed to God, performed in the direction of the Ka'ba in Mecca (*qibla*) and at specific times of the day, as announced by the *adhan* (call to prayer). Next comes *sawm*, the ritual fasting pursued from dawn to dusk during Ramadan, the ninth month of the Islamic calendar. The fourth pillar is *zakat*, a tax set at 2.5 percent of a Muslim's own net worth (although its accurate calculation is more complex than this suggests). Last is the *hajj*, the pilgrimage to Mecca which is to be pursued, if one has the means and health to do so, during the twelfth month of the Islamic calendar. (Mecca, the *qibla*, and the *hajj* are further discussed in Chapter 2.)

Muslims of Continental Asia

The Islamization of the Asian continent east of Persia proceeded in a tightly interlocked sequence of events, albeit not by design, as Hindus, Buddhists, and Shamanic peoples converted to Islam following their rulers or inspired by informal networks of knowledge, commerce, and spiritual allegiance. Non-Muslims embraced the new faith following a variety of paths and in ways that might have looked profoundly different. This variety manifested itself along the urban/rural and settled/nomadic divides, as well as across classes and professions, and amid changing historical-political circumstances.

Islam traveled overland following the expansion of the Abbasid Empire and its affiliated Islamized Turkic dynasties from the ninth century onwards, along a trajectory that moved from Khorasan and Transoxiana eastward into the Tarim Basin (today's Xinjiang Province in western China) and southward into Afghanistan and northern India.

The Abbasid Empire's territorial expansion and political unity had been sustainable only by establishing loose but stable relationships with other dynasties that controlled the edges of the Empire territorially and culturally, as mentioned at the beginning of this chapter. While the Empire granted them affiliation, in return these rulers paid tribute to the Caliph; this was intended at the discursive level (local states minted coins that showed allegiance to the Caliph) as well as territorially (Transoxiana became a bulwark against nomadic incursions), and financially, as the Caliphate received a constant supply of Turkic slaves, who were either sold on markets across West Asia, or absorbed by the army as soldiers (*ghulam*, *mamluk*, etc.). And where local rulers decided to rescind this affiliation and assert their own independent sovereignty, they minted their own coins and had Friday congregational prayer sermons dedicated to themselves.

Central Asia became a crucial site for the Islamization of the "far east" from the tenth century onwards. In the pre-Mongol period, Islamized dynasties were able to exert enough influence to effect conversions (as the Qarakhanids (992–1212), who converted *en masse* to follow the conversion of their leader, the *khan*; see Source 3.1 for the conversion of the Qarakhanid Satuq Bughra Khan (d. 955)), but there are too few sources from this period, and these are also heavily influenced by later narratives, to paint an accurate picture. The narrative of Sufi mystics' roles in converting Central Asia's nomadic peoples has dominated local imaginations of the past as well as scholarly literature for many decades. But this approach was largely based, first, on the reliability of later surviving manuscripts that projected a certain view of the region's Islamization; and second, on a scholarly sense that for nomadic peoples to be converted the message of Islam had to be simplified, supposedly something that only the Sufis would have been amenable to doing (as opposed to the jurists; see Chapter 3).[9]

Conversion of non-Muslim peoples across Asia mostly occurred gradually and non-systematically, as individual non-Muslims strived to insert themselves in newly constituted networks – whether these were military, financial, political, social, familial, or spiritual. They might have desired to obtain financial benefit from trading with Muslims as Muslims, enter the bureaucracy, marry a local woman, or enter the entourage of a Sufi order.

As seen in this chapter's opening discussion of the Ghaznavids, Turkic military slaves (converted as Muslims) were often able to rise through the ranks and obtain political-military power and territorial autonomy, which led to the further establishment of Islamized Turkic polities across Central Asia and northern India. Some early Arab traders had settled around the Bay's coast in Dhaka (today's Bangladesh) and Arakan (today's Burma/Myanmar) sometime in the tenth century. Yet, Richard Eaton has convincingly argued that the history of Bengal's Islamization is more accurately told as part of the Turkic expansion into the Subcontinent from Central Asia.

In fact, it was only after the Ghurids' takeover of the Ghaznavids in 1186 that Islam stretched significantly further across India. Under the military command of the former Turkic slave Qutb al-Din Aybak (1150–1210), the Ghurids entered Delhi in 1193, and then moved on to conquer Rajasthan, Awadh, Bihar, and Bengal. Mu'izz ad-Din Muhammad of Ghor (1149–1206) was assassinated shortly after, at which point Qutb al-Din Aybak proclaimed his autonomy, starting what came to be known as the Mamluk dynasty, the first in the string of five that would make up the so-called Delhi Sultanate.

The Turkic strand continued to rule the northern part of the Indian subcontinent. As recounted by the Moroccan jurist and world-traveler Ibn Battuta (1304–1377 or 1369), "the first who ruled in the city of Delhi with independent power" was Iltutmish (d. 1236), Aybak's slave-general, conqueror of Multan and the Bengal, defeater of the Ghaznavids, patron of Islam, and "the Sultan of the Sultans of the East," as his rule was sanctioned by the Abbasid Caliph in 1228/29. Iltutmish was also Aybak's son-in-law, as his allegiance had been further cemented through marriage. The Turkic sultans, then, continued to rule also through the reign of Radiyyah (d. 1240), reaffirming the dynasty's semi-independence and minting coins that glossed her name with the title "Blessed of the earthly world and of the faith."

A favorite of her father, Radiyyah had been raised as heir apparent, often shadowing Iltutmish in government and battle: "my sons are incapable of leading, and for that reason I have decided that it is my daughter who should reign after me," he is known to have declared. Upon Iltutmish's death, a feud ensued, but as she enjoyed the support of the Army, Radiyyah was soon after instated as Sultan. She reigned as an absolute monarch for four years, leading military campaigns and asserting her presence on the streets of Delhi, as she was known for roaming the markets, unveiled and dressed as a man, to keep abreast of events. After her untimely death, she was made "into a saint" as "a dome was built over her grave, which is now [mid-fourteenth century] visited, and people obtain blessing from it;"[10] in the eighteenth century she was still recalled as a capable ruler by local historians.

The Delhi Sultanate era (1205–1526) was characterized by the sustained political role of former Turkic slaves, influential women, and the further confluence between Central and South Asia by means of conquest, commercial and spiritual mobility, and diplomacy across the Himalayan region – here broadly meant to comprise Tibet, Nepal, and the northernmost areas of Pakistan. Parts of Nepal were annexed by the Sultanate in the fourteenth century, at the same time as the Kathmandu valley was being (briefly) invaded by a Bengali Sultan. By the fifteenth century, Muslim Kashmiri traders had begun to settle in Nepal[11] and had already become long-term residents in central Tibet;[12] concurrently, a Kashmiri Sufi had made an impact converting the Balti people in northern Pakistan and Tibet.[13] The Central Asian Sultan Sa'id Khan of Yarkand (r. 1514–1533) waged a "holy war" on Tibet, a seventeenth-century Balti prince invited scholars from Kashgar to contrast the spread of Shi'a Islam in his reign, and Samarqandi Sufis initiated Himalayan Muslims in a variety of orders in the eighteenth and nineteenth centuries.[14]

Since the Islamization of Baltistan in the fourteenth to fifteenth centuries, Muslim princesses were sent as brides for Ladakh's Buddhist princes "as promises of unity and peace … alleviating conflict" when the threat of a Kashmiri invasion might otherwise have seemed imminent. They were visible in court politics (sometimes even acting as dowager queens), and consistently stood out as patrons of both Islam and Buddhism, as they sponsored the arts, culture, and the building of both mosques and Buddhist monasteries. The memory of these women has remained impressed in Tibetan culture through the centuries, as they were integrated in Ladakh's traditional folksongs:

> The Royal Palace of Great Pashkum
> Is all aglow with the light of
> Sun and Moon.
> Not the light of Sun and Moon it is
> But the charming complexion of "Queen Muslim Bekim," the
>   Queen!
> Not the glow of the full moon it is
> But the charming appearance of
> Queen Muslim Bekim!
> Verily, Queen Muslim Bekim
> Does excel
> A hundred queens;
> Verily, Queen Muslim Bekim does possess
> The grace and charm of
> A thousand queens.[15]

The poem refers to the Kashmiri wife of King Drag Bumde (ca. 1410–1435) as *bekim*, probably a derivation of the Indo-Persian *begum*, but these Muslim queens of Buddhist kingdoms were more broadly known as *khatuns*, the title borne by Mongol women who played a public role. They might have been wives of sovereigns – Ibn Battuta recalls that "Among the Turks and the Tatars their wives enjoy a very high position; indeed when they issue an order, they say in it, 'By command of the Sultan and the Khatuns'" – or sovereigns themselves.

The same title of Khatun had in fact already identified Ilkhanid Mongol queens, such as Kutlugh Turkan Khatun (r. 1257–1282) and Padishah Khatun (r. 1291–1295); the latter also enjoyed the Islamic titles of "purity of the earthly world and of the faith" and "Sovereign of the world," or *Khadawand 'Alam* (as it appeared on her coins), combining a first word in Turkish and a second one in Arabic.[16] Such combination of Islamic and local symbols of legitimacy were not unique to Central Asia, but were common in Persia, South Asia, and Southeast Asia too.

In the meantime, the Mughal Empire (1526–1857) affirmed itself as a Persianate Muslim polity. Although the Mughal characterized themselves as Muslims, their rule had very little that was specifically "Islamic": the court was inhabited by diverse ethnic and linguistic groups; the population was ruled according to their respective religious laws; and the Hindu majority was treated as a *dhimmi* "protected minority" (see Box 1.1). It is on these grounds that Barbara and Thomas Metcalf have suggested that: "For the Sultanate rulers, as for the Mughal who succeeded them, Islamic ambitions focused on extending Muslim power, not on conversion."[17] The two regions that experienced the deepest process of Islamization in northern India were the western Punjab and eastern Bengal, notably areas that experienced relatively weak Muslim rule.

While Islam and Muslim rulers were asserting themselves in northern India, Genghiz Khan (d. 1227) had begun his takeover of continental Asia in the early thirteenth century. In 1258, his grandson Mongke Khan (r. 1251–1259) entered Baghdad, bringing an end to the Abbasid Empire. Alongside destruction and warfare, the Mongol invasion also brought political unity to Asia for the first time in history, from the eastern coast of China through the eastern shores of the Mediterranean.

Mongke Khan's reign did not last long, and as he died without designating a successor, the empire was divided shortly thereafter. From this internecine war emerged four polities, or Khanates: China came to be controlled by the Yuan Khanate under Kublai Khan; Persia's Ilkhanate initially included today's Iran, Azerbaijan, and parts of Turkey, and later expanded north into Armenia and Georgia; east into Turkmenistan and Afghanistan, and south into Pakistan; the Golden Horde, or Khanate of

Kipchak, stretched from eastern Europe to Siberia through the Northern Caucasus; and finally, Central Asia was ruled by the Chagatai Khanate, which controlled the Tarim Basin and the area between the Oxus/Amu Darya river and the Altai Mountains (thus including the cities of Bukhara and Samarkand) (see Map 2).

The Ilkhan Mahmud Ghazan (r. 1295–1304) was the first Mongol ruler to convert to Islam, and he pulled with him most of his tribes. Shortly after, Oz Beg Khan (1282–1341) of the Golden Horde embraced the new faith, ruling over several Muslim peoples. Worth noting is that the public status of Mongol women mentioned above was not affected by this wave of conversion: as witnessed by Ibn Battuta,

it is [Sultan Muhammad Oz Beg Khan's] custom to sit every Friday, after the prayer, in a pavilion … the sultan sits on the throne, having on his right hand the khatun Taitughli and next to her the khatun Kabak, and on his left the khatun Bayalun and next to her the khatun Urduja. Below the throne, to his right, stands the sultan's son Tina Bak.[18]

By the mid-fourteenth century, Tughluq Timur Khan (r. 1347–1362) took control of the eastern provinces of the Chagatai Khanate, thus leading to most Turkic peoples of Central Asia becoming Muslims. Upon his conversion (narrated in Source 1.1), Tughluq entered a mutually beneficial relationship with the local Sufis: they made proselytes and legitimized his power, while he provided them with infrastructures, most notably building and maintaining Sufi lodges (*khanaqa*s) and their shrines (for images of shrines, see Figures 1.2, 2.3, and 2.4). This illustrates how after the Mongol expansion new dynamics created the opportunity for Sufi *shaykh*s and ruling *khan*s to connect as agents of mutual legitimation.

Sufism had emerged as a tradition of asceticism and worldly withdrawal in eighth- to ninth-century Iraq. Largely in response to the lavishness displayed by the 'Umayyad and early Abbasid empires, it advocated the primacy of a self-effacing life of meditation and devotion oriented toward an individual quest to reach knowledge of, and a connection with, God. With time, other approaches and geographical centers competed with Baghdad, most notably Khorasan. The Khorasanian "way" (*tariqa*, or "order"), especially since the eleventh and twelfth centuries, demanded a stronger tie between disciple and master, and had a heavier accent on "training." This focus on the Sufi master led to three important consequences. First, the possibility of forging political alliances with rulers; second, the emergence of Sufi lodges as gathering places for students of specific masters; third, women – who had been widely present among the ranks of early

Source 1.1

The Conversion to Islam of Tughluq Timur Khan. Text by Mirza Haydar Dughlat (1499–1551)

Tughluq Timur Khan (r. 1347–1362) was a Turkic military and political leader, a descendant of Genghiz Khan, who came to power in the Chagatai Khanate in the mid-fourteenth century. His conversion, narrated below, led also to the conversion of the population of his Khanate, estimated at over 15,000 individuals. This text illustrates the close relationship between the Khan and a Sufi shaykh.[19]

At that time Tughluq Timur Khan was in Aqsu. When he had first been brought there he was sixteen years of age. He was eighteen when he first met the Shaykh [Jamal al-Din], and he met him in the following way. The Khan had organized a hunting-party, and had promulgated an order that no one should absent himself from the hunt. It was, however, remarked that some persons were seated in a retired spot. The Khan sent to fetch these people, and they were seized, bound, and brought before him, inasmuch as they had not presented themselves at the hunt. The Khan asked them, "Why have you disobeyed my commands?" The Shaykh replied, "We are strangers, who have fled from the ruined town of Katak. We know nothing about the hunt nor the ordinances of the hunt, and therefore we have not transgressed your orders." So the Khan ordered his men to set the Tajik free. He was, at that time, feeding some dogs with swine's flesh, and he asked the Shaykh angrily, "Are you better than this dog, or is the dog better than you?" The Shaykh replied, "If I have faith I am better than this dog; but if I have no faith, this dog is better than I am." On hearing these words, the Khan retired and sent one of his men, saying, "Go and place that Tajik upon your own horse, with all due respect, and bring him here to me."

The Moghul went and led his horse before the Shaykh. The Shaykh noticing that the saddle was stained with blood (of pig) said, "I will go on foot." But the Moghul insisted that the order was that he should mount the horse. The Shaykh then spread a clean handkerchief over the saddle and mounted. When he arrived before the Khan, he noticed that this latter was standing alone in a retired spot, and there were traces of sorrow on his countenance. The Khan asked the Shaykh, "What is this thing that renders man, if he possess [sic] it, better than a dog?" The Shaykh replied, "Faith," and he explained to him what Faith was, and the duties of a Musulman. The Khan wept thereat, and said, "If I ever become Khan, and obtain absolute authority, you must, without fail, come to me, and I promise you I will become a Musulman." He then sent the Shaykh away with the utmost respect and reverence. Soon after this the Shaykh died. He left a son of the name of Arshad al-Din, who was exceedingly pious. His father once dreamed that he carried a lamp up to the top of a hill, and that its light

Source 1.1 *(cont.)*

illumined the whole of the east. After that, he met Tughluq Timur Khan in Aqsu and said what has been mentioned above. Having related this to his son, he charged him, saying, "Since I may die at any moment, let it be your care, when the young man becomes Khan, to remind him of his promise to become a Muslim; thus this blessing may come about through your mediation and, through you, the world may be illumined."

Having completed his injunctions to his son, the Shaykh died. Soon afterwards Tughluq Timur became Khan. When news of this reached Mawlana Arshad al-Din, he left Aqsu and proceeded to Moghulistan, where the Khan was ruling in great pomp and splendour. But all his efforts to obtain an interview with him, that he might execute his charge, were in vain. Every morning, however, he used to call out the prayers near to the Khan's tent. One morning the Khan said to one of his followers, "Somebody has been calling out like this for several mornings now; go and bring him here." The Mawlana was in the middle of his call to prayer when the Moghul arrived, who, seizing him by the neck, dragged him before the Khan. The latter said to him, "Who are you that thus disturb my sleep every morning at an early hour?" He replied, "I am the son of the man to whom, on a certain occasion, you made the promise to become a Muslim." And he proceeded to recount the above related story. The Khan then said, "You are welcome, and where is your father?" He replied, "My father is dead, but he entrusted this mission to me." The Khan rejoined, "Ever since I ascended the throne I have had it on my mind that I made that promise, but the person to whom I gave the pledge never came. Now you are welcome. What must I do?" On that morn the sun of bounty rose out of the east of divine favour, and effaced the dark night of Unbelief. Mawlana ordained ablution for the Khan, who, having declared his faith, became a Muslim. They then decided that for the propagation of Islam, they should interview the princes one by one, and it should be well for those who accepted the faith, but those who refused should be slain as heathens and idolaters [...]

The Khan was circumcised, and the lights of Islam dispelled the shades of Unbelief. Islam was disseminated all through the country of Chaghatay Khan, and (thanks be to God) has continued fixed in it to the present time.

ascetics in West, Central, and South Asia alike – were now seeing their horizons limited due to the perceived impropriety of a male master/ female pupil relationship. In the early years, women had been seen as equally capable of achieving communion with God, as Islamic mysticism "left no room for the distinction of sex." In the twelfth century, al-Ghazali (d. 1111) had stated:

Consider the state of the God-fearing women and say (to your soul), "O my soul, be not content to be less than a woman, for a man is contemptible if he comes short of a woman, in respect to her religion and (her relation) to this world."

Figure 1.2 The shrine of Satuq Bughra Khan, Atush (Xinjiang, China).
© Chiara Formichi

This applied in historical terms, as "the first place among the earliest Muhammadan mystics" was given to a woman, Rabi'a al 'Adawiyyah of Basra (born ca. 717);[20] Rabi'a was credited with miracles and – possibly more importantly – with transforming "somber asceticism into genuine love mysticism," to borrow from Annemarie Schimmel. After centuries of practicing asceticism, being disciples of great masters, and participating (sometimes leading) community gatherings of *dhikr* ("remembrance" of God), by the twelfth century women disciples and their male masters were compelled to explore new ways to properly and "legally" pursue initiation ceremonies in their *tariqa*s without any direct touching.[21] But by the fourteenth century social norms of segregation had taken over in the institutionalized mystic orders.

In this *tariqa*-oriented, increasingly sectarian environment, the *khanaqa*s became centers for both teaching and conversion, as they retained their physical openness, allowing local poor and itinerant merchants (but not women) to take shelter. In their last transformation, *khanaqa*s became mausolea and shrines for the bodies of their past masters, and thus developed into pilgrimage destinations. By extension, the graves of other saints took on the function of bestowing blessings (*baraka*) and thus also the shrines of women mystics attracted many seekers of miracles (men and women alike) (see Chapter 2).

Sufism took shape as a form of Islam that was deeply rooted in the territory while also encouraging mobility both eastward and westward. Also, it opened a new way to win converts to Islam; in this period Sufism became key in the spreading of Islam in Central Asia, through the Tarim Basin, into northwest China (Gansu, Qinghai, and Ningxia), and possibly Tibet from the fifteenth and sixteenth centuries onwards. Sufism also remained important to the construction and projection of political power after the conquest of the Chagatai Khanate (in 1370) at the hand of the Muslim Turco-Mongol Timur Lang (known as Timur "the Lame" or Tamerlane in Europe, 1336–1405), as Naqshbandi Sufis held leading positions in the Timurid Empire (which stretched as far west as Baghdad, conquered in 1393). (Sufism is further discussed in Chapter 3).

By the beginning of the sixteenth century, what had been Timur's territory was controlled by four different polities: alongside the Shi'i Safavids (1501–1736) (see Box 3.1) who had emerged victorious in Persia, the Shaybanids took Bukhara in 1500 (the local Khanate would last until 1785, followed by the Emirate of Bukhara until 1920) while the Khanate of Khiva, on the eastern shores of the Aral Sea (1511–1920), emerged as an independent polity. The Yuan dynasty in China (1271–1368) remained the one of the four khanates that never had a Muslim leader, and yet, as testimony to the fact that Asia was indeed a profusely Islamized space, during the Yuan period many Muslims were involved in the administration of the new Empire.

Muslim merchant sojourners who had been coming "east" since the battle of Talas in 751, were joined by Sufis and "professionals" expressly invited by Yuan rulers. They were technocrats, scientists and military men. The Bukharan Sayyid 'Ajall Shams al-Din (d. 1279), for example, was appointed governor of Yunnan soon after the province's annexation by the Mongol in the late thirteenth century, and while he did not advance an Islamization agenda per se, he enabled Chinese Muslims to lead pious lives (building mosques, allowing religious education, etc.) while "provid[ing] them with a useful model for balancing one's obligations as a Muslim with those as subject of the imperial throne."[22] Muslims continued to come to China, and became an integral part of society, yet Islam remained associated with foreignness. In Lipman's words, Muslims were "familiar strangers."[23]

The Yuan era is also the time for which there is evidence of the cultural and intellectual exchanges that were occurring across Asia, and specifically within an Islamic framework. A case in point pertains to the sciences, such as medicine, pharmacology, and astronomy. In the late thirteenth century, the Yuan dynasty established medical academies in Beijing, which hosted several Muslim physicians, and Islamic pharmaceutical texts were translated in Chinese. If translation was a key element of knowledge transmission, the Mongols went even further, actually adapting and incorporating new, local research. This was the case with astronomy, as manuscripts have survived illustrating Islamic astronomical tables and explanations for calculating luni-solar eclipses and occultations of the moon based on observations made in China.[24]

Initially these texts were primarily used to compile calendars and almanacs for China's Muslim communities only. But by the Ming period, Islamic sciences were also used to the direct benefit of the Chinese establishment, as the title of Emperor, "Son of Heaven," created a direct connection between worldly authority and celestial movements. In fact, the official history of the founding emperor of the Ming dynasty, Hongwu (r. 1368–1398), explicitly mentioned Islamic astronomical sciences to justify his political legitimacy.[25] During the Ming era the Chinese and Muslim "Bureaus for the Administration of the Heaven" were merged, enabling collaboration and the emergence of a Chinese–Islamic system of calendrical astronomy. Portions (or versions) of the most influential *Huihui li* ("Islamic Calendar") manuscript were included in several texts, including: the official history of the Ming (*Mingshi*); the *Complete Books of the Four Imperial Archives*, a collection ordered by the Qing Emperor Qianlong (r. 1735–1796) listing the most valuable books ever written; the official history of the Korean Yi dynasty; and a unique copy of a related manuscript found in Tibet, with the main text written in Arabic but glossed in Mongolian and Tibetan.[26]

In the early decades of the Ming era (which lasted from 1368 to 1644), then, Muslims in the Empire were seen as "Chinese," whether as part of the military apparatus, the bureaucracy, sciences, or literary tradition (e.g. the *Han Kitab*, a new intellectual tradition that merged Islamic knowledge and Chinese frames of understanding; see Chapter 2). The case of Zheng He (1371–1433) is exemplary: a Chinese Muslim born in Yunnan, he was captured by the Ming army in the 1390s. After a career as a palace eunuch, this Muslim Chinese ethnic, who hailed from a landlocked province, was appointed as a naval admiral by the newly installed Ming Emperor Yongle (r. 1402–1424) with the task of leading expeditions to southern Asia and Africa and establishing a rapport with those trading Muslim populations.

But later in the fifteenth century, and into the Qing dynasty (1644–1911/1912), the Empire once again related to Muslims as "foreigners." This was the outcome of two shifts, one social and the other geopolitical. First, in the late Ming era, a general conservative turn enforced assimilationist policies on non-Han peoples. Second, in the eighteenth and nineteenth centuries the Qing dynasty advanced more assertive attempts at "integrating" peripheral regions into the Empire: the mass migration of Han Chinese into resource-bountiful Yunnan created a wedge between local Muslims and Han migrants, while claims to control the Tarim Basin accentuated the dichotomy between Chinese Muslims from the inner provinces (referred to as Hui) and other ethnic Muslim groups (such as the Turkic peoples of the Tarim Basin). (Xinjiang is discussed further in Chapter 7.)

Whereas frictions during the Qing era turned into conflicts, under the Ming the Hui had been better able to create alternative infrastructures for their cultural survival as Muslims, in both central China and Yunnan, or stay focused on Islamic education as a strategy "to save Islam." As suggested by Jaschok and Shui, "in the late fifteenth century respectable *nu junshi* [female religious scholars] existed, and women's talents and roles were acknowledged and approved by Muslims." Capitalizing on this tradition of female religious scholars, equal efforts went into boys' and girls' education, with communities setting up

schools for common Muslims women. As female religious schools became a main-stay of Central China and Yunnan, they came to be complemented with women's mosques (*nusi*) led by women scholars (*nu ahong*). Ultimately, women began to play a greater part in preserving and transmitting Islamic religion.[27]

Muslims of Maritime Asia

The ninth-century Persian geographer Ibn Khordadbeh recorded how seafaring traders from the Abbasid Caliphate reached as far east as Luqin (in today's Vietnam) and Qansu (Yangzhou) on the Yangtze River Delta. Arabs and Persians had in fact been trading along the Indian Ocean monsoon routes for centuries, as proven by the long-established Nestorian–Christian colonies scattered on the coasts of Arabia, India, and Southeast Asia, including Siam (today's Thailand; see Box 1.3). As suggested by André Wink, in the eighth and ninth centuries the Indian Ocean could have been considered an "Arab Mediterranean,"[28] in the sense that the Islamization of maritime Asia became an inevitable bypro-duct of commercial relations in the post-Mohammadan era.

Ships from southern Arabia or Persia (Siraf or Hormuz) called at ports on the east coast of India – either north, in Gujarat, or south, Malabar – before pushing off to Ceylon (Sri Lanka), the Bay of Bengal, and Siam's Ayutthaya. They would finally touch down on the northern coast of Sumatra before going through the Strait of Malacca, the gateway to the Spice Islands (today's Indonesia). Circumnavigating the Malay Penin-sula, some ships – and with them Islam – would redirect north to reach

Guangzhou, with a possible stop in Champa, today's Vietnam. Southeast Asia then had its own internal trading routes, along which Islam pushed south from Malacca to Java's northern coast (the *pasisir*), and further east to the Sulu archipelago (Southern Philippines). And it was this route that Zheng He navigated in the opposite direction in the fourteenth century, bringing Chinese Muslims to the north coast of Java (see Source 1.2).

Source 1.2

The Malay Annals of Semarang

The excerpt below is the beginning of the Malay Annals of Semarang, *offering a concise history of the early history of Chinese Muslim communities on the northern shores of Java. Although in itself a problematic text, this is an important source to understand the multiplicity of intra-Asian Muslim networks in the fourteenth-fifteenth centuries. This narrative centers around the story of Admiral Zheng He, and it is likely grounded on the Chinese records of the Ming maritime expansion. The text as we have it today comes from a 1964 Indonesian book.*[29]

[1. Introduction]

1368–1644
The Ming dynasty, which employed a very great number of Hanafite Muslim Chinese officials, reigned in China.

1403–1424
The reign of the emperor Ceng Tsu, called the Yung Lo period. This was the heyday of China in maritime matters.
1405–1425
The fleet of the Ming emperor of China, commanded by Admiral Haji Sam Po Bo [Zheng He], dominated the seas and shores of Nan Yang (South-East Asia).

[2. Beginning of the Chinese expansion]

1407
The fleet of the Ming emperor of China seized Kukang (= Palembang) which from ancient times had been a nest of Chinese pirates, non-Muslims, from Hokkien. Cen Tsu Yi, the chief of the pirates of Kukang, was taken prisoner and brought in chains to Peking [Beijing]. There he was publicly decapitated as a warning for the Hokkien Chinese all over Nan Yang countries. In Kukang the first Hanafite Muslim Chinese community in the Indonesian Archipelago was established. In the same year another was settled in Sambas, Kalimantan.

1411–1416
Hanafite Muslim Chinese communities were also established in the Malay Peninsula, in Java, and the Philippines. Java mosques were built in Ancol/

Source 1.2   *(cont.)*

Jakarta, Sĕmbung/Cĕrbon, Lasĕm, Tuban, Tse Tsun/Grĕsik, Jiaotung/Jo-
ratan, Cangki/Majakĕrta, and in other places.

[3. Settlements of Chinese Muslims in Java]

1413
The fleet of the Ming emperor of China put in for a month at Sĕmarang for
ship repairs. Admiral Sam Po Bo [Zheng He], Haji Mah Hwang, and Haji
Feh Tsin came very often to the Hanafite Chinese mosque in Sĕmarang for
divine service.

1419
Admiral Haji Sam Po Bo [Zheng He] appointed Haji Bong Tak Keng in
Campa to control the flourishing Hanafite Muslim Chinese communities
which were spreading along the coasts all over the Nan Yang countries.
(Note this was again done by the Japanese Army which appointed Marshal
Terauchi in Saigon, 1942–1945, to control all Japanese generals/
Saikosikikans all over the Nanyo countries.) Haji Bong Tak Keng
appointed Haji Gan Eng Cu in Manila/Philippines to control the
Hanafite Muslim Chinese communities there in Matan/Philippines.

1423
Haji Bong Tak Keng transferred Haji Gan Eng Cu from Manila/
Philippines to Tuban/Java to control the flourishing Hanafite Muslim
Chinese communities in Java, Kukang, and Sambas. At that time, Tuban
was Java's main port, with the kingdom of Majapahit as hinterland.
    Haji Gan Eng Cu became a kind of consul-general of the Chinese
government, the Ming emperor, having control of all Muslim Chinese
communities in the southern Nan Yang countries including Java,
Kukang, and Sambas. In respect of the still existing but degenerated
Majapahit kingdom Haji Gan Eng Cu became a kind of Muslim "Kapten
Cina" [Head of the Chinese community] in Tuban. But then, since the
Chinese fleet of the Ming Emperor dominated all navigation in the seas of
the Nan Yang countries, Haji Gan Eng Cu became also de facto harbour-
master in Tuban. As a reward for his services as a provider to the court of
Majapahit [of foreign supplies] from the harbour of Tuban he was given the
title A Lu Ya by the Majapahit Government. It was given to him by Raja Su
King Ta, Ruler [Queen] of Majapahit, 1427–1447 (Supposition: Haji Gan
Eng Cu is Aria Teja, and he is the father of Nyi Agĕng Manila who was
born in Manila, Philippines.)

1424–1449
His Excellency Haji Ma Hong Fu was appointed ambassador of the Ming
emperor of China at the court of Majapahit. Haji Ma Hong Fu was a son of
the War Lord of Yunnan, and a son-in-law of Haji Bong Tak Keng. On the
way to the court of Majapahit Haji Ma Hong Fu and his family were
escorted by Haji Feh Tsin who had already visited the court of Majapahit
three times as a roving ambassador. (Supposition: Putri Campa was the
wife of Haji Ma Hong Fu.)

Despite their long-standing existence, these networks received a boost when the Mongols conquered Baghdad in 1258: the Mongols themselves sponsored the establishment of Hormuz as a port with direct connections to China, to sustain their flourishing trade. The increase in the volume of commercial exchanges through maritime connections took place at the same time as the expansion of Sufi networks, further contributing to maritime Asia's exposure to, and affirmation of, Islam in the thirteenth and fourteenth centuries (see Chapter 3).

Each region and location experienced its own path to Islamization, but the embracing of this new faith seems to have resulted from a recognizable combination of factors along the oceanic route. First, Perso-Arab (male) Muslim traders settled along their routes to become local agents or taking temporary residence while waiting for the "return monsoon": in either case, they took local wives, their offspring forming the first kernel of local Muslim communities as they inherited the religion of their fathers (such as the Mappilas of Malabar, discussed below). Second was the perception that Muslim traders preferred to do business with other Muslims (along the Indian Ocean as well as the Silk Road), possibly because of the fact that Muslim societies respected trade, and had specific laws dedicated to its fair conduct. This attitude was embraced by individual traders as well as by local rulers whose main revenues came from commerce. Third, with the emergence of Islamic polities, many individuals with ambitions to rise in the new hierarchies chose to convert. Last but not least, some people who were exposed to the contents of Islam as a religious system embraced the new faith as their chosen path to connecting with salvation and the divine. Thus, as seen in the case of Central Asia, conversion was a result of multiple factors, ranging from individuals' spiritual encounters to changing political and military power structures.

The trading centers along the Indian coast had been small cosmopolitan entrepôts since the beginning of oceanic commercial connections, inhabited by Christians, Jews, Parsees, and others. With the spread of Islam in the Arab–Persian lands, these centers became dominated by Muslims, but remained surrounded by a solid and dense Hindu backdrop. The majority of the population and their rulers indeed remained Hindu, and uninvolved in commerce, even though the trade of Indian pepper and other luxury products (especially "spices," from incense to ginger, sandalwood, musk, and more) was very profitable. It was mostly the foreign Arab Muslims and the few mixed Arab-Indian Muslims who engaged in trade.

The Muslims of southern India – mostly located on the Malabar and Coromandel coasts – all claimed Arab and trading backgrounds, actively distinguishing themselves from the Muslims of northern India, who were either of Turkic origins or recent converts. They held this distinction in high consideration, and reaffirmed it in practical terms following the Shafi'i school of law (*madhab*, see Box 2.2), which had been predominant in southern Yemen. On the Malabari coast, then, trade was in the hands of the foreign Arabs and the Mappilas. It is unknown when this Islamic community first emerged, but the Mappilas were South Indian Muslims, the offspring of Arab men and local, low-caste women. Although locally they were seen as having low social status, they were the only community with direct access to the incoming Muslim traders. Similar dynamics were at play in Tamil Nadu, on the Coromandel coast.[30]

As narrated by Ibn Battuta, the Hindus kept these Muslims at a distance, considering them impure. Conversion of the local population was thus very slow. However, as in the thirteenth century considerable numbers of littoral Muslims joined the indigenous armies as mercenaries, and as a new wave of Arabs from southern Yemen – referred to as Hadramis, including *sayyid*s, Sufi *shaykh*s, and scholars – arrived in South India, the social status of Muslims began to change and Islam was more widely accepted. Whereas segregation remained a characteristic of the closed and introvert garrison cities of northern India, these open and outward-looking coastal entrepôts became sites of interaction and conversion, even though realistically speaking the phenomenon was probably limited in numbers and scope, mostly involving low-caste Hindus.

Between the thirteenth and early sixteenth centuries the coast of Malabar was still turning to Islam through local processes of conversion and increased trade. Far from being an exclusively "Arab" phenomenon, Muslim sojourners and settlers in Malabar continued to hail from all over the Indian Ocean, including those from Southeast Asia (Malacca, Sumatra, Pegu, and Tenasserim), northern India (Gujarat), West Asia (Mecca, Syria, and Turkey) and Persia. In fact, while Mappila Muslims were in control of the regional spice trade around southern India, it was foreign Muslims from the east and the west that connected the Mediterranean to China. The arrival of the Portuguese, and their establishing of port cities along the southern Indian coast, deeply affected these local dynamics.

Studying tropical Asia poses an additional challenge, as the humid climate has had a consistently negative impact on perishable manuscripts. The only reliable sources available to us today for the study of Southeast Asia are those made in stone. Thus, even though we can assume that Muslim merchants had been landing on the shores of Southeast Asia possibly as early as the ninth century, the earliest evidence of a Muslim polity and local society there dates back only to the fourteenth century. In historical terms the peak of Southeast Asia's Islamization was reached at the height of intra-oceanic commercial interactions, between the fifteenth and seventeenth centuries, what Anthony Reid has called "the age of commerce."[31]

But we also have an intermediate point, the Maldives, where we know that by the mid-twelfth century a Sultanate was established. These islands had been part of global trading networks for centuries, because of their strategic location in the Indian Ocean, their famed sailors, and the products they traded, including coconut fiber ropes (vital for ship operations) and cowry shells, almost exclusively sourced here and used as currency as far as China. A matrilocal society, much of the trade had been controlled by women for centuries; this fact might help contextualize Ibn Battuta's account of the Maldives, as upon his arrival there he found the place ruled by Sultana Khadija (1347–1379). Her three-decade rule – during which Ibn Battuta himself was appointed as *qadi* (judge of Islamic court) – was followed by another decade of female rule, as her daughter, Myriam (until 1383), and granddaughter, Fatima (until 1388) succeeded Khadija.

By the fourteenth century there are significant enough numbers of headstones populating the Muslim graveyard at Pasai (in contemporary Aceh) to determine that Islam had become a "local religion" in this port city on the western coast of Sumatra.[32] The role of Islam in Southeast Asia would continue to increase in the following centuries, intertwining with social, political, and economic dynamics.

Malacca was the first port of entry for Islam to Southeast Asia (see Map 3); its strategic location on the (homonym) Strait connected West Asia, India, maritime Southeast Asia, and China, making it a hub for traders from all these places, and thus a cultural entrepôt. As recorded in the Javanese chronicles, here *jawi* Muslims (i.e. Muslims from Southeast Asia) came to study, pilgrims boarded their ships to go to Mecca, and some – such as the sixteenth-century Sultan Mahmud – claimed that "Malacca was the right Mecca," erasing the need to go on *hajj* altogether (see Chapter 2 for more on substitute pilgrimages).[33]

Because of the flux of Muslim presence, and the absence of a single sovereign stretching his authority beyond his immediate environs, it is nearly impossible to draw the trajectory and chronology of the Malay Peninsula's Islamization, but the scattered sources available paint a picture in which by the fifteenth century, the king (*Raja*) of Malacca had taken on the title of Sultan, while also retaining a distinctively Hindu-Buddhist court ceremonial. Highlighting the latter factor, European observers argued that the early Islamization of Malaya had only left a mark through mysticism and other "folk" practices, with "the first task of the missionaries [being] to substitute for the Hindu epics tales of the heroes of Islam."[34] In fact, both the local legal code and practices of kingship, while still rooted in pre-Islamic Malay culture, also integrated Islamic principles (see Chapter 2).[35]

But as the trading interchanges also involved the Spaniards and Portuguese – who by then had begun to make substantive incursions into Southeast Asia – Christianity was making converts too. Malacca was eventually conquered by the Portuguese in 1511, displacing the local Muslim polity and effecting an important shift in commercial (and religious) power-balances. By the beginning of the seventeenth century the new faiths of Islam and Christianity had left a lasting mark on the region's maritime rulers.

Following the account of Tomes Pires, an apothecary from Lisbon who traveled to Malacca between 1512 and 1515, we can sketch the history of the Islamization of the Indo-Malay Archipelago. By then, the rulers of Sumatra had for the most part become Muslim, although those in the southern part of the island still embraced local beliefs. In a similar pattern, the hinterland of Central and East Java, as well as the island's western region, were not yet Islamized, while the northern coast – often called the *pasisir* – had been converted as far east as Surabaya (as also narrated by *The Malay Annals of Semarang*, Source 1.2).

The King of Brunei on the Borneo coast and the island of Tidore embraced the new faith in the mid-1400s, Ternate followed suit in the late 1400s, but no other Muslim ruler was to be found in the archipelago, as an inverse pattern had affected most of the eastern islands: rulers had mostly remained faithful to their indigenous beliefs, while individuals – merchants involved in the spice trade – had turned to Islam, confirming the trading factor in early conversions. Sulu, today in the southern part of the Philippines, had seen the establishment of its sultanate at the beginning of the fifteenth century, whereas Islam would make a dent in Patani (coastal Malay Peninsula) in the early sixteenth century – with the establishment of a Sultanate, ruled by, among others, four "Queens," between ca. 1584 and 1718 – and on the southern coast of Sulawesi in the late sixteenth (Buton) and early seventeenth (Makassar) centuries.

At the peak of this "age of commerce," across the strait from European-controlled Malacca, the Sultanate of Aceh was holding its ground. The era of Sultan Iskandar Muda (1607–1636) has been dubbed Aceh's "golden age," as the port city had established itself as a "bulwark of Islam" and pepper trade in the region.[36] But upon the untimely death of his son in 1641, the reign's stability was at stake because of European incursions and possible domestic unrest. Safiatuddin Syah was then appointed "Great Sultan and Illustrious King" of Aceh (*sultan al-muazzam wa-l-khaqan al-mukarram*), her legitimacy harnessed to both

---

Box 1.3   Siam

Islam in what is today's Thailand arrived and developed along at least three different paths. First are the provinces of Patani, Yala, Satun, and Narathiwat: although today these are located in the "deep south" of Thailand, they used to be independent or part of northern Malaya. After a century of coastal incursions from the King of Siam who wished to assert his military presence there, the British officially ceded the provinces to Siam with the Treaty of Bangkok (1909). Second were the Chinese Muslims who descended from Yunnan in the regions of Chang Mai and Chang Rai in the nineteenth century, either to escape the so-called Panthay Rebellion (1855–1873), or to trade in salt.[37]

Third were "foreign Muslims," who arrived to Siam as seafarers and traders from the West. They first populated the Siamese capital Ayutthaya, and then moved to Bangkok following the Burmese–Siamese war of 1767. Whereas Malay Muslims lived in their own communities in the south of the kingdom, these foreigners – and especially the Persians who had been using Ayutthaya as an alternative port to Malacca as early as the 1440s – came into close contact with the Siamese population and the court. Their socio-economic standing as traders allowed them to penetrate, and even influence, Siamese culture, bureaucracy and architecture.

In the early seventeenth century two Persian brothers restructured the department of foreign trade (*phrakhlang*), and while descendants from one of the brothers came to be in control of "the westward trade" for decades to follow, the son of the other brother became an associate of the future King Narai (1632–1688), thus gaining intermarriage within the royal family.

Persian influences started in the realm of overseas commerce, but expanded much further, spilling out into culture and architecture. In Ayutthaya, "*Wat* murals, manuscripts, and [Buddhist] scripture cabinets were adorned with adaptations of the Persian tree-of-life motif, complete with flora and fauna unknown in Siam." And some of the most luxurious mansions – including the French embassy – were styled on Persian architecture, featuring bath houses and Islamic-style pointed arches.[38]

The connection between Siamese royals and the Persians re-emerged over a century later. After the capital moved to Bangkok, the (currently still ruling) Chakri dynasty took control of the Kingdom. The mother of King Rama III was a royal concubine and herself a Muslim of Persian descent. King Rama III elevated her to the rank of Queen and built a mosque in her honor. The Masjid Bang Luang is still today a testament to the interaction between Persianate and Siamese cultures.

Islam and *'adat* (customs), and with no reference to her being female. As the religious scholars (*'ulama*) were integral part of the court apparatus, it is quite certain that the decision of having a female ruler was debated, and eventually accepted; the "state advisor" *shaykh-ul-Islam* Abdu Ra'uf al-Sinkili (see Chapter 2) recognized Safiatuddin as "deputy of God" (*khalifat Allah*), which she understood to mean the one

[who] manifests Allah's wisdom and blessings, who upholds Allah's laws, who clarifies those that are in doubt, whose shine brings forth Allah's light and goodness, who exhorts people to Allah's path, who treats Allah's creations with mercy, who dispenses Allah's justice with utmost care, who hides that which is ugly and forgives those who have sinned, and whose words are gracious.

As she herself illustrates, Safiatuddin – as well as her three female successors – established a practice of "queenship," to borrow Sher Banu Khan's term, which contrasted the cruelty of their male predecessors' coercive and absolutist regimes, and was inspired instead by mercy, tolerance, moral force, consensus, loyalty, and collaboration. The record shows that this strategy well served Aceh's economic interests in the age of commerce, and its political independence at a time when the Europeans had begun to infiltrate the pepper trade.[39]

Archaeological remains, European accounts, indigenous narratives and scholarly analysis, all point at "Islamization" as a process that took centuries to reach deep and wide across the region, to the extent that Merle Ricklefs has suggested that this process is in fact still ongoing.[40]

The maritime trading routes that connected West, South, and Southeast Asia continued north to the southeast coast of China, and were consistently dominated by Muslim merchants – both Arabo-Persians and eastern Asians. Mosques' steles and gazetteers confirm that by the tenth century there were sojourning Muslim merchants who had established themselves in the city of Guangzhou, and across the province of Fujian, the island of Hainan and the Champa region (see Maps 2 and 4). These sojourners would gradually settle, partly assimilating and partly retaining their Muslim identity, as testified by their mono-syllabic names: "Ma" for Muhammad, "Li" for 'Ali, "Pu" for Abu.

By the eleventh century, it was the Fujian port city of Quanzhou – known to the Arabs as Zaytun – that saw a rise in mosques and Tamil, Manichean, and Nestorian temples, as the Song established there a trade tax collection office, and power shifts in West Asia increased demands for luxury items. It was the Ayyubid (1171–1250) and Rasulid dynasties of Egypt that funneled new energy in the oceanic trade. Supported by the Mongol founding of the port city of Hormuz, on the Persian Gulf, direct relations between West Asia and China were established via South and Southeast Asia, thus also leading to a surge in the Muslim presence in Quanzhou (see Source 1.3).

While China had been for centuries the destination of Muslim merchants' land journeys, with the emergence of the Ming dynasty in 1368,

Source 1.3

Ibn Battuta Travels through China (1345)

Ibn Battuta was a religious scholar from Tangier, Morocco who set out to undertake his pilgrimage to Mecca and ended up traveling through Asia and back. It has not been ascertained whether he actually traveled as far as Southeast Asia, hence his account might include firsthand observations as well as tales conveyed to him by other travelers. Either way, his recollections provide us with a unique window in the life of Muslims from North Africa to India, Central Asia, China, and maritime Southeast Asia. Ibn Battuta was able to capitalize on a thick and wide network of Muslim merchants and political elites to forge transregional relations and gain access to local Muslim communities and establishments.[41]

The Chinese themselves are infidels, who worship idols and burn their dead like the Hindus ... In every Chinese city there is a quarter for Muslims in which they live by themselves, and in which they have mosques both for the Friday services and for other religious purposes. The Muslims are honoured and respected ...

On the day that I reached Zaytun [Quanzhou, Fujian province] I saw there the amir who had come to India as an envoy with the present [to the sultan] ... I received visits from the qadi of the Muslims, the shaykh al-Islam, and the principal merchants. Amongst the latter was Sharaf ad-Din of Tabriz, one of the merchants from whom I had borrowed at the time of my arrival in India ... these merchants, living as they do in a land of infidels, are overjoyed when a Muslim comes to them. They say "He has come from the land of Islam" ...

In one of the quarters of this city [Sin-Kalan, Guangzhou, Guangdong province] is the Muhammadan town, where the Muslims have their cathedral mosque, hospice and bazaar. They have also a qadi and a shaykh, for in every one of the cities of China there must always be a Shaykh al-Islam, to whom all matters concerning the Muslims are referred, and a qadi to decide legal cases between them ...

A few days after my return to Zaytun ... I chose to sail up the river ... after ten days' journey we reached Qanjanfu [Fuzhou], a large and beautiful city ... On our arrival, we were met outside the town by the qadi, the shaykh al-Islam, and the merchants, with standards, drums, trumpets and bugles, and musicians. They brought horses for us, so we rode in on horseback while they walked on foot before us. No one rode along with us but the qadi and the Shaykh al-Islam ... [W]ithin the third wall live the Muslims (it was here that we lodged at the house of their shaykh), and within the fourth is the Chinese quarter, which is the largest of these four cities [in one] ...

The land of China, in spite of all that is agreeable in it, did not attract me. On the contrary I was sorely grieved that heathendom had so strong a hold over it. Whenever I went out of my house I used to see any number of

Source 1.3 *(cont.)*

revolting things, and that distressed me so much that I used to keep indoors and go out only in case of necessity. When I met Muslims in China I always felt just as though I were meeting my own faith and kin.

Similar accounts of merchants, qadis, and shaykhs are given for Hangzhou (which he calls Khansa), further north on the river, as Ibn Battuta was traveling toward Beijing, the capital of the Yuan Emperor. Leaving Hangzhou, Battuta noted:

There are no Muslims to be found in these districts [between Hangzhou and Beijing], except casual travelers, since the country is not suitable for [their] permanent residence.

In fact, Hangzhou was the northernmost port city trading with West Asia via South and Southeast Asia.

sea voyages and Islam became key tools to advance imperial interests in asserting political legitimacy. Between 1405 and 1435, the Muslim Admiral Zheng He was tasked with leading seven expeditions along the centuries-old Muslim maritime routes, with the explicit design that his religious affiliation could help garner local support. Muslims in coastal China never built any polities, but they integrated into the imperial structure, and Islam influenced Chinese culture, politics, and science. With established coastal Chinese Muslim communities in Guangzhou, Quanzhou, Hangzhou, and Yangzhou, this potential advantage was reinforced by enlisting substantial numbers of Muslim interpreters, pilots, soldiers, and seamen. Zheng He's armadas reached all the way to the east coast of Africa and succeeded in establishing trading bases as they went along.

The success of this project, the undertaking of reverse-course voyages from East to West Asia, reinforced – and today bears witness to – the sense of an interconnected Muslim community around the Indian Ocean.

Conclusions

Islam traveled across the Asian expanse along land and maritime routes, as Muslims engaged in trade, proselytism, and conquest. While the territory and influence of Islamic political authority expanded, collapsed, and reached further once again, between the seventh and seventeenth centuries the realities and attributes of any given Islamic society varied greatly. This chapter has provided a bird's-eye view of the expansive movement of Muslims out of Arabia and into Asia, as Islam crossed the Oxus/Amu Darya river, following two main paths. First was the military expansion of the Arab Muslim Empire, which reached its territorial apogee under the Abbasids, spreading as far as Transoxiana and northwest India. Second was the movement of pilgrims, scholars, soldiers, and mystics – whose functional identities melted one into the other – across continental and maritime Asia, along the centuries-old Silk Road and the Indian Ocean networks.

These trajectories and dynamics of Muslims' expansion in the first millennium since Islam's emergence provide us with invaluable data necessary to see Asia as a historically cohesive space of Islamized interaction. The movement of ideas, goods, and peoples, whether as individuals or parts of political institutions, point to the interconnectedness of the region; the embedded interactions – sometimes collaborative, sometimes antagonist – testify to the suggestion that Muslims across Asia have imagined themselves as part of a religious community, the *umma*.

Source 1.4

Baba Palangposh

Baba Palangposh (d. 1699) was a seventeenth-century Naqshbandi teacher from Ghudjuvan, near Bukhara (Uzbekistan) who traveled to India and accompanied the Mughul Ghazi al-Din Khan Bahadur in his expedition to conquer the Deccan. As narrated by his pupil, Baba Musafir:[42]

Baba Palangposh arrived after some days, and he stayed in the bungalow beside the stream. He was ill with gripes ... I [Baba Musafir] submitted: "The enemies of Hazrat [polite circumlocution] have the illness gripes and the faqirs have been left behind at various places: and the rains are falling very heavily. You should stay here for a while. After the rains have finished, proceed in whatever direction your mind inclines!"

He said: "As you are pressing me to stay, listen! One dawn in Hasan Abdal [Punjab] I had a vision. The holy gathering of the leader of the Prophets [Muhammad] ... appeared ... I wished to kiss the feet of the Prophet, but he made a sign with his right hand and said in Arabic: 'First pay your respects to Sayyid Hamza!' ... 'Take this sword,' [Sayyid Hamza] said, 'and go to the army of Mir Sihab al-Din [Ghazi al-Din Khan Bahadur] in the land of the Deccan!' He gave the sword into my hand, and following his command I set out for the Deccan ..."

From the arrival of Baba Palangposh the star of /Mir Sihab al-Din's/ felicity was brought to the apex of fortune. In whatsoever direction he turned to confront the armies of the enemy, with /but/ a small body of men he was victorious over them ... /When his forces/ went to war, they saw that Hazrat Baba Palangposh always went forward in front of the army of Islam and would loose arrows upon the army of unbelievers.

By the sixteenth century, Muslim rulers across Asia had begun to look at the Ottoman Caliphate (in today's Turkey) to see their titles recognized, or to receive support as they engaged with the Europeans. In the 1520s several Muslim leaders asked for help from, or offered trading collaborations with, the Ottomans (from the Vizier of Hormuz to Indian corsairs and Sumatran Sultans), with the result that by 1538 the Ottomans "had managed to construct an enormous transoceanic coalition, linking Istanbul with allies across the entire breadth of the Indian Ocean from Shihr and Gujarat to Calicut and Sumatra."[43] But the Muslim community did not construct itself just in terms of religious politics, or in connection to a putative center of religious authority (more on the Ottomans and Asia in Chapter 4).

The experience of the Ghaznavid dynasty's emergence and expansion has brought to light the importance of local dynamics, and the relationship between politics, culture, and community-building in a new frontier. Under Mahmud of Ghazni, Islamization meant attempted obliteration of previous religious and cultural traditions – the fate of the idol of Somnath being emblematic of this trend – but also the sponsoring of knowledge production about non-Muslims. The next chapter will explore how these elements all came together, as pre-Islamic practices (decorative, structural, literary, etc.) came to be integrated, adapted, and appropriated in Islamized contexts, leading to various processes of negotiation that highlighted the endeavor by Muslims to give meaning to their "negotiated" practices and beliefs in Islamic terms.

Further Reading

Ahmed, L. (1992) *Women and gender in Islam: historical roots of a modern debate*, New Haven, CT and London: Yale University Press.

Atwill, D. G. (2018) *Islamic Shangri-La: inter-Asian relations and Lhasa's Muslim communities, 1600 to 1960*, Oakland, CA: University of California Press.

Chaffee, J. W. (2019) *The Muslim merchants of pre-modern China: the history of a maritime Asian trade diaspora, 750–1400*, Cambridge: Cambridge University Press.

Chaudhuri, K. N. (2008 [1985]) *Trade and civilisation in the Indian Ocean: an economic history from the rise of Islam to 1750*, Cambridge: Cambridge University Press.

Di Cosmo, N., Frank, A. J., and Golden, P. B. (Eds.) (2009) *The Cambridge history of inner Asia: the Chinggisid Age*, Cambridge: Cambridge University Press.

Donner, F. M. G. (Ed.) (2008) *The expansion of the early Islamic state*, Aldershot, UK: Ashgate/Variorum.

Eaton, R. M. (2011) *The rise of Islam and the Bengal frontier, 1204–1760*, New Delhi: Oxford University Press.

Elverskog, J. (2010) *Buddhism and Islam on the Silk Road*, Philadelphia, PA: University of Pennsylvania Press.

Golden, P. B. (1990) "The Karakhanids and early Islam," in Denis Sinor (Ed.) *The Cambridge history of early inner Asia*, pp. 343–370, Cambridge: Cambridge University Press.

Hussain, Y., Ibrahim, A., and Siddique, S. (1985) *Readings on Islam in Southeast Asia*, Singapore: Institute of Southeast Asian Studies.

Jaschok, M., and Shui, J. (2000) *The history of women's mosques in Chinese Islam: a mosque of their own*, Richmond, VA: Curzon.

Khan, S. B. A. L. (2017) *Sovereign women in a Muslim kingdom: the sultanahs of Aceh, 1641–1699*, Singapore: NUS Press.

Lapidus, I. M. (2013) *Islamic societies to the nineteenth century: a global history*, New Delhi: Cambridge University Press.

Lipman, J. N. (1997) *Familiar strangers: a history of Muslims in Northwest China*, Seattle, WA: University of Washington Press.

Mernissi, F., and Lakeland, M. J. (2012) *The forgotten queens of Islam*, Minneapolis, MN: University of Minnesota Press.

Milner, A. C. (1981) "Islam and Malay kingship," *Journal of the Royal Asiatic Society of Great Britain & Ireland* 113(1): 46–70.

Morgan, D. O., and Reid, A. (Eds.) (2010) *The new Cambridge history of Islam: Vol. 3, The eastern Islamic world, eleventh to eighteenth centuries*, Cambridge: Cambridge University Press.

Prange, S. R. (2018) *Monsoon Islam: trade and faith on the medieval Malabar Coast*, New York, NY: Cambridge University Press.

Reid, A. (1993) *Southeast Asia in the age of commerce, 1450–1680*, New Haven, CT: Yale University Press.

Wink, A. (2002) *Al- Hind: the making of the Indo-Islamic world*, Vols. 1–2, Leiden: Brill.

Figure 2.1 The Baiturrahman Mosque in Kutaraja (Banda Aceh, Indonesia).
© Collection Nationaal Museum van Wereldculturen. Coll. no. TM-60023672

Figure 2.2 Fort and mosque in Indrapuri (Aceh).
© Collection Nationaal Museum van Wereldculturen. Coll. no. TM-60008438

2 Becoming Muslim (Seventh to Eighteenth Centuries)

When the Dutch completed construction of the new Baiturrahman ("House of the Merciful") mosque (see Figure 2.1) in Kutaraja (now Banda Aceh) in 1881, the local population "had nothing else but ridicule" for it. The domed roof was compared to "a gourd," and the pink-and-blue color scheme reminded them of "the colorful paper decorations of a parade." In the eyes of the Acehnese, its structure "deviated so much from the traditional building style" that it was more "an exotic abnormality than a place of worship."[1]

As recounted by J. Kreemer, an officer at the Aceh Institute in the 1910s–1920s, the mosque had been built in a "beautiful Byzantine style."[2] The drum used to call believers to prayer had been replaced with a European clock, the floor plan was a Greek cross, the architecture referenced Islamic Spain and Mughal India, and the decorations were an Orientalist's dream, copying from the patterns of Egyptian mosques to the metal work of Gothic churches. The Dutch employed Chinese laborers from Java and deployed bricks from Holland, teak from Burma, marble from China, and cast iron from Belgium.[3] Rejecting all things Acehnese had been a conscious effort as the new congregational mosque was meant to mark a new era, being built as an act of good will after years of violent confrontation between the local resistance and Dutch colonial troops. For Christiaan Snouck Hurgronje (1857–1936), also a colonial officer based in Aceh (more on him later in this chapter), this mosque was "one of the many expensive mistakes that characterized the onset of [the Dutch] intervention in Aceh."[4]

Situated on the tip of Sumatra, the westernmost island of the archipelago, Aceh overlooks the Indian Ocean. From this vantage point, Aceh stood as the first point of contact with Muslim traders from Arabia, Persia, and South Asia: as recounted in Marco Polo's *Milione*, "owing to contact with Saracen merchants, who continually resort here in their ships, they [the inhabitants of Ferlac, in Northern Sumatra] have all been converted to the law of Mahomet." Ibn Battuta, a half-century later, talks of the local Sultan as a "lover of theologians. He is constantly engaged in warring for the Faith [against the infidels] and in raiding expeditions, but it is withal a humble-hearted man, who walks on foot to the Friday prayers."[5]

Although we don't know what Aceh's fourteenth-century congregational mosque looked like, we have a clear image of its seventeenth-century configuration, thanks to the drawings of an English traveler and subsequent descriptions and photographs of "traditional" Acehnese mosques from a number of visitors to the area. A structure with a square floor plan and a multi-tiered thatched roof is pictured in Snouck Hurgronje's *The Acehnese*; captioned as the Indrapuri mosque, this was one of the four "great mosques" in the region of Aceh (see Figure 2.2).[6] As argued by later scholars, and suggested by the Acehnese's own reactions to the new building in the 1880s, the paradigmatic mosque structure in Aceh, and elsewhere in the region, "evoked more the idea of a pagoda than that of a Middle Eastern mosque."[7]

Far from discrediting such design, in his masterpiece on Aceh, Snouck Hurgronje – who had spent substantial time in Mecca and was extremely knowledgeable about Islam as a theological, legal, and social phenomenon – reflects more broadly on the relationship between local traditions (*'adat* or *'urf*) and Islamic "ideals," reaching the conclusion that "The *adats* which control the lives of the Bedawins of Arabia, the Egyptians, the Syrians and the Turks, are for the most part different from those of the Javanese, Malays, and Achehnese, but the relation of these *adats* to the law of Islam, and the tenacity with which they maintain themselves in despite of that law, is everywhere the same."[8]

★★★

Rather than approaching Islam as a "new" paradigm superimposing itself on pre-existing rituals and cultures, this chapter focuses on the ways in which (groups of) individuals across Asia made sense of their actions, beliefs, and even aesthetics, "as Muslims."[9] As hinted at through the above illustration of the new Great Mosque of Banda Aceh, this chapter is aimed at highlighting the nuanced significance of "being Muslim" across the many manifestations of Islam as they emerged subsequent to the multidirectional encounters teased out in Chapter 1; and secondly, this chapter also puts into a broader context what is often taken to be the paradigmatic, ideal, or standard (some might say "orthodox") approach to Islam, as evidenced by the Dutch projection of what a mosque "should look like" in the late nineteenth century. The chapter thus explores ways in which Islamic rituals, texts, images, buildings, and legal systems, interfaced and interacted with local traditions during this process of

Islam's expansion across Asia; specific examples will look at China, Java, Malaya, Siam (Thailand), the Indian subcontinent, Afghanistan, and Central Asia.

The interaction between multiple religious traditions has often been described as "syncretic," thus assuming what Stewart and Ernst have explained as an "implicit or explicit contrast with 'pure'" religion. Syncretism rests "on the assumption that those observed have inappropriately mixed cultural and religious categories that are intrinsically alien to each other."[10] This was the predominant discourse in the analysis of Islam outside of the Arab world (see Chapter 9), as also exemplified by Western missionaries who channeled their fear and hostility when describing Islam among Inner Asia's Mongols as "either ingenuine or uncivilized" because of the interweaving of pre-Islamic and Islamic rituals. But as pointed out by Devin DeWeese, the renaming of a shamanic ancestor as a Muslim saint does not happen lightly, and in fact one should focus on "the extent of what has been 'let in' through 'nominal' Islamization ... For what has been 'let in' is the potential for more-than-nominal Islamization."[11]

Several scholars of Islam have approached the process of this encounter as a productive, rather than a negative, one: Merle Ricklefs has used the idea of a "mystic synthesis" to refer to the meeting of Islam and Javanese culture,[12] and Barry Flood has deployed "trans-culturation" for the encounter that took place in northern parts of the Indian subcontinent;[13] Tony Stewart has written about Islamic practices in Bengal as the imagination of "an Islamic ideal in a new literary environment" in which local "authors 'translated' their concepts into the closest locally available terminology,"[14] as Benite Zvi Ben-Dor has done in the context of coastal China when discussing the *Han Kitab* tradition (see below).[15] But Chinese-language Islamic texts that deployed Confucian and Daoist frameworks were not the only tradition in what is today China. Rian Thum has focused on the "*in*efficiency" of land-based networks across Central Asia as the setting for the creation of texts that were "firmly and obviously embedded in inter-Asian Islamic networks" but also "stripped ... of elements that made connection obvious."[16]

What is more, as Stewart and Ernst concluded, "every 'pure' tradition turns out to contain mixed elements; if everything is syncretistic, nothing is syncretistic."[17] Before plunging into the analyses of how the cultures and peoples of Asia became "Muslim" and how they negotiated this new identity, sense of aesthetic, and understandings of political power, it is, then, important to see how the Islam/pre-Islamic encounter was also crucial in the shaping of what came to be seen as Muhammad's orthopraxy.

Mecca as the Soul of Islam?

Pilgrimage to Mecca

In the contemporary imagination, Mecca and its yearly pilgrimage (*hajj*, the fifth pillar of Islam, see Box 1.2 and Box 2.1) are quintessential symbols of Islam. Yet, located a mere forty-five miles inland from the seaport of Jeddah, this oasis had already been a destination for pilgrimage in the pre-Islamic era (assuming an average speed of three miles an hour for a camel riding in a caravan, Mecca would have been one "good day's journey" from the coast).[18] The presence of water and its position along the caravan routes created the conditions for Mecca to become a trading hub and a destination for religious pilgrimages. Pagan Arabs flocked to the Ka'ba to pay tribute to their gods: the cube which hosts the black stone (likely a meteorite) was filled with votive statuettes, and the premises regularly witnessed the sacrificial slaughtering of cattle. This was the case until 630, when it is narrated that Muhammad entered the Ka'ba and "smashed" the idols (whether physically or figuratively is still debated).

[26]We showed Abraham the site of the House, saying, "Do not assign partners to Me. Purify My House for those who circle around it, those who stand to pray, and those who bow and prostrate themselves. [27]Proclaim the Pilgrimage to all people. They will come to you on foot and on every kind of swift mount, emerging from every deep mountain pass [28]to attain benefits and celebrate God's name, on specified days, over the livestock He has provided for them – feed yourselves and the poor and unfortunate – [29]so let the pilgrims perform their acts of cleansing, fulfil their vows, and circle around the Ancient House." [30]All this [is ordained by God]: anyone who honours the sacred ordinances of God will have good rewards from his Lord. (Q 22: 26–30)

[96]The first House [of worship] to be established for people was the one at Mecca. It is a blessed place; a source of guidance for all people; [97]there are clear signs in it; it is the place where Abraham stood to pray; whoever enters it is safe. Pilgrimage to the House is a duty owed to God by people who are able to undertake it. Those who reject this [should know that] God has no need of anyone. (Q 3: 96–97)

All things considered, Mecca's importance to Muslims rests on at least four key factors. First of all, as the birthplace of Muhammad (ca. 570) and the location where the message of Islam was first revealed to him, beginning in 610, this oasis (now a megacity) is taken as the birthplace of Islam. Second, its hosting of the Ka'ba made Mecca the hub of Abrahamic monotheism and a well-established pilgrimage site. Thirdly,

Mecca became the focal point of the ritual prayer, *salat*, as it is toward the Ka'ba that Muslims orient themselves when praying – even though, in the earliest months of the revelation, the direction of prayer, called *qibla*, was set on Jerusalem (Q 2:142–150). Lastly, Mecca was a place of longing for return: about a decade after the beginning of the revelation – a decade largely characterized by persecution – Muhammad and his supporters (*ansar*) were forced to leave Mecca and move (or migrate, *hajara*) to the oasis of Yathrib, later renamed as Madina an-Nabi (The City of the Prophet), or simply "Medina."

The *hijra* (migration) of 622 marked the year zero of the Islamic calendar (i.e. the *hijri* calendar) and sanctioned Muhammad as the political and military leader of the growing community of Muslims, in addition to his spiritual duties as prophet and teacher. This geographical rupture remained a key element of early Islamic history, as Muhammad continued to attempt to return to Mecca for political and military reasons, as much as for religious ones. In the wake of his military successes in the Hejaz, Muhammad tried to perform a pilgrimage in 628. Halted by his fiercest opponents (the Quraish), Muhammad failed in this attempt but succeeded in signing an agreement that would have allowed Muslims to perform the pilgrimage. The agreement proved unnecessary: accompanied by 90,000 followers, Muhammad conquered Mecca in 630, making of this town the capital of the emerging Muslim polity.

As we have seen in the verses quoted above (Q 22: 26–30), the Qur'an (and its exegetical commentaries, *tafsir*) narrate that the Ka'ba, or *bayt Allah*, "the house of God," had been originally built as a site of pilgrimage by Adam, and then restored by Abraham, the first monotheist (or *hanif*). Henceforth, the Ka'ba underwent multiple transformations, transitioning from being a destination of Abrahamic pilgrimage to an object of pagan devotion and eventually to featuring in the five pillars of Islam. Muhammad's message was thus couched as a reiteration of previous revelations, rooted in continuity. Yet, the Islamic revelation was also framed as a moment of rupture with Arab paganism.

Humanity had forgotten the path laid out by God, and Islam had come as a reminder, offering a way out of ignorance (*jahiliyya*). Muhammad walked the path of previous prophets (Q 2:87; Q 2:139), the Qur'an embraced previous revelations (Q 2:87; Q 4:136), and the peoples who had followed them were recognized and respected as monotheistic "people of the book" (*ahl al-kitab*, see Box 1.1) (Q 3:110–113). Islam thus presented itself as the most recent reiteration of an old message, while also intending to uproot Arab tribalism, factionalism, paganism, and patriarchy – all seen as causes for the corruption of the original status of harmony with God.

Box 2.1   The *Hajj* Rituals

Undertaken during the first half of the last month of the Islamic calendar (Dhul-Hijja), the *hajj* ritual takes place over seven days (although the average *hajj* tends to be longer than this, in terms of time spent in the Hijaz). Each pilgrim starts the performance of the fifth pillar of Islam by entering a state of purity (*ihram*), and donning two sheets of white cloth. This step symbolizes the equality of all pilgrims before God, but also allows each pilgrim to mark the transition into a spiritual dimension, "taking leave" from the mundane. This is a necessary condition for any Muslim entering the sanctuary (*haram*).

In the center of the *haram* is the Ka'ba, a cubic building fifty feet high, now empty with the exception of a risen small black stone. The Ka'ba is covered on the outside by a sacred drape of embroidered silk (*kiswa*) which is changed every year (panels being donated by various pilgrim-sending countries). In its proximity are the Station of Abraham (where his footprint is preserved), the well of Zamzam (the oldest spring in Mecca, and possibly the reason why this location emerged as a trading hub and pilgrimage site in the pre-Islamic era) and a pulpit. The hills of al-Safa and al-Marwa complete the scene.

The current ritual being a merger of the prophetic *'umra* and *hajj*, the pilgrimage is composed of two parts, one taking place in Mecca, and the other between Mina and the Plain of Arafat. The Meccan portion of the ritual includes the circumambulation (*tawaf*) of the Ka'ba and the running (*sa'y*) (or actually walking) between the two hills of al-Safa and al-Marwa, seven times each. This part is usually undertaken before and after the pilgrimage itself, which starts on the seventh day of Dhul-Hijja with a congregational prayer around the Ka'ba.

The pilgrims gather in Mina, whence they begin the actual pilgrimage to the Plain of Arafat and the Mount of Mercy, circa ten miles to the east. There they pray and meditate from sunrise until sunset (*yawm al-wukuf*), before returning to Muzdalifa and then onto Mina. It is on this second visit to Mina that each pilgrim performs the stoning of the Devil, throwing seven stones to a pillar (*jamrat al-'aqaba*) said to represent Satan himself. Before returning to Mecca, pilgrims celebrate a festival known as *'Id al-adha* (festival of the sacrifice) during which sheep, goats, and camels are slaughtered and distributed to the poor (a symbol of Ibrahim's slaughtering of a lamb instead of his own son, upon God's mercy after Ibrahim's readiness to obey his command). All Muslims celebrate the "Great Feast," whether they are performing the *hajj* or not, by slaughtering sacrificial animals and distributing the meat to the poor (see Bukhari, "The Sound" 25.104).

Once we take this perspective on the Qur'anic message and the Ka'ba, the *hajj* rituals (see Box 2.1) emerge as a vivid representation of the tension between continuity and change, as the Islamic tradition has retained several pre-Islamic elements of the pilgrimage itself while getting rid of others (such as the idols' statuettes).

But because of the narrative of continuity that surrounded the Ka'ba itself, modifications also needed to be explained as corruption of the Abrahamic tradition, a breach of monotheism. How, then, had the Ka'ba, the first house of God, the original place of monotheistic worship, become the ritual home of idolatry and paganism? The most widely accepted explanation was advanced by the Iraqi scholar Ibn al-Kalbi (737–819) who pointed to the nomadic background of the pilgrims. Unable to perform the pilgrimage as often as they desired, but committed to their worship, pilgrims, Ibn al-Kalbi suggested, took stones from the House and carried them along in their travels. Wherever they lived, they would then replicate a symbolic circumambulation of the Ka'ba by circling around the stone they had taken. The resemblance of these stones to human shape had eventually led to idolatrous practices. This explanation is important not as a historical account but as an indication of how much effort Muslim scholars were putting into identifying harmonizing common traits, as well as key differences, between the various manifestations of these pilgrimage rituals.

The pre-Islamic/Islamic transformation of the *hajj* pilgrimage was not the only nexus of change. Just as there had been much uneasiness in the early sources in addressing the relationship between the Abrahamic, pagan, and Islamic rituals, so there was difficulty in accepting the fact that the standardization of the *hajj* as an immutable Islamic ritual took shape over time, as a tradition *in fieri*. Muhammad himself had performed this ritual in different ways throughout his life. And in fact today's *hajj* rituals follow the canon established by Muhammad during his last pilgrimage, which he undertook right before his death.

During Muhammad's lifetime there appeared to be a distinction between a "lesser" and a "greater" pilgrimage: one called *'umra*, consisting of a purely Meccan set of rituals, as pilgrims circumambulated the cubic building, "ran" between the hills of al-Safa and al-Marwa, sacrificed the animals in the wider *haram* space, and shaved their heads. The other, back then referred to as *hajj*, instead brought the believers outside the oasis space and onto the Plain of Arafat. But the Islamic pilgrimage of today – regardless of whether it is performed during the month of Dhul-Hijja (thus claiming *hajj* status) or not (*'umra*) – combines these two traditions.[19]

Asia's Second Meccas and Other Substitution Pilgrimages

As rituals related to the *hajj* pilgrimage were shaped by pre-Islamic Arab pagan traditions connected to the Ka'ba, so Muslim pilgrimages in other parts of the world are the result of the encounter and negotiation between Islam and local pre-Islamic devotional practices (sometimes Hindu, sometimes Buddhist, Shamanic, or others), but they are consistently performed by Muslims as Islamic.

And while the pilgrimage to Mecca is beyond doubt a most formative experience for the Muslims who can embark on this journey, physical travel to Arabia and the performance of the *hajj* rituals illustrated above are not the only way Muslims have fulfilled the fifth pillar of Islam. In fact, the Abbasids built "second Meccas" on the eastern edges of the Empire to prevent their troops from leaving unstable conquered territory. The Palestinian geographer al-Maqdisi (945–991) wrote of a sanctuary near Nineveh, Iraq, which competed with Mecca as pilgrimage destination, with seven visits there corresponding to performance of the *hajj*. The same was said of circumambulations of the *mihrab* in the shrine of the Merinid Sultan Abu Yusuf (1258–1286) in Rabat, Morocco.

The origins of this phenomenon are in fact multiple, ranging from the logistical to the spiritual. In the seventh century, the 'Umayyads had lost control of Mecca and Medina when they moved their capital to Damascus (Syria), making the pilgrimage extremely difficult because of attacks by Arab Bedouin tribes. The Abbasids, whose capital was located even further away, were able to retain control of the holy cities and built the infrastructure necessary for safety and comfort (milestones, caravan paths, caravanserais, resting stations, and watering places). These routes survived the Abbasid collapse, but were all concentrated alongside the Mediterranean coast, in the westernmost area of Asia. Thousands of pilgrims gathered in Damascus, Cairo, and Baghdad at the beginning of the *hajj* season to continue onto Mecca, but their travels from Iraq, Persia, and Central Asia remained unsafe and unsupported until the fifteenth century. The Ottomans were the first dynasty to look eastward (or at least, the first one for which we have records of it doing so), but their commitment to "protecting" pilgrims coming from Central, South, and Southeast Asia was largely driven by political consideration. (see Chapter 4).

Alternative pilgrimage sites thus emerged due to political circumstances, physical distance, but also as a sign of devotional distance from "Mecca" as the "headquarters" of Sunni (and from the twentieth century onward, Wahhabi) Islam. Shi'a Muslims travel to

Karbala (near Kufa, Iraq) to commemorate the martyrdom of Imam Husayn (see Box 3.1), and while participating in one of the largest human yearly gatherings in the world, some see this pilgrimage as superseding the *hajj*. The Zikri Mahdavis of Baluchistan, a millenarian sect based in Southwestern Pakistan, regard a local pilgrimage to a shrine in Makran, their "holy city," as having the same merit as going on *hajj*.

"Second Meccas" also emerged from a variety of devotional practices, from a specifically Sufi discourse of rejecting external duties (including the five pillars) and placing much importance on their *shaykh*s, to the sacralization of relics of the prophet Muhammad. Sufis of various orders might privilege pilgrimage to the shrine of their founder, or other sites deemed important in their own cosmologies.

Adherents to the *tariqa* Qadiriyah in China, which in the seventeenth century spread throughout northwest China, maintain that pilgrimage to their Da Gongbei ("Great Shrine"), located in Linxia and housing the body of their founder Qi Jingyi (or Hilal al-Din, 1656–1719), is a valid substitute to undertaking the *hajj* to Mecca.[20] In fact, the town of Linxia itself (formerly Hezhou) will become known as "Little Mecca" among China's Muslims.

A sixteenth-century inscription located in Old Malda, Western Bengal, refers to its Friday mosque as a *thani ka'ba* ("second Mecca"). The shrine of Hazratbal, a neighborhood of Srinagar, Kashmir, is said to house a hair of the prophet Muhammad and is described as a "second Medina." A poem from the late seventeenth century celebrates the building of the mosque for this relic: "A voice from heaven announced: Kashmir has turned into Medina as a result of one hair of the Prophet."[21] In the words of a Kashmiri *pir*:

> Whosoever has seen the sacred hair of Muhammad,
> has had in reality the vision of the Prophet,
> [although] he is entombed in Arabia,
> his sacred hair sanctifies the *'ajam* [Persians, non-Arabs]
> he reveals the eternal reality of his radiance only to those in Kashmir
> who have an abiding faith and are spiritually illuminated.[22]

And in another case, Muhammad is compared to a beloved hero represented, in this eighteenth-century Punjabi poem, by Ranjha. In this example of South Asian Indo-Islamic love poetry, the birthplace of Ranjha is equaled to Mecca:

> The *hajji* go to Mecca, world by world,
> My Ranjhu is Mecca for me
> …

The *hajji* is within
the *ghazi* is within.
...
I have become a fool.
The *hajjis* go to Mecca.
We must go to Takht-i mir.
This is the road to Mecca.[23]

In Java, the graves of the nine saints (*wali songo*) credited with the Islamization of the island, and more broadly Southeast Asia, are known destinations of pilgrimage. Among them is the mausoleum of *Sunan Bayat* (between the towns of Yogyakarta and Solo), known to have performed miracles and thought to have lived in the early sixteenth century, the time of Java's transition from a Hindu-Buddhist empire to a Muslim kingdom. Visits (*ziyara*) to this grave site have been performed since at least the early seventeenth century by Sultan Agung (1593–1645, see below). Visits to the complex are best performed on specific days, with the timing calculated combining the Javanese and Islamic calendars; but as certain groups in Indonesia have been trying to dislodge the connection between Javanese and Islamic traditions, some visitors today might prefer actually avoiding traditionally held "special" days. And mirroring this tension, whereas "monuments in Hindu style surround Sunan's grave, the grave itself is purely Islamic, as it represents the Ka'bah in Mecca." What is more, according to the custodian, the sacredness of the place – and Indonesia's distance from Arabia – means that a *ziyara* to Sunan's grave can replace the *hajj* to Mecca. As suggested by Nelly van Doorn-Harder and Kees De Jong, "several Indonesian locations are considered to be cosmic centers that possess the same degree of spiritual power as can be encountered in Mecca."[24]

Many sites of substitution pilgrimages are still active in Kyrgyzstan, Kazakhstan, Uzbekistan, Turkmenistan, and Xinjiang. A legend recorded in the nineteenth century describes a mosque built near the Throne of Solomon at Ush, Kyrgyzstan, as being built by Abraham himself, on the model of Mecca; after naming it "The Mecca of the Persians," the legend goes on to stipulate that "whoever comes to this mosque during the Festival of the Sacrifice and performs a prayer with two prostrations, it is as though he makes the *hajj*."[25]

Narrations about the shrine of the "People of the Cavern" in Tuyuq (near Turfan, in Xinjiang) (see Figure 2.3), affirm that "some people argue that one pilgrimage performed at Ashab al-Kahf can be equated with a half-pilgrimage [to Mecca] (*hajliq*) and two pilgrimages to this place are equivalent to a full pilgrimage [to Mecca]."[26] In the early 2010s, pilgrims about to go on *hajj* to Mecca first undertook a visit to

Figure 2.3 Shrine of the People of the Cavern, Tuyuq (Xinjiang, China).
© Chiara Formichi

this shrine as a form of preparation. A 1947 poem dedicated to the shrine recites:

> Tuyuq is the second Mecca of God.
> Tuyuq is the travel-place of those who are successful,
> Tuyuq is the Paradise created by God.[27]

Locations scattered across the Muslim lands were then identified by local peoples as "second Meccas" or "second Medinas," holding the promise of ultimate blessing (baraka), whether bestowed through the holiness of an enshrined Sufi teacher, a relic of the Prophet, the memory of a miracle, or the aura of a (possibly mythical) ancestor. As suggested by Sophia Rose Arjana, "this enactment of a localized sacred space in relation to a holy city is common in the context of Islamic pilgrimages … due to ephemeral quality of sacred space, there is no one religious center around which all others necessarily revolve."[28]

Emerging Muslim Spaces

As foreign Muslims settled across Asia and local communities begun to emerge in the twelfth to fifteenth centuries, the landscape also began to change, albeit gradually. As seen at the beginning of this chapter, the "original" Great Mosque of Kutaraja on the island of Sumatra looked like a Hindu temple. As introduced in the previous chapter, Mahmud of Ghazni raided Jain and Hindu temples and repurposed some of their structural and decorative elements. Islamic practices, from ritual to the law, incorporated aspects of non-Islamic traditions, as we have discussed above in relation to the *hajj* to Mecca and other pilgrimages. In this section we see how the paradigms developed by scholars such as Ricklefs, Flood, Thum, Stewart, Ernst, and DeWeese, articulated at the very beginning of the chapter, manifest themselves in Islamic architecture, decorative arts, and ritual devotion.

Creating Muslim Spaces

Domes and minarets dominate our imaginary of Islamic architecture, as geometry, flowers, leaves, and calligraphy evoke Islamically compliant decorations. Yet, many mosques across Asia embody different referents: many of the oldest mosques in China look like pagodas – from the Huaisheng Mosque in Guangzhou, which is claimed to date to 627, to the Grand Mosque in Xi'an, built in the early Ming era, and the several Sufi shrines that dot Linxia's "Little Mecca" (see Figure 2.4); this style was even passed on to Chinese Muslim diasporas in Southeast Asia, as evident in the Panthay mosque built in Mandalay in 1868. And the structures of several mosques on the northern shore of Java and in peninsular Malaysia mirror Hindu temples, with their characteristic multi-tiered roof and square plant, as do several more in southern India (see Figure 2.2 at the beginning of this chapter).

But this repurposing of pre-existing models in a "new" Islamic context is not peculiar to "peripheral Asia." Arab nomadic tribes had an elaborate oral literary tradition but knew nothing about architecture or the decorative arts, as they knew little or nothing about bureaucracy, state administration, and courtly etiquette. Byzantium, the Hellenics, the Sasanians, and the Achaemenids made available readymade infrastructures to be used while the new Empire shaped its own, emulating and adapting these extant models to their own specific needs, in statehood as well as in the arts. And while some of this appropriation occurred in the context of military conquest, some was a two-way process of assimilation and integration.

The early Arab Muslim conquerors prayed in repurposed churches and temples in Syria and Palestine, and the first new buildings were modeled on them. The octagonal structure of the Dome of the Rock, built in 691 in Jerusalem, was inspired by Constantine's Church of the Holy Sepulcher, and the circular domed model had already been

Figure 2.4 Mosque, Linxia (Gansu, China).
© Chiara Formichi

recurrent in Roman mausolea. The 'Umayyad Mosque was built in
Damascus in the early eighth century after the Empire's capital moved
there: the chosen location had hosted a Phoenician site, turned pagan
Temple of Jupiter, turned Byzantine cathedral.[29] This heritage included

four square towers, one at each corner, known as *sawami*, i.e. hermits' towers. It is no coincidence, then, that the first case of purpose-built minarets as towers from which to perform the call to prayer (*adhan*) was requested by Caliph Mu'awiya (602–680) during his stay in Damascus. In 673, Mu'awiya ordered four towers to be added to the mosque of 'Amr, in Fustat, Egypt, to replicate the towers that surrounded the then "mosque" of Damascus, even though those were a clear pre-Islamic feature. Equally pre-Islamic was the model of the unique helicoidal minaret of Samarra, Iraq, inspired by the Babylonian *zikurrat*, the so-called "Tower of Babel."[30]

The dome, as emblematic of Islamic architecture as the minaret, finds its roots in Sasanian, Roman, and Hellenic palace architecture. Indeed, the dome made its inroad in mosque-building as princes began to patronize religious constructions and wished to mark them with a recognizable symbol of honor and prestige which connected them to Roman mausolea as well as pre-sedentary tent models.[31] Also Sasanian is the early model of Persian mosques, as Muslims either converted existing temples of fire or used them as models for their new mosques. This same square-based building would inspire the style of funerary constructions in Bukhara (also surmounted by domes, for the reasons explained above), as also seen in the Mausoleum of Mahmud of Ghazni (see Figure 1.1).

As had already happened under various dynasties in North Africa, the Levant, and Persia, when the Ghurids entered Delhi in 1193, the Friday Mosque (named the Quwwat-ul-Islam mosque, part of the Qutb Minar complex) was erected on the site of a pre-existing temple. Similarly to what Mahmud of Ghazni had done a century earlier (see Chapter 1), several Hindu icons were used at the main entrance to the mosque, "permit[ing] the perpetual commemoration of a singular victory."[32] At the same time, however, the Ghurids recontextualized non-Islamic artifacts in a positive manner: the entire construction of this Delhi mosque was in fact accomplished by repurposing pieces of over twenty Hindu and Jain temples, arranged following Iranian and Central Asian stylistic models.

Barry Flood shows how, parallel to conquerors' pillaging and re-using of pieces from pre-Islamic places of worship to build their own, some decorative or structural elements belonging to the "Indian" tradition were appropriated and seeped through, integrated with Islamic patters. At Ghazni, for example, the minaret of the Ghaznavid Sultan Mas'ud III (d. 1115) featured cut brick, which was only common in the temples and tombs of the Indus Valley.[33] A more vivid example is provided by the famous Taj Mahal, built by the Mughal Shah Jahan (1592–1666) as a tomb for his wife in the mid-seventeenth century. The choice of marble and bricks is thought to be a nod to the Hindu building practice of using white for Brahmin priests and red for Ksatrya soldiers; the mausoleum's dome is shaped as a lotus flower (which generally refers to purity in Hinduism, but also in the Buddhist and Jain traditions) and is surrounded by four smaller dome-shaped pavilions, used in the Hindu tradition to identify the location of cremation sites.

This pattern of adoption and adaptation characteristic of non-conquest contexts was prominent in southern India, where Islam arrived and spread through traders (see Chapter 1). Malabar, on the southwest coast of India, had been integrated in the larger trading networks of the Indian Ocean even before the emergence of Islam, and it is therefore very probable that some kind of places for Islamic worship existed in this area at an early date. Surely this was the case by the twelfth to thirteenth centuries, when the Malabar coast became a crucial stop for those engaged in the maritime trade between western and eastern Asia; this is testified by mosque architecture and by the existence of Muslim graves.

Small port towns along the Malabar coast accommodated a diverse population, which included local Hindus and foreign Arabs, Persians, Chinese, Javanese, Africans, etc. Mosques thus emerged as places of worship, education, and law-making for the local Muslims, the Mappilas, but also functioned as key elements in the logistical infrastructure needed by foreign Muslim traders, who would have otherwise been unable to procure food and shelter in this majority Hindu region.

The architecture reflected the fact that this Muslim minority's survival and economic privilege depended on the Hindu sovereign. As pointed out by Sebastian Prange, instead of transplanting Arabian or Persianate models (the latter becoming a mainstay across Central Asia), Malabar Muslims embraced the style of local buildings: not only they were better suited to the local climate – the multi-tiered roofs and open sides let the breeze flow through – but by using the same materials and craftsmen as their Hindu peers and avoiding a visual rupture, these features also allowed for integration in the local ritual and physical landscape. In fact, it was the inside of these mosques that marked their Islamicity and connection to Arabia: the space privileged congregation over procession; Qur'anic inscriptions in Arabic calligraphy were the dominant decorative feature; and a single semi-circular *mihrab* ("prayer niche") dominated the *qibla* wall.[34]

Southeast Asia's earliest mosques – dating from the fifteenth century onwards – also mirror the features of Hindu temples, as exemplified by the Indrapuri (Aceh) mosque featured at the beginning of this chapter (Figure 2.2), as well as the mosques of Demak (ca. 1479) and Kudus (ca. 1549), both on the northern coast of Java, and the (eighteenth-century) mosque of Kampung Laut located in northern Malaysia. The Demak and Kampung Laut mosques were both built in wood, on pillars arranged around a square plan, covered by a three-tiered roof, and only the latter included a minaret. The mosque at Kudus is most interesting because of its use of red brick, and the inclusion of a tower and portal that most starkly remind the viewer of Balinese Hindu temples.

Like Malabar's mosques, all of these buildings (and some others that can also be considered "traditional" in style), feature a single deep niche as *mihrab* and display elaborate Qur'anic inscriptions, making reference back to Arabia. Although it feels compelling to connect the mosque architecture of Malabar to Java and Malaysia, Hélène Njoto has noted that Java's Hindu-Buddhist temples from the seventh to the thirteenth centuries could have been the "indigenous" models for the early Javanese mosque, as they featured a square base with two concentric sets of pillars supporting a multi-tiered roof. This might suggest that "the Javanese and Malay mosque types should no longer be considered as sub-types of East Asian pagodas or Indian Muslim Mosques, but as worthy Southeast Asian innovations."[35]

Circulation of people, goods, and ideas existed and impacted the Islamicate world in all directions; not just "peripheral Asia," but also its core. In his fascinating study of the Yemeni Hadrami diaspora across the Indian Ocean, Engseng Ho has focused on the multi-directionality of travel, and how Hadramis' movement to Southeast Asia was never final, as these men – because they were mostly men – continued to straddle their Arab and *jawi* identities. A physical testament to this, besides the proliferation of shrines belonging to Hadramis who lived in Southeast Asia (known as *jawi* Hadrami), is the appearance of the verandah as an architectural feature in the Hadramawt valley in Southern Arabia in the late nineteenth and early twentieth centuries, as several of these *jawi* Hadramis re-settled west, taking with them bits of their Southeast Asian life.[36] Also pointing in the direction of a multidirectional circulation is the presence of Malay words in the Arabic language.

In the previous chapter we have seen how Persian Muslims influenced the bureaucracy and aesthetics of the Siamese capital of Ayutthaya, especially during the reign of King Narai (1632–1688), in the seventeenth century. Following the Burmese military victory against Ayutthaya in 1767, the royal palace was re-established in Thon Buri, today a neighborhood of Bangkok. At the time, this area was the kingdom's hub of commerce, military power, and wealth, hosting the Royal palace as well as several places of worship – a Lao temple, a Chinese shrine, a Portuguese catholic church, and a few mosques. Among them is the Ton

Son mosque, believed to be the oldest mosque in Bangkok, founded in the seventeenth century by the Cham community. Although it was renovated in the mid-twentieth century in a more distinctively Arab style, photos on site show that, at an intermediate stage, "the Ton Son mosque was rebuilt in 1827 [during the reign of Rama III] in a style similar to the Dusit Grand Palace [as a sign] of its royal sponsorship."[37]

Muslim merchants were as crucial to the economy of southern China during the Song (960–1279) and Yuan (1271–1368) periods, and thus the building of mosques in the tenth century is well documented in the coastal regions of Fujian, Guangdong, and Shanghai, and at a slightly later point in time in the Silk Road cities of Kaifeng and Xi'an. Because of heavy reconstruction projects that took place during the Ming dynasty (1368–1644), most of these mosques display a mixed environment of Islamic purpose and space organization, alongside Chinese models, techniques, and decorative elements. An early mosque in Quanzhou, for example, is characterized by a Central Asian and Iranian shaped entryway featuring a high arch with a rectangular frame (*pishtaq*), but in fact the technique used in the vaulting mirrors the one that had been used in China since the Han dynasty, indicating that "the architectural features observed today ... were clearly within the repertoire of builders in Quanzhou and across China at that time [i.e. in 1310]."[38]

A stele in the Huaisheng mosque of Guangzhou, Guangdong, claims its founding date to be 627, which is close to impossible. But what is of interest here is that its fourteenth-century plan strictly applied Chinese conceptions of space: the complex is oriented along the north–south axis, and its T-shaped worship space is confined by two gates, one at the south end, the other at the north end; arcades run along the east and west sides, enclosing a *yuetai*, a platform usually used for ceremonies in Buddhist and Daoist monasteries. Yet, although the *yuetai* is annexed to the southern wall of the prayer hall, to enter one has to make a sharp turn, as – to conform to Islamic parameters – the hall's entrance is on the east wall, faced by the *mihrab* on the west wall; and the southwest corner of the complex hosts a round minaret. As Nancy Steinhardt concluded, "Muslim worship could occur behind the facade of a thoroughly Chinese religious compound with a single alteration, namely the orientation of prayer space, and that accommodation to the tradition was not visible from the outside."[39]

Decorating Muslim Spaces

Allah's Apostle returned from a journey when I had placed a curtain of mine having pictures over (the door of) a chamber of mine. When

Allah's Apostle saw it, he tore it and said, "The people who will receive the severest punishment on the Day of Resurrection will be those who try to make the like of Allah's creations." So we turned it (i.e., the curtain) into one or two cushions.[40]

Calligraphy, geometry, and floral arabesques are the most characteristic elements of the Islamic decorative tradition. The presence of animals and people has been shunned from the sacred sphere, supposedly limited to the profane. The desert castle of Qusayr 'Amra, built by the 'Umayyads in north Jordan – now a UNESCO World Heritage Site – is the most notable example, displaying hunting scenes alongside naked women and a painting of six kings. And a series of events that occurred in the early 2000s – ranging from Islamic extremists' destruction of cultural heritage across West Asia, North Africa, and Afghanistan to the backlash to European publications of cartoons depicting Muhammad – would appear to confirm Islam's iconoclasm.

Although there is no clear rejection of figuration in the Qur'an, Muslims at different times and in different places have been concerned with their religion's perceived iconoclasm. A first example is from Java, where some of the earliest surviving examples of decorative implements in Islamic religious spaces appear to be concerned with avoiding iconography while retaining pre-Islamic imagery. The burial sites and shrines of Java's *wali songo*, the "nine saints" of Arab and Persian descent claimed to have Islamized Southeast Asia, were built between the fifteenth and seventeenth centuries, in styles combining Islamic sensibilities and Hindu-Buddhist patterns familiar to the craftsmen. Dutch drawings and photos taken in 1930 at the Mosque of Mantingan, near Jepara, Central Java – possibly built in the mid-sixteenth century and the burial site of Ratu Kalinyamat, the one woman listed as a *wali songo* – show this combination in the abstraction of zoomorphic carvings and guardian figures (in this case an elephant and monkey, but in others snakes or felines) that would previously have displayed clear animal features. The deployment of artistic patterns that are recognizably Hindu-Buddhist yet modified through stylization and abstraction, likely indicates early concerns with orthopraxy and the perceived ban on figuration, as craftsmen and commissioners deliberately pursued an Islamically compliant aniconic choice when crafting abstracted zoomorphic carvings (Figure 2.5).[41]

Mosques pre-dating the twelfth-century conquest of India by the Ghurid Turkic dynasty also seem to have abided by a strict avoidance of icons (aniconism) despite – or because of? – the conspicuous presence of Hindu imagery. Aniconism was also a form of "visual rhetoric of piety," used by the new Islamic order to demean Hindu traditions. After

Figure 2.5 *Mantingan*, elephant suggested in stylized lotus rods, leaves, and flower scrolls.
© Collection Nationaal Museum van Wereldculturen. Coll. no. TM-60054170

Mahmud of Ghazni conquered parts of Gujarat (1025), he proceeded to have the highly revered temple of Somnath destroyed, its central icon of Shiva *linga* looted, and later cast on the entrance threshold of Ghazni's Friday Mosque.[42]

Interestingly, though, before the emergence of stated prohibitions on figural decorations in mosques, the inclusion of such figural imagery (usually on re-used elements) was contextual. Besides the more intuitive difference between civil and sacred spaces (palaces and mosques, respectively), more nuanced distinctions were also made, as shown by Barry Flood.

The Friday Mosque at Delhi is dotted by scores of radiant lion faces, but the accompanying celestial nymphs were systematically erased. And whereas narrative figural scenes, such as the birth of Krishna, appear on the exterior lintels of this mosque's windows (as lion faces decorated the entrances of other Indo-Ghurid mosques), these same scenes were carefully erased in the areas closest to the *mihrab*.[43] The pillars comprising this *mihrab/qibla* area are then decorated with bell chains "adapt[ing] the iconography and rituals of the temple for aniconic worship; signs of the bell ring the worshipper's progression through the mosque and toward its mihrabs even as the bell is sounded by worshippers approaching the ... dwelling place of the deity."[44]

Of similar conception is the mosque at Kaman, a few miles south of Delhi. There, the entrance to the mosque's royal chamber displays intact zoomorphic carvings and defaced anthropomorphic ones. But the *mihrab* is framed by stones carved with vegetation, the Indic vine, a motif often used to sacralize Hindu temples' thresholds. Lotuses, enshrining ideals of purity and divinity, appear all around the prayer hall area, on the pillars, in the bays, and on the ceiling, and again on the *minbar* (pulpit).

Looking at the lotus motif allows us to see how flows of influences were interwoven and multidirectional. From Hindu India, the motif traveled further north, as we find it added to the cenotaph of the Ghaznavid sultan Mas'ud (r. 1031–1041) at Ghazni, and friezes dating from the late twelfth century feature a lotus chain band and a lotus vine similar to those found at Kaman. Several Indic elements are identifiable in twelfth-century Afghan Ghaznavid architecture, as Indian craftsmen were extremely mobile. Indeed, the marble carvings found on several monuments in Ghazni had their models in Rajasthan and Gujarat, and the anthropo-morphic and zoomorphic panel found there describing monkeys harvest-ing beans can be connected only to northern Indian decorative motives.

But in fact animal, human, and prophetic figurations have a docu-mented history within Islam. Although Arab idolatry made a deep mark in defining the boundaries of what was permissible in Islam, Muslims did not do away with figuration altogether, as shown by the presence of human figures on early Islamic coins. The 'Umayyad caliph 'Abd al-Malik, who reigned in the very early days of the Empire (685–705) and led the process of administrative unification, issued coins with a human face surrounded by the inscription of the *shahada*. Some were modeled off those representing the Sasanian king Khosrau II, and others imitated Byzantium's Justinian II. Whereas 'Abd al-Malik soon afterward switched to exclusively calligraphic aniconic coinage, images of rulers continued to crop up through history. Examples survive depicting the Abbasid Caliph al-Mustanjid (twelfth century), Egypt's Ayyubid Sultan Salah al-Din (dated 1215), and one showing the Artuqid Najm al-Din Alpi (1152–1176) of eastern Anatolia facing the Byzantine emperor.[45]

In Iran, possibly due to its population's majoritarian Shi'i identity, one still commonly finds portrays of Ayatollah Khomeini (1902–1989) and the Prophet Muhammad in paper publications, mosque courtyards, and wall murals. Some have defined this a modern phenomenon, fueled by the Iran–Iraq war of the 1980s (see Chapter 6), but in fact Persian manuscripts from the thirteenth century onwards often included miniatures of the Prophet and his companions, from the Turkish *Varqa va Gulshah* (1200–1250) to al-Biruni's *Chronology of Ancient Nations* (1307–1308) and the Timurid historian Hafiz-i Abru's *Collection of Stories* (ca. 1425).[46]

The origins of this practice are not agreed upon by scholars, but a possible explanation lies in the legacy of Mongol visual culture. As the Ilkhanids controlled Persia after the Mongol expansion, their acquaintance with Buddhist figuration trickled into their Islamic practice after conversion. From their perspective, figurative representations of the prophet were a way to celebrate Islam, and their vast and sustained patronage of the arts and religious infrastructures – likely driven by their desire to draw a political and propagandist advantage from having converted – helped the diffusion of their aesthetics.[47] Yet, the Turkish *Varqa va Gulshah* predates the Mongol invasion.

Parallel to this is the interaction between China and West Asia, which was partially discussed in the Introduction and Chapter 1. As West Asian patterns and motives influenced Chinese craftsmen, the Chinese repertoire of plants (e.g. the lotus), animals (such as the phoenix, dragon, or peacock) and specific Daoist and Buddhist emblems all left a mark on objects and art pieces found across the Muslim lands.[48] This was largely the outcome of traveling craftsmen and traders, who facilitated the exchange of ideas, from Arakan (Burma/Myanmar), the Muslim–Buddhist buffer zone between South Asia and Southeast Asia, to Turkey. Also in the sixteenth century, a Chinese *kendi* (a long-necked metal vessel used to pour water developed in India) decorated with Buddhist symbols and Arabic calligraphy was exported to Malaya. And at about the same time, Kirman's congregational mosque (in Persia) was decorated with tiles representing lotus blossoms and branches of a Chinese plum tree.[49]

One last locus of decorative interaction worth examining here is the Mughal painting tradition of the late sixteenth and seventeenth centuries. Usually referred to as the Indo-Persian style, artworks produced during the Mughal period have been described as embodying a refined Persian style and the Hindu realistic artistic vision. This interpretation largely rests on the life story of the second emperor of the Mughal empire, Humayun (1508–1556), who during his exile in Tabriz became intrigued by Persian miniature paintings. Upon his re-conquest of Delhi, Humayun was able to take the masters from Tabriz with him, to Kabul first and Delhi next. Humayun's son, Akbar (1542–1605, later to be known as Akbar "the Great"), learned painting from them and, upon becoming emperor in 1556, he formed a workshop in which the Tabriz masters worked together with local Hindu artists (see Figure 2.6).

Figure 2.6 "Radha Turns her Gaze Away from Krishna," page from the
Rasikaproya of Keshavadasa, 1665–80.
Photo courtesy of the Herbert F. Johnson Museum of Art, Cornell University

However, this was not the only source of inspiration for the Mughal style, as an artistic decorative tradition had already emerged at the cosmopolitan court of the Delhi Sultanate (from the fourteenth century onwards), which combined Persian, Turkish, Arab, and Chinese styles with the local tradition of illustrated texts. In books of this era, Persian motifs appeared in Hindu manuscripts; Mamluk elements found their way in Jain representations, as both rested on the absence of realism and stylization of images; and the prominence of the profiled figure in Hindu books made Sultanate iconography anthropocentric, characterized by expressive, "vitalist" bodies and faces. It was this "body-centric Indic compound that regrouped the rich and diversified non-Islamic and non-monotheistic cultures of South Asia"[50] that emerged in the pre-modern Sultanate painting. Likely seeping through in modern Mughal-Persianate artistic styles, it reinforced that era's political ritual of public appearance and portrayed imagery.

Behaving in Muslim Spaces

> The *adats* which control the lives of the Bedawins of Arabia, the Egyptians, the Syrians and the Turks, are for the most part different from those of the Javanese, Malays and Achehnese, but the relation of these *adats* to the law of Islam, and the tenacity with which they maintain themselves in despite of that law, is everywhere the same.[51]

The scholar Christiaan Snouck Hurgronje, professor of Arabic and Islamic studies at Leiden University, was also a colonial officer in the Dutch East Indies (today's Indonesia), who emerged as one of the leading "Orientalists" of his generation. While becoming fascinated by the Indies, his work in Batavia (Jakarta) and Aceh was mostly directed at developing colonial policies aimed at controlling Islam and Muslim subjects, as well as to bringing Aceh under Dutch military control.

Much of his policies and scholarly analysis were thus grounded in years of "fieldwork" conducted in Mecca and Aceh in the late nineteenth century, and noted the contrast between doctrine and actual practice as a feature common to Muslims worldwide. Far from concluding that Mecca was the center of a pure and unadulterated form of Islam intrinsically different from what he had witnessed in the Indies, Snouck Hurgronje's writings point to Mecca's Asian identity – as many of the teachers, students, guides, and pilgrims hailed from "across the Oxus" – and at the ultimate similarities in dynamics of interaction between local customs (*'adat* or *'urf*) and Islam.

The process of Islam's formation in Arabia and its spread beyond its original context was characterized by the interfacing of local practices and ideal standards. Leila Ahmed's argument that the public and social role of women changed at the time of the Abbasid period – a formative time for the interpretative textual edifice of Muslim societies – because of the influence of Byzantine and Sasanian models, can be expanded to other realms, locations, and historical periods without betraying the foundational idea that the reading of the Islamic scriptures was inevitably affected by established practices.[52]

Box 2.2   Islamic Law

The first chapter of the Qur'an invites Muslims to follow "the right path" set forth for them by God through the Qur'an and Muhammad, whose life example – transmitted through the centuries via the "sayings of the Prophet," or the *ahadith* (plural of *hadith*) – is taken as a model of behavior. Islamic legal traditions, then, have emerged from the implementation of principles embedded in these two key sources of inspiration, but it also ought to be stressed that historically the *sunna* (or "tradition," collectively referring to the Qur'an and *ahadith*) has not been used in isolation, but rather complemented by "local customs" (referred to as either *'urf* or *'adat*) and the process of human interpretation.

Among its many thousand verses, the Qur'an only makes direct references to a handful of requirements, including a specific set of ritual obligations toward God (*'ibadat*, commonly glossed as "the five pillars" although they appear as a group only in the *hadith* tradition and not in the Qur'an, see Box 1.2), norms detailing moral conduct, diet (e.g. the concept of *halal* food, and dress; see Chapter 8), and guidance principles for relations among human beings (*mu'amalat*), including family laws, property laws, economic relations, martial law, and criminal law. It is notable that, of the several legal realms touched upon in the Qur'an, explicit parameters for conviction and punishments are provided for five crimes only, the so-called *hudud* crimes: unlawful intercourse (*zina'*), false accusation of *zina'* (*qadf*), consumption of fermented or inebriating drinks (*shurb*), highway robbery (*qat'l-tariq*), and theft (*saraqa*). For example, in *sura* 5 ("The Feast"), the Qur'an states: "[38]Cut off the hands of thieves, whether they are man or woman, as punishment for what they have done – a deterrent from God: God is almighty and wise."

Whereas the Qur'an is understood to be "the word of God," the *ahadith* reflect the acts of Muhammad as a man chosen and guided by God. During the lifetime of Muhammad, but especially after his death, "sayings" about his decisions and actions were recounted by Muslims across the expanding Empire, and from generation to generation, as a way to keep the memory of his leadership and guidance alive. But as the *ahadith* also became a crucial source of the law, by the ninth century scholars of the law felt compelled to verify and codify the many circulating *ahadith*, thus leading to the creation of a recognized solid body of knowledge (as discussed in Chapter 1).

Box 2.2   *(cont.)*

Al-Bukhari (d. 870) and Muslim ibn al-Hajjaj (d. 875) assessed the "strength" of hundreds of thousands of "sayings" focusing mostly on their individual chain of transmission *(isnad)*, and thus researching the reputation of the transmitters, the plausibility of their physical encounter, the chronology of the chain, etc. Al-Bukhari, for example, sifted through 600,000 *ahadith* to compile a collection of only 2,750 "sound" *(sahih)* ones (the degree of strength goes from sound to fair to weak).

Between the eighth and ninth centuries, Kufa and Baghdad emerged as hubs of religious knowledge, including the law. As mentioned above, the *sunna* alone was not seen as enough to meet the needs of legal administration, and jurists (*'ulama*, *mujtahid*, *faqih*, *mufti*, etc.) were actively engaged in processes of legal interpretation *(ijtihad)* based on generally accepted "human sources" of the law. These included analogical deduction *(qiyas)*, consensus *(ijma')*, the personal sound opinion of a judge *(ra'y)*, and several other methodologies. Among the many scholars who engaged in legal interpretation, by the tenth to eleventh centuries some had emerged as leading personalities, giving rise to circles (or "schools," *madhahib*, plural of *madhhab*) based on methodological preferences. Those who are recognized today as "founders" of the four traditions of Sunni legal interpretations are Abu Hanifa (d. 767), Malik ibn Anas (d. 795), al-Shafi'i (d. 820), and Ahmad ibn Hanbal (780–855). Alongside them, the sixth Imam of the Shi'is, Ja'far al-Sadiq (d. 765), formalized the legal thought of most branches of Shi'ism (see Box 3.1).

By the twelfth century, legal practices had grown inconsistent and uncertain, to the extent that some scholars began to advocate for sustained homogeneity within each tradition. Jurists increasingly relied on replicating previous interpretations, and exegesis was now limited to only allow internal interpretation *(ijtihad fi-l-madhhab)* shifting into what came to be labeled "blind imitation" *(taqlid)*. As the social and political context of interpretation continued to change, past conclusions were often seen as inappropriate, leading to various waves of criticism and reaction from the thirteenth century onwards (see Chapter 3).

As we read in the initial quote, Snouck Hurgronje did not see the interaction between customs and Islam as undermining any perceptions or understandings of "orthodoxy." Despite his influence and recognized intellectual authority, his insights remained a minority opinion, largely ignored by his students and the administrators who succeeded him, who were instead influenced by the Indological tradition of Van Leur. Islam in Java has often been described by colonial and early post-colonial scholars as "a thin veneer" or an "easily flaking glaze" over the island's Hindu-Buddhist legacy (see Chapter 9). Evidence to support this statement would include Javanese Muslims' apparent allegiance to mysticism as a bridge between Hinduism and Islam; the architectural style of early mosques; sustained devotion for pre-Islamic deities, such as the Goddess of the Southern Ocean (Ratu Kidul); and the practice of visiting saints' shrines and making offers of flowers and food. Yet, more recent scholarship has offered new lenses through which to look at the interaction between Islam and its precursors in Java: whereas Islam provided the social infrastructure, the ritual vocabulary of belonging to a worldwide community, and the "outer identifying signs" of belonging, Javanese Muslims retained "the inner spiritual conceptions of the past."[53]

This conversation between Javanese and Islamic traditions continued for centuries. The seventeenth-century Mataram ruler Agung used several Javanese "indigenous" titles until 1641, when he was eventually invested with the title of Sultan by the *sharif* of Mecca. In Javanese literature he was said to have joined Ratu Kidul in a mystical marriage, while European visitors described him as a "pious Muslim" and one who had "died as a holy man."[54]

Merle Ricklefs speaks of Sultan Agung as "the reconciler." While he combined the Islamic lunar year and the Saka numerical sequence creating a new calendar, the Anno Javanico, several texts were composed at his court that similarly merged Islamic and Javanese paradigms. Among them, the most notable is the *Kitab Usulbiyah*, recitation or written copying of which was deemed to bring as much blessing as going on *hajj*, giving alms, reciting the Qur'an, or fighting a holy war. But far from being a "classical" Islamic text, its content is a reimagination of the past in which key Islamic personalities appear in Javanese settings: as Muhammad wins an argument with Jesus, leading to his conversion to Islam, Muhammad is wearing a crown with "Garudhas facing forward and backward, with teeth of precious rubies, gems for eyes and tongues of water jewels," thus mirroring the crown of the pre-Islamic Javanese Kingdom of Majapahit. Another text, "The song of the house of gold," illustrates Sultan Agung's political philosophy, describing a Javanese king as a pious Sufi warrior, ultimately merging Javanese martial kingship and Islamic piety:

> Take care and battle firmly.
> Let the scriptures [*sastra*] serve as your subjects.
> Let piety serve as your bow;
> let *dhikr* serve as your quiver,
> and the Qur'an as your arrows.
> ... Let there be destroyed
> desire and sensual pleasures,
> may comforts be defeated.

... Therefore you are given a position
by the Most Holy God,
because of your outstanding heroism on the field of battle.
... When you are consecrated as king,
don your royal garb:
let *khak* [reality] serve as your crown,
with *tarekat* [the mystical way] as its crest.
Struggle constantly,
sarengat [the law] serving as your lower garment.[55]

Javanese Muslims prayed five times a day, professed the *shahada*, fasted and paid their alms, buried their dead, went on *hajj*, and – mostly – followed dietary restrictions and implemented *hudud* punishments. Normative Islam helped navigate the "real world" created by a transcendent deity. But they also embraced Sufism as a medium to incorporate the supernatural, and continued to see the world as "unreal" – the creation of an immanent divinity – and therefore positing the unity of creation and creator.

Being Javanese and Muslim was an interlocked dimension, one fully dependent on the other. As summed up in the first half of the eighteenth century by Sultan Pakubuwana II (1711–1749), Javanese literature was one's left eye and Arabic literature was one's right eye: each was necessary to reach a complete vision of reality.

The Malay peninsula offers another example of how Islam inserted itself and conversed with a pre-existing order, both in terms of law and political authority (or kingship). When the British colonial officer Thomas Stamford Raffles (1718–1826) wrote about Malaya in the early nineteenth century, he stated that "in most of the [Malay] states the civil code of the Koran [was] almost unknown."[56] If family and commercial laws quite closely resembled *shari'a* models, criminal law as expressed in the early legal code, *The Malacca Laws* (*Undang-Undang Malaka*), countered many of the engrained principles of the *shari'a*: fines were prescribed for thieves, and several other Quranic penalties were substituted with *'adat* practices. Also, the ruler went under the name of *raja* – the pre-Islamic Hindu-Buddhist title – instead of Sultan, and fashioned himself as the "owner" of the law: "whomsoever transgresses against what has been stated in the [laws] is guilty of treason against his Majesty."[57]

Even though colonials saw this as contradicting Islamic principles and as a legacy of a pre-Islamic order, historical evidence shows that the Rajas were most enthusiastic about conversion to Islam. They converted – and "commanded" their peoples to convert – in response to an increased presence of Muslim merchants in the fifteenth century. At this point in time, "Islamic orthodoxy" was far from the golden ages of the Rightly

Guided Caliphs. Pre-Islamic Persian influences had emerged as early as the end of the 'Umayyad era, when the governors of Iraq incorporated "Persian principles to Islamic government" in the bureaucracy, urban architecture, and authoritarian forms of governance. The Abbasids and their vassals "creat[ed] a Persian empire in Islamic garb,"[58] and by the time their empire collapsed under the Mongols, the medieval Islamic tradition of kingship was in fact no longer Arab, but Persian, mirroring the transformation of women's social roles singled out by Leila Ahmed. Coins from this period show that rulers across the Malay peninsula had embraced multiple titles, including Sultan, Shah, "helper of the World and of the Religion," Caliph, "Shadow of God on Earth," and more.

Taking on titles that were neither grander nor inferior to *Raja*, and including some elements of *shari'a*, but not all, were equal indications of "the ruler's response to the Islamization of the Indian Ocean trade route."[59] And the Raja was in effect never described as a lax Muslim in the accounts of other Muslim travelers, neither by the Chinese Ma Huang nor by the North African Ibn Battuta.

This conversation between "Islam" and "the local" took place in Muslim majority and minority contexts alike. Besides the process of harmonization between local conceptions of power and Islam as pursued by rulers in Java and Malaya, Muslims in China also embarked on the creation of literary works that framed Islamic knowledge in Chinese Confucian paradigms. This body of literature, which began to emerge sporadically in the seventeenth century in coastal and "internal" China (e.g. Beijing, Nanjing, Yunnan, etc.), would later become referred to as the *Han Kitab* tradition.

By the Qing era, *Han Kitab* authors included translators and writers of original works, but their effort was also supported by the work of publishers, editors, and commissioners interested in projecting a specifically Chinese way of being Muslim, and a Muslim way of being Chinese. As argued by Zvi Ben-Dor Benite, "Chinese Muslim scholarship of the period began to reflect in important ways the growing sense of its producers that they were members of a distinct and distinguished Chinese intellectual tradition."[60] Their object of study was "a specific 'Dao' [way] – Islam."[61] And much of the impetus behind their work was the desire to ensure that new generations of Chinese Muslims, no longer acquainted with Arabic and Persian languages and literatures, would be able to perform Islam correctly. In the words of the first representative of this tradition, Wang Daiyu (1570s–1650s?), "The principles and Way [discussed] therein are all based entirely in reverence for Scripture, with reference to the commentaries, and I have not dared to interpolate my own personal feelings, to add or subtract, or divide the various scholars."[62]

One of the most representative authors of this tradition was Liu Zhi (?1670–1724), born in Nanjing shortly after the establishment of the Qing dynasty (see Source 2.1). He was well versed in Arabic and Persian, as well as in the Confucian, Buddhist, and Daoist classics, Chinese dynastic histories, and Jesuit literature. His intellectual breadth and depth, combined with the specific context of Qing repression and expectations of integration into Imperial norms, led him to push even further the interests of the *Han Kitab* scholars, concluding that what was recorded in the books of Islam was in fact no different from what was in the Confucian canon.[63]

Source 2.1

Selected Explanation of the Norms and Rites of Islam, by Liu Zhi (1710)

In this excerpt, the Nanjing-born Chinese Muslim scholar Liu Zhi (?1670–1724) explains the so-called "five pillars" of Islam in a Confucian framework, concluding that their practice will lead to the embrace of the "way" of heaven and man.[64]

Witness the real lord all the time, while resting [be aware of] its existence, while moving [be aware] of its transcendence, and the heart will not chase absurd [beliefs] [testimony as *nianzhen*]. Pray five times every day, [paying attention] to each [prayer's, *lizhen*] due time and to each [prayer's] due ablution. Fast for one month every year in order to control personal habits and desires [fasting as *zhaijie*]. Pay a tax on [your] wealth every year, in order to expand benevolence to the advantage of [all living] beings [almsgiving as *juanke*]. [Take part in a] pilgrimage to the heavenly gate [*tianque*] [once] in a lifetime, in order to approach with truthfulness and sincerity the remembrance [of God]. Once the five pillars [*wugong*] are accomplished, the *dao* of heaven is fulfilled …

Comply sincerely with the five norms [*wudian*], and the *dao* of man will be achieved.

The five norms are [binding] ruler and minister, father and son, husband and wife, brother and brother and friend and friend. In Islam, they are also called "five establishments" [*wucheng*]: the ruler and ministers establish the country, father and son establish the family, husband and wife establish the household, brother and brother establish [various] affairs while friend and friend establish morals, all [relationships being based] on immutable rites. Once the five norms are accomplished, the *dao* of man is achieved …

The ritual vehicle is called sharia [*sheli'er*] in Arabic, [a concept] jointly encompassing the way of heaven [*tiandao*] and the way of man [*rendao*], being all those norms [relevant to] the [religious] service.

Liu Zhi was not attempting a synthesis. Rather, he claimed that both "teachings" had the same basic principle. To this end, Liu Zhi's *Tianfang dianli zeyao jie* ("Selected Explanation of the Norms and Rites of Islam") reworked in Confucian paradigms the fundamental elements of Islamic ritual and law. Liu Zhi conformed to Confucian literary forms, but he also emulated Confucian pedagogy. Instead of arranging his book along the traditional distinction made in traditional Islamic *fiqh* (jurisprudence) books between dealings with other humans (*'ibadat*) and acts of ritual devotion (*mu'amalat*), he used the labels *dian* and *li*, respectively "norms" and "rites," then concluding the section on rituals and the five pillars of Islam stating: "Once the five pillars are accomplished, the *dao* of heaven is fulfilled."[65]

Liu Zhi ultimately framed a human and divine order acceptable to both the Islamic and Confucian (Qing) legal perspectives. In the eyes of the Qing establishment, Liu Zhi "upheld the Confucian principles of loyalty to the sovereign, respect by sons for their fathers, brotherly love, and so forth."[66] But Liu Zhi was not operating exclusively under Qing pressures. He was concerned about reinforcing and propagating Islamic "orthodoxy" for educational purposes. *Tianfang dianli* was then followed by *Tianfang sanzijing* ("Three-Character Classic of Islam"), a text focused on presenting the unraveling of the history of Islam as directly connected to a process of localization of Islamic law that retained its orthodoxy through the soundness and integrity of its transmission. By doing so, Liu Zhi was able to create a discourse that shunned legal interpretations formulated in the non-Chinese context, claims to "orthodoxy" by individuals who did not have a sound chain of transmission (*silsila*), and any attempts at Islamic scripturalism. In fact, the scriptures were "initial stones in an evolving legal path open to transformation and supportive of regionalism."[67]

Conclusions

The territory and influence of Muslim political authority expanded, collapsed, and reached further once again. In the meantime, the realities and attributes of any given society in terms of "being Islamic" varied greatly. Asia was characterized by multiple moments and forms of Islamization across time and place.

Mecca's appeal as the most meaningful site for Islam is largely rooted in the life story of the Prophet Muhammad and the early history of Islam. And while the resilient appeal of Arabia cannot (and should not) be denied, the transformation of Asia into a space of Islamized interaction through the multidirectional flow of peoples, ideas, and goods, led to Muslims giving an Islamically specific meaning to their actions, beliefs, practices, and sensibilities, even when these appeared to take form along different paradigms from those that emerged in Arabia.

Through the centuries, not only did Muslims find alternative locations for pilgrimage to fulfill their ritual obligation (out of practical or spiritual reasons) but also questioned Mecca's status as an ideal embodiment of Islamicity as an imagined construct. The "architecture" of the *hajj* rituals shows borrowings from pre-Islamic practices, as does the architecture of "classic" mosques in North Africa and the Arab Mediterranean; at the turn of the twentieth century, Snouck Hurgronje observed that in Mecca the fusion of local customs with "the law of Islam" was not different than in Java, Aceh, Malaya, or the Levant.

Muslim places of worship and general sense of aesthetic, rituals, and legal interpretations have, through time and space, adopted and adapted to what existed before the arrival of Islam, in Java, China, India, and Central Asia as much as in Arabia. This chapter has provided empirical examples and theoretical frameworks to explore and articulate how processes of Islamization (i.e. "becoming Muslim") necessitated negotiations and active engagement between past and new traditions, as Muslims carried their religious beliefs and passed them on, whether through trade, marriage, conquest, or other forms of knowledge transfers, without undermining their commitment to complying with the precepts of Islam.

Further Reading

Arjana, S. R. (2017) *Pilgrimage in Islam: traditional and modern practices*, London: Oneworld Publications.

Ben-Dor Benite, Z. (2005) *The Dao of Muhammad: a cultural history of Muslims in late imperial China*, Cambridge, MA: Harvard University Asia Center.

DeWeese, D. A. (1994) *Islamization and native religion in the Golden Horde: Baba Tukles and conversation to Islam in historical and epic tradition*, University Park, PA: Pennsylvania State University Press.

Ewing, K. P. (1988) *Sharī'at and ambiguity in South Asian Islam*, Berkeley, CA: University of California Press.

Flood, F. B. (2018) *Objects of translation: material culture and medieval Hindu-Muslim encounter*, Princeton, NJ: Princeton University Press.

Frankel, J. D. (2011) *Rectifying God's name: Liu Zhi's Confucian translation of monotheism and Islamic law*, Honolulu, HI: University of Hawai'i Press.

Gonzalez, V. (2016) *Aesthetic hybridity in Mughal painting, 1526–1658*, London: Routledge.

Hallaq, W. B. (2016) *An introduction to Islamic law*, Cambridge: Cambridge University Press.

Hefner, R. W. (2011) *Shari'a politics: Islamic law and society in the modern world*, Bloomington, IN: Indiana University Press.

Hooker, M. B. (2008) *Indonesian syariah: defining a national school of Islamic law*, Singapore: ISEAS.

Milner, A. C. (1982) *Kerajaan: Malay political culture on the eve of colonial rule*, Tucson, AZ: Published for the Association for Asian Studies by the University of Arizona Press.

Peters, F. E. (1996) *The hajj: the Muslim pilgrimage to Mecca and the holy places*, Princeton, NJ: Princeton University Press.

Petersen, K. (2017) *Interpreting Islam in China: pilgrimage, scripture, and language in the Han Kitab*, New York, NY: Oxford University Press.

Prange, S. R. (2018) *Monsoon Islam: trade and faith on the medieval Malabar Coast*, New York, NY: Cambridge University Press, Chapter 2, "The Mosque."

Ricklefs, M. C. (2006) *Mystic synthesis in Java: a history of Islamization from the Fourteenth to the early Nineteenth Centuries*, Norwalk, CT: EastBridge.

Sachiko M. (2017) *The first Islamic classic in Chinese: Wang Daiyu's Real Commentary on the True Teaching*, Albany, NY: State University of New York Press.

Schimmel, A. (1994) *Deciphering the signs of God*, Edinburgh: Edinburgh University Press.

Shokoohy, M. (2013) *Muslim architecture of South India: the Sultanate of Ma'bar and the traditions of the maritime settlers on the Malabar and Coromandel coasts (Tamil Nadu, Kerala and Goa)*, London: Routledge, esp. pp. 247–252.

Steinhardt, N. S. (2015) *China's early mosques*, Edinburgh: Edinburgh University Press.

Tagliacozzo, E., and S. M. Toorawa (2016) *The Hajj pilgrimage in Islam*, Cambridge: Cambridge University Press.

Tontini, R. (2016) *Muslim Sanzijing: shifts and continuities in the definition of Islam in China*, Leiden: Brill.

Zaman, M. Q. (2007) *The Ulama in contemporary Islam: custodians of change*, Princeton, NJ: Princeton University Press.

3 Networks and Renewal (Thirteenth to Nineteenth Centuries)

Figure 3.1 Mosque incense burner, Linxia (Gansu, China).
© Chiara Formichi

Of excellent qualities, how many have been entrusted?
My sources being preceptor after preceptor
Their fragrant scents were of the virtues I was granted
But how many were empty souls, deniers, of the manifest form?
Still in the Jawi aloes, the soothing freshness I set upon the brazier
There is the Jawi of these men, Mas'ud, of seasoned virtue.[1]

Abu 'Abd Allah Mas'ud b. Muhammad al-Jawi, [...] was once known as a great and famous skaykh in the city of Aden and surrounding areas. He was one of the greats, a shaykh and jurist of the people of 'Uwaja. He was a colleague of the great jurist Muhammad Isma'il al-Hadrami, who benefited all and whose turban was a blessing to their souls. He [al-Jawi] was a master of character and upbringing, from whom a great many of the greats benefited, including the shaykh 'Abd Allah b. As'ad al-Yafi'i and others.[2]

And he [al-Jawi] said to me: "A sign befell me this night that I was to dress you in the *khirqa*', and he put it upon me[3]... I never witnessed in any of these others the goodness of the way of the *tariqa* that I saw in the aforementioned shaykh – [that being] the fusion between the outer law (*shari'a*) and inner reality (*haqiqa*), good fortune and effort, great solicitude and facility with religious practice ('*ibada*), meticulous following of Sunna and abstention, excess in effacement and culture and humility, great inner knowledge and disclosure, good qualities and blessings."[4]

★★★

Myrrh and frankincense had been in high demand from the Mediterranean to China since ancient times, for both ritualistic and cosmetic uses. In Egypt incense burned all day long in temples, and the bodies of the dead were covered in a myrrh-derived unguent. In Rome, fragrances were similarly used in funeral processions and daily rituals. In China, incense smoke honored the ancestors. These were luxury products, as testified by the fact that in time of austerity, the consumption of such imported and "exotic" goods could be prohibited. Myrrh and frankincense were brought to the northern shores of the Mediterranean by caravans that traversed the Arabian Peninsula, as the hub of both production and trade of these goods was in Southern Arabia (Yemen). And when the Roman conquest of Egypt limited trade in the Mediterranean and thus led to the decline of Yemen's economic position in the second century of the Common Era, incense remained a source of wealth for Southern Arabia; not only was frankincense a sought-after luxury good across Asia, but Yemeni merchants also traded in other aromatic substances across the Indian Ocean.

Alongside the sustained production of its own resins, Yemen emerged also as an important international hub of trade for various fragrances in the thirteenth century, when camphor, sandalwood, and aloes from Southeast Asia entered the markets of the Muslim Empire, Europe, and China, through maritime trade. At this point in history, the most circulated fragrances were associated with *bilad al-jawa*, today's maritime Southeast Asia, as aloe wood was known as '*ud jawi*, and incense benzoin as *luban jawi*. As narrated by Chau Ju Kua in the thirteenth century, Sumatra's benzoin which "aroma is so strong that it may be used in combination with all other perfumes" was arriving in China via Arab merchants sailing from Yemen.

Also Abu 'Abd Allah Mas'ud b. Muhammad "al-Jawi"'s attribution (or *nisba*) indicates that the most important geographical connection for this Arabia-based scholar was thousands of miles to the east. The connection might have been established through birth, ethnicity, trade, or travel, but most important was that al-Jawi's existence was cast within the narrative of exchanges between Arabia and Southeast Asia, at a time when trade was flourishing across the Indian Ocean and further.

Abu 'Abd Allah Mas'ud was a revered scholar from Aden, in the Yemen, who lived in Mecca in the early to mid-thirteenth century. He dispensed his knowledge to future generations of 'ulama, instructing and directing them along the right path (the sirat al-mustaqim of sura al-Fatiha, the first chapter of the Qur'an), under inspiration from both the way of the law (shari'a) and the way of the soul (tariqa). He was a scholar of the law, and a Sufi master.

This chapter, then, follows an intertwined chronological-cum-geographical approach in order to achieve two main goals. First, it analyses how formal and informal networks of knowledge connected various "dots" across the Muslim lands. Second, it investigates the crisscrossing (and parallel existence) of "mystical" (Sufi) and legal approaches to "orthodoxy"; and whereas one could separate "the jurist" from "the mystic," "the traveler" from "the student," as the written materials we have fit one or the other literary genres, I deploy the broader (and all-encompassing) category of "scholar" ('alim, or 'alima if a woman; 'ulama collective plural) so to focus on how individuals contributed to a fluid constellation of intellectual exchanges which spanned across the geographical area of Islam's reach, creating a sense of community that went beyond the mere awareness of a common belief, or a specific approach to interpreting it.

The lives and religious-intellectual trajectories of several scholars whom – in Arabia as well as South Asia, Bukhara, Southeast Asia, and China – advocated and embraced adherence to Islamic law while also being prominent representatives of Sufi orders (with a dedicated focus to the Naqshbandiyah), illustrate how the impetus toward purification of practices deemed "new" (bid'a, evil innovation) had come from scholars representative of both "mystical" and "juridical" strains of thought, and how such inspiration had initially emerged as a concern in continental Asia.

Intra-Asian Mobility and Islamic Knowledge

Trade encouraged mobility, and with their goods traders also carried their knowledge, identities, and beliefs. Mobility, then, enabled the expansion of Islam's reach beyond its geographical core, and the creation of Islamic pockets across the Asian continent gave form to intra-religious networks, eventually strengthening the sense of community. The community of believers – the *umma* (see Box 0.1) – was from the very beginning a mobile, itinerant group. The Arabs belonged to nomadic tribes, the Empire reached from Spain to Sindh by 711, Arabo-Persian Muslim merchants had arrived on the coasts of southern India, Vietnam, and China by the early ninth century, and pilgrimages were a constitutive aspect of Islamic devotion.

Whereas Muslims traveled to places the world over (for trade as well as pilgrimages, as seen in Chapter 2), Mecca and Medina (collectively known as *al-Haramayn*, the two holy cities) remained important meeting points of such mobile a community, a destination for Muslims worldwide who sought *baraka* (blessing), knowledge (*'ilm*), and status. The *hajj* had become a vehicle to stimulate ordinary Muslims' mobility, providing motivation for travels (think about Ibn Battuta and how his *hajj* turned into a twenty-four-year trip around the world) or study; and these two goals were often intertwined, as proven by the use of the term *musafir al-'ilm*, or "knowledge-traveler." As recalled by Snouck Hurgronje in the late nineteenth century, "the great majority of the students come [to Mecca] from abroad," including Java, Malaya, Malabar, and Dagestan.[5] But it would be a narrow approach to assume that "Islam" and "Muslims" exclusively thrived in their connections to "the center."

The territorial expansion of the Muslim Empire stimulated mobility as much as religious knowledge: the Empire's borders were often occupied by Sufi mystics who attracted disciples to the *khanaqa*s (lodges) of Central Asia and sometimes also facilitated conversions. A third conduit for the mobility–knowledge nexus was the quest to verify the chains of transmission of the recorded *ahadith* (sayings of the Prophet, sing. *hadith*) and these individuals' life stories, a pursuit begun in the ninth century; the study of hadith (*ilmu'l-hadith*) had been a foundational part of *'ulama*'s formation in the Haramayn as a prophetic source of *shari'a*.

This mobile quest for knowledge dissolved the sense of a "center." Bukhara and its region were crucial sites for the consolidation of the study of the traditions of the prophet (*ahadith*) in the ninth to eleventh centuries; from the sixteenth century onwards, Muslims from the Indian Ocean rim were among the most prolific and engaged legal scholars based in Mecca; and one of the most influential lexicographers of the Arabic language was the South Asian Sharif Muhammad Murtada az-Zabidi (1732–1791).[6]

The parameters and boundaries of what constituted religious knowledge were themselves in flux. If in the earliest days being a scholar meant holding high standards of personal piety alongside knowledge of the word of God (the Qur'an) and of Muhammad's traditions and sayings (*ahadith*), through the centuries the focus shifted from being a pious repository of information to active interpretation according to increasingly canonized methods (see Box 2.2). Together with the institutionalization of ascetic practices into Sufi orders (*tariqa*) in the twelfth century, the sub-group most directly affected and gradually excluded from the *'ulama* were women.

'A'isha had been a sought-after source of prophetic examples and a "coveted legal authority," but with the eighth- to ninth-century concerns over forged *ahadith*, and the trend toward verification, women – who by then could no longer freely travel alone – were marginalized. Yet, the lives of some exceptional women have been recorded and we know that in Damascus an Umm al-Darda (d. 652) led assemblies for male ascetics while also being remembered as a *faqiha* (female jurist) who gave counsel to the 'Umayyad Caliph.

Once the *ahadith* corpus had been set and made available in written form, women from scholarly families were reinserted in these networks of piety, learning, and transmission. In the tenth to eleventh centuries, women enjoyed growing influence as *muhaddithat* – i.e. women renowned for their knowledge of the *ahadith*, their ability to transmit them to students, and to interpret them for the community – and *shaykhas*: "the learned woman, possessed of excellent virtues, the one with the best *isnads* [chain of transmission]... She had understanding and knowledge and was virtuous and pious as well."[7]

Among them was Fatima bint al-Hasan al-Daqqa (1000–1088) of Nishapur, "the product [Asma Sayeed has suggested] of a culture that exalted religious learning and piety among women as well as men." She had learned the Qur'an by heart, and she was a famous reciter as well as interpreter; she had been instructed in the *ahadith* corpus and could rely on a double network of kinship, as her father and husband were both acclaimed jurists and Sufis of their time. In fact, the harmonization of Sufi and legalist doctrines was also a trademark of Khorasan.[8]

Two "Ways"? *Tariqa* and *Shari'a*

The recent history of West Asia – especially the emergence of "Islamic reformism" in late nineteenth-century Cairo, and of Saudi Arabia as a Wahhabi state in the early twentieth century – has led to a view of mysticism as opposed to legalistic approaches to Islamic practices. As argued by Carl Ernst, "the beginnings of the modern study of Sufism lie in the colonial period ... stress[ing] the exotic, the peculiar, and behavior that diverges from modern European norms."[9] But they also saw Sufism as "heretical" within the Islamic tradition; in the words of Sir John Malcom, a British colonial officer in the early nineteenth century:

> [Mystics] are also accused by orthodox Mahomedans of having no fixed faith, but of professing a respect which they do not feel for religion, that they may smooth the path of those whom they desire to elude. They pretend, their enemy state, to revere the prophet and the Imaums [sic], yet conceive themselves above the forms and usages which these holy personages not only observed, but deemed of divine inspiration.[10]

However, even though the contemporary discourse on Islamic orthodoxy and "religious purity" has become inextricably harnessed to the vision of 'Abd al-Wahhab (1703–1792) and Saudi Arabia, it ought to be noted that the relationship between these two traditions has varied between the ninth century and today (on the fundamentals of Sufism, see Chapter 1).

Ahmad ibn Hanbal (780–855) – the namesake of the Hanbali school of law and the intellectual forefather of the seventeenth-century Wahhabi school of law (see Box 2.2) – was said to be on good terms with Bishr al-Hafi, an established Central Asian "saint" of his time, and was himself listed as a Sufi saint in the early eleventh century by the famous Hanbali scholar Abu Mansur al-Isfahani (who considered some contemporary Sufi masters as his own models); in eleventh-century Afghanistan we find traces of a "Hanbali mystic," and in Baghdad a widely distributed Sufi commentary of the Qur'an had been authored by a Hanbali. The twelfth-century founder of the Qadiri Sufi order was himself a Hanbali. A century later another Hanbali, Taqi al-Din ibn Taymiyah (1263–1328), agreed with al-Isfahani on the fact that an alliance was needed "between the [people] of the *hadith* and the [people] of the *tasawwuf*."[11]

Ottoman Naqshbandi Sufis in the fifteenth century "emphasized rigorous adherence to the *shari'a* and to the Prophet's *sunna* as central to their identity" while also engaging in mystical devotional practices and disengaging from politics and other wordly matters.[12] As Asma Sayeed suggested, the Hanbali focus on *hadith* as an example of prophetic conduct went hand in hand with ascetic piety. Where these traditions parted ways was, largely, at the devotional level, as several ascetics, later reconfigured as Sufis, came to "sanctify" their teachers (or masters) and turned, for example, their shrines into destinations of pilgrimages (see Source 3.1 and Figure 1.2).

Abidance to Islamic law and mystic spiritualism coexisted in different configurations for centuries, and whereas colonial and contemporary narratives of "good" and "bad" Muslims have led to the dichotomization of Muslims between seemingly moderate Sufism and fundamentalist

Source 3.1

Tazkira of the Qarakhanid Satuq Bughra Khan

This excerpt is part of the final page of the hagiography (tazkira) of the Qar-akhanid Satuq Bughra Khan (d. 955), one of the first Turkic rulers to convert to Islam and a follower of the Naqshbandi tariqa. This is a topical example of Central Asian Sufi literature that has survived as an oral and manuscript tradition. Whereas there is no information about the Four Imams mentioned here, the excerpt shows the survival and resilience of popular practices such as grave visitations and requests for intercessions from notable deads. For an image of the shrine, see Figure 1.2.[13]

The year was 390 [1000 AD]. The Imams drank the nectar of martyrdom on the 10th day of Dhu'l-hijja. Every year Yusuf Qadir Khan Ghazi made a pilgrimage to the blessed burial-place of the [Four] Imams. He gathered much alms, made the cauldron boil, lit the lamps, received people's entreaties, prayed, and praised God. And he used to say that whosoever was in need, if that person made a pilgrimage to the sacred burial places and circumambulated it, made the cauldron boil, lit the lamps and prayed, then on the day of judgement that person would be given a place in the shadow of the banner of the Imams, and they would perform intercession on their behalf. No one doubted that this was the truth ... Whoever reads the Imams' *tazkira* [hagiography], or, if he cannot read, listens to it – if he has conviction, performs charitable deeds, lights the lamps, recites the Qur'an, plays and praises God, he will find aid from the pure spirits of the Imams and will be esteemed in this world, and at the end of days he will be worthy of intercession.

legalist thinking, the contestation between "mystics" and "reformers" has mostly been just about forms of ritual devotion.

Ibn Taymiyah recognized some aspects of Sufism as valid (e.g. following the example of the Prophet and his companions, and advocating for a direct relationship with the scriptures), but he also condemned saint veneration and shrine visits, which he labeled "evil innovations" (*bid'a*) (see Source 3.2). He was not the only one to express concerns over these aspects of Sufism at a time of territorial and political fragmentation, as in the late Abbasid period the structural unity of religious and political authority was disappearing. Just a few decades earlier, the Central Asian Sufi 'Abd al-Khaliq al-Ghijduwani (d. 1220) is said to have pushed against what had become Sufis' concerns with worldly matters and peoples' veneration for "saints." By the second half of the thirteenth century, political power was in the hands of non-Muslims, and religious

Source 3.2

Taqwiyyat al-Iman, by Shah Isma'il Shahid (1771–1831)

In this mid-nineteenth-century text, the grandson of Shah Waliullah invokes the example of prophet Muhammad as guide for "correct behavior" for all Muslims. Likely the first text in the Urdu vernacular to be printed in South Asia, the Taqwiyyat al-Iman *was widely distributed and affected the devotional practices of tens of thousands of Muslims. In this excerpt, the author fiercely criticizes "holy men" for popularizing un-Islamic (Hindu) customs, seen as inevitably bound to foster* shirk *(associationism, polytheism). The very fact that such text was so widely available is indicative of the popularity of the criticized practices.*[14]

Nowadays people follow many paths in matters of faith, some hold on to the customs of the ancestors, some look to the tales of holy men (*buzurg*), and some follow the *maulavis*' words that they have cleverly devised out of their own minds. Some let their own reasoning interfere. Yet the best path is holding the word of Allah and the Messenger to be authentic, making it one's charter, and giving no entry at all to one's own opinion. Certainly, accept the stories of holy men or the words of *maulavis* if they accord with that word, but reject the rest. Give up any custom that is not in accord …

Often in a time of difficulty people call on their masters (*pir*), apostles, imams, martyrs, angels, and fairies … To ensure the child's life, one keeps a tuft of hair in someone's name, another puts on some chain or string in someone's honor, or perhaps clothing [blessed] in that name … In short, as the Hindus act with their gods, these false Muslims act with their prophets, saints, imams, martyrs, angels and fairies, yet they claim to be Muslims! …

[They defend themselves as follows:] "We are not engaged in *shirk* [associationism, polytheism] but only manifest our belief in the honor of the apostles and saints. If we held [them] equal to Allah, then it would be *shirk*, but we don't. We know that they are servants of Allah, his creation, and he bestowed on them their power. They exert power in the world through his wish. To call on them is to really call on Allah, to ask them for help is to ask Him. Those who are beloved of Allah can do whatever they want. They are our intercessors and mediators with him … the more we know them, the closer we come to Allah" …

Allah has specified many acts of veneration for himself, known as worship (*'ibadat*), for example prostration (*sijda*), bowing (*ruku'*), and standing with hands folded. Likewise, to spend money in his name or fast in his name. [Wrong acts include] undertaking a distant trip to a shrine in such a manner that everyone knows that one is going on a pilgrimage (*ziyarat*) – for example, calling out a master's name along the way or other such absurdities, or abstaining from killing animals, requiring circumambulation (*tawaf*), prostrating at a shrine, taking an animal there, spreading a covering (*ghilaf*) to fulfill a vow, making a supplication for worldly and religious matters,

Source 3.2   (*cont.*)

kissing some stone, rubbing one's face or chest against the wall, making supplication while holding on to the shrine's covering, circling it with light, becoming a servant (*mujawir*) of the shrine and rendering service like sweeping, supplying illumination, cleaning the floor, providing water for ablution (*wazu'*, *ghusl*), or righting people's encumbrances … Allah has assigned to his servants all this worship for himself alone …

[T]he lord Allah has had his servants taught that they should recall *his* name in their worldly acts and glorify *him*. Thus their faith stands firm and their deeds yield blessing (*barakat*). For example, one ought to make an offering to Allah in return for a vow, call on him in the time of trouble, and invoke him at the beginning of any undertaking …

Anyone who considers some prophet, imam, martyr, angel, or pir to be an intercessor of this sort with Allah, is truly associating others with him and is very ignorant. He understands nothing at all of the Lord's essence, nor of the power of this king of kings … Any intercession of a prophet or saint mentioned in the Qur'an or hadith is of this sort. Each person should call on Allah alone and fear him, make supplication to him, and acknowledge his sins before him, and know him as his master and protector … Allah is very benevolent and merciful. There is no need of intercession.

authority was largely held by the few surviving Sufi orders (*tariqa*s); they had strong ties with ruling dynasties (as mentioned in the case of the Eastern Chagatai Khanate, for example, in Chapter 1), and also exerted much power over the general population, largely by way of their charismatic *shaykh*s and stunning shrines. It was in this context that al-Ghijduwani and his followers advocated for a return to the primacy of what they perceived to be strong morals and religious integrity, and the abandonment of saint worship and intercessionist practices.

Other apparent contradictions involve the position of women in these configurations of religious practice and knowledge. On the one hand, in the early centuries ascetic Islam had privileged the "ethical vision" of the Qur'an (to embrace Leila Ahmed's analysis), thus allowing women to thrive in their circles, but the institutionalization of Sufi orders, with the secluded life of the isolated *khanaqa*s and the paramount importance assigned to the relationship between teacher and pupil, women were pushed out of this world. On the other hand, despite the fact that Hanbali scripturalism put women in a subdued position *vis-à-vis* their male guardians, thus largely limiting their role in society, "it appears that [in the thirteenth to fifteenth centuries] the Hanbalis [took] the lead over the Shafi'i in encouraging women's education," giving life to a group of recognized *muhadditha*s able to pass on their corpus of transmission to local and itinerant (male) scholars.[15]

Neither al-Ghijduwani nor Ibn Taymiyah garnered much support in their lifetime, but both names would become important in reconfigurations of Islamic practice in the modern era, as the distinction between Sufis and jurists became increasingly important in political, social, and educational terms. By the sixteenth century, legal scholars, especially in Ottoman West Asia, represented a formally trained class of professionals. Alongside the inevitable consequences in narrowing the spectrum of interpretation, this transformation also caused the definitive exclusion of women *muhadditha*s, *shaykha*s, and *faqiha*s. Whereas in more recent times, scholars have been able to trace the existence of female religious scholars in various locations across Asia (e.g. China, Maldives, and possibly Central Asia), there are barely no traces of their lives in the surviving manuscript traditions, and their role was likely limited to teaching and advising other women on matters strictly related to their being women.

"Intoxicated" Sufism, rooted in ecstatic practices and shrine devotion, was prevalent in the thirteenth century, and theological discourses that called for the need to "purify" Islamic practices and that directly challenged Sufism made little inroad during the Mongol period. Taqi al-Din ibn Taymiyah was often imprisoned and, being in repeated conflict with both the leading jurists and Sufis of his time, he was overall intellectually isolated. Yet, subsequently to the Mongol intervention, in the fourteenth to sixteenth centuries Sufi orders took shape as more structured institutions of devotion, learning, and obedience. On the one hand, this led to increased resonance of previous concerns over "intoxicated" practices (such as those expressed by al-Ghijduwani), thus effecting direct change among those with an inward orientation. On the other hand, the use of vernacular languages, connections to structures of power, and visionary elements caused both the further propagation of Sufism among the masses and the emergence of outright condemnation from the jurists, who were instead losing ground, echoing some of ibn Taymiyah's thoughts on Sufism. For Ibn Taymiyah's ideas and approach to start having a tangible impact on the scholars of the law we will have to wait until the early eighteenth century, most notably through the efforts of the Central Arabian 'Abd al-Wahhab (1703–1792). 'Abd al-Wahhab's vision – shortly afterwards espoused and promoted by the al-Sa'ud clan, and today institutionalized in the Kingdom of Saudi Arabia – was deeply informed by his isolated upbringing in the desert hinterlands as well as by his studying with the South Asian *muhaddith* Muhammad Hayya al-Sindi (d. 1750).[16]

The phenomenon of systematic Sufi contestation by legal scholars can thus be identified as a modern one. In fact, several scholars of Sufism agree that until the eighteenth century "there has never been any clear and uniform pattern of enmity between the jurists and the mystics," and that "Sufism was largely taken for granted as part of the fabric of daily life across Muslim societies from the Maghrib to Java."[17] The rest of this chapter, then, illustrates the lives of six religious scholars to narrate the history of Islamic thought in the thirteenth to eighteenth centuries as one of conversation and convergence between "the law" and "the soul" of Islam, echoing the example of our thirteenth-century Mas'ud al-Jawi who "fus[ed] the outer law (*shari'a*) and inner reality (*haqiqa*)" or the fourteenth-century Sufi *shaykh* Baha ud-Din Naqshband who "united religious law with the mystic path." (see Source 3.3).

Source 3.3

A Visit to the Shrine of Baha ud-Din Naqshband, by Sayyeda-ye Nasafi (d. 1707 or 1711)

This eighteenth-century poem describes the physical and theological grandiosity of the shrine of Baha ud-Din Naqshband in Bukhara with multiple metaphors and double-meanings (a common rhetorical device in Sufi poetry). Most notably, the poem establishes a direct connection between prophet Muhammad and Baha ud-Din, compares the shrine's garden to Medina's, and bears witness to the fact that shrine visits were common and valued in the eighteenth century; at the same time, the poem also stresses Baha ud-Din's commitment to combining mystical and legalistic approaches to Islam.[18]

> At dawn, the world-adorning sun
> disclosed paths to enjoyment everywhere.
> My mind cleared of vapors, I set out
> to make the rounds of the shrines.
> A garden rose up before my eyes from afar,
> renowned as the tomb of Shah-i Naqshband.
> Did I say "garden"? It is a garden like Medina,
> where tomb vaults thrust forth their proud chests.
> Immaculate pilgrims surround it in pure white,
> their robes like crying towels cinched at the neck.
> The Prophet called Baha' al-Din's spirit "son"
> and placed him in the cradle as the axis of the age.
> His miracles are as plain as full dawn.
> His prayers expect an answer, like lovers' eyes.
> His heart is aware of the secrets of divine truth;
> he has united religious law with the mystic path.

Convergence and Circulation

Mysticism and legal interpretation had been for many centuries represented two genres of literature, usually equally mastered by all accomplished scholars, men and women. As devotional approaches, they also coexisted side by side. However, with the historical development of Sufi orders as centers of political power as well as popular devotion, the field of Sufism shifted, creating spaces for contestation. Polarization of these two "ways" of understanding God grew gradually, eventually becoming a generally accepted reality. And conscious efforts to affect a re-convergence of Sufi and juridical methodologies took place in step, but this time in an exclusively male domain.

A key agent in this process was a prominent Sufi order, the Naqshbandiyah, which became known as the first order to ground itself in the legalistic tradition of *shari'a* compliance. This *tariqa* takes its name from Baha ud-Din Naqshband (1318–1389), a Central Asian Sufi master of the fourteenth century whose spiritual genealogy (*silsila*) connected him to al-Ghijduwani. All that is known about Baha ud-Din has been mediated by later followers of the *tariqa*, and it is thus difficult to determine whether he was really primarily concerned with eradicating Sufis' worldly attachments (or "extravagances") or not. Yet, it is attested that by the fifteenth century the Naqshbandi way was characterized by his followers' commitment to silent "remembrance of God" (*dhikr*) and other markers of "sober" Sufism, in the Ottoman Empire and Central Asia alike.

The origins and history of the *tariqa* Naqshbandiyah are distinctly rooted in Central Asia: besides the spiritual hallmark of al-Ghijduwani, Baha ud-Din Naqshband himself was born in a village near Bukhara, and it is in this city that he rests in a now rather lavish mausoleum (most recently renovated by the post-Soviet Uzbeki leader Islam Karimov, see Chapter 6). But today the Naqshbandiyah order has branches worldwide, from North America to China.

The earliest – and still most significant – international turn took place in the fifteenth century: Nasir al-Din 'Ubaydullah Ahrar of Tashkent (1404–1490) was a respected and leading follower of what was then considered to be the way of Baha ud-Din; he advocated for the implementation of Islamic law and regularly performed silent *dhikr*. But 'Ubaydullah Ahrar would be remembered mostly for his geographical expansion of the Naqshbandiyah, as he was the first to send deputies beyond Transoxiana. At this point in time various branches of the Naqshbandiyah stressed different aspects of devotion, nonetheless by the time of Ahrar's death, this *tariqa* had a strong presence across Central

Asia. And from there it was finding fertile soil to the west, in the Ottoman Empire, and to the east, both in the Tarim Basin and in India.

From the Ferghana Valley, successors to Ahrar were able to build upon a pre-existing Naqshbandi network around Altishahr and thus established the *tariqa* in the Tarim Basin in the late sixteenth and early seventeenth centuries. A century later, Khoja Afaq of Kashgar (d. 1694) expanded the Naqshbandiyah's influence to Qing China and Tibet by traveling first to the Tarim Basin and then to northwest China. The *tariqa* became important in northwest China in the late seventeenth to early eighteenth centuries thanks to the activism of Ma Laichi (?1681–1766), the son of a devotee of Khoja Afaq, and Ma Mingxin (?1719–1781), as they each established branches of the Naqshbandi order (Ma Laichi and Ma Mingxin are discussed further below).

But where it came to really thrive it was in South Asia, through the workings of the Afghan Baqi Billah (1564–1603, born in Kabul). The *tariqa* arrived in the Indian subcontinent in conjunction with the Mughal, as it had been connected to the family of its first Emperor, Babur (1483–1530). Baqi Billah was able to establish the first Naqshbandi *khanaqa* in Delhi, leaving a strong mark in the capital city and succeeding in reaching out to the broader population, instead of limiting his work to the imperial entourage. Among his many followers, two were to become important figures in the transmission and further expansion of the *tariqa* in the Subcontinent: Ahmad Sirhindi and Taj ad-Din al-Hindi (d. 1642).

Ahmad Sirhindi (1564–1624), the next *khalifa* of the order, was anointed as the "renewer of the second millennium" (*mujaddid alf saami*), as it was under him that the Naqshbandiyah took an even stronger revivalist bent, taking the moniker *mujaddida* (revivalist). Theologically, this was manifested as a refutation of *wahdat-ul-wujud* ("unity of being") in favor of the *wahdat-ul-shuhud* ("oneness of vision");[19] and politically, Sirhindi began a process of distancing the *tariqa* from the rulers, as since the reign of Akbar the Great (1542–1605) the Mughal Emperors had been advancing less *shari'a*-minded views of Islam in name of religious tolerance. It is at this point that the *tariqa* Naqshbandiyah becomes self-consciously, and openly, primarily concerned with the convergence of Sufi approaches to legally sound practices. In the Indian subcontinent, the *mujaddida* would later feed into other reformist efforts, contributing to the shaping of orthodoxy-concerned and politically engaged Islamist groups in the late colonial period (nineteenth to twentieth centuries).

Parallel to Sirhindi's shaping of the *mujaddida* strand in India was the consolidation of another approach to the Naqshbandi way advanced by Taj ad-Din al-Hindi, who had moved to Mecca after Sirhindi's appointment as *khalifa*. In Mecca, Taj al-Din gathered many pupils interested in the Sufi path and in his unwavering teaching of the *wahdat-ul-wujud*. Among Taj al-Din's students were two who featured most prominently as committed Sufis and well-known *muhaddiths*: Ahmad b. Ibrahim b. 'Alan (d. 1624) and Ahmad al-Nakhli (d. 1714). Both Ibn 'Alan and al-Nakhli contributed much to make the Naqshbandiyah acceptable in Mecca, their efforts supported also by two Medina-based Naqshbandis: *shaykh* Ahmad al-Qushashi (1583–1660) and his student Ibrahim al-Kurani (1615–1690). Notably, the impact of these two latter scholars was even stronger than the former, mostly because of the different nature of Medina's and Mecca's scholarly circles.

Mecca was the receiver of pilgrims from the world over, but their stay tended to be short. On the other hand, Medina attracted those who wished to advance the study of Islam, making this city a most cosmopolitan hub in the seventeenth century. If some pilgrims-turned-students returned home with a higher social and economic status granted by a (short) certified period of study in Mecca, many others settled in Medina, filling the rank and file of the city's religious circles (*halaqa*). Non-local residents, then, further enriched the spectrum of experiences and knowledge circulating there, giving this holy city a diverse outlook which allowed for an embrace of the breadth of Islam's reach and its intellectual implications. Similarly, such demographics provided a global platform to those who taught there: these study circles were held in Arabic language in an Arab city, but their members were representative of a truly multi-ethnic community.

Ahmad al-Qushashi had hailed from Jerusalem but spent most of his life in Medina, where he studied with many scholars from South Asia. His greatest pupil, the Kurd Ibrahim al-Kurani, was himself a celebrated scholar of *hadith* who drew his knowledge from across the Muslim lands, as shown by the chains of transmission of the *hadiths* he studied from al-Qushashi: first, al-Kurani held a traditional, extremely "strong" chain that from al-Qushashi moved on to North African and Egyptian scholars; second, al-Kurani cherished an alternative Sufi chain that connected him to India; lastly, he held a third line that reached back to the Andalusian Ibn 'Arabi (1165–1240), a famous mystic, and a well-recognized *muhaddith*.

By making these choices, al-Qushashi and al-Kurani set themselves up for a double impact. First, they rooted their *hadith* scholarship in multiple loci across the Muslim lands, while at the same time inserting these sources in a more conventional Arabia-based chain. Second, this diversification of knowledge exposed them to the mystical path and enabled them to see the possibilities in harmonizing the science of *hadith* with

Sufi knowledge, as shown by al-Qushashi's role in leading a reorientation of his Sufi *tariqa* away from esoteric practices and toward embracing *shari'a* as the necessary foundation to reach mystical truth, the *haqiqa*. As mentioned above, the *hadith* tradition was crucial also to the Sufis as prophetic examples of moral conduct, beyond (and in addition to) the commandments of the Qur'an.

Then it should not surprise that while based in the Arabian Peninsula, and actively making a Central and South Asian *tariqa* palatable to scholars based in Arabia, al-Qushashi and al-Kurani were able to attract pupils from all over the world. Among them was Khoja Abd Allah – who would inspire the establishment of a Qadiri center in China in the late seventeenth century through Qi Jingyi (or Hilal al-Din, 1656–1719) – and some of the most important *jawi 'ulama* of that time, who were all followers of the Naqshbandi *tariqa*. Both Abdu Ra'uf al-Sinkili (d. 1693) and Yusuf Makassari (d. 1699), for example, returned to Southeast Asia as Sufis, equally committed to the inner path and to legal doctrine. In Makassari's words: "let it be known, my fellows, exoteric devotion without esoteric one is like a body without a soul (*ruh*), whereas esoteric occupation without exoteric devotion is like a soul without a body."[20] Upon his return to Aceh, where he took the role of *shaykh-ul-Islam* under the reign of Sultana Safiatuddin, al-Sinkili dedicated himself to a conscious effort to harmonize *shari'a* and Sufism and make this "orthodox mysticism" the main approach for the Acehnese population, as he wrote in the local Malay literary language. Hence, even though there is no evidence of a structured presence of the order in Southeast Asia until the mid-nineteenth century (when the Naqshbandi center in Mecca would also become the most popular circle of instruction for *jawi* students), we know that individual *jawis* followed Naqshbandi practices in Aceh, Sulawesi, and Java as early as the late seventeenth century.

The connection between Sufism and *shari'a*-mindedness that had first emerged in the thirteenth century, retained a sustained presence through the eighteenth century and across Asia. Despite an apparent importance bestowed on Arabia, and the sense of a growing polarization between "mystics" and "jurists," the narratives of several Naqshbandi scholars show that this perceived need for religious reform and purification emerged from a variety of local circumstances as they manifested themselves across the Muslim lands, and eventually cross-fertilized each other via the circulation of scholars, pupils, and written materials that bridged the spiritual/legal divide. Focusing on the Naqshbandiyah, then, enables a reflection on the intertwining of the Sufi and legal paths across space in the long eighteenth century.

Muhammad ibn 'Abd al-Wahhab (1703–1792)

'Abd al-Wahhab hailed from the Nejd, the heart of Arabia, at a time when this central part of the Peninsula was still a politically fragmented and geographically isolated area of barren land inhabited by warring nomadic tribes, where the only "foreigners" passing through were southern Syrian and Iraqi *hajjis*. Like many of the local *'ulama*, 'Abd al-Wahhab traveled to "seek knowledge" from other scholars, mainly Hanbalis, but also the Hanafi Muhammad Hayya al-Sindi, who is often described in Wahhabi literature as "the spark that lighted Ibn 'Abdul Wahhab's path." In fact, it seems that Wahhab's vitriolic criticism of tomb visitations came from al-Sindi, who "was known to have been especially harsh in his criticism of established religious authorities for their lax attitude towards what he regarded as un-Islamic."[21]

'Abd al-Wahhab spent significant time in the towns of Medina and Basra, where he was faced by dramatically different realities from what he was accustomed to in the Nejd. His thought was deeply influenced by three elements: his origins in tribal Arabia, which in the eighteenth century still displayed many characteristics of its pre-Islamic society; the Medinan scholarly commitment to the revival of *hadith* science and to "bringing the Sufis back" to the *shari'a* (although several Sufi *tariqas* were themselves committed to it, as it was with the Naqshbandiyah); and Basra's mix of Sunni and Shi'a Muslims, which exposed him to a diversity of Islamic practices he had not experienced before (see Box 3.1). In this context, Hanbal's legacy of Sufi appreciation dissipated.

'Abd al-Wahhab's approach was soon characterized by an absolute commitment to God's unity and transcendence, which in practical terms manifested itself in a commitment to eradicating any form of idolatry (which he saw as any act of dedication to any other but God, including vow-making) and intercession (which he saw as prominent in the practice of shrine visits and saints' "veneration"). To him, both were signs of the Arab peoples' growing distance from the Qu'ranic message and from Islam as originally practiced by Muhammad and his companions: Islam was so corrupted by unlawful innovations (*bid'a*) that Arabia was once again in a state of ignorance (*jahiliyya*) and most Muslims could no longer call themselves Muslims. These are the roots of the Wahhabi practice of *takfir*, meaning labeling someone a *kafir*, an infidel, because they practice Islam in a different way.

This hardline position channeled much criticism from 'Abd al-Wahhab's contemporary peers. However, as the al-Sa'ud clan consolidated their power in the 1740s, they offered 'Abd al-Wahhab political support in exchange for his legitimation of their authority and

Box 3.1 Shi'ism

Upon Muhammad's death, Muslims found themselves in disagreement on who should be the leader of the *umma*. Muhammad had no male heir, and – some argued – he had left no clear designation. This position was in fact contested, as others contended that returning from what would be his last pilgrimage, Muhammad had indeed named his cousin and son-in-law, 'Ali ibn Abu Talib, as his successor when he had stated that "Of whomever I am the master (*mawla*), 'Ali is his master (*mawla*)." The statement was taken to embody both political and spiritual succession, as the term *mawla* was connected to closeness to God, and thus ability not just to rule but also to understand the divine message. It was in this historical context that the supporters of 'Ali came to be known as the Shi'a (i.e. "the followers of the *shi'at-'Ali*," the party of Ali), and the others as Sunnis.

In the following decades and centuries, the Shi'a came to pay more attention to the descendants of 'Ali and Fatima. The core of this group was referred to as the people of the house (*ahl al-bayt*), which included Muhammad, 'Ali, Fatima, and their two sons, Hasan and Husayn. As argued by Marshall Hodgson, after the establishment of Abu Bakr as the first Caliph ("representative") after Muhammad, "reverence for 'Ali and his Fatimid descendants ha[d] come to color in manifold ways the life of Sunni Islam," but others – namely, the Shi'a – "have come to give 'Ali and certain of his descendants an exclusive role in special religious systems" and, eventually, developed a specific legal corpus, referred to as Ja'fari *fiqh* (from Ja'far a-Sadiq, d. 765).

A second important watershed moment in the shaping of a Shi'a identity and consciousness was the Battle of Karbala (near Kufa, Iraq, 680), during which Husayn, his family, and a handful of supporters were attacked and ultimately killed by the 'Umayyad Army. The memory of Karbala is re-lived every year during the first ten days of the month of Muharram, usually through a series of daily, emotionally charged, readings of the account of the battle, culminating on the last day, 'Ashura. The discourse and propaganda leading to the Iranian Revolution of 1979 fully discharged the political potential of this memory, as revolutionaries often chanted the slogan "Every day is 'Ashura, every land is Karbala," and Zaynab – Husayn's sister and a strong figure in the Karbala narratives – was often depicted as the archetype of the defiant Shi'i woman.

From 'Ali, via his two sons, emerged the line of the *imam*s, or "guides," invested with spiritual leadership, exegetical authority, and – whenever possible – political power. There are a number of Shi'a "sub-sects" (including the Ismailis and Zaydis), but the largest group of Shi'as are the "Twelver," meaning that they recognize twelve *imam*s. In this view, (*al-Mahdi*) Muhammad ibn Hasan, considered the last *imam*, disappeared (going in "occultation") in the late ninth century; it is believed that he will return before the Day of Judgment.

Today, Shi'a Muslims represent a minority group globally, but at the national level they are the majority population in Iran, Iraq, Bahrain, Lebanon, and Azerbaijan, and are a significant minority in Pakistan and India.

deployment of his charismatic leadership to garner support from other tribes. Al-Wahhab was thus able to launch campaigns against popular traditions such as the veneration of trees, stones, and graves, often destroying the physical structures that had been built around them, with the support of the al-Sa'ud. Most infamous was his destruction of the shrine of Zayd ibn al-Khattab (d. 632), brother of the second caliph, 'Umar, and later (in 1802) the destruction of the tomb of Imam Husayn ibn 'Ali, located in Karbala, by Wahhabi followers. As 'Abd al-Wahhab couched the al-Sa'ud's military expeditions as a lawful *jihad* against the *kuffar* – never mind that these tribes considered themselves Muslims – the al-Sa'ud were able to further their territorial reach. The more established the al-Sa'ud became, the more power 'Abd al-Wahhab received: the extant opposition by other Arabian scholars (which had previously cost him expulsion) was quashed, he coopted and trained the *'ulama* who chose to stay, and thus he laid the ground for the Wahhabi hegemony of Arabia.

Shah Waliullah Dihlawi (1703–1762)

The Mughals had represented a period of political stability for South Asia since the sixteenth century, as had the Safavids in Persia and the Ottomans in West Asia, but with the death of Aurangzeb (r. 1658–1707), the Empire entered a phase usually defined as one of steady decline, ending with the British political takeover in the mid-nineteenth century. Similarly to other Muslim polities, the Mughal had established a firm bureaucratic infrastructure, in which the *'ulama* held a key role as intermediaries, thus eclipsing the social role that Sufis had held in the thirteenth to fourteenth centuries. That being said, some *'ulama* refused – or were denied – imperial patronage because of their views. Hence, when the Mughal Empire began to disintegrate, it was these sidelined *'ulama* and Sufi *shaykh*s who became popular leaders and authority figures. This phenomenon was visible in the Punjab and Sindh; the urban hubs of Delhi and Lucknow; and the rural areas of Bengal.

Whereas *'ulama* and Sufi *shaykh*s are often seen as belonging to opposite ends of the spectrum of Islamic learning, they unanimously pointed to the corruption of moral and religious standards as the primary cause for this environment of political and social collapse, thus initiating a process of renewal which centered around the need for closer attention to the *shari'a*. In fact, a key *mujaddid* ("renewer") of this period, Shah Waliullah Dihlawi (1703–1762), was known as both an *'alim* and a Sufi *shaykh* and was to be considered the intellectual ancestor of "virtually every Islamic movement in modern India."[22] Waliullah's impact was most marked in Delhi, but as his mission was taken on by his sons and other followers, his message spread across northern India. There, it remained influential well into the twentieth century and beyond, as the Deobandi movement claimed inspiration from his thought (see Chapters 4, 5, and 7).

Shah Waliullah started his career as a teacher in his father's *madrasa* (religious school) in Delhi, and he remained committed to teaching throughout his life. As an *'alim* who practiced in the absence of a Caliph, his primary concern was to offer his audience clear and approachable interpretations of the *hadith*s, providing instructions to navigate their daily life under uncertain political circumstances. Although he was a firm believer in the need for *ijtihad* to overcome the current state of things, Shah Waliullah reserved this interpretative enterprise to the scholars, proscribing that the general population should instead follow the Hanafi *madhhab* and the guidance of its learned interpreters. A second aspect of his scholarship focused on the unity of God, as he attempted – with only partial success – to reconcile the *wahdat-ul-wujud* with *wahdat-ul-shuhud*. Thirdly, he sought to settle the most vicious aspects of Sunni and Shi'a discord, at a time when Shi'ism was gaining ground in the courts and streets of South Asia.

These three pillars of Shah Waliullah's thought were carried further by his descendants, following two parallel paths. On the one hand was his eldest son, Shah Abdul Aziz (d. 1824). Like his father, he was known and respected as both a reformist teacher and a Sufi *shaykh*, but within the changing socio-political context of rising British influence, this *hadith* scholar focused his efforts on rectifying Delhi Muslims' orthopraxy by way of juridical exegesis and the issuing of *fatwa*s. These included daily guidance in terms of inheritance, family law, etc., and also suggested rectifications for how to conduct oneself when visiting the shrines of saints, for example. Yet, Shah Abdul Aziz was still far from fully abandoning or condemning local practices. This step – partially advancing from Shah Waliullah's last will, which encouraged Muslims to reject pre-Islamic customs – was taken on by Sayyed Ahmad Barelvi (1786–1831). Well-educated but impoverished, this Indian Arab of prophetic descent (*sayyid*) had first studied at the school of Shah Waliullah with his grandson Shah Isma'il (the author of Source 3.2), to later become himself a leading *'alim* of his time.

Unlike Shah Abdul Aziz, Shah Isma'il and Sayyed Ahmad Barelvi believed that the solution to this period of Muslim underachievement lay in destroying the current society through *jihad* in order to then build a new one in which Muslims were fully committed to practicing Islamic law; Sayyed Ahmad Barelvi and his followers would eventually confront the British and the Sikhs, albeit unsuccessfully, in 1826. In his writings he advocated for an unwavering commitment to *tauhid* (unity of God), and the condemnation of Shi'ism (as well as Sunnis' adoption of Shi'i practices, such as Muharram commemorations for Husayn's martyrdom, see Box 3.1), "false" Sufism (referring to esoteric *tariqa*s), and local customs (most notably, shrine visitation and intercession).

Ma Laichi (?1681–1766) and Ma Mingxin (?1719–1781)

After the Muslim merchants, bureaucrats, and scientists who had crossed Central Asia from the Tang period onwards, the emergence of Naqshbandi communities in northwest China represented a second wave of Islamization from the west, one that occurred parallel (and in contrast) to the development of the specifically Chinese Muslim literary tradition of the *Han Kitab* (discussed in Chapter 2). While Liu Zhi (?1670–1724) and other *Han Kitab* authors in coastal China and Yunnan translated and produced new scholarship adopting Islamic principles in a Confucian framework, Ma Laichi and Ma Mingxin traveled to Mecca, Yemen, and Central Asia (Bukhara and Kashgar), and possibly even India, collecting "'pure' texts from West Asia" and enhancing "their ability to interpret them," ultimately gaining "symbolic capital" and "add[ing] to their influence on potential converts to the Sufi ways."[23]

Both Ma Laichi and Ma Mingxin had been educated in an environment that put emphasis on adherence to the *shari'a* as well as practicing *dhikr* and reading mystical texts, and they were thus similarly committed to guiding their communities toward a purified form of Islamic rituality. Both were ordained as Naqshbandi *shaykh*s, yet they belonged to different generations (and thus different sub-traditions) of Naqshbandis, leading to wildly different outlooks. For Ma Mingxin, his studies with al-Kurani's disciples in Yemen were so formative that they led him to embrace a voiced, or "loud" (*jahri*), form of *dhikr*; to uphold the primacy of merit over genealogical descent to determine succession within the order; and to see "political and social reforms [as] a crucial focus" for Naqshbandi understandings of "renewal" (*tajdid*), as it was for Hayya al-Sindi, Waliullah, 'Abd al-Wahhab, Sirhindi, and the Southeast Asian al-Sinkili.[24]

However, these stands of Ma Mingxin clashed with several tenets that Ma Laichi had inherited from the Central Asian Naqshbandi tradition (Ma Laichi was a second-generation follower of Khoja Afaq). First, he practiced "silent" *dhikr* (which had led to this sub-branch being referred to as the Kahfiya, or "silent" group). Secondly, Ma Laichi adopted the importance of genealogical succession among descendants of the prophet Muhammad by arguing for the hereditary quality of the position of the order's *shaykh*; in his analysis of Ma Laichi's leadership, Jonathan Lipman has suggested that his ability to mirror within this Islamic institution the specifically Chinese model of corporate lineage turned the *menhuan* ("the Muslim saintly lineage of northwest China") into an effective tool for controlling local elites and guaranteeing their support.[25] Combined with Ma Laichi's advocacy for unconditional subordination to the (non-Muslim) Qing (1644–1911/1912) authority, the Kahfiya order's ability to adapt to its social and political environment allowed it to thrive during a period of harsh repression, without compromising its reformist agenda.

The case of Sufism in Gansu allows us to see how even if the impetus toward ritual purification had been reinforced by periods of study in West Asia, the historical trajectory of the Naqshbandiyah's consolidation in northwest China as an order that inspired activism, conformity to the *shari'a* and supra-local networks, had more to do with Central Asian models and Gansu's own local socio-political dynamics, than with Arabian ideals of reform and orthopraxy.

'Abd al-Nasir al-Qursawi of Bukhara (1776–1812)

Bukhara had been the bastion of Hanafi traditionalism in Central Asia for centuries, enjoying a process of rejuvenation in the second half of the seventeenth century and becoming a preferred destination for scholarly training over Kabul and Dagestan in the eighteenth century. By then, the improvement of caravan routes in the Kazakh steppe had allowed for better connections between the Khanates and Transoxiana, facilitating the influx of spiritual travelers who were attracted to the region by its many shrines. Yet, it was isolated from the "western" Muslim empires by the Safavid block. Hence, even though the Russian Empire incorporated Central Asia and its Khanates only in the 1860s (establishing a Governor General of Turkestan in 1867, see Chapter 4), the eighteenth-century scholarly circuit already connected Bukhara to the Russian Empire, bringing together Muslims from Transoxiana and the Volga-Ural basin.[26]

This was also a time of renewed religious freedom and institutional-ization, as in the northern Volga region the Empire allowed for the establishment of a Spiritual Assembly of Muslims in 1799. It is within this context that winds of reform picked up in Bukhara, under the guidance of 'Abd al-Nasir al-Qursawi. Some scholars have suggested a Wahhabi influence on al-Qursawi's commitment to *ijtihad*; however, there is no evidence of it at this point in time. In fact, the connection between Central Asia and the greater West Asian and North African regions (i.e. the Ottoman Empire, Egypt and the Arabian Peninsula) would only emerge after al-Qursawi's death, reaching consolidation in the late nineteenth century. Instead, al-Qursawi traced his intellectual genealogy back to the Naqshbandi-Mujaddid Ahmad al-Sirhindi via the Bukharan *khalifa* Ishan Niyazquli at-Turkmani (d. 1820).[27]

Al-Qursawi's approach was rooted in the rejection of all theological traditions that had emerged since the death of Muhammad, arguing that these "innovations" had impeded Muslims from practicing the com-mandments of the Qur'an. Inevitably, this reformist message caused conflict between al-Qursawi and the established Hanafi *'ulama* of Bukhara: his books were burnt and he was sentenced to death for heresy in 1808. In exile, he found refuge in his home village. There, he con-tinued to develop his interest in *fiqh* (advocating for direct engagement with the scriptures for all Muslims) and God's transcendence, but con-flict with the traditionalists did not subside. Al-Qursawi died in Istanbul, in 1812, on his way to perform the *hajj*. His work did not end, however, as later scholars – collectively referred to as the *jadids* – embraced it as the dawn of Muslim reform in Central Asia (see Box 3.2).[28]

Shaykh Da'ud al-Fatani (1769–1847)

As 'Abd al-Wahhab was forging his alliance with the al-Sa'ud, and spread his influence across the Arabian Peninsula, a few dozen refugees from the Sultanate of Patani (in north Malaya/south Siam, later Thailand) were arriving at Mecca, displaced by the Buddhist King of Siam who had taken over their land in 1786. The most prominent of these men was Shaykh Da'ud bin 'Abd Allah al-Fatani. After arriving as a refugee, he undertook the *hajj* at the first given opportunity, then resumed his studies, and eventually became a teacher in the *masjid al-haram* (Mecca's main mosque). Through his holding of this prestigious position, which was rarely occupied by non-Arabs, al-Fatani's *jawi* students formed a network of religious scholars who were key in facilitating a cultural

Box 3.2   Jadidism

Jadidism developed among a small (but vocal) group of Central Asian scholars at the turn of the twentieth century as they reflected on issues of "reform" within the context of encroaching Russo-European influences. While they had deep roots in al-Qursawi's commitment to *ijtihad*, this concern with "religious reform" emerged amidst a specifically contextual new interest in reforming Islamic education. This was a phenomenon primarily focused on a "new method" of teaching the Tatar language which relied on phonetics (Turkic languages were taught using the Arabic alphabet phonetically, rather than syllabically) and with broader issues of cultural reform. Theological debates seemed then irrelevant, and manifestations of pan-Islamism were rather limited, often couched in semi-secular terms under the influence of similar developments in the Ottoman Empire, but the political and religious implications of the jadidist program were unavoidable.[29]

Whereas until the eighteenth century the intellectual hub of Central Asia was in the cities of Samarkand and Bukhara, these heartlands of Khorasan were to slide in decay following their annexation by the Russian Empire, moving the center of reform westward and thus creating the conditions for the emergence of jadidism as a program of cultural (and religious) reform.

The Russian conquest of the Khanates in the 1860s had brought about dramatic socio-cultural transformations: Muslim Central Asia was seen by the Russian Empire as barbarian, fanatic, and despotic, to the extent that the self-branded "progressive" Empire advanced its own *mission civilisatrice* as the British and French had done in their colonies. Not only was this discourse embraced by some Muslim scholars – feeding into the reformist analysis – but it also informed imperial policies. Hence, instead of embarking on a program of internal reform, the Empire eliminated all existing Islamic institutions in what was then referred to as "Turkestan"; following the withdrawal of any form of state support for Islamic bureaucracy and education, Bukhara and Samarkand were eclipsed as centers of Islamic knowledge, and standardized primary education was introduced using vernacular languages. The legacy of the reformist approach which had emerged in Bukhara, Samarqand, and Kabul in the late eighteenth and early nineteenth centuries was then carried forward by the Volgan, Uralian, and Siberian Muslim students who had returned to European Russia, further reinforced by new discourses on Muslim decadence.

Within this context, post-conquest jadidism was a response to the Russian critique of Muslim society and an attempt at empowering Russian Muslims to be part of this new society without having to abandon their cultural and religious forms. Some local *madrasa* remained in operation, but most of Central Asia's Islamic intellectual activity took place in a network of Ottoman, Tatar and Central Asian scholars. The Ottoman Empire, later "Turkey," was an important locale for the *jadid*s; on the one hand was the historical legacy of Ottoman attempts at asserting the Caliph's authority over them, symbolically represented by the Treaty of

Box 3.2   *(cont.)*

Kucuk Kaynarca (1774) which, following the belligerence between the Ottomans and Russia over the Northern Caucasus, sanctioned that despite its military loss, the Ottoman Sultan-Caliph was granted the role of religious representative of Crimean Tatars: "As to the ceremonies of religion, as the Tatars profess the same faith as the Muhammadans, they shall regulate themselves, with respect to His Highness [the Ottoman Sultan], in his capacity as the Grand Caliph of Muhammadanism, according to the precepts prescribed to them by their law."

But on the other hand, this also reflected the impact of Ottoman reformers' endeavors; the *jadid*s took on the moniker "Young Bukharans" as a reference to the "Young Turks" who advocated for constitutional reforms in the Ottoman Empire. But Mecca and Cairo were also crucial intellectual hubs for the enriching of Russian Muslim thought. It was with the return – permanent or temporary – of a few prominent reformers that some schools gradually embraced the "new method" beginning in 1881.

As was the case in South Asia, this approach to reform and renewal took two seemingly opposing directions: on the one hand were those who called for a renewal of Islamic moral education alongside the limiting of its influence in the public sphere and a deeper embrace of Western modernity (in education, politics, dress, technology, etc.); on the other hand, there were those who saw the concept of *ijtihad* to mean a return to the example of the Prophet and his companions. In both cases, Russia's Muslims were trying to differentiate themselves from the state's Orthodox Christian imprint and to project and reinforce the *umma*'s aura of respectability in an environment of increasing material wealth.

renaissance that eventually enabled Patani to become a regional center for religious learning in the nineteenth century. As argued by Francis Bradley, "Shaykh Da'ud was the principle figure that directed this process [of fusion of Arabian and Southeast Asian Islamic intellectual traditions] via writing, translating and advocating reforms."[30] A few decades later, the *jawi* scholars Shaykh Nawawi al-Bantani (1813–1897) and Shaykh Ahmad Khatib al-Minangkabawi (1860–1915) were also allowed to teach within the confines of Mecca's mosque, further enhancing both *jawi* identity in Mecca and making Mecca's educational profile more cosmopolitan.

The displacement of a literate and educated elite – which was comparatively more religious than the general Patani populace and which became convinced that their political-military defeat had been a consequence of their religious laxity – created a physical and scholarly bridge between Mecca and Southeast Asia, between ideals of orthodoxy and reform.

Once in Mecca, Shaykh Da'ud studied with other *jawis*, such as al-Palimbani and al-Banjari, but also several Arab *'ulama*. He mastered *'ilmu al-hadith*, *tafsir*, and jurisprudence under the guidance of the most prominent teachers, including the then president of Cairo's al-Azhar (al-Shanwari) and his predecessor, al-Sharqawi. But his framework was also affected by regular life in Mecca. Upon his arrival, Shaykh Da'ud had performed the *hajj* and immersed himself in the local lifestyle, and during the fasting month of Ramadan he was once again faced by the difference of religious practices between Arabia and Patani. Shortly after, he became more vocal in his suggestion that the defeat of Patani had been sent by God as punishment because the community had been practicing Islam loosely. In the years that followed, his lectures and writings were mostly focused on legalistic issues, from slaughtering to *salat*, in an effort to "rectify" Islamic practices among the *jawis*. Patani had lacked a textual tradition, religious instruction being pursued orally. Hence, in the very beginning Shaykh Da'ud spent much time translating Shafi'i texts in Malay, advancing the reformist vision that Patani Muslims would thus be able to restore their community if they practiced a purified version of Islam.

But Shaykh Da'ud studied also *kalam* and *tasawwuf*, wrote a number of works inspired by Sufism, and was eventually inducted in the Khalwatiyyah and Shattariyah *tariqa*s. This he did not see as a contradiction of his commitment to a legalistic, "proper" form of ritualistic Islam. In fact, both *tariqa*s he was a member of, were considered "sober" ones (like the Naqshbandiyah), and his Sufi writings consistently pointed at the need to reform "intoxicated" *tariqa*s and to bring them in line with Shafi'i *fiqh*.

Shaykh Da'ud was in Arabia during 'Abd al-Wahhab's lifetime and in Mecca during its Wahhabi period (1805–1818). And some of his thinking overlaps with Wahhabi approaches to Islam – a return to the *hadith*, the need for purification from *bid'a*, condemnation of esoteric Sufism. Yet Shaykh Da'ud was also so clearly not a Wahhabi: he himself embraced Sufism, he was – and remained – a committed Shafi'i, studied with al-Azhar scholars, and while he encouraged "proper" Islamic practices, he also pursued an intellectual synthesis of Arabian and Southeast Asian traditions. Although during the Wahhabi period of Mecca Shaykh Da'ud concentrated his efforts on translating Shafi'i legal codes, during the period of Ottoman presence (1814–1818) he penned two works that would have encountered Wahhabi opposition, as they openly supported local Patani and Southeast Asian traditions.[31]

The Nineteenth Century

Even though "Islamic reformism" has been framed in the twentieth century as a direct response to the wide spread of Sufism and its "intoxication," traditional forms of devotion remained rooted across the Muslim lands (see Source 3.2).

Nile Green has vividly captured the multifaceted reality of twentieth-century Islamic devotion, suggesting that "in the absence of state religious monopolies, modernization enables the ritual, organizational, material and ideological productions of a dizzying range of Muslim religious firms whose visions, whether rationalizing or enchanting, answer to the needs of the heterogenous Muslims of an uneven world." In the specific case of Bombay – but also in many other locales across Asia – shrine veneration and saints' devotion proved stronger than reformism in reconnecting migrant workers and laborers with their roots, and thus a steadier anchor at a time of change.[32]

Another counter-argument to the dichotomization of reformism and Sufism was the role of Sufis in leading the reformist movement. Building on Sirhindi and Waliullah, the Deobandi school, for example, created a movement which, Brannon Ingram has argued, "sees Sufism as inseparable from Islamic legal norms. These, in turn, are inseparable from Islamic ethics and politics, broadly conceived." Yet these scholars have been consistently labeled as "fundamentalists" and "Wahhabis" to imply an anti-Sufi devotional streak.[33] As there had been many Hanbali mystics in the tenth to twelfth centuries, in the eighteenth to nineteenth centuries many pioneers of the Islamist movement had come from Sufi backgrounds. Most notable is the case of the al-Azhar reformer Muhammad 'Abduh (1849–1905), who in his youth was attracted to mysticism and asceticism, and whose initial attraction to Jamal ad-Din "al-Afghani" (1838–1897) was through mysticism: "there arose the sun of truths, who clarified for us their subtle intricacies. (So it came to pass) with the arrival of the perfect sage, truth personified, our master Sayyid Jamal al-din al-Afghani."[34] But they all struggled with the perceived "excesses" of Sufism, as also discussed by 'Abduh's student, the Syrian Rashid Rida (1865–1935); the *tariqa* Naqshbandiyah was Rida's spiritual home for a while, but he eventually distanced himself from all Sufi practices:

I was striving to follow the Sufi Way by leaving the best food and being satisfied with a little wild thyme with salt and sumac and by sleeping on the ground etc., until it was no longer any trouble deliberately to leave the best food available. But I tried to accustom myself to put up with dirt on my body and clothes, which is not lawful, and I was unable to do so.[35]

Conclusions

The intellectual biographies of these scholars have led us through an exploration of how mysticism and legal approaches to Islamic practice did not take shape as mutually exclusive, but rather as intertwined, dynamics. Shah Waliullah Dihlawi and 'Abd al-Wahhab were born in the same year and developed similar platforms, but their mind-sets were radically different, as a Sufi inclination enriched Dihlawi's reformist perspective. Similarly, Shaykh Da'ud al-Fatani emerged in Mecca as a famed scholar of *hadith* and jurisprudence deeply concerned with "proper" ritual, but also as a spiritually rich man ordained in multiple Sufi orders and committed to not repudiate his Southeast Asian roots. This dual track of reformism and Sufism sustained itself also further east, as the Chinese Ma Laichi and Ma Mingxin both complemented a desire for orthopraxy and ritual purification – which they had garnered during periods of study in Yemen and Arabia – with the Naqshbandi path. Through the teachings of the Naqshbandiyah, both Ma Laichi and Ma Mingxin expressed and spread commitment to a return to the scriptures and a rejection of *bid'a*, which in northwest China mostly manifested itself as the absorption of Chinese traditions into Islamic practices.

Secondly, the focus on the Naqshbandiyah allowed to center these dynamics in Asia, as this Central Asian order spread to the Indian subcontinent and influenced developments also in China and Southeast Asia, ultimately bringing Asia in the spotlight when exploring scholars' concerns (and interventions) about "deviation" and "orthodoxy."

Dihlawi and 'Abd al-Wahhab's connection was forged in Arabia, but indirectly (they don't seem to have ever crossed paths), as they studied with the most eminent *muhaddith* of that time in Medina, the South Asian Muhammad Hayya al-Sindi. Arabia is neither the center nor the instigator for reformist desires, even if it sometimes landed itself as a meeting location. Hence, without denying the crucial role played by Mecca and Medina as gathering places for scholars coming from all corners of the world, this chapter has taken into consideration alternative routes and networks of religious learning that connected the *umma* across geographical boundaries.

Echoing Albert Hourani, the reformist ideas that would be broadcast from Cairo's al-Azhar at the turn of the twentieth century, had in fact been "in the air" for much longer and well beyond the traditional centers of Islamic knowledge.[36] Taking Hourani's insight further, the next chapter explores how Muslims in Central, South, and Southeast Asia intersected with Cairo's socio-religious reformism and with Ottoman attempts at capitalizing politically on the Caliph's spiritual authority on the "global *umma*." But far from being the subjects of West Asia's initiatives, Muslims "beyond the Oxus" often become the main drivers behind transnational Islamist movements, policies, and strategies.

Further Reading

Azra, A. (2004) *The origins of Islamic reformism in Southeast Asia: networks of Malay-Indonesian and Middle Eastern 'Ulama' in the seventeenth and eighteenth centuries*, Crows Nest, NSW: Asian Studies Association of Australia in association with Allen & Unwin.

Baljon, J. M. S. (1986) *Religion and thought of Shāh Walī Allāh Dihlawī, 1703–1762*, Leiden: Brill.

Bradley, F. R. (2016) *Forging Islamic power and place: the legacy of Shaykh Daud bin Abd Allah al-Fatani in Mecca and Southeast Asia*, Honolulu, HI: University of Hawai'i Press.

Commins, D. D. (2006) *The Wahhabi mission and Saudi Arabia*, London: I. B. Tauris.

Cooke, M., and Lawrence, B. B. (2005) *Muslim networks from Hajj to hip hop*, Chapel Hill, NC: University of North Carolina Press.

Dudoignon, S. A. (1996) "Le réformisme musulman en asie centrale: du 'premier renouveau' a la soviétisation, 1788–1937," *Cahiers du monde russe: Russie, Empire russe, Union soviétique, États indépendants* 37(1/2) (special issue on Islamic reformism in Central Asia).

Farquhar, M. (2017) *Circuits of faith: migration, education, and the Wahhabi mission*, Stanford, CA: Stanford University Press.

Metcalf, B. D. (1982) *Islamic revival in British India: Deoband, 1860–1900*, Princeton, NJ: Princeton University Press.

Voll, J. (1975) "Muḥammad Ḥayyā al-Sindī and Muḥammad ibn 'Abd al-Wahhab: an analysis of an intellectual group in eighteenth-century Madīna," *Bulletin of the School of Oriental and African Studies, University of London* 38(1): 32–39.

Weismann, I. (2007) *The Naqshbandiyya: Orthodoxy and activism in a worldwide Sufi tradition*, London: Routledge.

Figure 4.1 Blue and white headcloth with Arabic calligraphy.
© Collection Nationaal Museum van Wereldculturen. Coll. no. TM-5663-2

4 Pan-Islamism and Nationalism (Nineteenth and Twentieth Centuries)

Dated to the late nineteenth century, the headcloth (*kain kepala*) depicted here (Figure 4.1) is decorated with *batik* technique to incorporate the pseudo-calligraphic representation of the words "Allah" and "Muhammad" and the signature of one of the Ottoman Sultan-Caliphs (called a *tughra*). This object, then, draws interesting connections between Southeast Asian artistic techniques, ideas of authority and power, and pan-Islamic politics.

The wax-resistant *batik* technique of textile decoration was usually practiced by women who drew patterns with a hollow metal "pen" that allowed the hot wax to flow down slowly. After soaking the cloth in a color bath, the wax was melted, revealing the white patterns on dyed background. Found in many places worldwide, it became characteristic of Java's textile industry around the fifteenth and sixteenth centuries, as Islam was taking a foothold in the region. From the same period are Malay epics which mention headcloths either as symbols of authority worn by war-chiefs, courtiers, and messengers, or as protective talismans, deemed to carry supernatural powers.[1] The latter kind was said to be decorated with Islamic quotations and worn by those setting out on a quest or engaging in warfare. Embedded on the cloth was Arabic calligraphy, embodied by the wearer as protection, regardless of whether the script was properly represented or only vaguely recognizable (i.e. pseudo-calligraphy).

Traffic between eastern Asia and the Ottoman Empire had been sustained for centuries, but following his own proclamation of "the Ottoman Sultan as Caliph of the Muslim World" in 1876, Caliph 'Abdulhamid II (1842–1918, r. 1876–1909) undertook several propaganda initiatives to project his religious authority onto Muslims who lived outside of the Ottoman territory. As tensions in Europe were on the rise, this strategy was pursued in hope of political support from other Muslim populations under the control of rival imperial powers. However, at the turn of the twentieth century, Malay-language readers in the Dutch East Indies seemed more interested in the Ottomans' nationalist military campaigns and court intrigues than in their pan-Islamic propaganda.[2]

When in the 1910s the Ottomans turned to the *umma* for political support, but received none, it became evident that previous invocations of the Ottoman Caliphate's Islamic authority – so recognizably embedded in this *kain kepala* – were rooted in its potential to provide supernatural power, not political alliance. The *tughra* – which had made its way to Southeast Asia as part of the Caliphal pan-Islamic propaganda – had in fact become a protective talismanic symbol deployed by Javanese and Sumatran warriors as they fought the Dutch in their effort to achieve an independent nation-state.

★★★

The lands that by the fifteenth century had been integrated through Islamization straddled cultural similarities and differences. The processes that had made Asia a Muslim space had also led to the influence of Asia on Islam, as these two "entities" engaged in conversations and exchanges while retaining their own peculiarities. But the sixteenth century saw the arrival of a new actor, as Europeans began to move, and assert their presence, on the Asian stage.

What had started as the European age of explorations in the late fifteenth and early sixteenth centuries soon turned into a commercial enterprise, and eventually – by the beginning of the eighteenth century – into European Imperialism. By the late 1800s, the Russian Empire incorporated most of Central Asia; the British had political control of South Asia, Malaya, Burma, and Hong Kong; the Dutch ruled over the East Indies; the French had Indochina (corresponding to today's Vietnam, Cambodia, and Laos); and the Spanish held the Philippines until 1899, when the United States took over (see Map 5). The only independent nations, at least formally, were Siam (today's Thailand, under the Cakri dynasty), Japan (under the Meiji dynasty), and China (under the Qing dynasty), although they were under indirect pressure from various Western powers throughout the nineteenth and twentieth centuries. Much of the world's *umma* was under non-Muslim rule (both European and Asian), and imperialism deeply affected the way that Muslims practiced Islam as a form of religious devotion as well as how they thought about Islam as a source of governance.

At the same time as Europe was engaging with the wider Muslim world, the Ottomans were emerging as the new leaders of the *umma*, adopting the title of Caliph and taking control of most of the former Islamic Empire, from Egypt to Iraq. But the Ottoman demise during

World War I, compounded with the general state of subjugation across the world, stimulated a lively intellectual discourse, as Muslim scholars tried to explain the reasons for their condition, forged a path toward independence, and explored options for the re-constitution of a central Islamic authority. But it also ought to be remembered that "resistance" was only one mode of interaction between Muslims and colonizing empires, as in several circumstances and contexts Muslims cooperated with their political opponents, and outsiders' knowledge and political praxis were taken as inspiration by Muslim intellectuals.

This chapter first explores the relationship between the Ottoman Caliphate and Muslims who lived outside of its sphere of political control, paying particular attention to issues of authority, directionality, and agency, as the Ottomans faced defeat and Muslims worldwide discussed the future of this political and spiritual leadership. While colonized peoples addressed issues of self-determination and nationalism, the crisis (and later collapse) of the Ottoman Caliphate unfolded, informing those debates.

Hence, the following pages also investigate how Islam intersected with, contributed to, and informed nationalist anti-colonial movements across Asia. Muslims in colonized territories were impacted differently by Islam and the European presence, and although "the assumption is that Muslims, due to their piety and the nature of their faith, naturally resist ... nation-states," the history of Muslim peoples in the early twentieth century shows that many among them were inspired by, or even provided support to, imperial orders, European manifestations of culture, and the very idea of a nation-state.[3]

The flow of peoples and ideas, the relationship between a putative center of Islam (located in the Ottoman Empire, today's Turkey) and "outer Asia," and reflections on how (or whether) to integrate Islam in the nation-building process are explored through the cases of the Dutch East Indies, British India, and the Soviet Union, their engagement with imperialism and Islam, pan-Islamic aspirations, and the rise of nation-states, local politics, and transnational intellectual discourses.

From the Center Out?

On November 14, 1914 the Ottoman Grand Mufti (or *shaykh-ul-Islam*) issued a legal opinion (*fatwa*) calling the *umma* to wage a *jihad* (here used to mean "religiously justified war," see Chapter 7) against colonial Europe, leveraging the fact that the head of the Ottoman Empire was also the Caliph, hence the spiritual guide of the *umma* worldwide. The text, known as the "Jihad Fatwa," incited "Muslims living under the sovereignty of Britain, France, Russia, Serbia Montenegro, and their supporters" "to resort to jihad" as these "enemies of the Islamic Caliphate are trying to – may God forbid – extinguish the divine light of Islam by attacking the seat of the Caliph and the Ottoman nation" (see Source 4.1).

Source 4.1

The Ottoman Jihad Fatwa (1914)

This text is the full English language rendering of the fatwa *(legal opinion) issued by the Ottoman* shaykh-ul-Islam *in 1914, as an attempt to rally international support within the* umma *against opposing European powers in the theater of World War I.*[4]

QUESTION: Would it be a religious duty for all the Muslims in all countries, whether young or old, infantry or cavalry, to resort to jihad [here used to mean exclusively "religiously justified war"] with all their properties and lives, as required by the Quranic verse of Enfiru, if the Sultan of Islam declares war and calls the entire population under arms, when there is an enemy attack against Islam and Islamic countries are extorted and pillaged and Islamic people are enslaved?

ANSWER: It would.

QUESTION: In this way, would it be a religious duty for them to declare war against Russia, Britain and France and their helpers and supporters, who are enemies of the Islamic Caliphate and trying to – may God forbid – extinguish the divine light of Islam by attacking the seat of the Caliph and the Ottoman nation with battleships and land forces?

ANSWER: It would.

QUESTION: In this way, when success depends on all Muslims to resort to jihad, would it be a sin and a major rebellion if they – may God forbid – refuse to do so and would they deserve the wrath of God and the punishment for this great sin?

ANSWER: They would.

QUESTION: In this way, would the abovementioned state, who are fighting against the state of Islam deserve to be killed and burn in infernal fire if they, deliberately or under coercion, murder Muslim people, destroy their families and fight against the soldiers of the state of Islam?

ANSWER: They would.

QUESTION: In this way, would the Muslims living under the sovereignty of Britain, France, Russia, Serbia, Montenegro and their supporters deserve severe suffering if they fight against Germany and Austria, who are helping the Ottoman government, because it would be harmful for the Caliphate of Islam?

ANSWER: They would.

With this issuance, the Ottoman Empire was attempting to rally support from individual Muslims, calling upon their sense of duty to defend the Caliphate, and thus capitalizing on the theological, ritual, and political feelings of belonging to the *umma*. The proclamation was intended to make ripples from Europe to the Dutch East Indies and the Philippines. But rather than emerging from a religiously inspired concern (or even Islamist strategy), the Jihad Fatwa was mostly a response to the end of the old Ottoman–British alliance, which had terminated with the onset of World War I. At the time, some observers even suggested that the *fatwa* had been issued under pressure from Germany, the new ally of the Ottoman Empire.

The *fatwa* not only represented the most direct attempt at reaping the fruits of the Ottoman pan-Islamic propaganda, but was also the Caliphate's most blatant failure at that. This should have not come as a surprise: in previous years much effort had gone into translating pan-Islamic, pro-Ottoman propaganda materials in Arabic, Turkish, Persian, Urdu, Tatar, and Chinese and then distributing them across Asia through the network of German consular offices (e.g. in Batavia/Jakarta, Beijing, and Shanghai). But Asia's Muslims proved to be the hardest to reach: not only were they far away and with limited resources, but also their imperial masters – Russia, Britain, and the Dutch – were actively involved in censorship, customs control, and the screening of returning *hajji*s.

Even before the Ottoman Empire (and its ally, Germany) had begun to lead direct pan-Islamist propaganda to garner political and military support from the *umma*, the Ottomans had sought to expand their spiritual reach over the *umma*. Mostly, they had tried to do this by capitalizing on the image of the Caliph as the protector of all Muslims to "incorporate a subaltern appeal for better treatment of the colonial oppressed ... [but] Pan Islamism had to avoid appearing anti-imperialist" because, as concluded by Cemil Aydin, "the Ottomans still sought good relations between empires, and they used pan-Islamic ideology to pursue that harmony, not a clash of civilization."[5]

Building on some past (intermittent) occasions on which the Ottoman Caliph had been able to assert himself as the spiritual leader of Muslims outside the Empire's territorial confines, in the late 1800s the new Ottoman constitution (1876) provided the framework for the intended impact of the Jihad Fatwa, as it announced "the Ottoman Sultan as Caliph of the Muslim World." This, combined with the fact that the Ottomans were the last independent Sunni Muslim polity still standing, contributed to the prestige of the Empire in the eyes of the wider *umma*. Caliph 'Abdulhamid II thrived in this newly refashioned position: "Everyone knows that a word from the caliph, the head of the Muslims, that is I, would suffice to inflict a great harm to the English authority in India."[6]

During his reign, 'Abdulhamid II undertook major infrastructural projects to "unify" the *umma*, such as building the Hejaz railways and repairing the Ka'ba, the mosques at Medina, Karbala, and Najaf, and the family tomb of 'Ali ibn Abu Talib. He also promoted himself as the sole religious leader of the *umma*, establishing a monopoly on the printing and distribution of the Qur'an and providing *'ulama* to Muslim communities worldwide (e.g. in China and South Africa). In this multi-pronged propaganda effort, the Empire also supported the publication of pan-Islamic pamphlets and newspapers in Turkish, Arabic, Urdu, and other Islamicate languages; they trained small military contingents across the Empire, providing both martial and religious pan-Islamist instruction; and they sent emissaries to Africa as well as Central Asia, India, China, Malaya, the Dutch East Indies, Japan, and the Philippines.

'Abdulhamid II was most involved in the pan-Islamic effort, its political advantage becoming most clear in the late 1880s to the early 1910s. But while a Caliph could ask for *fatwas* to be issued and railways to be built, he still needed the intellectual legitimation that only a respected scholar could carry. So it was, that in 1892 Jamal ad-Din "al-Afghani" (1838–1897) joined the caliphal court (see Box 4.1).

Box 4.1   Jamal ad-Din "al-Afghani" and the Roots of Pan-Islamism

Born in Iran into a Shi'a family, Jamal ad-Din – often referred to as "al-Afghani" because of his claimed Afghan descent – had a peripatetic life. He spent time in Afghanistan (1860s), India (at around the time of the 1858 rebellion), Cairo (1870s), Istanbul (1869 and again in the 1890s), Paris (1880s), Britain (1884), and Iran and Russia (mid-1880s). In most cases, his move to the next place was due to his expulsion by British or pro-British authorities. With a background in Islamic philosophy, Jamal ad-Din's thought was first and foremost impacted by Western imperialism, which he began to oppose in his early days in Afghanistan. His political legacy built on the combination of a classical education and anti-imperialism, with a commitment to teaching (which characterized the decade he spent in Cairo) and a belief in the ability of the *umma* to come together regardless of sectarian, ethnic, or linguistic differences (Jamal ad-Din was known for his attempt at minimizing differences among Shi'is and Sunni, which was what had brought him to the Ottoman court in the first place). Jamal ad-Din's pan-Islamism sought the unification of the *umma* against Western encroachment through the internal reformation of the *umma* itself, as he eloquently explained to Caliph 'Abdulhamid II in 1885, while suggesting he should be preaching this approach to Muslims in India and Central Asia.

Throughout his life Jamal ad-Din had been mostly concerned with anti-British imperialism in Afghanistan, India, Persia, and Egypt, but he had also taken an anti-Ottoman position, accusing the Egyptian provincial government of having caused the political and financial crisis of the 1870s. Yet, his suggestion that Muslims could confront the West only if they united regardless of ethnic, linguistic, or sectarian identities – the roots of pan-Islamism – was congenial to the Caliph, who was fighting for the loyalty of Iraq's Shi'is against the (Shi'i) Safavid Shah of Persia. The Caliph thus embraced the vision of a unified *umma* (i.e. "pan-Islamism") as a tool to further affirm his authority – political, military, territorial, or spiritual – over Muslims worldwide *vis-à-vis* his neighbors, and less so against European powers.

To Jamal ad-Din, however, "pan-Islamism" was a solidarity network primarily meant to help individual nations to achieve independence from European colonialism. It was only in later years, and only temporarily, that this vision was transformed in a political ideal aimed at uniting the worldwide *umma* under a Caliph. Also, the "unity of the *umma*" was but one aspect of a broader strategy to address the problem of non-Muslim rule, as to Jamal ad-Din the political subjugation of Muslims worldwide was the outcome of Muslims' own internal conflicts as much as of their religious laxity (echoing the concerns of the reformers discussed in Chapter 3). Whereas pan-Islamism would have a more decisive impact in later years, the need for reform was to have immediate resonance in the Empire and with Muslims worldwide. Jamal ad-Din had begun to express this vision in 1881 on the pages of *The Indissoluble Bond* (*al-urwa' al-wuthqa*), which he edited in Paris with his Cairene student Muhammad 'Abduh (1849–1905), and continued to advocate for these reforms until his death. His legacy was taken forward by 'Abduh and the latter's disciple Rashid Rida (1865–1935). Although they did differ in some nuances, the three agreed that the internal reformation of the *umma* required a renewed interpretation of the scriptures (*ijtihad*, see Box 2.2), the pursuit of socio-religious self-improvement, and the incorporation of Western technology and sciences in Islamic education.

Jamal ad-Din and 'Abduh had formulated what is now referred to as "Islamic modernism" or "reformism" as a reaction to the Western encroachment on Muslim lands as well as local elites' adoption and absorption of Western models of knowledge and power, which they claimed were leading to their abandonment of Islam as a guiding principle of conduct. Notably, these two scholars (and Rida later) related differently to Western knowledge. Jamal ad-Din was more decisively opposed to the West, while 'Abduh was rather interested in engaging with it (especially with its approach to education and its technological advances) at the same time as he advocated for retaining the authenticity of Islamic authority. Rashid Rida, the youngest among this first generation of political reformists, had himself received an eclectic education, mastering the natural sciences and foreign languages as well as the Islamic tradition. He thus had a deep-seated commitment to the incorporation of Western methodologies. Rashid Rida was not the only Muslim to be fascinated – or at least appreciative – of certain aspects of Western culture, as seen in the cases of the Indian Sayyid Ahmad Khan (1817–1898), whose intellectual approach came to be labeled "Occidentalism," and the Russian Tatar Ismail Gasprinskii (1851–1914) (see Sources 4.2 and 4.3).

Even though Jamal ad-Din had an outward and transnational vision – having engaged directly with Muslims in India and Central Asia – the impact of his thought was mostly limited to the Ottoman Empire. It was only when Rashid Rida moved to Egypt to join 'Abduh, that Islamic reformism gained a broader audience through its periodical *al-Manar* (*The Lighthouse*) (see Box 4.2).

Besides its local readership in Egypt, which included both local Arabophone Muslims and foreigners who had come to Cairo for their studies – Cairo had been picking up as an alternative destination since the pro-Wahhabi Saudi monarchy had dramatically limited individuals' freedom of expression, thus reducing the range of intellectual stimulation which had come in the form of teachers and books (see Chapter 3) – the impact of Cairene reformism was also amplified by *al-Manar*'s distribution abroad, which took place through pilgrims, merchants, and scholars who carried the pages and ideas of the journal as far as China, Japan and the Dutch East Indies.

All propaganda aside, the Ottoman commitment to pan-Islamism seemed to fall short when Muslim rulers asked for help. Whereas in religious terms the Ottoman Caliphate channeled its influence toward affirming its own authority over the *umma vis-à-vis* Western authorities, this was envisioned exclusively in the spiritual and religious realm. On the military and political levels the Caliphs tended to encourage peace and harmony between Muslim subjects and their colonial masters: in 1798, the Ottomans discouraged the Sultan of Mysore, in southern India, from forming an alliance with the French to push back against the British, as Napoleon was indeed a common enemy of Britain and the Ottomans;[7] in 1857 'Abdulhamid's father, Sultan 'Abdulmecid (r. 1839–1861), issued "a proclamation advising Indian Muslims to remain loyal to his British allies"[8] and thus to refrain from joining the Rebellion; *Jawis* complained to the Caliph about having to live under

Source 4.2

Sayyid Ahmad Khan's Occidentalism

Sayyid Ahmad Khan was an English-educated Indian man employed in the colonial service. His efforts went into educating British India's Muslims along the lines of Western education, without however erasing their Muslim identity. Besides establishing the Mohammadan Anglo-Oriental College, later renamed Alighar Muslim University College, Sayyid Ahmad Khan also published extensively to reach a broader audience. Here below are two excerpts; one is from an essay weighing the status of women in the Islamic scriptures and societies vis-à-vis British laws and society, where he concludes that Muslim societies need to engage further with the West to actualize the Qur'anic mandate. The other is an blunt exhortation for India's Muslims to embrace English customs in order to achieve "civilization."[9]

Women

Advanced countries loudly proclaim that men and women were created equal, that both hold equal rights, and that there is no reason why woman should be thought of as less important or less worthy of respect than man ... Yet we observe that up to this day in no advanced country has woman been given importance or equality to men in rights and authority, to the extent she has been given in Islam. England greatly favors the freedom of women, yet when its laws relating to women are examined it is discovered that the [English] people have considered women quite insignificant, unintelligent and valueless.

According to English laws, when a woman marries, she is considered to have lost her separate existence, and her distinctive individuality is absorbed into that of her husband ...

Now consider how woman is honored in Muslim law, and how her rights and authority have been conceded to be equal to man's ... upon reaching adulthood she assumes authority and is capable of every kind of agreement, just like a man.

There is no special restriction upon a woman which is not also upon a man, except that which she has taken upon herself in terms of the wedding contract, or the restriction relating to the private parts of her body which differ by nature from man's. Thus, in truth, in the religion of Islam man and woman are considered equal in a way which does not exist in any other religion or in the law of any nation.

But it is a most astonishing fact that all advanced nations strongly criticize the condition of women in Islam. And there is no doubt that in actuality the condition of women in the advanced nations is considerably better than that of Muslim women or women of Muslim countries, although the situation ought to be the reverse ...

Source 4.2   *(cont.)*

At this point the thing for which we wish to argue is simply good treatment of woman by man ... Doubtless, as far as we know, there is considerable progress being made in these particulars regarding women, in the advanced countries. But in Muslim countries there is no progress in these areas, and in India there are such unworthy and humiliating carryings-on that one can only cry out, May God have mercy on us!

People who connect these evils with the religion of Islam are surely mistaken. In fact, to the extent that there is deterioration in the condition of women in India, the only cause of this is a failure to observe fully the regulations of the Muslim religion. If its principles were brought into practice, no doubt all these evils would be eliminated.

In addition, there is another strong reason for this: Muslims today are uncivilized ... Muslims, despite the fact that their religious law regarding women was much higher than the laws of the rest of the world, on account of being uncivilized, have treated women so badly that all the nations laugh at the condition of Muslim women. Because of our inherent evils, and because the whole Muslim community everywhere is in the same state, (with perhaps some minimal exceptions willed by God!) all nations criticize our religion.

Assuredly, then, this is no time for us to let our zeal flag, or to let our conduct go uncorrected, or to fail to show by our conduct the proof of Islam's enlightenment – for our religion is enlightened.

On Being Uncivilized

When man performs a good act in an uncivilized way, that which is essentially good makes an impression on people's hearts, and the depravity of the savage style in which the good act was done, is hidden from the eyes. The effect of superior education, however, is that it eradicates that savage conduct, and nothing remains but pure goodness ...

It is a matter of extremely good fortune for a man to be born in, or immigrate into, a country – and receive his education there – where educational facilities are plentiful and where learning and refined culture are widespread ...

These thoughts stir me up to induce my community to mix with a civilized community and to go to a refined country. I am forever sorrowful to think that even those virtues which are present in our community are uncivilized ones. Worldly dealings, meeting with one another, the friendship of friends, the piety of the pious, the wealth of the wealthy, all are in a state extremely lacking in refinement and cultivation. If they are adorned with fine teaching and training, it will be a tremendous improvement for man both in this life and in the life which is to come.

Box 4.2 *Al-Manar* and Its Impact

Al-Manar (*The Lighthouse*) was first published in 1898, a year after its founding editor – the Syrian Rashid Rida – had arrived in Cairo to join 'Abduh, whom he saw as the foremost thinker in Islamic reformism. Whereas Muhammad 'Abduh had received a traditional *'ulama* training in *tafsir* (interpretation) and *fiqh* (jurisprudence), only later in life becoming committed to the adoption of Western models of education (under the guidance of Jamal ad-Din "al-Afghani"), Rida had himself been exposed since childhood to an eclectic education in the natural sciences, languages, and Islamic traditions. The articles on *al-urwa' al-wuthqa* resonated with the young Rida who had been familiar with both the Sufi al-Ghazali (d. 1111) and the legal scholar Ibn Taymiyah (1263–1328), the earliest pioneers of Islamic reform (see Chapter 3 on Sufism and legal reformism), and who view *ijtihad* (legal interpretation) as permissible only within the framework of *maslaha*, the greater good of society. Despite this conservative approach, Rida, like other reformists, continued to advance the idea that European dominance on the *umma* had been caused by its own weakness, as represented by its fragmentation, the stagnation of religious scholars, and the tyranny of rulers. And thus, he advocated for the unity of Muslims and a renewal of the Caliphate.

The impact of *al-Manar* went much further than West Asia. The influence of Jamal ad-Din, Muhammad 'Abduh, and al-Azhar in general had been latent among Russia's Muslims since the late 1880s, when Jamal ad-Din had visited St. Petersburg. But it became most evident starting in the 1910s, as Russia enjoyed a short spell of freedom, and between 1908 and 1918 Russian Muslims were able to access the ideas broadcasted on the pages of Rashid Rida's *al-Manar* in their own language, through the magazine *al-Shura*, which was published in ottomanized Tatar language. Another key publication was *Tercuman*, started by Ismail Gasprinskii in 1883 as a platform to advocate educational reforms and modern sciences, as well as pan-Turkism and pan-Islamism.

A similar timeline applied to Southeast Asia. *Jawi* Muslims had often contributed articles, or asked for *fatwa*s on the pages of *al-Manar*, already in the 1890s, and the Arab magazine had been circulating in the region for several years, mostly smuggled by returning pilgrims and students, since colonial authorities were concerned with the potential revolutionary impact of pan-Islamism and reformism itself. The first channel of Cairene reformism in the Malay language emerged in 1906; *al-Imam* was published in Singapore with the contribution of several men from the Minagkabau area of Sumatra, but it lasted only a few years, later followed by *al-Munir* launched in Sumatra. By the 1910s *al-Manar* had inspired several reformists to print magazines in the Dutch East Indies, Singapore, and parts of Malaya.

In northern South Asia the ideas of al-Azhar were propagated through the pages of the periodicals *al-Hilal* and *al-Balagha*, which between

Box 4.2 *(cont.)*

1912 and 1930 brought the ideas of al-Azhar to South Asia's reformists, under the editorship of Abu al-Kalam Azad (1888–1958); an Indian Muslim nationalist, later a member of the Congress in the 1940s, Azad was a firm believer in Jamal ad-Din's anti-imperialism and *al-Manar*'s ideas. In the South, instead, *al-Islam* started publication in the late 1910s and set out to propagate its ideas in Malayalam language (1918). Its editor, the Muslim reformer Vakkom Moulavi, had already been an advocate for the education of women as well as the fashioning of a "modern education" for all Mappila Muslims in Kerala.

The latest and furthest local adaptation of *al-Manar* was in China, as the magazine *Yuehua* began to publish translated articles from *al-Manar* and *Nur al-Islam* (the latter being al-Azhar's bulletin) as well as other Islamic periodicals from overseas (in Arabic, Malay, Turkish, etc.) as late as the 1930s. This exposure of China's Muslims to the global reformist movement was by and large the result of a first batch of students officially sent from the Shanghai Islamic School to al-Azhar in 1931; the following year more were sent from the Chengda Normal School, located in Beijing, further amplifying and broadening the impact of *al-Manar* in East Asia.[10]

non-Muslim rule in 1873, and a few years later (1898) some of them, whom were Hadramis, asked Istanbul to be recognized as Ottoman citizens on account of their Yemeni origins, but all to no avail;[11] in 1899 Muslims in Sulu (Southern Philippines) recognized American sovereignty after the Caliph guaranteed that they would enjoy freedom of religion under the new administration; and in 1900 the Caliph preliminarily agreed to exert his influence to stop Chinese Muslims' involvement in the anti-foreigners Boxer Rebellion (although by the time his envoys arrived in Beijing, the uprising had already been quashed by the Qing).[12]

Hence, when the Jihad Fatwa was issued in 1914, reactions were mixed. According to Jacob M. Landau, this was the outcome of five factors: first, the absence of any structured organization able to ensure the distribution of the text; second, the Entente powers' ability to stonewall the initiative in their colonies; third, the fact that in 1914 the Ottoman government was mostly secularist and anti-Caliph; fourth, the cooperationist approach of some Muslim leaders in the colonies; and lastly, theological exegesis did not allow for warring alongside a Christian power (Germany) against other Christian powers.[13] A sixth explanation needs to be added, though: the Ottoman Caliphate had been·prolix in its pan-Islamic propaganda but had not delivered in terms of material assistance to Muslims under imperial rule, thus alienating any potential forthcoming support.

Agency at the Peripheries

If pan-Islamism had failed as a political ideology that spread out from a religious and political center to a periphery, thus proving unable to coalesce the global *umma* to help the Caliphal Empire, its spirit was alive across the Muslim lands, shaping how Muslims envisioned anti-colonial struggles. Before anti-colonial movements worldwide took a definitive turn away from internationalism (whether this had been framed within the paradigm of Communism, anti-Imperialism, or Islam) and toward nationalism in the 1930s, two phenomena kept pan-Islamism alive. On the one hand were the intellectual and logistical efforts of Russian/Soviet Muslims who saw themselves passed from one internal colonizer to the other; and on the other hand was the perceived imperative of having a Caliph, which sparked one last push toward transnational coordination in the 1910s and 1920s. In both cases, international congresses, gathering Muslims from all over the world, were a crucial space for sharing ideas, channeling efforts, and taking stock; and whereas Islam was a primary element of inspiration, other non-religious, sometimes Western, ideologies also contributed to the debates (e.g. labor movements, Communism, ethno-national self-determination, etc.).

The peak of this activity was reached in the early 1920s, yet the first organizational manifestation of pan-Islamism can be identified in the general Muslim congress held in Cairo in 1907 and organized by the Crimean Tatar (i.e. Russian Muslim) Ismail Gasprinskii. Gasprinskii had received a mostly secular education, but he had also traveled extensively at the heart of the Ottoman Empire and Egypt. After working in the political establishment in Crimea for several years during the Tsarist era, he shifted his focus toward writing, first and foremost addressing his concern for the consequences of Russia's religious-cultural assimilation policies and systematic discrimination against its Muslim population. In reaction to this reality, and inspired by the Young Turks movement as well as the *jadids* (see Box 3.2), he advocated the need for Russia's Muslims to become conversant in the official language (Russian) while holding fast to their own identity as Muslims and Turkic peoples (thus capitalizing on both pan-Turkism and pan-Islamism).

Gasprinskii's initiative found its origins in a series of local gatherings he had coordinated in Russia starting in 1905, as the Russo-Japanese war had allowed pan-Islamism (and to a certain extent pan-Turkism) to make a leap from the cultural and religious spheres into politics. The first convention had taken place in Crimea in 1905, and had called for a union of all the Muslims of Russia, equality of rights for Russians and Muslims, and freedom of education and press for Muslims under the Tsar; a second meeting, held less than a year later, established this Union of Muslims of Russia as a pan-Islamic platform in the Empire. The Third Convention of Russia's Muslims met in mid-1906, gathering almost a thousand participants, and stating an openly pan-Islamic agenda, not just in form – as it changed its name into the Union of Muslims (*Ittifak-i Muslimin*) – but also in substance: as claimed by Abdurreshid Ibrahim (1857–1944) on that occasion, "The relationship of Muslims does not depend on a party – consequently, union is necessary not solely among the Muslims in Russia, but among the Muslims on the entire globe."[14]

Of Bukharan descent, Abdurreshid Ibrahim had become a representative of the *jadid* movement both in terms of educational methodology and religious reformism (and at the same time was also a Naqshbandi, following in the long tradition of Sufism-*cum*-reformism explored in Chapter 3). He was educated in local religious schools in Tara and Kazan (Tatarstan) first, and Medina and Istanbul later. After working for a few years as a *madrasa* teacher and as a *qadi* in Tara (north of what is today Kazakhstan), Ibrahim was forced to leave Russia; after that, he spent his time between advancing the pan-Islamic and pan-Turkic agendas in Istanbul, and traveling across the Muslim lands, from Egypt to Western China and onward to Japan. If his travels were crucial to physically connect Asian Muslim reformers and to consolidate their efforts, his activities were even more important to the instillation of pan-Islamic ideas in Japan, with the support of the pan-Asianist political association Kokuryukai ("Black Dragon Society") (see Source 4.3).

In the 1920s, as Japan was laying the ideological foundations of its expansion across Asia (1931–1942), some Japanese political activists saw Islam as "indispensable both to the establishment of Pan-Asianism and to the completion of Japan's imperial mission."[16] Even though Japanese intellectuals who felt so deeply about Islam and pan-Asianism were few and far between, they represented a broader reality in which Islam was seen as anti-Western and a good anchor for mobilization. As recently argued by Martin Kramer,

Source 4.3

The Future of the Japanese from the Perspective of Religion (1910), by Abdurreshid Ibrahim

The writings of Abdurreshid Ibrahim, a Russian Tatar Muslim deeply invested in Japanese politics, represent well the intellectual connections established by Japan between pan-Asianism and pan-Islamism. The excerpt below is the concluding essay to the first volume of his book The World of Islam and the Spread of Islam in Japan, *originally published in Istanbul in Ottoman Turkish in 1910. A position later embraced by the Japanese establishment as the Empire spread across (Islamized) Asia, this essay points at the political and economic advantage for Japan of cooperating with Muslim causes and forge an alliance with extant pan-Islamic transregional networks.[15]*

For many reasons, I have come to the conclusion that the Japanese will receive the honor of knowing Islam. First, the customs, morals, and lifestyle of the Japanese are appropriate to beautiful Mohammedan morals, with no detectable differences between them; hence, if a Japanese person and a Siberian Muslim were travelling together, it would be impossible to tell which was Japanese and which was not ... They will not hesitate at all from entering this path [of Islam]. It requires some degree of effort on our part to achieve this end because, today, there is no [easy] way of informing the Japanese of the truth of the religion of Islam. They do not know Arabic or Turkish, and there are no books in foreign languages that explain the truth of Islam in suitable terms ...

Apart from the above, there are a good number of political reasons for the Japanese to accept Islam. If the Japanese accept Islam, Muslims in China would undoubtedly be a ready market for Japanese products. Half of the population of Manchuria are Muslims. When the Japanese accept Islam, they will be able to occupy these areas without lifting a sword. In addition, the islands of the Indian Ocean will cooperate with the political aims of the Japanese, for 20 million Muslims are ruled by a small country like Holland. These Muslims are always ready to throw themselves into the bosom of the Japanese – the only way for them to be free of Dutch oppression is to seek asylum with Japan. The future advancement of the Chinese is a very important issue for the Japanese as well, for if the Chinese manage to achieve significant progress the Japanese will face greater and greater difficulties. At the same time, 100 million Muslims within China will be loyal friends to the Japanese and their ideological servants. Hence, from this perspective, the spread of Islam in Japan will provide a great political advantage to the Japanese. There are many other aspects to be considered. There are about 30 million Muslims within Russia, which is a great enemy of the Japanese. And even if we do not take into consideration the India factor, the area covering the Malay Peninsula and Singapore

Source 4.3   *(cont.)*

which constitutes the southern part of Asia includes seven Muslim emirates that will grateful for Japanese support ...

I myself have greatly desired that the Japanese become familiar with Islam and, while I was in Japan, I gave a great deal of careful thought to the question and indeed saw some degree of success. If our Muslim ulema make some effort in this regard, undoubtedly the prospects will be very bright ... [T]oday there are some very distinguished men who have been conferred the honor of Islam ... But the important point is to find a way for senior government officials to turn toward Islam. The real accomplishment is to have Islam accepted as an official religion. If one works with careful preparation, all these things can be realized.

Islam was eagerly taken up by Japanese pan-Asianists in the first half of the twentieth century ... and did not abate after 1945 ... That interest in Islam endured the demise of the government-sponsored Greater East Asia Co-Prosperity Sphere clearly indicates that Islam was more than a political expedient for at least some Japanese.[17]

Back in Russia, the Muslim congresses had little to no traction, at home as abroad, regardless of the enthusiasm of some leading members. In Russia, quarrels within the party and the return to Tsarist authoritarianism led to the dissolution of the Union. In Cairo, the 1907 gathering received a cold reaction from the local intelligentsia and politicians, and sharp criticism from Rashid Rida, who had been unimpressed with Gasprinskii's focus on economic issues and his mere nod to Islam as a religious system and pan-Islamism as a spiritual-*cum*-political enterprise.

But its failure to generate any direct outcome notwithstanding, the 1907 Cairo congress lay the foundation for what would follow in the 1910s and 1920s in response to the crisis of the Ottoman Caliphate and, shortly after, its abolition, as Muslims with pan-Islamic aspirations often called for gatherings to take place in Europe and West Asia.

The global stage of pan-Islamist and more generally anti-colonial groups was largely a men's world, but at the local level women across Asia became involved – to various extents – in the movement for self-determination. Women wrote opinion pieces and letters, took to the streets, or limited their impact to their family and neighbors through education, often invoking models of Islamic womanhood drawn from the time of Muhammad's life. But besides their direct involvement in politics, women were also indirectly deployed in the struggle, their bodies and minds used as sites of contestation between clashing ideals of "progress." The worlds of representative politics and religious authority allowed men to speak for and about women, but the burgeoning press of the early twentieth century also allowed women to express their own ideas to larger audiences.

The Caliphate Movement between Pan-Islamism and Nationalism

Even though the Ottoman co-optation of pan-Islamism had yielded very few results in the 1900s and 1910s, Muslims from all over the world had been able to gather and debate the future leadership of the *umma*; inspired by the original vision of Jamal ad-Din "al-Afghani," the unity of the *umma* was understood not as a political formation (i.e. a global caliphate ruling over all Muslim peoples), but rather as a solidarity movement in which Muslims would come together against imperial powers (the British first of all) regardless of ethnicity, language, or sectarian affiliation. This message became particularly powerful as the more general anti-colonial discourse was gradually "nationalized" with the emergence of pan-Arabism, pan-Turkism, and other ethno-linguistic nationalist movements. And the idea of Muslim solidarity was also embraced by political leaders who sought non-Islamic forms of governance.

The weakening of the Ottoman Empire had started with their defeat at the hands of the Russians in 1878, but the Caliphate's spiritual authority had been challenged at its own peripheries since at least the mid-nineteenth century. Then, Muslims in northern Syria had expressed their interest in establishing an "Arab" Caliph of Muhammadan descent, referring to the then Sharif of Mecca, Husayn (1853–1931), the man of prophetic lineage who (at least nominally) held the role of protector of Mecca and Medina. Soon after, Bukharan Muslims also entertained the possibility of electing the Sharif of Mecca as their Caliph. Joining several European diplomats and more disappointed Syrians, Jamal ad-Din expressed the thought that the days of the Ottomans were ending. 'Abdulhamid II himself was aware of these challenges, but he thought of them as British machinations to increase control over their colonial subjects. As he declared in an interview, "England's aim is to transfer the Great Caliphate from Istanbul to Jidda in Arabia or to a place in Egypt and by keeping the Caliphate under her control to manage all the Muslims as she wishes."[18] To his credit, the British did connive with the Sharif of Mecca: in 1916 they collaborated in launching an "Arab Revolt" against the Ottomans, during which Husayn was hailed as "the king of the Arabs and the caliph of all Muslims."[19]

Despite 'Abdulhamid II's efforts to frame the Empire's fragility as a colonial machination and to ground its legitimacy on Islamic credentials, criticism of the Caliphate was coming from all parts of the *umma*, as there was an increased sense that the Ottoman dynasty had steered away from the "right path." Corrupt in their customs and politics, the Ottoman Empire was no longer seen as the best suited candidate for the caliphal role. The press in the Dutch East Indies reveled in the stories that came out about the life of the sultan and his court entourage, often pointing at his lascivious lifestyle or cruelty toward the women in his harem. Eventually, the idea of a Hijazi Sharifian Caliphate was popularized among Muslims worldwide in the very early 1900s through *al-Manar*.

The actual abolition of the Caliphate came in March 1924. In the conviction that the future of Turkey as an independent and modern nation rested on the separation of religion and politics, and that the future of Islam was in individuals' piety, not in its connivance with politics, Mustafa Kemal (1881–1938) – a military officer who had made a name for himself during the Ottoman-Greek war, and who would eventually be known as Ataturk, "father of the Turks" – abolished first the Sultanate (i.e. the political face of the Ottomans) and two years later its spiritual and religious counterpart, the Caliphate.

Muslims the world over followed the transformation of the Ottoman Empire–Caliphate into the Republic of Turkey and mulled over who would become their spiritual and religious leader. After all, that was *their* Caliph too, regardless of the political squabbles and general discontent of the previous decades. Mustafa Kemal's actions turned the possibility of an alternative Caliphate as debated in the previous times into a necessity, and thus fueled the *umma*-wide effort to find a new leader.

By mid-1924 the pan-Islamic discourse had already taken on a life of its own, separate from the politicking of Istanbul. In fact, Sharif Husayn arranged for his nomination as Caliph immediately after, and then called for a Muslim congress to take place in July, during the *hajj* season, to rally broader support. Pledges of support came in a flurry from the Levant as well as India and Southeast Asia. But in October of the same year 'Abd al-'Aziz Ibn Sa'ud (1875–1953) conquered Mecca, leading to Husayn's abdication and the establishment of Saudi control over the Holy Cities. Now the intellectual rivalry between Cairo and Mecca was to play out in the realm of politics, too. The year 1926 saw two congresses convening back to back: in May representatives from across North Africa, Arabia, and West Asia, as well as South Africa and the Dutch East Indies, gathered in Cairo; in June they moved to Mecca, where they were joined by even more representatives hailing from India,

Afghanistan, Turkey, and the Soviet Union. Neither congress reached any definitive conclusion about the Caliphate nor strategies to pursue "Muslim unity."

From a pan-Islamic pan-Asian perspective, it is of great interest to note that Indonesian delegates were also present at the Tokyo Congress held in 1939 and hosted by the Greater Japanese Muslim League. A reflection of both Asia's engagement with pan-Islamism and Japan's imperialist agenda in the 1930s and 1940s, the Congress gathered representatives from the Soviet Union, China, Indonesia, and Japan.

Even though none of these congresses reached any consensus on who the new Caliph should be, or how to pursue a cogent pan-Islamic strategy, knowledge of these events, and the direct experience of participating in them, were catalysts for Muslims who lived further away from Cairo and Mecca. As Muslims worldwide had been discussing alternative solutions for years, in private circles as much as in public forums, these events sparked a deeper affinity for pan-Islamic identity as well as anti-colonial, nationalist desires.

The Indian Subcontinent

In response to the crisis of the Ottoman Empire, a group of concerned Indian Muslims gathered in 1919 to establish the All-India Khilafat Committee, with a pro-Ottoman and anti-British outlook. It was this avowed anti-British commitment that allowed the forging of the Hindu–Muslim nationalist alliance in 1919–1921, which in turn established Ghandi's non-cooperationist and non-violent movement. In February 1920, the president of the Bengal Provincial Khilafat Conference, Abu al-Kalam Azad, delivered his presidential speech reminding his audience of the Constitution of Medina issued by Muhammad in 622; in that occasion the messenger of Islam had defined the *umma* as composed of Muslims and non-Muslims alike. With these words Azad was calling for a solid collaboration between India's Hindus and Muslims. This collaboration was crucial to advance the anti-colonial movement, as it had also been the contribution of women, both Hindu and Muslim, who carved a niche for themselves, strong by virtue of the fact that their traditional roles as mothers and wives could allow them "to retain influence while expanding their realm of activity beyond the household."[20]

The Khilafat's 1919 founding conference had seen in attendance Sunni Muslims alongside Shi'is, Ahmadis, and Hindus. In fact, the Khilafat Committee showed inclusivity also from within the Sunni Muslim community, as demonstrated by the educational backgrounds and political visions of its key members, which spanned from the Islamist to the secular end of the spectrum. The Khilafat movement took root at a time when Islam in the Subcontinent was being reimagined. The movement was able to coalesce Muslim intellectuals who took a variety of routes toward "reform," from the Western-influenced thought of Sayyid Ahmad Khan of Alighar to the scripturalist approach of Deoband, here represented by the *'ulama* Mahmud al-Hasan (1851–1920). Other important figures were the brothers Muhammad Ali and Shawkat Ali of Alighar College and their teacher Abdul Bari (d. 1926) of the Farangi Mahal *madrasa* (school), both located in Lucknow, and Abu al-Kalam Azad.

In South Asia, the encounter between Islamic reformism and imperialism flared in the aftermath to the Rebellion of 1857, as reformism had previously been a mostly apolitical phenomenon. Three *'ulama*, followers of Shah Waliullah of Delhi (see Chapter 3), established a school in the town of Deoband, northeast of Delhi (1867). The Dar-ul-'Ulum *madrasa* was innovative for a number of reasons; modeled on the bureaucratic style of British educational institutions, it was run by professional staff, offered a set course of study, required pupils to take standardized examinations, was hosted in formal classrooms, and released a yearly report on its activities and finances. Within this "modern," "Westernized" structure, the pupils studied Greek and Arab philosophy; astronomy, logic, and geometry; but also the Qur'an and *hadith*, which formed the core of their education, not only as sources of the law but most importantly as models of life. Deoband's reformism was, however, different from that of 'Abd al-Wahhab and others who rejected *taqlid* and mysticism. While calling for a purified form of Islam, Dar-ul-'Ulum taught the books of Hanafi *fiqh*, and its *fatawa* incorporated – rather than condemned – Sufi practices into its disciplined religious life. Innovations were a concern, but only when they pertained to ritual (*'ibada*) or threatened the unity of God (*tauhid*), such as pilgrimages to the graves of saints and participation in *sama'* performances (musical sessions that were said to induce ecstasy). Deoband's teachers were among the leading Sufis of their times, mostly influenced by the Naqshbandiyah, but all belonging to multiple *turuq*, thus without casting themselves as *shaykh*s of a specific order.

Having emerged after the Rebellion and the consequent British crackdown on Muslims, Deobandis were largely apolitical, focusing on theological and scripturalist studies. Yet, under the leadership of Mahmud al-Hasan with his ties to the Khilafat Committee, the legacy of Deoband's Dar-ul-'Ulum became split between those who remained apolitical quietists and those who sided with Mahmud al-Hasan. Al-Hasan's approach was also bifurcated, as he was openly seeking pan-Islamic connections (he was imprisoned in Malta between 1917 and 1920 after an attempt at reaching out to Turks in the Hijaz) while at the same time joining Gandhi's Indian National Congress and thus arguing for a single, secular post-colonial country. A small group of *'ulama* eventually split to establish the Jamiat Ulema-i Islam (1945) in support of the plead for a separate state for India's Muslims which was being advanced by the Muslim League (see Chapter 5 on the formation of Pakistan).

Notably, the border between northwest British India and Afghanistan had become dotted by a chain of Deobandi *madrasa*. The combination of al-Hasan's influence on these schools, and the fact that in the early twentieth century Afghanistan was one of the few Sunni independent countries, allowed for the emergence of Afghanistan as a Deobandi-inspired hub of dissent against the King, who advocated in favor of Western-styled modernity (as discussed in Chapter 7).

Similar to, but distinct from, the Deobandi Dar-ul-'Ulum was the Nadwah school in Lucknow, established by another successor to Shah Waliullah and Khilafat supporter, Shibli Nu'mani (1857–1914). Nu'mani recognized the need to embrace the West, but within an Islamic perspective. Grounded in the knowledge of the *hadith* and a mastery of both Arabic and Persian, he firmly advocated a return to the scriptures and the establishment of a society ruled by the *shari'a* – this is what pulled him toward the Khilafat's pan-Islamic ideals, and it was with this goal in mind that in 1898 he established the Nadwah school, even though he never reached the theological conservatism of Deoband. Lucknow hosted two other important centers of knowledge transmission. First, the Farangi Mahal, a *madrasa* which encapsulated "the rationalist traditions of Islamic scholarship derived from Iran"[21] as it had been established, in 1694, by the scion of an eleventh-century Sufi from Herat (Afghanistan), possibly himself the descendant of a Medinan companion of Muhammad. While in broader terms the Farangi Mahal had become a voice of dissent against the British in the late nineteenth and early twentieth centuries, in the specific context of the Caliphal crisis, Abdul Bari emerged as an influential pan-Islamist *'ulama* who contributed greatly to solidifying Ottoman prestige in India and in voicing India's Muslim support for Caliph 'Abdulhamid.

Second was the Alighar Muslim University College, initially named the Mohammadan Anglo-Oriental College. Despite the fact that it stood at the opposite end of reformism from the Deobandi and Farangi Mahal schools, some of its most eminent alumni were equally involved in the Khilafat movement. The school was established in 1875 by Sayyid Ahmad Khan, who had spent time in Britain and who would become a representative of what has been labeled "Occidentalism," or a fascination with the West (Source 4.2). Amidst criticism from all sides, Ahmad Khan embraced the idea that not only was Islam compatible with progress, but that religion – and religious education – should be sidelined in favor of secular ideas. In politics this view was being expounded by the All-India Muslim League (established in 1906), while in education it was reflected in the Mohammadan Anglo-Oriental College. Modeled on Cambridge University, Aligarh aimed at facilitating the entrance of India's Muslims into the government service by providing them with a "modern" education, focused on the sciences and broad humanities alongside a non-denominational theological education, but without denying or eliding their Indian Muslim identity.

Notable alumni of Alighar, however, were not all "Westernized" or "loyalist." And among them were also the 'Ali brothers of the Khilafat movement, outspoken champions of the Ottoman Caliphate cause and opponents of the British, so much so that they were both interned during the entire duration of Turkey's belligerency. In their absence, their mother (Abadi Banu Begum) and their wives became equally important leaders of the movement, abandoning previous practices of seclusion (*purdah*) to become involved in religious nationalist politics and community. In 1917, Abadi Banu Begum wrote to a prominent Hindu political leader:

I fear this letter will surprise you a good deal not only because it comes from a total stranger, but also because the writer is a Muslim woman brought up in the old orthodox ways according to which women are seldom supposed to address any communication to strangers, and never to men ... But these are extraordinary times, and things are changing so fast that no one should feel astonished if an old woman like myself addressed, at the sacrifice of a little orthodoxy, a letter to one so universally respected and reverenced as yourself on a subject which fills at present the minds of all.[22]

A few years later, she further pushed the boundaries of *purdah* practices, speaking to a mixed political gathering in Punjab: "She lifted the veil of her burqa to speak to the crowd, explaining that all present were like her sons and daughters, and thus there was no reason to maintain purdah before them."[23] Women had a prominent role in the anti-British mobilization as they collected funds and instilled nationalist and religious values in mothers and children. As Gail Minault suggested, "Women had a role to play" in each and every aspect of the Khilafat's political effort.[24]

At the end of the war, in 1919, Shawkat 'Ali emerged as the most prominent Khilafat leader, leading the alliance with Ghandi and supported by his brother, Muhammad, as well as the already mentioned Abdul Bari and Abu al-Kalam Azad. Abu al-Kalam Azad became one of the key ideologues of the Khilafat movement in virtue of his ability to straddle pan-Islamism and nationalism, and his being the living example of the eclectic reality of India's Muslims. Azad was born in Mecca, and his *silsila* included Shah Waliullah Dihlawi and Ahmad Sirhindi. Yet, he had been an admirer of Ahmad Khan's rationalism and reformism, while also being a protégé of Nu'mani's and a writer for Nadwah's bulletin. The youngest among this group of nationalist pan-Islamists, Azad remained involved in Indian politics until his death in 1958: he covered the role of India's minister of education and was deputy leader of Congress through the partition of the Subcontinent into the two nation-states of India and Pakistan, remaining committed to the view of a single multi-religious national *umma wahida* (see Box 0.1).

The Dutch East Indies

At the end of World War II, after the Japanese occupation (1941–1945) and as the Dutch attempted to re-enter the archipelago (1947–1948), the people of Java witnessed the proclamation of three Republics, each at the hands of a different Muslim leader: Sukarno's nationalist republic in 1945, a communist republic in 1948, and an Islamic state in 1949. This was the physical manifestation of the intellectual fragmentation that hit the Indies' anti-colonial movement in the 1920s. In the 1910s the port city of Surabaya, in the northeast corner of Java, was bustling with anti-colonial dissent: it was in this city that Sukarno (1901–1970, leader of the nationalist movement and first president of Indonesia), H. O. S. Cokroaminoto (d. 1934, founding father of Sarekat Islam, the most influential Islamist party in late-colonial Indonesia), and several leftist leaders started their political activism. Sukarno boarded at Cokroaminoto's home and married his daughter; Sarekat Islam's leadership embodied communist ideals as much as political Islamic goals; and many of the communist leaders were Muslims. In virtue of these intersectionalities, the Indonesian anti-colonial movement had emerged as a non-ideologically driven desire for the advancement of the local population, guided by ideals of social, economic, and political justice.

Speaking at the Fourth Comintern Congress in Moscow in 1922, Tan Malaka (1897–1949, the most prominent among Indonesia's communists) criticized the Russian General Zinoviev for suggesting a distancing from pan-Islamism by arguing that "in the East Indies ... We have cooperated with the Islamists," and further explaining that

Pan-Islamism now means the brotherhood of all Muslim peoples, and the liberation struggle not only of the Arab but also of the Indian, the Javanese and all the oppressed Muslim peoples. This brotherhood means the practical liberation struggle not only against Dutch but also against English, French and Italian capitalism, therefore against world capitalism as a whole ... This is a new task for us. Just as we want to support the national struggle, we also want to support the liberation struggle of the very combative, very active 250 million Muslims living under the imperialist powers.[25]

Shortly after, Cokroaminoto published his "Islam and Socialism" booklet (1924), and Sukarno issued "Nationalism, Islamism and Marxism" (1926), each an attempt to show commonalities and bridge differences; similarly, they collaborated in the non-partisan "Agreement of Indonesian People's Political Association" (established by Sukarno in 1927). Yet, Sarekat Islam had already started to fragment, with the split between a "red" (communist) and a "white" (Islamist) wing in 1923, and Sukarno's endeavor had failed by 1929. Although there is no clear indication of what caused this reconfiguration of political groups along ideological lines in 1920s Java, it is a fact that this happened alongside fervent debates over the Caliphate question, the same question that in India had led to the collaboration of Muslims and Hindus, Sunnis and Shi'as, modernists and traditionalists.

A Central Caliphate Committee was established in Surabaya not earlier than October 1924. Until that point, public opinion in the Indies had been overall unconcerned with the Ottomans' defeat, and was supportive of Mustafa Kemal's actions, arguing for the need to "renew" the caliphate: the Indies' press had been reporting on "unislamic" behavior by the Ottomans since the late 1800s, and on Mustafa Kemal's military bravery since the late 1910s. Yet, in late 1924 Cokroaminoto clearly stated the need for the existence of a Caliph and, most notably, that this was most relevant to Muslims who lived under non-Muslim rule. On these grounds, Indonesian Muslims should have taken a leading role in determining the future of the Caliphate.

On that occasion, then, the Committee drafted a proposal to be presented at the 1924 Cairo congress; this suggested a new form of caliphal institution, to be grounded in consultation, representation of Muslims worldwide, and election of the Caliph himself. By the time that the 1926 congresses were announced, the Indies' Muslims had polarized: the debate over a Cairene versus a Meccan Caliphate drove the *madhhab*-oriented traditionalists away from those who supported Ibn Sa'ud's conquest of Mecca. Additional difficulties were raised by the financial barrier imposed by distance; Dutch fears of pan-Islamism and their stonewalling of international travel; and mixed feelings over whether "Muslims at the centre" would listen to the suggestions of this "peripheral" community.[26]

Nonetheless, Cokroaminoto was able to travel to Mecca for the 1926 congress, accompanied by a representative of the reformist Muhammadiyah organization and two Javanese Hadramis; there, two more Mecca-based *Jawi* scholars (a traditionalist and a reformist) joined the congress as Indonesians. Despite the strength of the Indies' contingent, and the excitement and conviction that they had expressed back home, the record said of them that "They did not say a word, and avoided any commitment."[27] This was a very different depiction from that of the Indian delegation, which deeply impressed the audience.

The political experience of Muslims in both British India and the Dutch East Indies converged on the importance that pan-Islamism was to take as an internationalist platform capable of supporting Muslims' nationalist aspirations. But if the Indian Khilafat movement had emerged as a unifying force in South Asian politics, pulling in representatives of multiple political ideologies, the Dutch Indies' experience was marked by the fragmentation of the anti-colonial front as much as that of the Islamist wing. Another crucial difference was the way in which Indian women had been able to carve a role in the religious political movement in the 1910s and 1920s.

Even though scholars generally agree that women in Muslim Southeast Asia have enjoyed important social roles through history, and we have seen that in pre-colonial Aceh and Patani there were female Muslim sovereigns, it appears that women's political activism in the Dutch East Indies was limited. Cokroaminoto's Sarekat Islam had women members, and since at least 1918 it also had associated women's organizations, reflecting its diverse identity. Recognizing "the need to draw more women and youth into the movement," Cokroaminoto encouraged the establishment of even more groups across Java. By 1933, Sarekat Islam – now constituted as a nationalist Islamist party – had a woman on their central leadership board. But unlike their Indian sisters, neither emancipation nor political activism – whether in a nationalist or pan-Islamic framework – were part of the party's agenda. While women in Java and Sumatra wrote about the 1931 Lahore Women Congress, and invoked the experiences of Turkey, Egypt, China, Japan and India as examples of women's emancipation movements, their social activism in the late colonial period hinged exclusively on girls' education as the locus of societal salvation against the influence of Western models of behavior. As Sally White suggested, "their activities thus appeared to have been a mixture of social activism, addressing the needs of women workers and peasants, and of religious reform,"[28] but not nationalist politics.

The Japanese occupation government, established in 1941, put much effort into re-structuring and centralizing political groups in Java, Sumatra, and the other islands. Even though this did not translate into an increase in political space, Japan's intervention contributed to the shaping of a better organized independentist movement, which was now made of groups able to see beyond their narrow ethnic or linguistic identities. This centralization of the political landscape had two important consequences: on the one hand, it forced ideological opponents to work together; on the other, it played factions off against one another. These new Islamic parties effected important change in the religious political leadership, as the factionalism of colonial-era parties was forcibly removed, and career politicians were sidelined by socially oriented scholars. This also meant that Japan initially favored the Islamic nationalist movement, but regularly shifted its support between the traditionalist and modernist wings. By 1943, as Japan began to discuss Indonesia's independence, their conversation partners were the secular nationalists.

Representatives of different political organizations from across the archipelago were gathered by the Japanese authorities to discuss and reach an agreement over the ideological foundations of the independent state. Amidst much debate, Sukarno's voice dominated. Since his early days in politics in the 1910s, Sukarno had advocated for a non-confessional state as a necessity to ensure the country's geopolitical unity. In the intervening years he invoked the examples of Turkey, Afghanistan, and Iran as successful Muslim countries which had set Islam aside in favor of a nationalist state. And so it was that on June 1, 1945, he delivered a speech announcing that the Indonesian Republic would be based on the "Five Principles" (Pancasila) of nationalism, humanitarianism, deliberation among representatives, social welfare, and belief in One God. The Islamist wing's request to add a clause affirming "the obligation for adherents of Islam to practice Islamic law"[29] was eventually denied, and Sukarno's vision of a non-confessional Indonesian Republic was instead consolidated.

Central Asian Muslims

The second All-Russian Muslim convention, held in Kazan (Tatarstan) in mid-1917, passed a resolution stating the cultural and political unity of all of the Empire's Muslims and started the formation of a Muslim army, but the strengthening of the pan-Islamic movement in Russia was halted by revolutionary turmoil. The October Revolution and the civil war that followed it led to the fragmentation of the Muslim population and the diversification of their circumstances between those in European Russia (Crimea), the North Caucasus, and Central Asia.

The conquest of Central Asia by the Tsar had taken place between 1866 and 1893. Some areas had been absorbed into the Empire (such as the Kazakh–Kyrgyz areas), while others had been left with a degree of autonomy (e.g. the Khanate of Khiva and the Emirate of Bukhara); nonetheless, in much of non-European Russian territory, social relations had been tense between Russian ethnics and local peoples. Russians tended to be involved in the bureaucracy, and as settlers they were given land that would have otherwise belonged to the (largely peasant) local peoples; food rations were unequally distributed, favoring the Russian population, and Russian cultural and linguistic traits were favored in the public sphere.

The experience of Russian Turkestan was itself very varied, as the region that came to comprise what today are Turkmenistan, Uzbekistan, Tajikistan, and Kyrgyzstan, plus the southern portion of Kazakhstan (between the Aral Sea and lake Balkhash) was to be subject to different regimes of control. At the end of 1917, this region had at least five, if not more, centers of gravity: a Soviet government established itself in Tashkent with the support of Russian ethnics and the communist government; Kokand proclaimed autonomy under the leadership of politicized "natives"; Bukhara remained a self-governed emirate, and Khiva a self-governed khanate; attempts were being made to pull China's Xinjiang into the Soviet sphere; and there were a number of rebellious groups that claimed sovereignty over their own "ancestral" territory. In this context, the Provisional Government, in the hands of Russians, "utilized the Soviet government and party machine to intensify the economic and political exploitation of the native populations. The Revolution, therefore, brought to the Moslem areas not the abolition of colonialism, but colonialism in a new and much more oppressive form."[30]

The fragmented territorial authority and Soviet violence and oppression affected direct consequences for the local political administration as well as for what had been, briefly, the appearance of a pan-Islamic union across the Empire. The assertion of Soviet authority over Turkestan took several months, and was not peaceful; in the process, the unpopularity of Bolshevik rule and Tashkent's refusal to grant self-rule to the local people became a source of concern for Moscow. In April 1918, under instruction from the central government, the Fifth Congress of Soviets announced the formation of the Autonomous Republic of Turkestan. Even though on this occasion Muslims and Russians were presented as equal, Muslims were given positions of authority only at the end of 1919, once Turkestan became fully integrated into the Soviet system.

Shortly afterwards, the first report on Soviet Turkestan concluded that the transitional government had perpetrated the same discrimination as the Tsarist regime had, pushing Lenin to impose preferential policies for the local populations, in fear that "Soviet misrule there [in Turkestan] might have an adverse effect on Communist efforts in the Middle and Far East and alienate those Moslem nationalists."[31] In these early years, then, Muslims were given economic privileges as well as complete freedom of religion and education; plus, Soviet propaganda was expressed in clear pan-Islamic terms. These accommodations allowed for the emergence of a strand of national Muslim Communism: publications from the first decade of Soviet rule show a clear focus on pan-Islamic goals, ranging from the rejection of European culture to demands for a Muslim Communist Party and the creation of a Muslim state. Yet none of these goals were to be obtained on any scale, and the years leading up to the 1924 re-drawing of Central Asia's boundaries were marked by the peak of Islamist anti-Soviet resistance.

These dynamics are best exemplified by the events surrounding the so-called Basmachi rebellion. The assertion of Soviet authority in the early months of the Revolution had been violent, bringing Islam to the fore as the one unifying element of the oppressed. The first confrontation between local Muslims and Soviet rule pitted the authority of Tashkent against Kokand, which had obtained political recognition from a number of urban centers across the Ferghana Valley, but not from any of the other constituted rulers. The majority of the Muslim population of Kokand fled and hid in the mountains as soon as the violence started, and those who remained were killed by the Russian soldiers, who first looted and then razed the city to the ground. Following their victory, the Army had moved on to Bukhara. There, they thought they could rely on the support of the *jadid* modernist Islamic intelligentsia, which had been sidelined by the Emir, who held instead to "traditionalist" Islam. *Jadid*s and traditional *'ulama*, understanding the Revolution and its context differently, had decided to take separate paths after the First Turkestan Muslim Congress (which had gathered in Tashkent in 1917) and set up parallel organizations, leading to intellectual and armed conflict across the region. Bukhara repelled the military attack, forcing Tashkent to recognize the Emirate's autonomy. The rest of the territory, however, was populated by Muslims under the rule of "new" colonists.

Many Kokand Muslims had fled the rape of their city, and more followed, joining other inhabitants of the Ferghana Valley who had suffered Soviet and Russian abuses. Usually referred to as "Basmachi," likely meaning "bandits," these rebels took on the aura of freedom-fighters. They were highly fragmented along ethnic and tribal lines and were rarely able to work together; infighting was frequent. A transformation took place, however, in 1920, as the Red Army deposed the Emir of Bukhara and put the *jadid*s in power of the pro-Bolshevik People's Soviet Republic.

By the end of 1921 the history of Bukhara was to intersect with that of Enver Pasha, the leader of the Young Turks Revolution of 1908, who had recently become estranged from Mustafa Kemal. Leaving Ottoman Turkey, Enver went to Russia to join the Congress of the Peoples of the East in Baku. The Bolsheviks had for years advanced the idea of "revolutionizing the East" to topple European capitalist, bourgeois, and colonial regimes. The *jadid*s, however, turned the class struggle envisioned by the Bolsheviks into a "national" one. While the Young Bukharans led national and cultural reforms, establishing public education and health systems, traditional *'ulama* and other Muslims challenged the Soviet authority. It was to Bukhara, then, that Enver was sent by the Soviets in an effort to encourage popular support for the new regime; however, his own interest was more in tune with the rebels. Enver wanted to lead a pan-Islamic and pan-Turkic rising.

After a rocky first encounter, Enver was able to reach the Basmachi area and unite several of these groups to fight against Soviet rule, while also receiving support from the Young Bukharans, whose expectations of autonomy had not been met. Although not all the Basmachis were accepting of Enver Pasha and his political visions, his self-styled claim to being "Commander in chief of all Islamic troops, son-in-law of the Caliph and the Representative of the Prophet"[32] allowed him to lead these bands of mountain rebels to some success. In early 1922, his forces controlled the eastern side of the Bukhara region, and people in the Ferghana Valley thought that if he had had broader support he would have been able "to raise all Turkestan against the Bolsheviks."[33] Enver Pasha died in battle in August 1922. The fighting continued for a few months, as the news was not widely circulated; but by the end of the year popular support had withered, effectively bringing the rebellion to an end.

Starting in the mid-1920s, Soviet rulers changed their approach toward their minorities, embracing a policy of "indigenization" which focused on local ethnic identities. Instead of favoring Muslim peoples and their leaders, Muslim cadres were expelled from state organs, and the idea of national Muslim Communism was systematically undermined, ultimately pushing for a deeper integration and assimilation of

Muslims to Soviet culture. The politicization of a single national Islamic identity was seen as a serious threat to the integrity of the Soviet state. It was with this goal in mind that Stalin, at the time Commisar of Nationalities, led the reconfiguration of Soviet territory in Central Asia in five republics, each with its own language, predominant ethnic identity, economic interests, and new boundaries. Both the Khanate of Khiva and the Emirate of Bukhara were each divided between the Uzbek and Turkmen Soviet Socialist Republics in 1925, and shortly afterwards the Uzbek republic itself was further divided to allow for the creation of the Tajik Soviet Republic.

Ideals of Progress

Taking stock of the failure of previous strategies, by 1926–1927 the Leninist policy of indigenization of nationalities was reformulated as centered on gender. With gender now a substitute for class, the Muslim women of Central Asia were to become the "victims of the oppressive structures of patriarchal Islamic society" and "latent revolutionary allies."[34] Notably, the implementation of this approach varied across the republics, and the 1920s and 1930s witnessed multiple national forms of "reform" (or rather, to use the Soviet expression, "attack against old ways of life") which ranged from eliminating polygamy and illiteracy to abolishing seclusion and veiling.

In Uzbekistan and Azerbaijan, then, liberation came to be equated with unveiling and the elimination of seclusion, even though in previous decades these practices were not seen as a hindrance: "even though we still wear the veil, we are nonetheless free" declared a woman meeting Lenin in Moscow in 1921.[35] The previous year, a delegate at the First Congress of the Peoples of the East, held in Baku, had stated:

The women of the East are not fighting merely for the right to walk in the street without wearing the chador, as many people suppose. For the women of the East, with their high moral ideals, the question of the chador, it can be said, comes last in priority. If the women, who form half of every community, are set up against the men and do not enjoy the same rights, obviously it is impossible for society to progress; the backwardness of Eastern societies is irrefutable proof of this.[36]

This policy of reform, intended to integrate Central Asia into the Soviet cultural sphere, was embraced by some – and their voices were diligently recorded in the official narrative – but also opposed by many others, both men and women. Although hundreds of women unveiled, at least as many refused to leave their homes uncovered; if many men escorted their wives and daughters to "unveiling ceremonies," several others subscribed to the clerics' view that "the unveiling of women entails the debauchery of the entire world."[37]

Decades later, these same "paradigms of enslaved and liberated womanhood" were used in Maoist propaganda among China's Muslim minorities (see Figure 4.2). Even though Confucian values had also restricted the freedom of Chinese women in "the past" of "feudal oppression," Jaschok and Shui have noted that "minority women were seen as still more greatly affected by lingering legacies of sexual oppression," with the head-dress "serv[ing] as a most poignant symbol of dependency." The official newspaper for post-Revolution Muslims victoriously announced, in 1959, that "to walk the path of equality, some [Muslim women] had removed their head-dress." Short of that, within this discourse, Muslim women could not foresee reaching liberation if they continued to listen to their religious leaders, who were said to argue that "if Hui women go outside, and their skin and hair are displayed in public, this is damaging to [the faith]; after death they shall enter [purgatory]."[38]

Communist cadres were not the only people focusing on women's bodies as a site for societal progress. European colonial authorities were walking the same path in North Africa (e.g. the French in Algeria, see Box 6.3), and a few Muslim politicians and intellectuals across Asia were advancing the same strategy, albeit each party had its own vocabulary. In 1925, Mustafa Kemal banned the wearing of the *fez* for all Turkish men, enforcing instead European-style hats and more general Western dress as a sign of being "a civilized man." Similarly, he discouraged – but did not ban, yet – women's veiling: "Let them show their faces to the world, and see with their eyes ... Don't be afraid. Change is essential, so much so that, if need be, we are prepared to sacrifice lives for its sake."[39]

This effort to "modernize" the former Ottoman Empire was taken, by some Muslims, as a model of reform from within the Muslim tradition and thus became a source of inspiration ideologically in contrast to, although in practice aligned with, communist and colonial visions of liberation. King Amanullah of Afghanistan and Reza Shah Pahlavi of Persia had been also advocating for the "unveiling" of women, starting with their own wives and daughters.

Groups of Muslim women across Asia saw in these experiments interesting points of departure to advocate for change in their own

Figure 4.2 Anti-veiling state propaganda mural (Xinjiang, China).
© Chiara Formichi

environments, as these countries were seen as examples of reform inspired by and within Islam. If Abadi Banu Begum had stretched the boundaries of *purdah* without challenging its principles, other Muslim women in India compared their condition to that of other Muslim contexts to advance a different solution. By the late 1920s, Turkey, Iran, and Afghanistan had become main points of comparison:

> The purdah which is found amongst the women of Behar [Bihar Province, in northeast India] is not found in any country of the world. Turkey, Persia, Afghanistan are Islamic countries, but in these countries also the ladies have got freedom to a great extent. Behar cannot boast of even this much freedom. There ladies are confined within the four walls of their houses and no one can hear their voice, let alone see their faces – the evils of purdah are obvious. I will here only refer to one and that is, it is impossible to educate our girls properly under this custom ... It appears that the women of Turkey and Persia have freed themselves from the trammels of 'burqa' and that even in Afghanistan this reform has commenced.[40]

Similarly, newspaper articles from the 1920s and 1930s in the Dutch East Indies show that discussion over the donning of the *kudung*, or head scarf – notably a recent introduction – was placed on a theological as well as contextual level. The writer S. Z. Goenawan, who refused to wear the veil, embraced contextualization, suggesting that

> every person indeed has different types of opinions, for example about the meaning of a verse of a hadith ... We acknowledge that there is this verse and hadith about the kudung (more precisely: head scarf), but we consider, what is the meaning and purpose of it, while among the Muslim women of Syria, Turkey America, etc. whose thoughts are clearer than ours, they don't give priority to the kudung ...[41]

But as in Soviet Muslim Central Asia, in Java and India women came forward to argue in favor of head covering and seclusion. At a local conference in Lucknow, Begum Wazir Hasan argued that

> there was nowadays a considerable body of Mussalmans who favoured a total abolition of purdah, following the examples of Turkey and Afghanistan. The speaker's personal opinion was that purdah in India would certainly have to be reformed, but not to the extent desired by the admirers of Western.[42]

In the 1910s, head covering in Java and Sumatra was an exclusive marker of women who had been on the *hajj* to Mecca, but by the early 1920s Islamic reformist organizations in the Dutch East Indies had begun to argue that covering one's head was a religious duty. And going beyond scripturalism, reformist women argued that the *kudung* "was a useful, even rational piece of clothing, that it was 'modern.'"[43]

Contextualization was thus not only used by those advocating for unveiling, but also to their counterparts, as in Java and Sumatra reformist organizations – which advocated veiling and segregation of the sexes – were deeply involved in education (secular and religious) as a crucial element of personal development and social activism, and, as articulated by Nelly van Doorn-Harder, to many of them "progress" meant a return to the teachings of the Qur'an.[44]

Notably, after the 1911 Republican Revolution in China, local "scholars began to link progress in women's status and education with the significance of *nusi*," women's mosques which since the sixteenth and seventeenth centuries had been hubs of female Islamic education. Between the 1920s and 1940s, upper-class Muslims in Yunnan, the northwest provinces, and Beijing sponsored the establishment of schools for women which concurrently imparted secular and Islamic knowledge.[45]

Hence, let's conclude with the words of a reformist woman from Java, writing in the early 1940s in response to the overwhelming success of Mustafa Kemal's reformist discourse on the Indonesian nationalist political elite:

Their kudung is clearly different from our kudung. Our kudung just covers the head, and we wear the veil not because we are enslaved, but because it is a command of Islam, which will bring happiness, and wearing it doesn't hinder us in the pursuit of knowledge and our obligations.

They throw away their kudung (which covers their faces) to achieve progress. And we wear the kudung (which just covers the head) to achieve progress.

What sort of progress will lead to happiness and succeed in its purpose, not wearing the veil or wearing it? Check it out yourself![46]

Conclusions

The rapid technological advances which took place in the second half of the nineteenth century – most notably steam shipping, the opening of the Suez Canal, and printing – allowed for increased exchanges and communication across Islamized Asia. The intellectual vitality that enveloped Cairo and Mecca reached many across Asia, whether directly through travel or indirectly through publications. And indeed, the direct influx of news and reflections from the greater Ottoman Empire onto Asia occurred at a turning point in global political history. As World War I eventually brought about the collapse of the Ottoman Empire and the end of the Caliphate in 1924, at the same time reinforcing the European colonial presence, Muslim communities worldwide became involved with pan-

Islamism, whether as a reflection of their interest in the resurgence of a caliphate, or as a strategic component of their anti-colonial efforts, further reinforcing the sense of community and belonging. But most notably, Muslims in Central Asia, British India, and the Dutch East Indies became main initiators of forums to discuss the future of the Caliphate.

This chapter has followed the impact of the Caliphal crisis across Asia with a focus on the Dutch East Indies, British India, and Soviet Muslims. In each of these locales Muslims came to embrace pan-Islamism as a rallying point to achieve independence, even though their frames were largely shaped by local understandings and experiences of culture, religion, and politics.

European colonial powers had become obsessed with the potential threat of pan-Islamism, understood by them as a politicized form of Islamic solidarity that was set to bring Muslims together in an anti-colonial movement. Whereas Muslims the world over did discuss ideals of belonging that could in some ways be understood as a global network of solidarity, in anti-colonial movements across Asia the primary desire was the establishment of independent nation-states, sometimes within the frame of Islam, other times within that of secularism, as Muslim political leaders and intellectuals did not all embrace a fully confrontational stand against Western ideas.

Further Reading

Al-Rasheed, M., Kersten, C. and Shterin, M. (2013) *Demystifying the caliphate: historical memory and contemporary contexts*, New York, NY: Columbia University Press.

'Aziz, A. (1967) *Islamic modernism in India and Pakistan, 1857–1964*, London: Oxford University Press.

Casale, G. (2010) *The Ottoman age of exploration*, Oxford: Oxford University Press.

Gelvin, J. L., & Green, N. (Eds.) (2014) *Global Muslims in the age of steam and print*, Berkeley, CA: University of California Press.

Hassan, M. (2016) *Longing for the lost caliphate: a transregional history*, Princeton, NJ: Princeton University Press.

Karpat, K. H. (2001) *The politicization of Islam: reconstructing identity, state, faith, and community in the late Ottoman state*, New York, NY: Oxford University Press, esp. chapter 10.

Keddie, N. R. (1966) "The pan-Islamic appeal: Afghani and Abdülhamid II," *Middle Eastern Studies* 3(1): 46–67.

Khalid, A. (1998) *The politics of Muslim cultural reform: Jadidism in Central Asia*, Berkeley, CA: University of California Press.

Landau, J. M. (1990) *The politics of Pan-Islam: ideology and organization*, Oxford: Clarendon Press.

Metcalf, B. D. (1982) *Islamic revival in British India: Deoband, 1860–1900*, Princeton, NJ: Princeton University Press.

Minault, G. (1982) *The Khilafat movement: religious symbolism and political mobilization in India*, New York, NY: Columbia University Press.

Nakamura, M. (1983) *The crescent arises over the banyan tree: a study of the Muhammadiyah movement in a central Javanese town*, Yogyakarta: Gadjah Mada University Press.

Qureshi, M. N. (2009) *Pan-Islam in British Indian politics: the politics of the Khilafat Movement, 1918–1924*, Leiden: Brill.

Ricklefs, M. C. (2007) *Polarizing Javanese society: Islamic, and other visions, c. 1830–1930*, Honolulu, HI: University of Hawai'i Press.

Roy, O. (1986) *Islam and resistance in Afghanistan*, Cambridge: Cambridge University Press.

—— (2000) *The new Central Asia: the creation of nations*, New York, NY: New York University Press.

Teitelbaum, J. (2001) *The rise and fall of the Hashemite Kingdom of Arabia*, New York, NY: New York University Press.

Northrop, D. T. (2004) *Veiled empire: gender & power in Stalinist Central Asia*, Ithaca, NY: Cornell University Press.

Figure 5.1 December 1947: Lady Nusrat Haroon (C), Moslem League activist and heiress to a sugar fortune, surrounded by her numerous daughters, daughters-in-law & grandchildren, while posing in front of large portrait of her mother & father & her siblings, at home.
Photo by Margaret Bourke-White © The LIFE Picture Collection via Getty Images/Getty Image

Muslim South Asian women were deeply involved in the movement for social reform in late-colonial India. Joining forces with their Hindu sisters in the All India Women's Congress (AIWC), they advocated for women's advancement in the social, legal, and educational spheres. As argued by Elisabeth Armstrong, "women from newly independent and still colonized nations in Asia and North Africa honed … a solidarity of commonalty for women's shared human rights, and a solidarity of complicity that took imbalances of power between women of the world into account."[1]

But the scope of women's associationism was much broader than women's rights. On the one hand, it created a stage for transnational anti-colonial solidarity: "I appeal to you, women around the world, to mobilize public opinion in favor of freedom and democracy, and to proclaim your desire to see it established in all colonial countries," proclaimed a member of the AIWC at the 1945 International Congress of Women.[2] In fact, women's organizations were one of the avenues through which activists, artists, politicians, and intellectuals in emerging post-colonial nations across Asia (and Africa) advocated for their rights and collaborated transnationally. In the post-colonial era, internationalism took shape in a variety of forms,

from liberal internationalists with considerable faith in the international order and the United Nations in particular; to feminists, trade unionists and farmers' representatives who believed the inequalities they fought were best addressed at the international level; to radical internationalists who, rather than fight for Afro-Asian inclusion, sought to overthrow the international order and remake it.[3]

But notably, religion was not seen as an ideology around which to coalesce. At the Asia-Africa conference held in Bandung in 1955, which often epitomizes the internationalism of this era, Indonesia's President Sukarno and his wife donned local Islamic headgear, and posed for photographs with Nasser of Egypt and the Prince of Saudi Arabia, but Islam was not spoken of as a common ground for international cooperation. Against a backdrop dominated by the Cold War and the emergence of the non-aligned movement, transnational Islamic solidarity and (pan)Islamist gatherings were in fact a rarity.

On the other hand, women's associationism provided a setting for Muslim women to enter the public sphere with a social, religious, and political agenda. Lady Nusrat Haroon, here sitting with the female members of her family (Figure 5.1), was a leading organizer in the women's sub-committee of the Muslim League, the political organization that beginning in 1940 advocated for Pakistan as a separate state for India's Muslim population.

In 1931, Begum Mohamed Ali – who had already made a name for herself in the Khilafat movement –

made a stirring appeal to Moslem ladies to come forward to help their men in the work for Islam. Those who wanted to keep their veils on might do so and those who wanted to come out of *purdah* were welcome to follow their resolve. But, whatever they chose to do, it must be remembered that progress without Muslim women was an impossibility.[4]

Muslim women in British India collected funds, advocated for girls' education, visited voters door-to-door, cast their ballots, and ran for elections campaigning for the implementation of Islamic law.

In the mid-1930s, "founding father" of Pakistan Muhammad Ali Jinnah (1878–1948), still argued that "religion should not enter politics" and that the All-India Muslim League was only concerned about minority representation.[5] As further elaborated by a leading woman of the time, Begum Ikramullah, "the demand for Pakistan was an assertion of our separate, independent, religious and cultural existence. We feared and objected to the assimilation being attempted, for we were proud of our culture and wanted to keep it intact. We wanted political power to enable us to preserve it."[6] At the end of the decade, Jinnah was still pushing against the idea of Pakistan as an "Islamic State," "too shrewd and too secular" to accept his colleagues' call that "the only way to solve the problem ... was to enforce the 'Law of Islam.'"[7]

At the same time, the Muslim women of the League entered the realm of political activism invoking the early days of Islamic history, upholding Islamic law as protective of their rights (*vis-à-vis* customary laws), and without challenging Islamic parameters of propriety, as it had happened in the days of the Khilafat movement. In 1947, they participated in acts of civil disobedience, leveraging the *purdah* system in their favor, as their bodies could not be touched by policemen and other male figures of authority. While Jinnah had his sister sit next to him during public events, many women still preferred to stay behind the curtain while making religio-political demands for this nation and fellow women.

After the partition of British India and the establishment of Pakistan as a Muslim state in 1947, the tension between ideals of modern nation-building and desires to preserve a religious identity – often situated in family law, education, and women's bodies – was not resolved. In the decades that followed, the *'ulama* exerted themselves to affirm the Islamic character of this secular Muslim state, while social *da'wa* groups operated at the grassroots, concerned with the call to re-Islamize their fellow citizens.

***

Colonial empires had brought together otherwise separate Muslim communities, further fostering the idea of an interconnected *umma*. But as pan-Islamic solidarity moved into the background and nationalism to the foreground, in the immediate post-colonial era, efforts were mostly concentrated on the nation-state. In this setting, Muslims in many corners of the world sought avenues to re-insert Islam in state and social structures, giving life to a variety of outlooks for the Islam-and-Nation conglomerate.

Islam had been an important force in the anti-colonial movements that spread across Asia in the late nineteenth and twentieth centuries, but it was not the only path toward independence, as leftist, secular, and other ideologies of self-determination also contributed to the intellectual environment surrounding political activism between the 1920s and 1960s. Under the pressure to create "modern" states based on a Western paradigm, "secular nationalism" emerged as the victorious force across most of the Muslim lands. Yet Muslims continued to rethink the process of state formation, and re-articulate its shape, throughout the twentieth century.

This chapter begins an exploration of how, in the second half of the twentieth century, some Muslim constituencies strived to make Islam a more prominent element in their nations' political, social, and personal spheres. Similar dynamics affected Muslims from North Africa to Southeast Asia, yet in this phase – differently from earlier and later years – their efforts were neither coordinated nor interconnected through religious networks in any substantial way, as transnational solidarity took place along different ideological lines. It was only beginning in the late 1960s that a transnational vision of Islamic activism begun to emerge. What characterized this phenomenon in the first two decades after the end of World War Two was its rootedness in local political concerns and strategies.

How did Islam interface with nation-states in the immediate post-war era? What kind of contestations and negotiations were taking place between established governments and their Muslim peoples? The first part of this chapter focuses on the twenty years that followed the end of World War II, analyzing the socio-political dynamics that affected the two largest Muslim countries in the world, namely Indonesia and Pakistan (which until 1971 included also today's Bangladesh), and the Soviet Republics of Central Asia.

In these contexts, Islam was a dominant facet of individual identities, but states did not uphold it as a primary source of ideological inspiration. The conversations and contestations that ensued, addressing the relationship between Islam and secularism as foundational ideologies, took place in a variety of ways, sometimes playing out in the realm of formal politics (representative organs, constitutional assemblies, elections), and sometimes outside it, both in peaceful and violent forms; *jihad*, as observed by Ayesha Jalal, was a most effective tool of political opposition to secular modernity as implemented by Muslim nationalists.[8] On the one hand, the debate was about how to engage with the established authority (including the question of whether to play the political game or withdraw from it, i.e. performing a *hijra*); but on the other hand, it was also about how to shape a religiously minded society for the Muslim community, either leading a gradual and peaceful *da'wa* to change society bottom up, or by leading armed warfare to impose a top-down Islamically conformed state structure.

In Indonesia, the twenty years following the Japanese withdrawal (1945–1965) were marked by vocal movements attempting to Islamize the semi-secular state (see Chapter 4) established by President Sukarno (1901–1970, president 1945–1967): some did so through parliamentary politics, some through education and *da'wa*, and others pursued armed rebellion. The second case-study is that of Pakistan. Since its partition from India in 1947, the traditional *'ulama* repeatedly attempted to affirm the Islamic political character of what was established as a secular Muslim state, while social *da'wa* movements concerned themselves with their call to re-Islamize their fellow citizens, without any direct interest in institutional politics. The Central Asian republics are a peculiar case, because whereas the framework of colonialism is usually deployed to characterize Western empires with overseas territories, Northrop has suggested that "the USSR, like its Tsarist predecessor, was a colonial empire [as] power in the Soviet Union was expressed across lines of hierarchy and difference that created at least theoretically distinct centers (metropoles) and peripheries (colonies)."[9] The case of Central Asia is also a cross-over in terms of minority–majority relations, as the Central

Asian Republics were Muslim majorities incorporated into the Soviet atheist and culturally Christian (Orthodox) state. In the 1940s to 1960s, then, the autocratic and atheist regime of Moscow was able to control religion by embedding it in its bureaucratic structure while Soviet Muslims also found ways to express their religiosity through alternative modes of piety, ultimately enabling Islam to remain an important social and political force in this secular/atheist state.

The question of Muslims' relationship to their religious identity and the nation-state was not limited to Muslim-majority contexts, though. Hence, the second part of this chapter explores the impact of colonialism and post-colonial nation-state formation on Muslim minorities, keeping an eye on the historical processes that brought these communities into existence as minorities (since minority communities emerged as such through geopolitical transformations), their position in contemporary states, and their identity; in particular, the chapter focuses on Muslim minorities in India, Burma/Myanmar, and Singapore.[10] By focusing on three countries that used to be British colonies, the discussion problematizes the too-often deployed explanation of exclusive colonial responsibility in creating ethno-religious tensions (without absolving colonialism from contributing to this reality), and points instead to a diverse set of trajectories and outcomes. Cursory references to other communities of Muslim minorities have been made in previous chapters (especially Chapters 1, 2, and 3), and further, the cases of Thailand, the Philippines and China are explored in detail under the rubric "Framing Resistance in Jihad" in Chapter 7.

The case studies in this chapter differ on many counts, but they also illustrate how similar dynamics affected Muslim communities across Asia, regardless of state ideology, demographics, and path to independence.

Muslim Majorities and the Post-Colonial Order

Indonesia

Following the Japanese occupation of the Dutch East Indies/Indonesia in the early 1940s, the project of shaping the new nation-state was bestowed upon Sukarno. On August 17, 1945, Sukarno issued the proclamation of independence of the Indonesian Republic. While it projected an aura of consensus and unity, as had the Pancasila speech previously (Chapter 4), this document did not reflect the hopes of all ideological streams.

Most relevantly here, the religious wing (represented by the "colonial" Sarekat Islam, "Japanese" Masyumi, and other social groups that had sprung up between the 1920s and 1940s) still demanded a more prominent role for Islam. Despite the efforts of Vice-President Hatta (1902–1980), the preparatory committee concluded that Indonesia only had a chance as an independent nation if no mention of Islam was made in the constitution. The provision demanding that Muslims comply with *shari'a* laws (known as the Jakarta Charter), was scrapped from the final draft and replaced by a declaration of freedom of religion.

To appease the representatives of the Islamic parties, Sukarno then qualified that this constitution was "temporary," "quick," and only applicable to the period of revolution, promising that "later in the future ... if we live in a safe and orderly state, we will gather once again the elected representatives of the people, who will enable us to make a more complete and perfect constitution,"[11] thus implying that Islamic parties would have a chance to Islamize the state if they gathered the majority of votes. The promise that the elections to form a new constitutional assembly would be held soon after the Dutch departure reinforced both the framing of the Pancasila constitution as a stepping-stone toward the realization of an Islamic state, and the viability of re-opening the debate with the secular nationalists. But as elections were withheld, the decade following Sukarno's proclamation of independence was characterized by political contestation across the archipelago.

In the meantime, religious scholars, politicians, and intellectuals became involved in a rich debate on the relationship between the semi-secular Pancasila ideology and Islam. Books and pamphlets were published either affirming the compatibility of these two frameworks and reassuring pious Muslims that a Pancasila state would allow them to pursue devout lives without obstacles, or arguing that to fulfill their religious duties, Indonesia's Muslims had to bring about a formal Islamic state. Among the latter group were some who engaged in writing, some who chose politics, and yet others who preferred armed confrontation. The bulk of the Islamic party Masyumi launched a campaign in favor of a "holy war" and of practicing a policy of non-cooperation (*hijra*, see Box 6.2) with the Republican and Dutch governments in order to establish Indonesia as an Islamic state. But Masyumi was quick to clarify that its envisioned path to an Islamic state of Indonesia was to be pursued through parliamentary consultation, thus engaging with Sukarno's politics.

Historical circumstances led some groups of Masyumi members to go a different way, especially since an unexpected Dutch military intervention in the archipelago facilitated the formation of militant armed groups committed to challenging the fledging – and now destabilized – Indonesian state. Members of the Communist Party proclaimed a Communist

Republic in Madiun, East Java, in 1948, while the Darul Islam group proclaimed an Islamic Republic in West Java in 1949. Whereas the Madiun movement was eradicated immediately, the Darul Islam remained active in Java, Sumatra, and Kalimantan (Indonesia's Borneo) until 1965, gathering the members of the Islamist factions who envisioned a more assertive, violent approach.

The inner area of West Java, the mountainous and impervious region of Priangan (in the Sunda region), became the hub of the Darul Islam. This area had traditionally been a Masyumi stronghold, thus enabling Islamic troops to receive support from the local population (which valued Masyumi as the local authority), as well as to absorb disbanded police troops and Japanese-era militias. The Republican authority and Masyumi should not have been in competition with each other, as they were both on the same front of the anti-colonial struggle. However, the tensions arising from the Republic's negotiations with the Dutch and Masyumi's commitment to integrating Islam in the new state inevitably resulted in divergent agendas. On the one hand, Sukarno agreed to cede West Java to the Dutch, and Republican troops were ordered to exit the region; on the other hand, the Islamic party proclaimed the establishment of an Islamic "safety zone" as a first step toward an Islamic "new state" of West Java.

Between the end of 1947 and the beginning of 1948, the Darul Islam (comprising former Masyumi political officers and militant troops in West Java) had reconstituted themselves under the label "Islamic State of Indonesia and the Islamic Army of Indonesia." This transformation marked a further shift, as in March 1948, the representatives of various local Masyumi branches (now constituted in the Islamic State) nominated a leader (*imam*) for West Java's *umma*, issued a call for armed *jihad* against the Dutch, and prepared the grounds for the establishment of an Islamic law "special zone."[12] Even though the Darul Islam, the central branch of Masyumi, and the Republican army, all collaborated and shared some goals, it became gradually clear that the central Masyumi could no longer support the political aspirations to independence of West Java's population. Islamic State troops were instructed to "reach power in a tactful way, succeed in taking control of the Republic, and include it[s territory] within the Islamic state."[13]

The Darul Islam struggle continued through the 1960s, but important shifts took place in the meantime. While the Islamic State leadership saw its efforts as "the continuation of the independence struggle, following on from, and in line with, the August 17, 1945 proclamation,"[14] albeit in a different form, by mid-1949 relations between Sukarno's republic and the Islamic State were severed by the proclamation of a territorially defined "Islamic State of Indonesia." Headquartered in West Java, this new state, an alternative to Sukarno's Pancasila republic, was expanding into Sumatra, South Kalimantan, the Moluccas, Sumbawa, and the Lesser Sunda Islands, in the eastern portion of the archipelago. In the meantime, the Masyumi central branch and other Islamic parties defended the Islamic State as an anti-colonial entity.

The Masyumi central branch and the Darul Islam/Islamic State had taken separate paths to affirm the need for a stronger presence of Islam in the new Indonesian state. Yet, Masyumi and other Islamic parties came to the fore to defend the Islamic State as a "self-defense movement"[15] against the Dutch. On June 30, 1950 the cabinet of the Indonesian federative state issued a declaration stating that "The government respects the DI's ideology as one of the political streams" of Indonesian politics, however since the Darul Islam was causing disorder in society, the government had the duty to restore peace.[16]

This narrative was not to last much longer, though, since the Dutch formally withdrew from Indonesia at the end of 1949, turning this conflict into one that pitted the Islamist DI against the Pancasila republican state. And the political environment continued to change, as in 1953 Sukarno successfully completed the transition from a federal structure to a "unitary" state. Within this new context, the Darul Islam/Islamic State had lost all claims to legitimacy: the colonial threat had vanished, and the proclamation of a unitary state had eliminated the possibility for the Islamic State of West Java to become an autonomous province within the federal structure.

As the post-unification government became overwhelmed with the needs of internal security, challenged by regional rebellions across the nation (most notably in Aceh, Western Sumatra, South Sulawesi, and the Moluccas), the Darul Islam was labeled "a rebellion" and its leader an "enemy of the state."

Notably, Indonesian women have been largely absent from political narratives of the revolution and its immediate aftermath, and women did not appear in the ranks of Masyumi leadership, even though they were active in its component organizations (see Chapter 4 for women in Sarekat Islam). But Nahdlatul Ulama (NU), the largest Islamic organization in Indonesia, and at the time a political party, had a different approach. Through the 1950s NU was aggressively recruiting in its affiliated women's groups to "educate young, devout Muslim women of high morality who were knowledgeable, responsible, and charitable and wanted to spend their energy in the service of their religion and nation."[17] Women participation was seen as important for the male and female leadership alike. Young women were exhorted to "Join the political developments of the fatherland like all those who are members of a political party;" this was the key to gaining more votes, as well as to being heard and to gaining positions of power. In fact, not only did women occupy leadership positions on the highest boards of NU in the 1950s and 1960s, but they also conducted political training and campaigning ahead of the 1955 elections, and filled some of their seats in Parliament. One of them recalls how "at school I was on leave for almost a year to have time for campaigning. On horseback we visited the remote villages to lobby for votes; Anshor, the NU branch for young men, provided guides and protectors" to guarantee the propriety of her travels and engagements.[18]

Masyumi had continued to show support for Darul Islam, issuing statements in favor of an Islamic state – or an Islamically compliant state – but this position was not shared by Muslim voters across the archipelago. The 1955 elections (postponed since 1945) took place on the backdrop of the non-Aligned movement's Asia-Africa conference in Bandung, the Islamist rebellion, and the fragmentation of the Islamic political front between traditionalists (Nahdlatul Ulama) and modernists (Sarekat Islam and Masyumi). The Communist Party (Partai Komunis Indonesia, PKI) emerged as the second largest party, causing fears that communism might be poised to reach national power; the further fueling of extant social tensions eventually led Sukarno to proclaim a nationwide state of emergency and declare martial law in March–April 1957.

Within two years, the return to power of military officers allowed for the convergence of political and military views on the "regional rebellions" and the launching of a systematic anti-guerrilla offensive in West Java in 1959. Unable to overcome the Islamic State forces, in 1960 the Army forcibly coopted the civilian population and by 1965 all the Darul Islam/Islamic State leaders were arrested or executed.

As the anti-Islamist repression succeeded, other groups had been at work to ensure that communism would not emerge as the established ideology either, affirming a form of technocratic secular nationalism as the exclusive base of the Indonesian state. In fact, 1965 was also the year of an alleged communist coup which allowed the military, and specifically General Suharto (1921–2008), to lead a systematic effort to eradicate communism and take power as president (1967–1998).

Numbers are impossible to confirm, but estimates suggest that between 500,000 and one million people (actual and suspected members of the PKI, their families, and many ethnic Chinese) were killed in the twelve months following the alleged coup on September 30, 1965, with many more men and women tortured, assaulted, or raped. As several army battalions in Java were thought to be infiltrated by the PKI, much of the killing was pursued by ordinary citizens, mobilized by members of Muhammadiyah, the Nahdlatul Ulama's youth wing (NU *ansor*), rural *'ulama*, and former Darul Islam activists. Communists were labeled as *kuffar*, and killing them was regarded as equal to participating in a holy war. NU women also played a role on this stage, as they had been organized into semi-military groups as well:

> We moved from an unruffled existence of preaching and giving courses in preparing a corpse for burial to rallying in the streets against the Communists. We climbed barricades and demanded that the Communist women's organization, Gerwani, would be removed from the National Association for Women's Organizations [Kowani]. We went ahead at high speed, and after that we could never go back to the traditional Muslimat NU activities. We were now fully involved in society and politics.[19]

In the second half of the 1960s, Muslim engagement with the Indonesian nation-state was set on a diametrically opposite track from the previous twenty years, when Islamic activists had challenged the constituted authority of the semi-secular Pancasila state. Political Islam came to be coopted as an underground force, kept out of the public sphere; instead, individual piety was encouraged by Suharto's new regime as a marker of anti-communism. Beginning in 1966, the government deliberated the obligation for all Indonesians to declare affiliation to one of five officially recognized religions (Islam, Catholicism, Christianity (Protestant), Hinduism, and Buddhism) and in its five-year plan it dedicated funds to the building of mosques throughout the country, on a village-by-village basis.

Under the Suharto regime, then, Muslim organizations retreated from political engagement and focused instead on *da'wa* activities, returning to a large extent to their colonial patterns in which men and women focused on education, health, and charity.

Pakistan

> The Hindus and Muslims belong to two different religious philosophies, social customs, and literature[s]. They neither intermarry nor interdine together, and indeed they belong to two different civilizations which are based mainly on conflicting ideas and conceptions.[20]

So spoke Muhammad Ali Jinnah at the All-India Muslim League gathering held in Lahore in 1940, thus reiterating other vague ideas of separation and identity politics that had previously been advanced by the poet-*cum*-ideologue Muhammad Iqbal (1877–1938) and other Indian Muslim intellectuals. As the idea of Pakistan as a separate state became paramount after 1940, the political effervescence generated by this step led to increased popular participation, of both men and women, in the League's activities.

However, in these early days of the idea of Pakistan – which literally means "the land of the pure," but actually came about as an inclusive name for the five regions where the majority of India's Muslims lived, i.e. the Punjab, the Afghan region, Kashmir, Sindh, and Baluchistan (as Bengal was advancing its own demands for independence) – visions were deeply contested, and it was not so very clear that geopolitical separation was envisioned as the best solution at that time. In fact, in those regions they held a demographic majority, meaning that Muslims were already in control of the administration, and both the Punjab and Bengal had a large measure of autonomy. But even though in the early 1900s the Muslim League and the Khilafat movement had collaborated with Gandhi and Congress, forming a Hindu–Muslim anti-colonial resistance, British policies during the 1930s had fomented sectarian identities, leading to serious concerns over the status of Muslims as a minority in the future state of India, as articulated by Begum Ikramullah (see the beginning of this chapter).

Jinnah's words came at the right time to provide a clearer ideological vision and actual scaffolding for the so-called Pakistan Movement, as several Muslim politicians, scholars, and intellectuals came increasingly to see an advantage in separation. By then the British were keen on pleasing the Muslim constituency to gain their support in the war effort.

In the post-war period, then, Jinnah claimed the role of "sole spokesman" for Muslims, advocating for the two-nation solution. The suggestion that a separate nation-state be created for the Subcontinent's Muslims gained support from Muslim leaders of various backgrounds, ranging from followers of Shah Waliullah Dihlawi (1703–1762) to the modernists, such as Sayyid Ahmad Khan, the "apolitical" Deobandi-derived Tablighi Jama'at, and the Khilafat movement, but it also incited opposition among Islamic groups.

Abu A'la Mawdudi had established the Jama'at-e Islami (JI) in 1941 as a religio-political group which stood in stark contrast with all other extant ones. On the one hand, it openly opposed the Indian National Congress because of its secularism; on the other hand, it criticized the All-India Muslim League because of its Westernized elite and its demands for separation into a Muslim nation-state, which Mawdudi deemed in itself an "un-Islamic" idea. Further, in opposition to both Congress and the League, Mawdudi argued that women were valued as mothers, wives, daughters, and sisters but should not have a public presence, either in politics or in the professions. On another level, JI was reflective of a "fundamentalist" Islamist imprint, which rejected Westernization (embraced instead to various degrees by Sayyid Ahmad Khan of Alighar, the Muslim League, and Muhammad Iqbal), as much as Islamic trad-itionalism and Sufism. Hence, Mawdudi and his JI envisioned a fully Islamized state grounded in the scriptures and led by a cadre of Islamic intellectuals who were "modern" in purely Islamic terms.

As mentioned above, the idea of Pakistan as a separate nation was mostly supported by individual groups who felt threatened in their minority status, but Muslims in the Punjab and Bengal felt strong in their position. Hence, in order to rally popular support in Punjab,

---

Box 5.1   Abu A'la Mawdudi and Sayyid Qutb

Mawdudi's religious-*cum*-political vision was not to remain confined to South Asia, as it traveled both east (to Indonesia and Malaysia) and west, where it inserted itself in the Islamist milieu opened in 1920s and 1930s Egypt by Hasan al-Banna (1906–1949) and the Muslim Brotherhood (see Box 6.1). Sayyid Qutb (1906–1966) became an active member, and later a leader, of the Egyptian Muslim Brotherhood upon his return from a two-year journey to the United States, a trip he had undertaken as a civil servant in the Education Ministry. Shortly after returning to Egypt, Qutb made arrangements to go on *hajj*. It was in Ta'if (Arabia), sometime in 1951, that he first encountered the work of Mawdudi, thanks to the mediation of the South Asian scholar Sayyid Abu Hasan Nadwi (d. 1999), who provided Qutb with Arabic translations.

Mawdudi's writings were influential on Sayyid Qutb as they helped him crystallize and better frame concepts and views he had elaborated by observing Egypt's own reality. In particular, it was Mawdudi's con-ceptualization of God's sovereignty (*hakimiyya*), *'ubudiyya* as the self-deification of the worldly ruler, *jahiliyya* as a modern reality, and *jihad* as legitimate conflict, that left a mark on the Egyptian *ikhwan*. Notably, Mawdudi's impact on Qutb is often downplayed; yet, as Qutb had died a martyr, executed by Gamal Abdel Nasser's Arab-Socialist regime (Chapter 6), public criticism of his thought was not accepted from within the Muslim Brotherhood's circle. Following Qutb's execution and Nas-ser's broader suppression of political Islam in Egypt, the Muslim Brotherhood's Supreme Guide, Hassan al-Hudaybi (1891–1973), felt the need to undermine some of Qutb's most extreme positions, as these had led some young Brothers to advocate for the excommunication (*takfir*) of Egypt's political and military establishment. To achieve that goal, al-Hudaybi bypassed Qutb altogether, by exclusively criticizing Mawdudi, and thus making explicit the South Asian influence over the Brotherhood.

Jinnah coopted Sufi *pirs* (masters) to spread the idea that Islam was "in danger" unless "Pakistan" became a separate state; he advocated for a united Muslim front, and leveraged individuals' sense of religious loyalty (David Gilmartin presents a telling collection of electoral posters in his contribution to *Islam in South Asia in Practice*).[21] As Barbara and Thomas Metcalf argue,

> for the average Muslim voter [in 1946], Pakistan came to mean two things at once. It was, as a modern nation-state for India's Muslim peoples, the logical culmination of the long process of colonial Muslim politics. At the same time, however, as a symbol of Muslim identity, Pakistan transcended the ordinary structures of the state. As such, it evoked an ideal Islamic political order.[22]

With so many different understandings of what the idea – and later reality – of an independent state of Pakistan meant, the nation-state project was bound to be pulled in multiple directions. Most emblematically, Muslim scholars and politicians hailing from Deoband envisioned Pakistan as an Islamic state implementing Islamic laws and social norms, while both Jinnah and Iqbal thought of Islam as a culture and as a religious, moral, and political, system which would provide Pakistan's Muslims with a broad set of values, not a blueprint for government.

The British accepted the two-nation solution, Jinnah emerged as the "Father of the Nation," and in 1946 Pakistan took shape as a secular state. Yet, the vast majority of the country's politicians agreed that Islam should be the foundation of the new nation – the state of Pakistan had, after all, been created to accommodate the region's Muslim population. Upon Jinnah's premature death the various factions begun to raise their voices in hopes to take control. The newly appointed (Deobandi *'alim*) *shaikh-ul-Islam* of Pakistan demanded the transformation into an Islamic state, and Mawdudi's Jama'at-e Islami (JI) – effecting a turnaround – demanded an Islamic constitution affirming "the supreme sovereignty of God" and *shari'a* law as the law of Pakistan.

After 1948, Mawdudi and the JI became the new leaders, shaping the conversations and Pakistan's early constitutional debates. Funneling the support of both traditionalists and modernists, Mawdudi eventually succeeded in presenting a unified vision, enshrined in the Objectives Resolution (see Source 5.1). This text sanctioned the primacy of God's sovereignty but also the importance of "principles of democracy, freedom, equality, tolerance and social justice, as enunciated by Islam." First promulgated in March 1949, the Objectives Resolution would become the preamble to Pakistan's constitution in 1956, and retained as such through the 1962 and 1973 rewritings.

Source 5.1

Pakistan's Objectives Resolution (1949)

This text was promoted by Abu A'la Mawdudi after Ali Jinnah's death. It sanctioned the primacy of God's sovereignty alongside the importance of democratic principles for Islamic politics. In 1956 became the preamble to Pakistan's constitution, demanding the adherence of all other laws to Islam.

1. Sovereignty belongs to Allah alone; but He has delegated it to the State of Pakistan through its people for being exercised within the limits prescribed by Him as a sacred trust;
2. The State shall exercise its powers and authority through the chosen representatives of the people;
3. The principles of Democracy, freedom, equality, tolerance and social justice as enunciated by Islam shall be fully observed;
4. The Muslims shall be enabled to order their lives in the individual and collective spheres in accordance with the teachings of Islam as set out in the Holy Quran and Sunnah.
5. Adequate provision shall be made for the minorities to freely profess and practice their religions and develop their cultures;
6. Pakistan shall be a Federation;
7. Fundamental Rights shall be guaranteed;
8. Judiciary shall be independent.

During the first decade of its existence, Pakistan suffered much instability, especially as the Punjabis affirmed themselves as the majority, marginalizing all other ethno-linguistic groups, and tensions also emerged on the intra-Muslim sectarian front. The bureaucracy and military were the only fully functioning structures, leading to the formation of a highly technocratic state grounded in secular authoritarian rule. With few exceptions in the realm of family law, Pakistan's legal system was still based on English common law, while the country's full name remained, for the time being, "Islamic Republic of Pakistan."

This ambivalence between secular and religious ideologies came to the surface most clearly in 1953, when a court tasked to establish the facts of a sectarian riot decided to push its mandate further and thus analyze the relationship between the Pakistani state, ideals of liberal democracy, and the principles of an Islamic state. The court's final report concluded that the riots had been caused by the influence of the 'ulama over matters of the state, and consequently glorified the civil administration as the only agent able to keep order. Yet, the report's inability to differentiate between the 'ulama's elaboration of the historical experience of the

Islamic state, on the one hand, and their theological elaborations, on the other, paradoxically created the impression that a coherent Islamic state system actually existed at the time in Pakistan, and that it was being legitimated and validated by a "secular" court.

In 1956 Pakistan issued its first constitution. Enshrining the Objectives Resolution of 1949 as its preamble, the text declared that Pakistan's laws could not contravene Islam. Yet, what this meant remained unclear. Mawdudi's JI and other Islamist groups were caught in a bind: their campaigning had been successful enough to effect a change, but the state was unable and unwilling to act upon it.

With the rise of General Ayub Khan and his military regime in 1958, Pakistan moved further along the spectrum of secular order, as evidenced, for example, by a renaming process that eliminated the "Islamic" attribute from the country's official name. Islamist groups, and JI specifically, saw their movements further restricted through bans, arrests, and closure of facilities. It was in this context that JI opted to side with secular parties to advocate for democracy (the only environment in which JI could further expand), forging an alliance with a Muslim League faction, the Bengali ethno-nationalist Awami League, and a Marxist party. Maududi embraced pragmatism and argued that an Islamic state could only be established through electoral politics. However, the political fragmentation of the Islamist front meant that the 1970 elections were won by the Awami League (39 percent), followed by the Pakistan People's Party (18 percent) led by Zulfiqar 'Ali Bhutto (1929–1979). These results precipitated the country into a civil war which eventually ended with the separation of its eastern and western provinces (i.e. today's Bangladesh and Pakistan, respectively), indicating that ethno-nationalism could supplant – or even be stronger than – religious brotherhood. This realization threw the country into an identity crisis which consequently led to a religious conservative turn throughout the 1970s: Bhutto opted to sideline the Pakistan People's Party's socialist orientation and advance instead an Islamization campaign, with the primary intent of instilling a sense of national unity to this now-maimed nation. In the decade that followed, first Bhutto and later Zia ul-Haqq (1925–1988) shifted the laws and norms of Pakistan to better conform with ideals of Islamic Sunni orthodoxy, priming Pakistan to become a supporter of Saudi Arabia (see Chapter 6).

While Pakistan's Islamic parties saw their sphere of influence narrowed and restricted by Ayub Khan after 1958, nonpolitical groups were able to further their activities. Most prominent and successful among them was the Tablighi Jama'at (TJ), a group that had emerged as an offshoot of the Deobandi movement in the 1920s, when its founder, Muhammad Ilyas Kandahlawi (d. 1944), sought to engage the Muslim peasantry of northern India. Abandoning the scholasticism of Deoband and marginalizing the importance of texts, Kandahlawi focused instead on encouraging "nominal" Muslims to perform ritual obligations and to pursue an Islamic way of life. Rather than pointing at legal exegesis, Kandahlawi preached by example, his own and that of the Prophet Muhammad. Embracing "the mission of the prophets," Kandahlawi became an itinerant preacher, and structured his Jama'at around the principle that *da'wa* was the duty of every Muslim.

The emergence of the TJ as a grassroots movement that advocated individual regeneration and eschewed political engagement was extremely contextual to India in the 1930s and 1940s. As communal tensions and politics began to infiltrate the conversation on independence, Hindu proselytizing groups were active in "reclaiming" Hindus whose ancestors had converted to Islam; on the other hand (Deobandi) Muslim scholars and intellectuals split between those who supported demands for a separate Muslim state and those who wished to work with Congress. Kandahlawi continued to advance a quietist, apolitical stance. At the time of Kandahlawi's death in 1944, the TJ started to look beyond its hub in Mewat and northern India, and under his successors' leadership the group has reached Southeast Asia, West Asia, post-Soviet Central Asia, Africa, Europe, and North America.

The TJ has no formal structure, its activities being coordinated locally; yet, it has been able to retain a commitment to Kandahlawi's methodology and – most notably – the commandment of not getting involved with politics. In the context of Pakistan, it was this staunchly apolitical stance that enabled the TJ to continue to operate under the authoritarian rule of Ayub Khan, and through which in later years, in conjunction with Zia ul-Haqq's interest in further Islamizing Pakistan's administration and military, this group was encouraged to gain followers within the higher echelons of the state.

Soviet Central Asia

In the decades before the Soviet involvement in World War II, Islam in Central Asia had been reconfigured in a Marxist-Leninist framework, as the central government in Moscow accentuated ethno-national identities. On the one hand there were geopolitical transformations, as Stalin (1878–1953) divided the region into ethno-nationally defined "union republics," giving Central Asia the outlook still extant today. Russian Turkestan was first split into the Uzbek and Turkmen Soviet Socialist Republics (in 1924), with the former containing the Tajik Autonomous

Soviet Socialist Republic; then came the separation of the Tajik ASSR as an independent republic, and the formation of a new Kyrgyz SSR. On the other hand, Moscow also worked toward eradicating religion from peoples' lives, following Marxist-Leninist ideology: the *jadid*s (see Chapter 3) were derided as "bourgeois" and "old intellectuals" and came to be substituted by a new Soviet elite that had no connections with traditional networks of authority; Islamic values were dislodged from the public discourse and arena; religious schools, courts, and benevolent associations were abolished; *'ulama* were persecuted, mosques converted into "productive" spaces, and the veil was banned in name of women's emancipation and liberation (see Chapter 4). But World War II was to change everything.

The pre-war ideological and physical attack on Islam was suddenly halted, and religion came to be deemed necessary to carry the population through the hardships of war. Mosques (and churches) were re-opened across the Union, and in 1943 the central government facilitated the establishment of an office for Islamic affairs, named the Spiritual Administration of the Muslims of Central Asia and Kazakhstan (SADUM). Headquartered in Uzbekistan, and placed under the chairmanship of a Naqshbandi *shaykh* from Tashkent (and his successors, as the same family held the position until 1989), SADUM was the only organization of its era that defied ethno-nationalist boundaries.

SADUM's scope was very clearly bound and defined. Its primary mandate was to rally Muslim support for the war effort and to advance a religious discourse that highlighted the concurrence of Islamic and Soviet identities (and lifestyles). As with the jadidist experiment, SADUM officials promoted the purification of Islam from local practices and historical vestiges, and encouraged dedication to the nation-state and a modern education. SADUM issued *fatwa*s that supported the integration of Muslims into Soviet society by, for example, declaring Ramadan a non-obligatory duty for those engaged in physical labor; condemning visits to tombs and shrines as un-Islamic; and upholding "honest work" as an Islamic virtue, thus addressing the social problems of absenteeism and drunkenness.

Similar negotiations were evident in the realm of education. SADUM was allowed to run its own school to train its future cadres: the Mir-i Arab *madrasa* was re-opened in Bukhara in 1948, but it admitted no more than a dozen students each year, and only several years later a few more were trained at the Imam al-Bukhari Islamic Institute of Tashkent. Hanafi traditionalism was abandoned in favor of practicing direct *ijtihad* (interpretative effort), with its *madrasas* ditching *fiqh* commentaries and favoring instead the study of Arabic,

Qur'anic recitation, *tafsir*, and *hadith* primary texts alongside geography, the social sciences, and the Uzbek language. Starting in 1945, SADUM was also allowed to send a few pilgrims to Mecca every year, but Central Asian Muslim youth would have to wait until the mid-1960s to be sent abroad to study.

Religion had thus been re-allowed in the Soviet Union, but through SADUM Islam became embedded in the state's apparatus, reflecting the imprint of Soviet ideology and subjecting it to the prevalent political winds. Hence, while Nikita Khrushchev (First Secretary of the Communist Party, 1953–1964) suppressed Islam once again after the emergency of World War II had ended, in the 1960s and 1970s Islam reappeared as a tool of Brezhnev's (General Secretary of The Communist Party, 1964–1982) foreign policy as he attempted to establish contacts with other Muslim (Arab-Socialist) nations (Chapter 6).

For Muslims in the Soviet Union, their religious identity had become an aspect of ethnic belonging: "Being Muslim came to mean adherence to certain cultural norms and traditions rather than adherence to strictures that were directly validated by the learned tradition."[23] It was this transformation of Islam into an intrinsic element of ethnic identity that allowed it to work with, rather than against, the established authority. As concluded by Adeeb Khalid, displays of public piety – even during Khrushchev's anti-religious campaigns of 1959–1962 – should not be considered "a priori subversive or even political, [as] for the vast majority of Central Asians, being Muslim was *not* repugnant to being Soviet."[24]

That being said, there were ways of being a Central Asian Muslim that did not conform to the example envisioned and offered by SADUM and the authority of the Soviet state. By the mid-1960s the Soviet regime recognized that in the past several decades, its Muslim territories had experienced the emergence of a form of Islam "parallel" to that of SADUM. Besides the fact that the Soviet Union's isolation from the outside world had left limited opportunities and resources for the expression of religious piety, and had fostered localized forms of ritual at the grassroots, Central Asian Muslims were also responding to the sheer scarcity of religious infrastructure, and (discreetly) voicing their dissatisfaction with SADUM's intellectual and spiritual narrowness.

The scarcity of registered places of worship led, for example, to the leader of a collective farm in Ferghana Valley hosting a formal event for Ramadan without seeking official permission from the local Soviet authority or SADUM offices (1958). A couple of years later, the chairman of another collective, in Uzbekistan this time, had used money from the budget to rebuild an old mosque. And between 1945 and the 1950s, an unregistered mosque in southern Uzbekistan was hosting up to seventy Muslims for regular prayer, about 300 on Fridays, and over 2,000 on festivals.[25]

Central Asian Muslims found their environment limiting not only in terms of material resources, but also in the range of acceptable forms of piety. Once the main pillar of Central Asia's Islamic society, the Sufi *tariqa*s had almost disappeared after being the target of the Stalinist purges of the 1920s and 1930s. At the height of ideological communism, the master–pupil relationship was seen as a form of feudal exploitation and as sectarian in nature; but in addition to that, Sufism also had a track record of political involvement in the Northern Caucasus and Central Asia, making the Soviet regime uncomfortable with this "extreme mystic manifestation of Islam [which members] led a parasitic way of life, performed public mysteries and ecstasies, which stirred up fanaticism, as well as religious dances, and adhered persistently to the idea of the *gazavat*, the war against 'infidels.'"[26]

Sufism had, however, managed to survive by going underground and finding support among the local elites, to the extent that in the 1940s and 1950s *shaykh*s (locally referred to as *ishan*) were still able to recruit new pupils across all strata of society, including the Soviet establishment. Sufism was still so prevalent that *imams* openly criticized *ishanism* as un-Islamic during Friday sermons, and civil officials advanced the suggestion that SADUM should issue a *fatwa* on the topic. The activities of *ishan*s elicited little more than talks from Soviet cadres, who went no further than calling for local clerics and officials to take "administrative" measures against them through the 1950s. But the Khrushchev years, marked by renewed anti-religious campaigns, eventually hit Sufism hard: shrines were closed or destroyed, and *shaykh*s persecuted and imprisoned.

Another group of unaffiliated religious leaders were the *otine*s, women knowledgeable in religious matters – ritual and theological – who exerted influence and commanded authority in their extended families and local communities. Their role, ascertained since at least the late eighteenth century and probably going back to pre-Islamic Shamanism, was to guide women into proper conduct, advising them on all kinds of matters, and ultimately to preserve Islamic practices and knowledge for the younger generations. They were often wives of *'ulama*, and their status might have been equivalent to that of the *'ulama*, albeit possibly enhanced by their versatility: *otine*s taught the Qur'an in all-girls schools, recited prayers at community events, and led *dhikr* ceremonies and congregational prayers for women, as well as leading them on pilgrimages to local shrines. As a Soviet scholar writing in the mid-1920s recalled:

During the zikr, the *otine*, (literally schoolteacher), the one who memorized the Qur'an, the *hafiz*, sings spiritual songs. She is considered a good reciter and is in general, highly well regarded ... It is the talent of the *otine* that makes the zikr more animated.[27]

But from the mid-1920s onwards, women religious leaders were pushed underground, first by the purges and then by a patriarchal vision of Islam. SADUM opened a few religious schools, and while Central Asian Muslim men were gradually able to insert themselves in international networks of education, *otines* were left behind, excluded from these institutionalized spaces of knowledge transmission. Cut off from formal religious education, and unable to read the few books that had survived the Stalinist purges (as these were written in Arabic and Chagatai Turkish, languages and scripts no longer taught in the Soviet era), the knowledge of the *otines* was based exclusively on what was passed on to them orally by their mentors.

And yet Islamic practices survived the Soviet onslaught, retreating in the private sphere of domestic piety and rituals, and it was largely these women, the *otines*, who kept Islam alive in Soviet Central Asia by spreading and reinforcing religious morals among other women. By the mid-1950s the Soviet establishment was deeply concerned about their "fanaticism," "popularity," and "authority." Reporting on the wife of a Kyrgyz imam, herself a local religious leader, a Soviet document stated:

[Mustafina] leads discussions encouraging the view that Muslim women should be God-fearing, that Muslim women should not entertain themselves with music, dancing, and songs, that they should not walk around with the heads uncovered [and] the imam and the qadi Shokirxo'jayev are well aware of Mustafina's statements, but do nothing to stop her.[28]

A third front of resistance to SADUM's commitment to reconcile "Islam" with Soviet life was taken on by locally renown scholars. Perusing and teaching traditional texts of Hanafi *fiqh* to pupils gathered in (illegal) study circles (*hujra*, referring to the cells in which *madrasa* students lived), these scholars criticized SADUM's approach, contending that it betrayed Central Asia's tradition of tolerance of local customs (*'adat*) and legal eclecticism. By the 1980s the *hujra* landscape had become more complex, as traditionalist Hanafi teachers were sidelined by foreign-influenced *ikhwani*, Salafi, or Wahhabi youth (Chapter 6). In this constellation of study circles scattered across the region, there were two scholars who defined the terms of the conversation in the 1950s and 1960s.

Muhammadjan Hindustani (1892–1989) was born in a small village in the Ferghana Valley. At the age of twelve he left for Kokand to study the Qur'an, and from there he pursued further studies in Bukhara, Balkh (Afghanistan), Tashkent, Jalalabad (back in Afghanistan), and

Kashmir, where he was trained at a Deobandi school. His adult life was also rather itinerant, but not by choice, as he was often arrested during the Stalin years. It was after the death of Stalin in 1953 that he was able to settle in Dushanbe (Tajikistan). While he taught Urdu at the Institute of Oriental Studies of the Academy of Sciences, he also ran a *hujra* that provided a full curriculum, comparable to that of traditional *madrasas*. His pupils mastered Islamic law, doctrine and ethics, but also Arabic language and Islamic cosmology, astronomy, philosophy and medicine. And in line with the *madrasa* tradition, Hindustani's approach was faithful to the Hanafi school, striving for the reconciliation of *shari'a* and local practices, and uninterested in challenging the authority of a non-Muslim ruler insofar as Muslims were able to practice their religion – a reality guaranteed, in his eyes, by the embedding of Islam into Central Asians' ethnic identity. Several of his students would become representatives of the next generation of religious leaders. Among them was Hakimjon Qori (b. 1898), who, however, saw his ideals better reflected in the teachings of Ibn Taymiyah and the Wahhabi school of thought. Born in Margilan (Ferghana Valley, Uzbekistan), Hakimjon eventually distanced himself from Hindustani after studying with representatives of the South Asian *Ahl-i Hadith* and being exposed to materials published in Saudi Arabia and made available through SADUM (see Chapter 6).

Despite their existence outside of the Soviet sphere of control, these forms of personal piety, *hujra*s, Sufism, and the *otine*s were not direct channels of contestation in the 1940s to 1960s era, but rather gray areas that had resulted from an untold process of negotiation between the state and this Muslim society. Then, "parallel Islam" was rarely the target of repressive policies as anti-religious policies were most often directed at reducing the institutional presence of religion in society.

The uninterrupted decades of Soviet policies had led to a full separation of the public sphere of subject–state interaction (characterized and dominated by Soviet atheist modes of being) and the private sphere of religious devotion. What is more, the latter's construction as a marker of ethno-cultural identity also affected the potential impact of foreign Islamic discourses: as Islam had become an integral part of Soviet Central Asians' identities, these Muslims struggled to see Islam as a bonding element with Muslims from other parts of the Union or the wider world. Uzbeks celebrated al-Biruni and Ibn Sina, Timur's expansion to South Asia, and Samarqand's history, all as aspects of their local ethnic identity, rather than reflecting a potentially "pan-Islamic" one. They were appointed as diplomats in other Muslim countries, and fought in the Soviet Army in large numbers, also in Afghanistan: the idea of Islam as an aspect of local culture was so engrained that, even as Central Asian republics became the showcase of a successful socialist path to development for the entire world to see (and especially for Arab-socialist countries, as Khrushchev's campaigns "proved a desirable asset for the Soviet leadership" on the international stage),[29] they remained largely impenetrable to transnational ideals of Islamic solidarity or Islamist politics until the late 1980s.

In the past some of these populations had waged anti-Russian (both Tzarist and Soviet) rebellions under the banner of Islam, yet after decades of assimilation, Central Asian Muslims remained committed to their Soviet identity even amidst the Islamized resistance to the Soviet invasion of Afghanistan, which coalesced Muslims from the world over (see Chapter 7). The sentiment is best represented by Muhammadjan Hindustani, whom in his "Answers to those who are introducing inadmissible innovations into religion" stated:

You praise the Afghan mujahidin, believing that they are waging a true jihad. But their jihad is the destruction of Muslim mosques, the murder of those who pray, the confiscation of people's property, the murder of women and children. Is this truly jihad? This is nothing other than the destruction of holy places and the annihilation of sacred things. In particular, an ancient robe of Allah's Prophet was preserved in Kandahar – may Allah bless and preserve it! And they burned it! Is this really holy jihad? No, not by any means![30]

Muslim Minorities and the Post-Colonial Order

Muslim communities had emerged across continental and maritime Asia as the result of human movement (see Chapter 1), which translated into the formation of Muslim pockets along (mostly) trading routes. Muslims had become long-term residents in key nodes of the northern Silk Road and in Tibet, along the coastal areas of India and Southeast Asia. These communities were often surrounded by non-Muslims – Confucians, Buddhists, Hindus, etc. – but they remained connected to other Muslims through those networks of mobility, and often enjoyed various degrees of autonomy. The appearance of Europeans across Asia from the fifteenth century onward was to change things dramatically, as they established their own trading posts and, later, colonial states.

European Empires across Asia disrupted the links that kept Muslim communities in touch with each other, creating, in fact, minority communities. What had been self-reliant polities on the southern coast of India, with sustained relations with other Muslims east and west, became isolated units within the Hindu-majority, European-dominated British Raj. The

Sultanate of Patani, on the Malay Peninsula, was ceded by the British (who controlled Malaya) to the King of Siam (their northern neighbor), thus turning Patani Muslims into a minority group ruled by the Thai Buddhist King. The Muslims of the Sulu Sea, whose Sultanate had been part of the Indo-Malay sphere, were forced under the control of Spanish (Christianized) Philippines. Muslims of the Tarim Basin had for centuries been part and parcel of Turkic Central Asia, but the Qing conquest of the area and the subsequent creation of Xinjiang as China's "new province" in the late nineteenth century turned the Uyghurs into a minority group.

Minorities, then, are a politically contingent construction, the outcome of geopolitical re-shapings initiated by imperialistic policies. As suggested by Ilyse Morgenstein Fuerst, "minoritization does not refer solely to the demographic realities of a particular location, but instead to the systematic process by which elites deny power or access to a group through the implementation of power, be that local, linguistic, economic or political."[31]

India

The British took political control of the Subcontinent in the second half of the 1800s, after the (Muslim) Mughal dynasty had ruled a Hindu-majority population for several centuries. The British approach to administering this varied and stratified population was through a clear and stated policy of communalization, meaning that the colonial state dealt with its subjects on the basis of their religious affiliation. Laws, education, taxes, etc. were all determined on the basis of communal belonging. Since the mid-1800s, the British further stressed "differences between and among Indians on the basis of religion" eventually "creat[ing] an image of India's Muslims as a unitary whole" different from, and often opposed to, the territory's Hindus.[32]

As seen when re-tracing the history of the emergence of Pakistan as an independent nation-state, several local politicians had embraced that same approach in order to guarantee infrastructural protection for the Muslim minority. While some saw this as possible through reforms within a Hindu-majority context, others became convinced of the necessity of a separate state tasked to advance Muslim interests. Despite the establishment of Pakistan and the large numbers of Muslims (and Hindus) who crossed the demarcation line, India's remains today the third-largest Muslim population in the world, surpassed only by Indonesia and Pakistan.

The act of Partition was one marred with horror, as some ten million people migrated and possibly another million died in the process. In addition to the overwhelming number of deaths, Gandhi himself became victim of his involvement with Partition, as he was assassinated by a Hindu extremist after his decision to share some of India's assets with the new Pakistan. The Hindutva movement – which first emerged in the anti-colonial milieu as a push to identify "India" as "Hindu" and to reject all other religious groups as foreign – had begun to make a visible impact in Indian politics, and would not stop.

Following these events, the Indian Congress came to be mostly inspired by a rejection of communal politics; the 1950 constitution was harnessed on secular principles of non-denominational bias (even though the term "secularism" does not appear in the text, see Source 5.2), it abolished religious identification of electorate and parliamentary seats,

---

Source 5.2

Islam in Secular India, by Mushir Ul-Haq (1972)

Graduated from Nadqat al-Ulema in Lucknow, Mushir ul-Haq is an academic and public intellectual based in India. In this excerpt, he reflects on the shifting meaning and acceptability of "secularism" for India's Muslims before and after the Partition of 1947.[33]

The Constitution of India designates the country a "Sovereign Democratic Republic" but makes no mention of "secularism." For the last two decades Indians have been talking of secularism, yet the term remains vague and ambiguous. One may, therefore, be justified in asking: what does secularism really mean – especially in the Indian context? ...

It should be remembered that when India became independent the makers of the Indian Constitution had hardly any alternative to taking secularism as their guideline. The leaders of the Independence Movement were so committed to a noncommunal and non-religious policy that even after the partition of the country they could not retreat from their stand. The Muslim community of India also welcomed the idea of a secular state because they feared the alternative would be a "Hindu state" ...

All through the freedom struggle hardly any national leader dared to question the importance of religion. The leaders of both the Hindu and the Muslim communities most of the times used a religious vocabulary in their speeches and writings to achieve political ends. In the case of the Hindu community one may say that religion did not mean a codified and systematized set of principles, rather it was understood in term of higher moral values. But this cannot be said about the Muslims. Religion to them was not just moral values: it was the *Shari'a*, a system, an institution: Muslims were told this time and again ...

Source 5.2   (*cont.*)

Thus secularism and secular state are to be accepted or rejected on the basis of the *Shari'a*. The secular state, as we have seen, has a precedent in Islamic history and is, therefore, acceptable, but secularism as a doctrine is believed to be incompatible with Islam. Since no serious effort has so far been made to explain to the Indian Muslims – as it has been done in the case of Turkey – that "secularism" is a foreign word, and in Islamic society it can be interpreted quite differently from what it is understood in a Christian society, naturally we find the Indian Muslims still groping after the meaning of secularism ...

On the question of secularism, however, Indian Muslims appear broadly divided into two sections. The first group, in a minority and rather contemptuously called "secularist" includes mostly modern educated Muslims who hold that religion, as a faith, can co-exist with secularism. The second group, led by the *'ulama'*, stands by the view that religion is not only faith but *Shari'a* also. Faith may co-exist with secularism, but *Shari'a* cannot ...

There are then two groups of Indian Muslims – the "secularists" and the "nationalist" *'ulama'* – who are suspect in the eyes of many Muslims, but there is little hope of their joining hands. These two are quite different from each other. They have practically nothing in common in their education, or mental make-up, or in their approach to this world and the next, in short, in anything. The only point common to them is that both are frowned upon by the generality of the Muslims, of course, for different reasons altogether.

In short it can be said that the Indian Muslims are in a dilemma: so far as the secular state is concerned, it is acceptable, for one thing, no alternative is available and, for the other, a secular state guarantees religious freedom. But the philosophy of secularism is considered to be a poison for religious life.

and advocated the development of a code of civil law that would not hinge on religious affiliation. But in the decades that followed, Hindu–Muslim relations were to become tense.

Beginning in the 1980s, the century-old reality of having mosques built on Hindu temples (Chapter 2) became contested: the dispute surrounding the Babri Mosque in Ayodhya (Uttar Pradesh), and its eventual destruction by activists of the World Hindu Organization in 1992, snowballed episodes of Hindu–Muslim violence across the country. The turn into the twenty-first century has been marked by the rise of Hindutva as a government platform, as the BJP, or Bharatiya Janata Party, increased its power in the late 1990s and through the 2010s. In what Barbara Metcalf has described as close to "a betrayal of the secular values of Nehru and Gandhi,"[34] a coalition government led by the BJP won the 1998 elections. In the early 2000s, fueled by the impact of the US-led "war on terror" and India's own economic stagnation, anti-Muslim sentiments and actions grew exponentially, with Muslims labeled as privileged, disloyal, and unassimilable, and ultimately made "a scapegoat for problems not of their making."[35] A 2006 government report showed the discrimination, educational disadvantages, and economic difficulties faced by Muslim communities across the country.

Most recently, conflict has revolved around the issue of cow slaughter; considered sacred by the Hindus as the symbol of the Goddess of fertility, cows are commonly eaten by other religious groups in the Subcontinent. Not only have twenty-four (out of twenty-nine) states promulgated legal restrictions or bans on the slaughtering of bovines, but also "cow protection" groups have been known to attack violently, intimidate, or even kill Muslims and Christians, without incurring into any legal prosecution. By the late 2010s, members of religious minorities and civil society groups felt that the BJP rule had made them the targets of religiously motivated discrimination and attacks on their persons and property and generally more vulnerable.[36]

Burma/Myanmar

Upon their takeover of Arakan (today's Burma/Myanmar's Rakhine State) in the 1820s, the British found the region promising in terms of natural resources but scanty in potential laborers. Drawing on their experience in the Straits Settlements, the British soon devised plans for diverting Chinese and Indian migrants away from Singapore, Malacca, and Penang and toward Lower Burma instead. The arrival of "foreign" Muslims (alongside "foreign" Christians, Buddhists, and Hindus) created a sense that the local demographics were changing due to colonial immigration policies, and late nineteenth-century trends eventually led to a characterization of Islam in Akyab (a harbor city on the Bay of Bengal) as Indian and foreign. Yet, in earlier decades British officers had noted that Muslims were indigenous to the region: "the Mussulman population of Akyab, however, is not, as elsewhere in the province, alien, as they have for the most part been settled in the province for many generations,"[37] "[they have] been so long in the country that it may be called indigenous"[38] stated the 1872 census report; "There are few or no indigenous Hindus, though there is a considerable indigenous Mahomedan population in Arakan,"[39] reinforced the Superintendent in 1881. Yet, while in 1883 Mr. Mac-Neill had made no mention of Islam,[40] in 1891 the Census report identified Islam as "of comparatively recent introduction" to Arakan, while indigenous Muslims were still identified in other areas as "Burman-Muslims." By 1901, Hinduism, Islam, and Christianity were labeled as "foreign" religions, the affiliates of which were to be considered outsiders to Burma's social fabric.

What had started as a conversation between colonial officers on whether Islam and Muslims were "indigenous" or "foreign" to Burma (and more specifically Arakan) was to develop into a deeply politicized question from the 1920s onwards. As Britain planned the separation of Burma from British India (effective from 1938) and as the nationalist movement picked up momentum, the status of Burma's Indians and the need to prove indigeneity to advance claims for citizenship became crucial aspects of Burma Muslim identities.

International political shifts added fuel to the nationalist debate that took shape as "Burma for the Burmese Buddhists" (instead of "Burma for the Burmese").[41] Even though scattered instances of "Muslims" among various "indigenous race-groups" can be encountered in the 1921 and 1931 censuses, the overall category of "Burman-Muslims" gradually disappeared and Muslims came to be classified as foreign "Indo-Burmans."[42] Today, visiting cities across Burma/Myanmar, but especially Mandalay and Yangoon, one sees ethnically defined Muslim communities, and the many mosques that still dot these cities are clear representations of this ethno-linguistic reality. In Yangoon, mosques are named after various ethnic groups, such as the Cholia (from Tamil Nadu), Nishapuris (from Persia), and Surtees (Gujarati), and Mandalay's "Chinese" (or "Panthay") mosque has a pagoda-styled minaret.

The nationalist discourse that cemented around the idea of Burma as a Buddhist nation has been most recently reaffirmed by the Ma-Ba-Tha ("Patriotic Association of Myanmar") and the 969 movement (which is specifically anti-Muslim) in the 2010s, when being Burmese (*Bar-Ma*) was regarded as equivalent to being Buddhist, and being Muslim as equivalent to being foreign. Low-stakes disagreements in the town of Meiktila (located in central Burma, between Mandalay and the new administrative capital, Naypyidaw) set local mosques and entire Muslim neighborhoods ablaze in 2013; this incident was in fact amplified by previous clashes in Rakhine State, where a year earlier over 200 Rohingya Muslims had died and thousands had been displaced. The term Rohingya has been used by Muslims in Rakhine, as they identify themselves as an indigenous group of Muslims with historical roots to Rakhine (or Arakan, as the region was called until the 1970s). On the other hand, the Burma/Myanmar government and military have refused to acknowledge the Rohingya as a legitimate indigenous group, arguing instead that they should be considered illegal immigrants, "Bengalis" who entered Burmese territory after the establishment of British Burma. The latest census, conducted in 2014, did not include the term Rohingya, and – more generally – did not make ethnic and religious data available to the public, making it impossible to know the actual number of Muslims in Burma/Myanmar and their ethnic affiliation. Estimates suggest that 4.3 percent of the country's population is Muslim.[43]

Anti-Muslim violence has since snowballed across the country to crystallize itself in what has come to be referred to as the "Rohingya crisis" in Rakhine State. After decades of violence, in August–September 2017 the military launched a "clearance operations" against Rohingya militants, but the systematic destruction of villages and persecution of women and children caused the "world's fastest growing refugee crisis."[44] As over 700,000 people were displaced between August and December 2017, seeking refuge in Bangladesh where they joined another 200,000 who already populated refugee camps,[45] the United Nations asserted that Burma/Myanmar's military commanders "should be investigated and prosecuted for the 'gravest' crimes against civilians under international law, including genocide" alongside murder, rape, torture, sexual slavery, persecution, and enslavement.[46] According to the Arakan Project, there are about half a million Rohingyas left in Burma/Myanmar (including over 100,000 internally displaced persons), at least as many in Saudi Arabia, a further 350,000 in Pakistan, almost a million in Bangladesh, 150,000 in Malaysia, 5,000 in Thailand, and 1,000 in Indonesia.[47]

Singapore

In August 1965, when Malaysia and Singapore took separate paths to post-colonial independence, Singapore's Muslims found their position completely reversed: after over a century of being the majority (ethno) religious group in British Malaya, Singapore's Muslims became a rather small minority, accounting for 14 percent of the island-state's population. Even though this island is located at the southern tip of the Malay Peninsula, and was a place of transition and trade where Muslims hailed from Malaya as well as Arabia, South Asia, Java, and many other regions of the Indo-Malay Archipelago, the Muslim population of Singapore remains largely Malay (circa 85 percent)[48] and, as in Malaysia, in Singapore "Malay" tends to equate to "Muslim" too.

The ruling Chinese-dominated People's Action Party acknowledged this historical change by enshrining the "special position" of the Malays in the new state's constitution:

The government shall exercise its functions in such a manner as to recognise the special position of the Malays, who are the indigenous people of Singapore, and accordingly it shall be the responsibility of the government to protect, safe-guard, support, foster and promote their political, economic, social, and cultural identity and the Malay language.

This opening was placed alongside a statement of religious freedom. Despite being limited by the primary concern of harmony, the text seemed to provide a relative sense of cultural identity preservation for the territory's Malays (and Muslims more generally).

Following in the steps of the British, who by the late 1950s had set up *shari'a* courts and a registry of Muslim marriages as part of their establishing a state bureaucracy in their colonial territories, the Singapore state enacted the Administration of Muslim Law Act (AMLA, 1965) and formed the Islamic Religious Council of Singapore (MUIS, 1966) with the task of issuing *fatwas* and managing *zakat*, *waqf*, the *hajj*, *halal* certification, and all *da'wa* activities; in later years, the state – through MUIS – took on the job of granting permits and providing some funds to build mosques and run religious schools. The state has thus been supporting, at least infrastructurally, its Muslim minority.

On the other hand, the Singaporean establishment has been perceived as concerned (if not outright suspicious) about Malay (Muslims)'s political and spiritual allegiance; thus, Malays have felt limited in their military service involvement (in roles and ranks), as well as in their actual freedom to display their religiosity in the public sphere. The mandate to ensure respectful intra-ethnic (or "intra-religious") interactions in the name of "religious harmony" has often taken over individual freedoms. One notable step in this direction was the promulgation of the Maintenance of Religious Harmony Act (MRHA) in 1990[49] in response to Christian proselytization efforts as well as the global Islamic resurgence; second, the 1998 amendment to the AMLA disallowed *shari'a* courts from adjudicating any multi-faith divorce cases; and more recently, the government reaffirmed the secular principles of Singapore's public sphere by upholding the ban on headscarves in public schools and having MUIS issue a *fatwa* in support of such decision.

Hence, despite the infrastructural accommodation of Muslims in the Singaporean state, the prioritization of stability and secularism (which some scholars have defined as a form of authoritarianism,[50] pointing to the state's interest in regulating and controlling religion) have been alienating portions of the Muslim population and causing MUIS's influence to decrease. What is more, the Muslim communities of Singapore have lagged behind their peers in terms of academic achievement, occupational placement, and, ultimately, wealth, creating more reasons for social discontent.

Conclusions

If the Khilafat and anti-colonial experiences created solidarity networks harnessed on religious identities and the idea of an interconnected *umma*, the emergence of nation-states set new priorities and frames of reference. Most notably, in the "post-colonial moment" – roughly the two decades that followed the end of World War II – transnational networks of solidarity took shape alongside leftist, Third-Worldist, labor unionist, or feminist ideologies, not religion. This era would prove exceptional in that way, with Islam only occasionally emerging as a site of connection among individual political leaders (e.g. at Afro-Asia conferences), or as a diplomatic tool deployed by non-Muslim states with large Muslim populations (e.g. the Soviet Union).

Marking the transition to the era of independent nation-states, this chapter has thus offered windows on how Muslims, in both majority and minority contexts, have interfaced with broader societal communities and states to (re-)define the role of religion. From the specific case studies of Indonesia, Pakistan, the Soviet Republics of Central Asia, Singapore, India, and Burma/Myanmar we can draw some comparative reflections. First of all, Islam was rarely accorded a preferential status in Muslim-majority countries, and often just as a reflection of ethnic identities; second, whereas colonial policies and boundaries had important consequences for post-colonial orders, the leaders of independent nation-states exerted much autonomy in (re-)shaping their countries, and the role of religion therein; third, desire for a more prominent role of religion did not exclusively mean the establishment of an "Islamic government" or the implementation of *shari'a* laws at the national level, but often translated into the religious renewal of society; and, despite the existence of international networks, in this long "post-colonial moment" Islam was mostly deployed alongside, and affected by, local developments.

Hence, as secular ideologies came to rule Muslim communities, some sectors of these populations set themselves to re-insert Islam in the picture, sometimes in the realm of politics, sometimes in society, through either peaceful or violent means. But regardless of their intellectual scope or strategic modalities, the territorial unit of reference remained the nation-state. And this was also evident for Muslim minority communities, even when their self-identified cultural-geographical expanse did not match political boundaries. Minorities' concerns and desires pertained to their being recognized as legitimate constituencies with their own self-determined identities.

Beginning in the 1960s, however, the secular nationalist platforms encountered increasing difficulties due to economic crises and social discontent, and thus the seeds of national-level bottom-up Islamization bore fruit. Religiously minded political activists and intellectuals started to look beyond their national boundaries to seek solidarity and alliances, strengthening their demands and organizations, reclaiming the idea – and reality – of a transnational *umma*.

Further Reading

'Aziz, A. (1967) *Islamic modernism in India and Pakistan, 1857–1964*, London: issued under the auspices of the Royal Institute of International Affairs by Oxford University Press.

Calvert, J. (2010) *Sayyid Qutb and the origins of radical Islamism*, New York, NY: Columbia University Press.

Crouch, M. (ed.) (2016) *Islam and the state in Myanmar: Muslim-Buddhist relations and the politics of belonging*, New Delhi: Oxford University Press.

Formichi, C. (2012) *Islam and the making of the nation: Kartosuwiryo and political Islam in twentieth-century Indonesia*, Leiden: KITLV.

Ghassem-Fachandi, P. (2012) *Pogrom in Gujarat: Hindu nationalism and anti-Muslim violence in India*, Princeton, NJ: Princeton University Press.

Harvey, B. S. (1977) *Permesta: half a rebellion*, Ithaca, NY: Cornell Modern Indonesia Project, Southeast Asia Program, Cornell University.

Jalal, A. 1994. *The sole spokesman: Jinnah, the Muslim League, and the demand for Pakistan*, Cambridge and New York, NY: Cambridge University Press.

Kahin, A. (1999) *Rebellion to integration: West Sumatra and the Indonesian polity, 1926–1998*, Amsterdam: Amsterdam University Press.

Kahin, G. M. T. (1952) *Nationalism and revolution in Indonesia*, Ithaca, NY: Cornell University Press.

Kepel, G. (1985) *Muslim extremism in Egypt: the prophet and pharaoh*, Berkeley, CA: University of California Press.

Khalid, A. (1998) *The politics of Muslim cultural reform: Jadidism in Central Asia*, Berkeley, CA: University of California Press.

(2014) *Islam after communism: religion and politics in Central Asia*, Berkeley, CA: University of California Press.

Laffan, M. F., Prakash, G., and Menon, N. (Eds.) (2018) *The postcolonial moment in South and Southeast Asia*, London: Bloomsbury Academic.

Long, R. D. (2015) *A history of Pakistan* (first ed.), Karachi: Oxford University Press.

Metcalf, B. D. (2002) *"Traditionalist" Islamic activism: Deoband, Tablighis, and Talibs*, ISIM Papers 4, Leiden: ISIM.

(2009) *Islam in South Asia in practice*, Princeton, NJ: Princeton University Press.

Metcalf, B. D., and Metcalf, T. R. (2012). *A concise history of modern India* (3rd ed.), Cambridge: Cambridge University Press.

Osman, M. N. (2018) "The secular and the religious in the management of Islam in Singapore," *Journal of Muslim Minority Affairs* 38(2): 246–262.

Osella, F., & Osella, C. (Eds.) (2013) *Islamic reform in South Asia*, Cambridge: Cambridge University Press.

Pipes, R. (1964) *The formation of the Soviet Union: communism and nationalism, 1917–1923* (rev. ed.), Cambridge: Harvard University Press.

Ro'i, Y. (2000) *Islam in the Soviet Union: from the Second World War to Gorbachev*, New York, NY: Columbia University Press.

Schimmel, A. (1980) *Islam in the Indian subcontinent*, Leiden: Brill.

Tasar, E. (2017) *Soviet and Muslim: the institutionalization of Islam in Central Asia, 1943–1991*, New York, NY: Oxford University Press.

Verghese, A. (2016) *The colonial origins of ethnic violence in India*, Stanford, CA: Stanford University Press.

Figure 6.1 Indonesian domestic workers participating in
a demonstration in Hong Kong.
© Kees Metselaar

Young Indonesian women have been migrating to the Arab Gulf as maids and nannies since the oil boom of the 1970s and 1980s, but after the economic rise of Asia, work in Taiwan, Macau, and Hong Kong became much more attractive, partly because of notorious negative living conditions in the Gulf, and partly because of East Asia's closer proximity to home. But whereas in the Gulf Indonesian workers were able (if not coerced) to follow an Islamic lifestyle, in predominantly Chinese settings Islam was seen as a foreign entity.

As Way Yip Ho suggests, "at the same time as employers struggle to understand – and often willfully refuse to accommodate – the religious needs of Muslim Foreign Domestic Workers (FDWs), the sheer presence of veiled women and the mere encounter with a non-pork diet pressures Chinese employers to acknowledge this cultural and religious difference."[1] Muslim FDWs have been known to be forced to eat pork, pray in bathrooms while hiding from their employers, or wear "hats" to cover their heads. But through the years, and especially since the mid-2000s, Islam has become a most visible presence in Hong Kong.

On Sundays, groups of women are now seen in the island's iconic Victoria Park praying or holding religious education circles. The Kowloon Mosque, for decades an exclusively South Asian and male-dominated space, is now much more diverse, with flocks of Southeast Asian women attending (and even organizing) events there. At the same time, more Hong Kong middle-class families have become aware of what it means to be a Muslim.

This major shift, which has forced Hong Kong Chinese to face Islam on a daily basis, as maids pray, fast, request pork-free food, or wear a headscarf on their day off, was not the mere outcome of changing demographics – Indonesians are now both the largest Muslim group and the largest immigrant group in Hong Kong – but was most of all the result of these women's growing interest in embracing and displaying more outward forms of personal piety. For some, this was a reaction to an overwhelmingly secular culture; for others, it was a way to re-discover themselves after difficult encounters with drugs and alcohol abuse, or to make sense of their world after enduring physical abuse; or, more simply, it was a safe space in which to foster friendships, meaningful relations, and a support network, with other women with similar stories.

Ultimately, Hong Kong (like Taipei, Macau, etc.) has become an important site for the Islamization phenomenon that since the 1970s has enveloped much of Asia, the so-called *da'wa* movement. Displays of piety, such as wearing a headscarf or participating in Islamic education circles, have been primarily about expressing one's religious identity in an effort to connect with other communities on the grounds of religious affiliation.

Transnational connections, fostered by more widely accessible technologies of travel and communication, intertwined with socio-political shifts across Muslim societies from the 1960s onwards, ultimately contributing to shaping a self-consciously "global *umma.*" In Figure 6.1, in which Indonesian FDWs participate in a July 1 demonstration protesting against China's 1997 annexation of Hong Kong alongside a variety of other groups, members of the Indonesian Muslim Migrant Alliance (GAMMI) are self-identifying as migrant workers, but also as Muslims, through their institutional affiliation (clearly marked on the banners they hold) as well as their headscarves. In fact, GAMMI had been established in 2006 with a dual identity, being concerned with both labor rights of FDWs and their members' connection with Islamic beliefs and practices.

★★★

We have seen how Pakistan, Indonesia, and Soviet Central Asia's struggles to renegotiate the role of Islam in their respective state-structures and societies from the late 1940s to the mid-1960s were largely stimulated, driven, and shaped by domestic concerns (see Chapter 5). Men and women joined national Muslim groups and they took a variety of paths toward individual reform and spiritual strengthening, as well as institutionalization of religious political systems, some through peaceful engagements (*da'wa*, politics, and education) and others embracing political violence. The late 1960s open a new era, when nation-based movements intersected with various strands of intellectual, political, and spiritual devotion generated abroad.

While often the spotlight will appear to be on the influence of foreign and transnational phenomena – such as the Egyptian Muslim Brotherhood, Ayatollah Khomeini and the Iranian Revolution, the Saudi Arabia-based Muslim World League, the Jerusalem-born Hizb ut-Tahrir, or the Indian Tablighi Jama'at – the primary goal of this chapter is to investigate how domestic socio-political transformations across Asia generated a need for reconfigurations of Islamic piety, thus creating fertile soil for these "exogenous" groups. Case studies range from the consolidation of political Islam within government structures in Malaysia to the intellectual impact of the Iranian Revolution among disenchanted Indonesian youth, the religious awakening of post-Cultural Revolution China, and the spread of *da'wa* movements in the post-Soviet Central Asian Republics.

Highlighting the inherently transnational as well as profoundly national character of new imaginations of piety between the 1960s and the 1990s (whether in political, activist, or exclusively spiritual terms), this chapter marks Asia as integral to the picture of global Islam by following the multidirectional intersections between local desires to reframe patterns of Islamic devotion and international *da'wa* and solidarity networks.

Reactions to Secularism

After World War II, the outlook of several Asian and African countries, from Morocco to Iraq, China, and Indonesia, was characterized by secular nationalism and state-directed economic development. The sidelining of religion progressed hand in hand with widespread education and urbanization, but since many developmentalist targets were missed, the only tangible outcome was a disconnected and crumbling social landscape. The 1960s and 1970s then came to be shaped by disillusionment with secularism, and the consequent quest for an alternative mode of being, favored the emergence of Islamic revivalist movements.

Able to garner popular support among the merchants, the (largely underemployed) educated middle-class, internal migrants, and students by offering them a solid structure for community life, the Islamic vision provided an alternative system that encompassed "moral guidance, social justice, solidarity, work cooperation, and political goals."[2] What is more, in this environment Islamic scriptures did not provide a past reality to copy in current times, but were rather a source of inspiration capable of adaptation to contextual circumstances.

If not unique in its experience, Egypt emerged as a trailblazer in this process of reimagined piety that saw the confluence of social engagement, Islamic devotion, and (often but not necessarily) political activism. Gamal Abdel Nasser (1918–1970, president 1956–1970) obtained political-military control of Egypt in 1952 after years of turmoil and scheming. But although he had received support from the Muslim Brotherhood (see Box 6.1), Nasser had eventually created a state shaped by secular norms: laws, courts, education, consumer values, gender

---

Box 6.1   The Muslim Brotherhood

The Society of the Muslim Brothers was established by Hasan al-Banna (1906–1949) in 1928, as an organization focused on contrasting Western modernity and secularism in late-colonial Egypt. Al-Banna, inspired by Rashid Rida (see Chapter 4), hinged the Society's work on the principle of *da'wa* as an individual obligation. This path of reform focused on Muslims and the role of education, and was located within mosques, which the Society saw as "schools [for] the commoners, the popular universities and the colleges that lend educational services to the young and old alike."[3] This idea of *da'wa* as a personal duty, combined with a critique of institutionalized religious knowledge, ultimately created the structure for the popularization of *da'wa* as an informal process of reform. Even though the Qur'an exhorts men and women alike, the Society remained largely a men's effort, with its women's section – Muslim Sisters – relegated to the role of teachers within the family. But just a decade later, Zaynab al-Ghazali (b. 1917) established an independent Society of Muslim Ladies. Initially only concerned with providing charitable services, in the late 1940s and 1950s this Society trained women in "the art of preaching." Notably, al-Ghazali refused to merge with al-Banna, even though she actually took the reins of the Muslim Brotherhood when Nasser arrested its most prominent leaders. A similar dynamic has emerged in more recent times, as in the early 2000s women members of the Egyptian Brotherhood stepped in during Hosni Mubarak's repression. As Saba Mahmood pointed out, al-Ghazali's activism "occurred at the height of the early nationalist period in Egypt wherein the status of women and their visibility in public life was made a key signifier of the new nation, an emphasis that later declined."[4]

---

roles, etc. were all aspects of Egypt's public sphere and society which were modeled on a Western understanding of modernity. Seeing this about-face, the Muslim Brotherhood begun to voice their discontent; their opposition gained much traction under the leadership of Sayyid Qutb (1906–1966), leading to a brutal repression of political Islam in general and to the execution of Sayyid Qutb in particular.

When a year later, in what is usually referred to as the "Six-Day War" (June 1967), Israel occupied territories home to over one million Arabs and previously administered by Egypt, Syria, and the Palestinian government (namely, the Sinai Peninsula, the Gaza Strip, the Golan Heights, and the West Bank of the Jordan river), Egypt's military failure became a rallying point for Muslims whose political concerns had been marginalized and repressed during the Nasser regime, but also more widely. The year 1967 was then a first wake-up call announcing that the path undertaken by many Muslim-majority countries was not serving their populations well. As had happened in the late nineteenth century *vis-à-vis* Europe, political-military inadequacy was once again interpreted as a sign of religious insufficiency, and thus it fomented the desire for a reinvigoration of Islamic values.

The Arab–Israeli conflict continued on, taking a variety of forms. Following another Israeli victory in 1973, oil-producing Arab countries led a boycott against the US and other Western countries that supported Israel. The boycott itself was a failure in the immediate terms of the war, but in the long run it ensured Saudi Arabia's economic wealth: oil prices quadrupled in a matter of weeks, and by 1976 the Kingdom had become the largest oil producer in the world. In the following years, Saudi Arabia raised its selling prices while reducing supplies, filling its coffers even more rapidly. These new monies were then channeled toward domestic infrastructures (such as roads and new urban developments) and – more relevantly for the outside world – to support the "export" of the Saudi religious ideology, Wahhabism.

This mobilization of Islam as a social (and sometimes political) force was soon to intersect with parallel transformations across the Asian continent. Re-centering the conversation on Asia, Pakistan comes sharply into focus, as after the secession of Bangladesh, the 1970s were marked by the deployment of Islam as a tool of national unification.

Zulfiqar 'Ali Bhutto (1929–1979) issued a new constitution, which in 1973 sanctioned Islam as the state religion and required a commitment from civil servants to "strive to preserve Islamic ideology." All laws were to undergo review for Islamic compliance, and all school children were to take Islamic education classes; by 1974 the Ahmadis were declared non-Muslims because of their belief that there had been another prophet after Muhammad. But 'Ali Bhutto also projected Pakistan on the international Islamic scene, hosting the second Islamic Summit conference (1974), which revolved exclusively around the Palestinian question and the need for Muslim solidarity worldwide.

Despite Bhutto's readiness to appease the religious elite, in 1977 General Muhammad Zia ul-Haqq was able to stage a coup and takeover, with the support of the Pakistan National Alliance, a group combining diverse ideological strands but overall under the control of Mawdudi's Jama'at-e Islami (JI). Mawdudi had stepped down during the Bhutto era due to health issues, and after a period of stagnation the movement had re-emerged as a government-allied force that actively contributed to the Islamization of the Pakistani state. After decades of opposition, JI was finally operating alongside a political leader amenable to establishing an Islamic state as envisioned by Mawdudi, as Zia ul-Haqq continued to advance a clear, steady, and thorough agenda of Islamization. A key

watershed moment for Pakistan came in the year 1979: although Mawdudi had died in Buffalo, NY, after a last attempt at medical intervention,
Zia ul-Haqq promulgated four ordinances to codify in the country's
criminal code adultery, wrongful accusation of adultery, theft, and alcohol consumption (the so-called *hudud* crimes, see Box 2.2).

As it happens, 1979 – the opening year of the fourteenth Islamic
century – was a turning point in the relationship between Islam and
politics, not just for Pakistan but for Muslims across the globe. In the
same week that Zia ul-Haqq passed the Hudud Ordinance, Ayatollah
Khomeini (1902–1989) was allowed to return to Iran from his Parisian
exile; succeeding in unifying all factions of the anti-Shah movement, he
was thus shortly thereafter (on February 11) able to proclaim the Islamic
Republic of Iran as a Shi'i theocratic state.

A fourth event worth noting here was Saddam Hussein's appointment
as president of Iraq in July, following his own take over and purge of the
ruling Baathist Party. As he domestically suppressed the Shi'i majority
(alongside the Kurdish minority), by the end of the year Iraq and Iran
had entered a territorial and religio-ideological war that would last eight
years, costing hundreds of thousands of lives. Lastly, on Christmas Eve,
the Soviet Army invaded Afghanistan, triggering a ten-year war that
pitted communism against Islam (this is the focus of Chapter 7).

These individual events were to become deeply interconnected on
the global plane: first, in combination with the rise of Saudi Arabia, the
Iranian Revolution politicized the Sunni–Shi'a split, as witnessed by
the Iran–Iraq war and Zia ul-Haqq's Islamization policies (which exacerbated sectarian relations in Pakistan). Second, the Iran–Iraq war led to
a drop in oil supplies to the West from both countries – this was partly
due to a decrease in production, but also to the rescission of contracts
between Iran and the USA. This second oil crisis in less than five years
ultimately allowed for the strengthening of Saudi Arabia as an international force. Not only was Saudi Arabia able to increase oil prices at
will, but also – and more importantly – petro-dollars were funneled into
the further assertion of the Saudi state as the defender and promoter of
(Wahhabi) Islam on the global scene.

Further interconnecting these threads, in the 1980s the Cairene Muslim
Brotherhood found its way to Malaysia, and there it intersected with local
socio-political developments; disenchanted Indonesian youth read the
works of the Iranian revolutionaries 'Ali Shariati and Khomeini; Bangsa
Moro independentists from the Philippines encountered Mu'ammar
Ghaddafi of Libya, while Syrian students were inspired by the Pakistani
Mawdudi; and Arabs went to fight the anti-Soviet *jihad* in Afghanistan.
Chinese Muslims were re-connected to the global *umma* shortly after

Box 6.2   The Vocabulary of Islamic Activism

The strategies and efforts of Muslims in the late colonial and early post-colonial era might have been "new" compared to previous decades, but their models were deeply grounded in the history of Islamic civilizations. Their choice of terminology shows this connection to "the tradition," but also highlights the necessary tweaks and changes in nuance necessary to adapt to the (inevitable) changes in circumstances.

Hijra

The memory of Muhammad's migration from Mecca to Medina in 622 was referenced by groups who advocated forms of separation from environments they deemed non-Islamic, often defined as *jahiliyya*, again an early Islamic term which connoted "ignorance" of Islam. *Hijra* came to mean political non-cooperation with colonial authorities, non-engagement in party politics, the creation of self-reliant segregated communities (see e.g. the Darul Arqam in Malaysia, Chapter 8), and many other things. The concept of *hijra* hinges on the assumption that the surrounding environment is not only "ignorant" of the Islamic revelation (as it was in the case of pagan Arabia), but – more dramatically – because of its rejection of Islam. These concepts, then, have often been invoked in conjunction with the idea of *takfir*, a term related to *kafir* ("infidel") and literally meaning "marking someone as infidel." Fringe groups (e.g. ISIS today, but many others in recent history) and others with a broader presence (such as the Wahhabis), have embraced *takfir* as a way to exclude Muslims who embrace different persuasions (in terms of legal interpretation, political affiliation, etc.), to marginalize them or – in violent contexts – to deem their killing permissible. *Takfir* and *jahiliyya* were devised as political strategies in the twentieth century by Abu A'la Mawdudi (Pakistan) and Sayyid Qutb (Egypt) (see Box 5.1).

Da'wa

In the Qur'an God exhorts believers to "Invite to the Way of your Lord with wisdom and beautiful preaching, and argue with them in ways that are best and most gracious" (Q 16:125). It was this invitation or "call" (*da'wa*) that had allowed for the formation of a community of Muslims in Mecca. By the eighteenth century, and more prominently in the twentieth century, *da'wa* reflected an effort by Muslims to "redirect" other Muslims on the "right path" (e.g. Tablighi Jama'at in South Asia and Central Asia, see below). University campuses became key areas of operation for *da'wa* groups, which fashioned their work as "education" (*tarbiya*), conducted in small gender-segregated study circles (*halaqa*) that often turned into a student's new community, or "family" (*usra*). This idea of study cell as "family" was first introduced by the Egyptian Hasan al-Banna, who in 1928 established the Muslim Brotherhood (Ikhwan al-Muslimin) as an organization aimed at reconnecting the local youth to an "Islamic way of life." By the 1960s the Muslim Brotherhood and its methods had spread well beyond Egypt's boundaries (see Box 6.1).

Deng Xiaoping instituted the Open Door Policy (1978); and some scholars in the Muslim Soviet republics were able to obtain copies of the works by Qutb and Mawdudi, circulating them in illegal study circles.

Malay Brothers, Malay Sisters

In May 1969, Malaysia's capital (Kuala Lumpur) and other urban centers across the country were shaken with riots, mostly targeting the local Chinese minority. Racial tensions had been simmering since the provisional results of the general elections had indicated less support for the multi-ethnic ruling coalition (the National Front, Barisan Nasional, BN): Malays appeared to be as disappointed with the Malay party (UMNO) as the Chinese were with their own representatives.

The Barisan Nasional had ruled post-colonial Malaysia as a coalition party that embodied the compromise between the recognition of Malays' political prominence (the Malay party, UMNO, led the coalition) and the integration of the "immigrant" Chinese and Indians; members of these communities had been granted citizenship but were still seen as foreigners, despite the fact that they had been present on Malayan soil for multiple generations, often going back to the eighteenth century. This provision, often referred to as "the bargain," had been enshrined in the 1957 constitution, and had institutionalized the silo-like structure of Malayan colonial society, which for almost 200 years had separated the Chinese miners and shop-owners from the Indian plantation laborers, and the latter from indigenous peasant Malays. This separation affected all subjects, as all political associations in the 1940s and early 1950s envisioned their goals in terms of ethno-nationalism, despite the common anti-colonial goal.

The riots, then, were a sign that this precarious and artificial balance was fracturing. In an attempt at reaching a new balance, in the 1970s the coalition government launched a platform of "National Principles" (Rukun Negara, not so different from Indonesia's Pancasila), while also introducing reforms to reinforce the socio-economic position of the Malays vis-à-vis the Chinese. But these reforms, aimed at restoring stability and national unity, in fact led to a further disaggregation of society.

Malay quotas were set for the public sector, private enterprises, and higher education, at the expense of Chinese and Indians. Increasing numbers of Malays (men *and* women) left the villages and became urbanized, entered the bureaucracy, and attended universities, in Malaysia and abroad – in the West, as well as across Asia.

Hand in hand with these economic reforms, affirmative action was also promoted in the cultural sphere, with the primary language of education shifting from English to Malay. This move, alongside the economic reforms, snowballed a series of social transformations that led to an identity crisis for the Malays. By constitution, a Malay was someone who practiced Malay '*adat*, spoke the Malay language, and practiced Islam. But as "Malay traditions" were being gradually eroded by "modernization" and urbanization, and as the Malay language became the national language, the Malays were left with just Islam as their defining identitarian element, as Judith Nagata has argued.[5]

Until the 1960s Malaysian politics and society had been exclusively organized along ethnic lines, trumping any other political project (e.g. women's rights or labor unionism). Post-1969 policies (inadvertently) changed this, and religion emerged as a marker of political identity. Even though these policies had actually imagined the Malays as an ethnic group, stressing race as the primary marker of "affirmative action," the "Malay-ization" of the public cultural sphere, together with the erosion of traditional values, led to the re-definition of "being Malay," no longer as a three-point identity but as a primarily religious one.

Looking at the big picture of transforming society, we can see how migration to the cities created, in general terms, a sense of loss of the (extended) family network and community. Kuala Lumpur had attracted many Malay (Muslim) youth, but the city itself had been predominantly inhabited by non-Muslims, and thus lacked an infrastructure of Islamic networks and displayed a greater ethno-religious diversity than any rural village (*kampung*) in the Peninsula. A last unsettling aspect of urbanization related directly to gender dynamics, as in the 1970s many unmarried young women had found financial independence and social emancipation through employment in the electrical and manufacturing industries.

It is against this domestic backdrop of socio-political transformation that the "foreign" models of Islamic devotion and activism inserted themselves in Malaysia. As in Egypt, the combination of state-driven development, urbanization, access to higher education, erosion of traditional values and social structures, and political discontent all shaped an environment favorable to processes of reimaginations of piety as a tool to transform society. Their influence in Malaysia was channeled in student and youth groups who focused on renewing Malay Muslims' call to Islam, as well as in political parties.

At the societal level, then, many Malays came to focus on their religious identity. In the 1970s a handful of Malay university graduates established the Muslim Youth Movement of Malaysia (ABIM), whose activities aimed at renewing Malay Muslims' religious piety and know-ledge; their intellectual legacy evidently rested on the Egyptian Muslim Brotherhood and Mawdudi's JI. Under ABIM, *halaqa* study circles were implanted all over the country to propagate the Muslim Brotherhood-inspired educational method (*tarbiya*), and true to this legacy, women – who traditionally had played active roles in society – were embraced only as second-tier members. ABIM activities were segregated along gender lines, and women's professional engagements were allowed only if their primary roles as mothers and wives could be preserved.

Some Malays had been exposed to Muslim Brotherhood ideas as early as the 1940s and 1950s, mostly through travel to Arabia and Egypt and through the circulation of Ikhwani publications. Another line of transmission had taken place in Malaya itself, as upon Nasser's ban of the organization in 1954, several Ikhwanis traveled to Malaya, and were occasionally employed at Malayan universities. Yet others came into contact with the Muslim Brotherhood and Mawdudi's ideas in the west, as North American and British universities in the 1970s had become breeding grounds for both the socially oriented *da'wa* movement and political Islamist groups.

At its inception, the leaders of the Islamist party (the Pan-Malayan Islamic Party, PAS) had been deeply informed by the Muslim Brotherhood: one had studied in Egypt and had attended lectures by Hasan al-Banna and Sayyid Qutb; another had published magazines and translations to introduce reformist ideas and Qutb's own works to Malay Muslims. But this was just a phase, and the influence of these groups never succeeded, for example, in curbing the participation of women in the party. Under the leadership of Datin Sakinah Junid – wife of PAS chairman Datuk Asri (1969–1982) and previously active in the anti-colonial movement – PAS established a women's section, the *Kaum Muslimat*, which "fully endors[ed] women's contributions to public social life through voluntary service or as teachers" but saw them as unsuitable for leadership over men.[6]

In the immediate post-riot years, PAS entered into an alliance with the ruling coalition, and thus re-oriented its focus on ethno-nationalism, openly rejecting the *da'wa* effort and the Muslim Brotherhood's vision. The 1980s marked a third phase, as the influence of Islamism on Malaysia's socio-political scene forced a leadership change and the embrace of what Dominik Müller has defined "an ideologically 'de-racialised', newly Middle Eastern-inspired and more internationalist – although still highly localised" brand of Islamism.[7] In this new framework, inspiration came largely from Iran and Khomeini's vision of a political leadership of the *'ulama* (*velayat-e faqih*). In the early 1980s, PAS cadres restructured the party to resemble Iran's government, implementing the Ulama

Leadership blueprint by creating a superior post for a spiritual leader (mirroring both Iran's Supreme Leader and the Muslim Brotherhood's General Guide, or *murshid 'amm*) who oversaw a consultative council. To appease those concerned about PAS taking Shi'i Iran as a model, the party also issued a renewed affirmation of PAS as a Sunni institution.

The narrative of the Islamization of post-colonial Malaysia is then one characterized by the constantly moving intersection of the social with the political and of the local with the foreign. It can be tempting to stress the role of the "global Islamic revival" and the impact of international *da'wa* groups and networks of solidarity in Malays' refashioning of their identity as primarily Muslims. Yet, it ought to be noted that even though the government (UMNO) had initially remained anchored to ethnic-based identity politics, from the 1980s onwards the Malaysian state became the primary sponsor of Islamization. Under Mahathir's leadership, and with the support of ABIM co-founder Anwar Ibrahim, UMNO created the image of the Malay party as an Islamic party (although not everyone agreed with that), leading a process of Islamization that was controlled, top-down, development-friendly, and openly disengaged from foreign Islamist networks.

While Mahathir supported the strengthening of "state Islam" (as indicated by the establishment of an Islamic university, medical centers, Islamic courts, and *shari'a*-compliant banks), he also proved his readiness to eradicate any form of Islam that might have threatened the established authority of the state (e.g. the quashing of the Darul Arqam movement; see Chapter 8). Mahathir's priorities were multifarious. Besides keeping control of the Islamization process and political primacy, he also drove the economic advancement of the Malays. Under his tenure as prime minister, Malaysia emerged as a successful case of Asian capitalism (notably possible only because of the intervention of a developmentalist state and a curbing of civil liberties). The combination of these approaches eventually led to a projection of Malaysia as a modern, developed, stable, and Islamized country.

In this phase of Malaysia's history, social-economic reform increased women's education and employment in white-collar jobs, while the emergence of *da'wa* as a "normalized cultural practice," to borrow from Aihwa Ong,[8] also allowed them to "carve out a religious space for themselves in a modernizing Muslim society, thereby strengthening their Islamic identity." Hence, even though politically (and in terms of religious hierarchies) they might have been subjected to male authority, Sylva Frisk has suggested that Malay women in the early 1990s "construct[ed] themselves as religious actors and as religious persons, and by this process transform[ed] the practice of Islam in Malaysia"[9] (see Source 6.1)

Source 6.1

Minah's Veiling

This first-person account tells of the encounter between anthropologist Sylva Frisk and one of her informants, Minah (not her real name), in Kuala Lumpur in the mid-1990s. Frisk was conducting research on the position of women in the da'wa *movement, exploring ways in which women were able to carve out spaces of their own in usually male-dominated arenas. This excerpt looks back in time at Minah's relationship to the* da'wa *movement and her own deliberations over veiling.*[10]

When I [author Sylva Frisk] met Minah she was a professional woman in her mid-thirties. She was unmarried and devoted much of her spare time to Muslim charity work and to religious studies. She was born [in the 1950s] in a village on the east coast of Malaysia but was quite young when she was sent to a boarding school on the west coast. Her father had been the village *ustaz* [teacher] but he had been very particular about providing his children with a good secular education. He was therefore very pleased when Minah was offered the chance of doing her secondary education in an English-medium boarding school ... After secondary school, she chose to further her science studies at university in Kuala Lumpur. Minah told me that it was in her final year at college, in 1972–1973, that something happened to her that made her aware of her Muslim identity. There was a public holiday on account of the Chinese New Year and some students were arranging a day seminar on Islam. A friend of hers was involved and invited her to come along. Minah expressed this as a turning point. She said that it was the first time that she realized that religion was part of who she was. Overnight, she started to wear the *tudung* [headscarf] and *baju kurung* [Malay women's tunic]. She remembered that she only had three sets of *baju kurung* and she wore them out completely in just six months. Before this she used to wear short skirts and T-shirts like everyone else. Minah's newfound identity was, however, not strong enough to last. When college was over and she started to work, she found it difficult to stay with Islam. After about a year and a half she took off her scarf. Her own reflections about this were of two sorts. First, she believed that her awakening to Islam happened too fast, overnight. Second, she described the situation in 1973 as difficult for someone in *tudung*. Almost nobody was covered at that time and people used to stare art her. She said that she felt like an "alien." Nobody else at work was covered and she found it very difficult to keep it up without support from someone else. Her interest in Islam was still strong and she took part in religious activities and tried to learn as much as possible about her religion. About fifteen years later, times had changed and Minah was ready again. The *dakwah* [*da'wa*] movement had spread far beyond the university campus and veiled women had become an everyday sight. Minah started to cover again in connection with performing the hajj. Since then, her commitment to Islam has just grown stronger, making her increasingly secure in her Muslim identity.

Box 6.3   The Veil and Politics

The veil has been interpreted by white men (but also women, and secular Muslims of both sexes) as a symbol of women's oppression and, as such, as the stumbling block on women's paths to advance in Muslim societies.[11] Several women scholars have placed under the spotlight "colonial feminism" and the obsession of British (Leila Ahmed),[12] French (Marnia Lazreg),[13] and Americans (Lila Abu-Lughod)[14] over the veil. In mid-1958 – just a few years before Algeria gained independence – a group of French generals brought into the North African capital bus-loads of Algerians from the countryside, staging them as supporters of the colonial regime. On that occasion, during "a well-choreographed ceremony," the few women present were "solemnly unveiled by French women" as a symbol of Europe's drive to free and emancipate women.[15] More recently, the US invaded Afghanistan pledging – among other things – to rescue Afghan women from the Taliban.

During most of New Order Indonesia (1967–1998), veiling was forbidden in public schools and government offices, and the appearance of headscarves there in the 1980s and 1990s was a marked sign of socio-political dissent against the state and traditional culture. Similarly, the veil was a political symbol in the revolutionary movement that brought the fall of the Pahlavi Shah and the emergence of the Islamic Republic of Iran in 1979 (and in 2018 "unveiling" became a public symbol of resistance). In Western China (Xinjiang province) villages and cities are plastered with government-sponsored advertisements marking veiled women as conservative, and uncovered ones as "modern." In Hong Kong, every Sunday public places are flooded by Indonesian Foreign Domestic Workers who wear the headscarf on their "day off" to express a religious aesthetic that is often denied to them in everyday life by their employers. The Taliban enforced the *burqa* (or *chadri*) on all women living in the territory they controlled in 1990s Afghanistan, but historical and anthropological studies have shown that the *chadri* emerged as an empowering tool, a "mobile home" that enabled women to participate in society while maintaining the integrity of their moral and religious requirements.

The politics of veiling is, then, a complex phenomenon, as government efforts to control societies through the policing of women's bodies and dress have been recorded in Europe, America, and Asia alike, and regardless of whether a state was promoting veiling or unveiling (Chapter 4).

Da'wa in Central Asia

Partly as a reaction to the long-lasting Soviet suppression of religion in the public arena, partly because of the opening of their borders to foreign Muslims, the fragmentation of the Soviet Union in the 1990s translated, among other phenomena, into the emergence of political Islam in the newly independent republics of Tajikistan, Uzbekistan, Kazakhstan, Kyrgyzstan, and Turkmenistan. Yet, it would be a mistake to assume that the Islamic resurgence affected these Muslim populations only from the 1990s.

Following the ebbs and flows of the Soviet regime, Islam had seen its position shift through the decades. While the USSR was moving toward a domestic identity crisis, which it faced by encouraging the re-discovery of its peoples' roots to "reinvolve and reinvigorate a citizenry which was rapidly sinking into drunken, degenerate indifference,"[16] internationally the Soviet Union also needed to strengthen its alliances. The tumult of the Khrushchev years (1953–1964) had dealt a hard blow to the country, but Brezhnev's takeover in 1964 (until 1982) introduced some stability under the guiding principle that the Soviet Union had reached the second-last stage before obtaining communism, "the period of mature socialism."

Against the backdrop of the Cold War and the Sino-Soviet split (1963), Moscow thought it convenient, in the mid-to-late-1960s, to rally support from Arab nations which belonged to the non-Aligned movement but also embraced a form of economic socialism. To achieve this goal, the Soviet leadership continued to involve SADUM and to loosen restrictions previously imposed on its Muslim populations. Central Asian students were sent to study at religious institutions in Egypt, Syria, and Libya, and SADUM 'ulama traveled on friendly diplomatic missions, while Arab delegations were welcomed to visit the successful reality of Central Asia's communist development.

As the Six-Day War unfolded, Central Asia's Muslims demonstrated in support of the Arabs, participating in solidarity conferences, condemning the Israeli aggression as colonialist and imperialist, and requesting Soviet organizations to send them as volunteers to help the Arabs. In 1970 Tashkent hosted a conference "For the Unity and Cooperation of Muslims in the Struggle for Peace, Against Imperialist Aggression," giving further audience to the calls for transnational Islamic unity, as did the Samarkand International Islamic Conference held in 1974 to celebrate the 1,200th birthday of Imam al-Bukhari. These efforts were lauded in Arab West Asia, as political and religious leaders expressed gratitude to the Soviet government for its support.[17]

A decade later, a new thread connected the Soviet Union to the Arab world: oil. As Russian oil production sunk in the mid-1970s, the government begun to groom relations with Saudi Arabia, thus allowing a steadier flow of Wahhabi literature to enter Central Asia, and complementing the already present reformist literature which had begun to seep in during Brezhnev's opening-up in the 1960s.

SADUM had since the beginning embraced Islamic modernism, as it was better suited to advancing Soviet-friendly Islam than traditional Hanafi thought (as seen in Chapter 5). But in this new phase, SADUM, as the official Muslim body of Soviet Central Asia, had also become the receptacle of donations. Its library, then, housed copies of the literature that foreign Muslim delegations were bringing along; and all extra copies were distributed among unofficial (or unregistered) *'ulama* with connections to SADUM. This influx of foreign literature created a new dynamic. Increasing numbers of students were interested in modernist Islam, but unable to be absorbed into the official *madrasas*, which still accepted only a score of students each year, they went to study in unregistered *hujras*.

Whereas in the 1950s and 1960s *hujras* offered a different curriculum from SADUM, focusing almost exclusively on deepening their members' understanding of the Hanafi tradition, in the 1980s students in unregistered circles were exploring the writings of Ibn Taymiyah and more recent authors, including Hasan al-Banna, Sayyid Qutb, and Mawdudi. And while political shifts across the Muslim lands might have encouraged the 1980s popularization of scripturalist Islam and some forms of religiously inspired political activism, these phenomena mostly had "indigenous roots," as Eren Tasar argues.[18]

From its inception, SADUM had embraced a return to the scriptures and a rejection of local practices with the overall goal of forging a Soviet-Muslim identity, but under Brezhnev the Soviet state came to tolerate "gray spaces," and SADUM developed a "symbiotic relationship" with unregistered *'ulama*. The disputes among scholars – between those who argued for the validity of the Hanafi school (*taqlid*) and those who advocated for a direct interpretation of the scriptures (*ijtihad*) – were largely dogmatic and theological, rather than a political confrontation with the state.

In this context, the term "Wahhabi" came to describe (incorrectly) anyone who rejected Hanafi *fiqh* and any other strand of *ijtihad*-oriented scholarship and favored instead Salafi-inspired interpretations of the scriptures. But it is also true that beginning in 1980 the Soviet state had pressured SADUM to establish relations with the Muslim World League (MWL) in an effort to limit the impact of the Iranian Revolution and the Afghan *jihad*. Even though the MWL had been invited for sheer political reasons, Soviet Central Asian Muslims now received preferential treatment during the *hajj*, and were eligible for scholarships to study in North Africa and West Asia, facilitating the circulation of foreign materials.

As noted by Muhammadjan Hindustani (1892–1989, see Chapter 5), "several of the ulama had begun to gradually diverge from Hanafite doctrine"[19] in the late 1970s, largely under the influence of the Ikhwani and Wahhabi literature that had begun to enter the country, causing much factionalism among Muslim scholars. The first student of Muhammadjan Hindustani to break away was Hakimjon Qori; however, his "Wahhabi" inclination (in the rather loose sense of referring to any "fundamentalist" or "puritanical" approach in Soviet Central Asia) remained focused exclusively on theological matters. On the other hand, Rahmatullah-alloma (1950–1981) and Abduhvali Qori (b. 1952) – who had studied with both Hindustani and Hakimjon – condemned their teachers' "collaborationist" relation with the Soviet establishment and plunged into politics, forging connections with foreign Muslim students who provided access to the writings of 'Abd al-Wahhab, Mawdudi, and Sayyid Qutb. Reading these Islamist thinkers without the guidance of either SADUM or traditional teachers, they came to advocate for a more aggressive display of piety, the propagation of Islamist ideals, the establishment of an Islamic state (which they called Musulmanabad), and the use of force.

International connections played a key role in getting new readings into the country and steering the conversation toward politics. The state security apparatus (KGB) in Tashkent recognized the potential threat of politicized Islam as brokered by foreign students, but when it stipulated that they could no longer socialize with local Muslims, nor attend local mosques, it was already too late. By 1977–1978 the transformation had already taken place.

As in the early 1980s the Soviet Union embarked on a trajectory of gradual economic reform, and later in that decade it experienced a fragmentation of political authority, these groups were able to push their agenda to bring politicized Islam to the surface, publishing and distributing materials, changing their appearance, and challenging established authority. Local Islamist and revivalist groups were joined by "imported" groups, as foreign preachers were allowed in, literature flooded bookstores and libraries, and Islamic infrastructures were financed from abroad. Leading countries in these efforts were Pakistan, Saudi Arabia, and Turkey.

But if in the early years after *perestroika* Central Asian governments proved open to international Islam, this phase was rather short-lived. The new (secular, "sovietized") leaders who took the helm of Central Asian politics in the 1990s had initially accepted Islam as a necessary element of their citizens' national identity, following the Soviet example; however, the political bent taken by several groups, and their forging of international connections, turned Islam into a security threat.

Islam Karimov was elected Uzbekistan's president in 1991, and remained in power until his death in 2016, maintaining a strong grip on the country. On the one hand, he encouraged private displays of Islamic piety such as *hajj* and ritual prayers, tolerated a certain degree of societal Islamization (including polygamy), and welcomed opportunities to use Islam as a legitimizing force. The renovation of the shrine of Baha ud-Din Naqshband in Bukhara in the early 1990s, made possible through the financial contribution of Turkey, was such an example. On the other hand, though, Karimov's stand on non-governmental Islamic groups was firm. Demonstrations protesting Westernizing and secular reforms (e.g. the adoption of the Latin script), and demands for the implementation of *shari'a* laws, were regularly crushed; and legislation was passed to limit the social and political influence of religion. Uzbek Islamist leaders have "disappeared" and major mosques converted in civil public places.

In the 1990s the strongest challenge came from a militant Salafi group, the Islamic Movement of Uzbekistan (IMU). The movement was established in Afghanistan with the collaboration of Tajik Islamists with the goal to strive for the creation of an Islamic state all across Muslim Central Asia (including Xinjiang), but the US invasion of Afghanistan in 2001 led to the decimation of IMU, which only remained active in the Ferghana Valley. It was at about this same time that a new group started to emerge in the region, especially in Uzbekistan and the Ferghana Valley: the Hizb ut-Tahrir.

The Hizb ut-Tahrir, literally meaning "Liberation Party," has strived for a global caliphate projecting a social, *da'wa*-based (some say utopian) strategy, since the 1950s. The group was founded in 1953 as an underground political party by Taqiyuddin an-Nabhani (1909–1977), an al-Azhar graduate and a judge in the *shari'a* court of Jerusalem. Its foremost aim was to challenge the creation of the state of Israel (1948) and pave the path for a movement that would bring about a new Caliphate. For an-Nabhani this was necessary, as Saudi Arabia had been established as a dynastic monarchy and the Khilafat movement of the 1910s and 1920s – in all of its various geographical manifestations – had failed. But whereas the Khilafat had grown hand in hand with nationalist aspirations (see Chapter 4), an-Nabhani envisaged a truly global caliphate, thus expressly challenging the formation of post-colonial "bounded" Muslim nation-states.

It is against this backdrop that post-Soviet Central Asia appealed to Hizb ut-Tahrir's central leadership as a new playing field, challenging the secular authority of the Uzbek state and its neighbors. While it started its activities in the mid-1990s as a clandestine group targeting Uzbek ethnics and largely dipping into the region's prisons for new recruits, by the early 2000s the group had been able to expand its reach in the region, operating in the open, confronting both the state and other Islamist groups, and recruiting members of all ethnic groups and various backgrounds.

Whereas women have been largely disengaged from party politics in Uzbekistan, Hizb ut-Tahrir has proven particularly successful in recruiting them into its rank and file to the extent that estimates suggest up to 10 percent of the group's membership is constituted by women. Hizb ut-Tahrir advocates gender segregation and a rather conservative understanding of gender roles in the family, however:

> Women have the same rights and obligations as men, except for those specified by the *shar'i* evidences to be for him or her. Thus, she has the right to practice in trading, farming, and industry; to partake in contracts and transactions; to possess all form of property; to invest her funds by herself (or by others); and to conduct all of life's affairs by her.[20]

The organization has gathered support worldwide from women, who populate parallel branches regularly organizing conferences, educational events, etc.

In the Central Asian context, women seem to join the organization for a variety of reasons, ranging from their desire to continue the struggle of their (male) relatives who have been imprisoned, to allegations that women left alone by husbands who work seasonal jobs in Russia receive financial support from Hizb ut-Tahrir in exchange for their affiliation. As they are so rarely involved in politics, women are seen as extremely effective members, able to distribute (illegal) literature, recruit new members, and conduct attacks without raising too much suspicion from police forces. As a local analyst suggested,

> "Women's interest in this party might be linked to the fact that the party itself puts emphasis on working with women, and that is because – according to Central Asian traditions – there is a lower possibility of women being prosecuted [by the state]."[21]

Marked early on as a threat to the established authority, Hizb ut-Tahrir is not registered with the Uzbeki government – a key requirement for any religious organization – and has thus been illegal there since its inception; Kyrgyzstan and Tajikistan both banned it in the early 2000s, following the example of several other countries worldwide. As Karagiannis argued, Hizb ut-Tahrir has been able to carve out a niche in the region "as the only alternative to despotic and corrupted leaderships due to its diverse political agenda, simplistic program and non-violent political methodology."[22]

The early 2000s were a growth period also for other foreign Islamic groups in the region, and most notably two groups that find their origins in the Indian subcontinent. One is the Ahmadiyya; despite being considered heretical in Pakistan, Saudi Arabia, and a few other Muslim-majority countries, this group was able to gain new followers in relatively tolerant Kyrgyzstan until 2011, when the organization's registration was suspended for security reasons. The other is the Tablighi Jama'at (TJ), which possibly made its first appearance in Central Asia in the 1960s or 1970s, as students from the USSR were sent to study in India. A second wave of TJ expansion occurred in the early 1990s, when Tablighis from India and Pakistan traveled to the region. In more recent years the directionality seems to have become inverted, as Central Asian Tablighis are regularly found in the group's training centers in India, Pakistan, and Bangladesh. TJ started making a dent among Central Asia's Muslims in the post-9/11 era, probably thanks to its avowed apolitical and peaceful stance, which allowed it to proselytize more or less freely. That being said, Tablighis are also very visible, as they don the South Asian-styled *salwar kamiz* outfit, leading to mixed reactions.

The divergent treatment of TJ across Central Asia offers a window on this region's countries' response to the Islamic revival. In 2014, the newly appointed state *mufti* of Kyrgyzstan was a renown Tablighi leader, and its members there are not only free to pursue their *da'wa*, but they also enjoy a good degree of public recognition, partly because of the freedom accorded to religious groups in general, and partly as a result of cultural affinity. Tablighis' focus on "the basics" of Islam, their accommodation of indigenous practices, desire to eradicate alcohol and drug abuse, and itinerant lifestyle are all elements seen favorably by the government, which recognizes the peculiarities of a formerly nomadic, recently Islamized population. At the other extreme is Uzbekistan, where Tablighis are often arrested and imprisoned, and lumped together as "radical Islamists" with members of the IMU and Hizb ut-Tahrir. In between are Tajikistan and Kazakhstan. If the Tajik state does not recognize the TJ as a legal organization, largely because the government-allied Islamic party fears it as a potential competitor, in Kazakhstan TJ activists are mostly allowed to preach freely, even though in more recent years some have been imprisoned. Such diversity reflects a variety of political regimes, but also the fact that neither TJ nor Hizb ut-Tahrir is just a Central Asian organization; rather, they rely on broader regional networks and implement different strategies to achieve similar goals in the region.

Awakening in China

While West Asia and Muslim populations in many other areas were witnessing or experiencing the political changes that in the 1980s would lead to these reimaginations of Islamic piety, China was undergoing Mao's Cultural Revolution (1966–1976). As with pre-war Soviet policies and Khrushchev's renewed anti-religious campaigns, in 1950s China, religions – from Confucianism to Islam – were seen by the Maoist regime as a form of superstition propagated by feudal warlords to sustain the socio-economic status quo (following Marxism-Leninism) and as a form of foreign influence and infiltration (reflecting the approach of late nineteenth-century Qing political discourse). In the early years, Christian missionaries were expelled and Buddhist and Daoist monks and nuns were forced to return to "secular" life. But as the country fell deeper in the years of the Cultural Revolution, general repression gradually transitioned toward an attempt at completely eradicating religion. Places of worship and education were destroyed, books were burnt, and minorities became the target of violent repression. In July 1975, thousands of Chinese soldiers led a military attack on several villages in Shadian (Yunnan), killing hundreds of local Muslims belonging to the Hui ethnic minority group.

Mao Zedong's death in 1976 and the emergence of Deng Xiaoping as leader of communist China signaled the beginning of a new era characterized by a rejection of the Cultural Revolution, an attempt at social reconciliation, and, most famously, the re-insertion of China in the global economic market. In terms of religious policies, Deng Xiaoping recognized that Mao's eradication policies had actually led to a further entrenchment of religious beliefs. The Bureau of Religious Affairs was re-opened in 1979, followed by the re-establishment of Islamic Associations in all regions with considerable Muslim population, not only in Hui areas but also in Xinjiang, where a relaxation of religious policies was seen as necessary for improving economic relations with Central Asian states.

As new roads were built and borders were opened, China's Muslims went on *hajj*, traveled abroad to study, and fostered connections with other Muslim communities across the country, across Asia, and beyond. Muslims were allowed to perform daily ritual prayers in mosques, don Islamic clothes, display Islamic paraphernalia on the walls of their homes, fast during Ramadan, and celebrate canonical festivities, and in certain circles these behaviors conformed more and more to their West Asian models. The 1980s saw a spree of mosque-building as the government contributed to this endeavor, also as compensation for the many mosques that had been destroyed during the Cultural Revolution (to the extent that there are probably more mosques in China now than there were before the Cultural Revolution). Often the architectural style came to embrace Arab models, adopting domes and minarets and shunning the pagoda-like structure of older buildings (for local Chinese mosque architecture see Chapter 2).

But alongside many "conventional" mosques, many communities took the opportunity to refurbish extant women's mosques (*nusi*) or build new ones. And as pointed out by Jaschok and Shui, "the growth [of the *nusi* economy] laid a necessary material foundation for the development of women's religious culture."[23] Through the 1980s, then, many women's religious schools (*nuxue*) opened in Yunnan and the northwest provinces, usually attached to local mosques (possibly but not necessarily women's mosques) and financed locally by members of the community. At the same time, hybrid schools also sprang up, instructing young women in the official Chinese curriculum as well as religious subjects, the Arabic language, and Arabic Islamic canonical texts. This latter shift marked at once both a reorientation in vectors of knowledge production and trans-mission, and a change in gender dynamics: as traditionally women's religious texts had been in Persian, female *ahong*s were unable to teach the Arabic texts that constituted the core of the reformed curriculum, and male teachers became crucial to advance girls' education.

The Arabic script was re-introduced for the Uyghur and Kazakh languages, and mosques were rebuilt, first with government support and then, as economic conditions improved, through private donations – local and foreign. In 1985, the government funded an Islamic seminary in Urumqi (Xinjiang), and another one was built in 1988 in Yinchuan (Ningxia), marking a shift toward the de-centralization of religious education. However, as during the Cultural Revolution books had been burnt and teachers "reformed," knowledge and teaching materials had to be sought abroad. A note is necessary here to clarify that, even though current discourses in the People's Republic of China suggest that the 1980s were the time when Xinjiang's Uyghurs became "radicalized," fostering connections with their geographical and cultural neighbors in Central Asia and Pakistan, joining in the IMU, training as *mujahidin* in Afghanistan, or studying in Pakistani *madrasa*s (Chapter 7), debates among Uyghurs at the time were centered on the connection between ethno-nationalism and Islam, and most of the literature that made its way to the region from Saudi Arabia or Pakistan took the form of theological (rather than political) texts.

Not all Muslims in China experienced or participated in these pro-cesses of reimagination of piety, but the timing of when they were allowed to express their religiosity contributed to a religious awakening informed by global trends. Places that had previously been isolated came into contact with their regional hubs, and with increased communication and economic exchanges with West Asia came also efforts to "reconvert" or "re-Islamize" Muslims who were perceived as "ignorant" or "heterodox." The opening-up of China, with its enormous population, was not only appealing to those who, on the global market, sold material goods, but also to those who had new modes of religiosity to offer.

In 1981, the Saudi-based MWL visited China on an invitation from the PRC's Islamic Association, with the stated purpose of "obtain[ing] first hand information about the conditions of life of the Muslim community in China, and to offer, within the broader framework of Islamic cooperation, all possible moral and material help."[24] The League is an international organization, yet its being headquartered in Saudi Arabia causes it to be perceived as a body of the Kingdom and as committed to advancing the agenda of Saudi Arabia, including the spread of Wahhabism. Notably, relations between China and Saudi Arabia had already begun to warm up in the mid-1950s, with the establishment of the Islamic Association of China and Zhou Enlai's mediation to re-open *hajj* opportunities for Chinese Muslims.

The delegation visited the main coastal cities and traveled to Xinjiang, consistently noting the poor conditions of the mosques and the lack of educational institutions, Islamic literature, and even copies of the Qur'an; their report concluded that Chinese Muslims "did not seem very enthusiastic about Islam. Their souls seemed to have petrified and lost fervor in the absence of Islamic activity."[25] The League's delegation thus offered immediate support, in the form of literature and financial help (for a total of $1 million, for a current value of c. US$2,700,000) "for the repair of mosques and the education of their children," and made several recommendations, each one of which pointed to increased contact between Saudi Arabia and China's Muslims to "prevent their assimilation,"[26] mirroring dynamics that had been playing out already with the rest of Asia as well as Africa. However, each and every action of the League was to be approved by the state-controlled Islamic Association, meaning that little influence and impact was actually achieved (see Source 6.2).

At about the same time, in 1986, a group of Tablighi Jama'at missionaries arrived in China from Malegaon (in the western Indian state of Maharashtra), for a four-month *da'wa* tour. Salafi Islam and the TJ are the two revivalist movements that, through individual *da'wa*, have made the most inroads in China in the post-Mao era. But while they both promote a form of unadulterated Islam, rejecting all aspects of "Chinese" Islam, they differ in methodology (Salafis are scripturalists, whereas the Tablighis focus on ritual practice) and in their historical trajectory in China.

China's Salafiya emerged as a byproduct of interactions between East and West Asia, with Hui Muslims going on *hajj* and on study trips to Arabia and Cairo between the 1920s and 1930s. During his *hajj* of 1936,

Source 6.2

"Recommendations of the Muslim World League's Delegation to China," 1981

After Deng Xiaoping's re-opening of China's doors in the late 1970s, the Saudi Arabia-based Muslim World League was able to send a delegation to assess the conditions of China's Muslims. The delegation was concerned about the visible assimilation of the Hui, and the poor socio-economic status of the Uyghur, even though their religious strength seemed to be higher. The Delegation offered a series of recommendations to improve China's Muslims' infrastructures, education, and connections to other Muslim countries.[27]

The Muslim World League should continue giving all possible help to these Islamic Associations with the purpose of educating Muslims there about their faith and practice.

Though lacking in some respects, the efforts of the Islamic Association of China symbolize the desire on the part of the Chinese Muslims to preserve their Islamic identity and these efforts should be encouraged in every way.

The delegation suggested that the Muslim World League should approach various universities both inside and outside the Kingdom to make necessary arrangements for the admission of Chinese Muslim students into these universities. It would also arrange to bring over young students under 15 years of age to the Kingdom for receiving instruction in Islamic sciences and provide them with special facilities, so that when they go back they could re-enkindle the light of Islam in these far off lands ...

The next round of contacts with Chinese Islamic Associations should include two training courses, one in Peking and the other in Urumchi, to train Imams and religious speakers and to increase their ability to speak Arabic ...

Finally, we also propose that the Muslim World League should take up with the Islamic Association the issue of provision of facilities to Chinese Muslims for the performance of Hajj. The Association should in consultation with the Chinese government facilitate the Hajj journey ... We also propose that invitations to perform the Hajj on the sponsorship of the Muslim World League should every year regularly be extended to selected leaders of the Chinese Muslim Community.

the Hui Ma Debao encountered a Salafi *da'i*, Muhammad Habib Allah (also referred to as Habibullah, Huzandi, or Said Buharla, a testament to his being from Bukhara), and the two traveled to China to establish schools and spread Salafi thought in Gansu and Qinghai. Locally known as the "Faction of the Prophet's Teaching," the Salafiya was from the outset focused on purifying Islamic practices from localized cultural adaptations, and on instilling "Arab" modalities of ritual, opposing shrine veneration, incense burning, and Sufi mysticism. It was on these premises that the movement was persecuted and opposed as "heterodox" and "foreign" during China's Republican period (1912–1949). In 1950, however, the Salafiya had two mosques and several *imam*s in Hezhou (today's Linxia, in Gansu Province), and having positioned itself as a nonpolitical movement, the Salafiya saw a steep increase in its numbers following the domestic political crisis of the 1970s and the prominence of Islam internationally.

Nobody in China had instead ever heard of the Tablighi Jama'at before the 1980s. The re-awakening of Islamic piety in 1980s China has been framed in internal debates as pitting an "authentic" way of life modeled on the one crafted in the Arab center of Islam against the "inauthenticity" of Chinese Islam, yet Matt Erie has pointed out that this narrative "belies the imagined connection with Saudi Arabia,"[28] as in fact the history of China's Islamic resurgence was more closely connected to the peripheries of Central and South Asia than its Arab hub: the orthodoxy-driven Chinese Muslim intellectual tradition of the eighteenth century merged Persian and Arabic texts with Confucian ones; the first wave of Salafism arrived from Mecca, but via a Bukharan scholar; and the Tablighi Jama'at finds its roots in the northern part of the Indian subcontinent.

Reading Khomeini in Indonesia

The transition from Sukarno's presidency (1945–1967) to Suharto's New Order regime (1967–1998) took place at the same time as the Six-Day War, as Iran entered its revolutionary phase, and as Muslims across the world experienced a "resurgence" of piety. Suharto opted to continue Sukarno's policy of marginalizing Islam as a potentially anti-nationalist force, yet his regime also endorsed and supported personal piety as a measure against communism. With a two-pronged approach, the regime contrasted fears of a Communist return by supporting the "revitalization" of Islam as an aspect of individual piety, while it also set out to actively suppress the last vestiges of political Islam.

To counter Suharto's policies, in 1967 former Masyumi leader Mohammad Natsir established the Indonesian Islamic Mission Council (DDII, Dewan Da'wah Islamiyah Indonesia) as an Islamizing force "from below," although its ultimate goal remained the achievement of a stronger link between Islam and the state. The broadening of its activities from the 1970s onwards was made possible mostly through Saudi Arabia's religious philanthropy, which followed the increase of oil prices and the distribution of "petro-dollars" across the global *umma*.

A different strategy was embraced by other former Masyumi members who, under the impression that the regime had chosen Islam as its political ally, in 1968 requested the reintegration of the Jakarta Charter in the constitution (Chapter 4). Their pleas went unanswered.

In the repressive climate of Suharto's autocratic regime, Islam took an increasingly activist stance, and the distinction between piety and politics became difficult to retain. One early move of the regime had been to stop sending Indonesians to study in Arab West Asia and North Africa (Cairo, Mecca, and Medina had been favorite destinations) and instead to sponsor graduate programs in the UK, North America and Australia in order to create a new elite of religious intellectuals committed to a "modern" approach to Islam and to the separation of religion and politics. But for the young people who remained in Indonesia, the mosque became the only gathering place.

Amidst opposing domestic tensions and fervor across the Muslim world, between the end of the 1970s and the early 1980s, Indonesia's university students were able to take advantage of New Order policies and re-channel their grievances toward the regime in religious-intellectual terms, consolidating prayer and *da'wa* groups in a model similar to that of the Muslim Brotherhood and Jama'at-e Islami. By the mid-1980s the *usra* (family, circles) movement had achieved a strong presence across the country, with high school and university students gathering in mosques across Java and beyond. Like their peers in Egypt and Malaysia, they avidly read and discussed the works of the most prominent Islamic intellectuals, Hasan al-Banna, Abu A'la Mawdudi, and Sayyid Qutb.

Although the *tarbiya* (training) and *usra* movements are broadly identified with Sunni Islam, at the time these groups were also open to the literature that was emerging from Iran's Shi'i context. The most discussed author was Ali Shari'ati (1933–1977), closely followed a few years later by Murtadha Motahhari (1919–1979) – a choice that reflected the early stages of the Revolution, when leftist groups were prominent in the anti-Shah movement. Indonesian *usra* members gave no thoughts to "sectarian" allegiances, fascinated instead with a Revolution that, in the Indonesian press, was represented as a liberation movement against a Western-controlled despotic Shah, and as one that stood in defense of the weaker strata of society.

Until the mid-1980s, public debates on the Iranian Revolution had been limited to government politics. Indonesian periodicals mostly followed Western press agencies in assessing Khomeini's reforms, Iran's economic situation, and its position in international politics, leaving untapped the issue of religion. It was only in the context of the Suharto regime becoming concerned with the potential spread of the Iranian

Revolution's anti-establishment activism, and rising concerns with anti-Islamic extremism, that anti-Shi'a discourses were endorsed by the Indonesian state. In 1983–1984, the government had the Council of Ulama (MUI) issue a recommendation (*tawsiya*) warning Indonesian Muslims against the danger that Shi'a Islam might upset the country's social harmony.[29] The text elucidated, albeit succinctly, the theological and juridical differences between Sunni and Shi'a Islam, but the motives were political. The *tawsiya* represented a political response to the Iranian Revolution.

Far from closing the debate on the Iranian Revolution or Shi'ism, the issuance of the *tawsiya* awakened Indonesians' interests in this "new" Islamic movement, thus acting as a catalyst for discussions. While readers sent letters to newspapers and magazines asking for reading suggestions to acquire deeper knowledge of Shi'i Islam, its presence in the Indonesian archipelago, and the meaning of the Revolution and its religious and social dimensions for the Indonesian people, new publishing houses sprang up to fill the newly opened market created by the Iranian Revolution. The most prominent ones hailed from the *tarbiya* movement.

The first and most active of such enterprises was Mizan, established in 1983 by a group of students belonging to the Salman Mosque in Bandung, West Java. Masjid Salman, built in the early 1970s, was the first mosque on the Bandung Institute of Technology (ITB) campus, and it soon became representative of the *da'wa* circle that took shape there and nationwide. From its beginning, Mizan anticipated the eclecticism of the decades to come. The first book it published was a translation of Sharaf al-Din al-Musawi's *al-Muraja'at*, a famous epistolary debate that had allegedly taken place in Peshawar in the 1910s between the Sunni head of al-Azhar University in Cairo and a Shi'a cleric from Lebanon. This text, aimed at illustrating "what Shi'a Islam is really about," went through two editions within six months. Musawi's *al-Muraja'at* was followed by translations of works by Ali Shari'ati, Abu A'la Mawdudi, Sayed Nawab Haider Naqvi, Sayyid Qutb, and Yusuf al-Qaradawi, to name a few. These monographs were joined by a number of edited volumes compiled by the editors of Mizan, in which the influence of Iranian revolutionary thought was evident. Hence, Mizan was not just committed to translations, but more broadly to bridging the Sunni–Shi'a divide

Yogyakarta, in Central Java, was also emerging as an important center for the *da'wa* movement, equally crucial to the spread of Iranian thought. Ali Shari'ati's lectures appeared in Indonesian in 1984 as the translation of a 1982 government edition from Mashhad, Iran. The introduction had been written by Amien Rais, who a decade later would become the President of Muhammadiyah (the second largest Islamic organization in Indonesia), but in 1984 had just obtained his doctoral degree from the University of Chicago and had been nominated chairman of the Jamaah Shalahuddin, the *da'wa* community that congregated at the Gadjah Mada University campus mosque in Yogyakarta. Combining his studies at Chicago with his earlier training at Cairo's al-Azhar, and with a dissertation addressing the evolution of the Muslim Brotherhood of Egypt, his profile fitted well with the modernist *da'wa* mission of the Jamaah.

Jamaah Shalahuddin's *da'wa* activists were being exposed to multiple Islamic intellectual influences, as their reference books featured Shari'ati together with Qutb, Mawdudi, Iqbal, and al-Ghazali.[30] Shari'ati and Mutahhari had the strongest appeal to students and young people because of their fascination with the Iranian Revolution, as well with the socialist underlining of these intellectuals' writing. Shalahuddin press, then, reflected the group's varied taste in a similar tone to Mizan's, and further pointed to the connection between the *tarbiya* circle and the spread of Shi'a thought.

During this period of the Islamic resurgence, it was authors considered representative of socially engaged, left-leaning Islamic thought, and inspired by Third-Worldism, who were more widely read. The introduction of "Shi'i literature" in the 1980s was not a conscious attempt to socialize Shi'ism as an alternative approach to Islam, but rather the result of a general fascination with the social-religious movement that had led the Iranian Revolution, regardless of sectarian concerns.

The Iranian Revolution and the Islamic Republic's missionary activities that followed it are often seen as the trigger for conversions and the formation of legalistic (Ja'fari *fiqh*) Shi'i Islam outside the historical centers of the Muslim world, including Southeast Asia. However, in Indonesia, Twelver Shi'ism appeared much later (mostly in the 2000s), while in these early years following the Revolution, Shi'i "sympathizers" remained inspired by the intellectual sophistication of Shi'a thinkers and their engagement with metaphysics and logic, rather than Khomeini's political platform.

Conclusions

This chapter has emphasized how Islamic activist ideologies traveled from one country to another, following multiple geographical vectors and contributing to the shaping of local envisioning (or reimaginations) of piety beginning in the 1980s.

The influence of Egypt's Muslim Brotherhood in the establishment and political assertion of Malaysia's Islamist party PAS, the impact of Iran's revolutionary intellectuals among Indonesia's activists, the Saudi World League's interest in fostering connections in China, and the booming of relations across the border between former Soviet Central Asia and Pakistan all show how the reimagination of piety that occurred across Asia in the second half of the twentieth century had its roots in phenomena that built on the idea of the transnational *umma* as a community of belonging, but it was also "hyper-national" in nature. These case studies are, then, useful for understanding in some detail how international networks of piety found fertile soil to implant themselves in Asia as Muslims there became disenchanted with the secularist experiment.

The year 1979 was a milestone on the road to a socially and politically engaged global *umma*, not only because the establishment of an Islamic republic in Iran proved to Muslims worldwide that Western-style orders could be toppled, but also because it created the conditions for broader conversations about Islamic activism. By the late 1990s, Islam had become a strong presence in the Asian public sphere, as Muslims found ways to insert their religious, social, and political values and frames of references into public discourses and practices. At the same time, the Soviet invasion of Afghanistan, which took place at the end of 1979, offered an additional stage for these developments, in the form of a platform for the concrete application of these ideas on the grounds, as anti-Soviet resistance was to become dominated by an Islamist discourse, turning Afghanistan into the site of a local *jihad* pursued by an international community of fighters.

Further Reading

Erie, M. S. (2017) *China and Islam: the prophet, the party, and law*, Cambridge: Cambridge University Press.

Esposito, J. L. (Ed.) (1990) *The Iranian Revolution: its global impacts*, Miami, FL: Florida International University Press.

Fuchs, S. (2014) "Third wave Shi'ism: Sayyid 'Arif Husain al-Husaini and the Islamic Revolution in Pakistan," *Journal of the Royal Asiatic Society* 24: 493–510.

Karagiannis, E. (2011) *Political Islam in Central Asia: the challenge of Hizb ut-Tahrir*, London: Routledge.

Kepel, G., and Roberts, A. F. (2014) *Jihad: the trail of political Islam*, London: Tauris.

Khalid, A. (2014) *Islam after communism: religion and politics in Central Asia*, Berkeley, CA: University of California Press.

Lapidus, I. M. (1997) "Islamic revival and modernity: the contemporary movements and the historical paradigms," *Journal of the Economic and Social History of the Orient* 40(4): 444–460.

Meijer, R. (2013) *Global salafism: Islam's new religious movement*, New York, NY: Oxford University Press.

Mervin, S. (2010) *The Shi'a worlds and Iran*, London: Saqi.

Mitchell, R. P. (1993) *The Society of the Muslim Brothers*, London: Oxford University Press.

Müller, D. M. (2014) *Islam, politics and youth in Malaysia: the pop-Islamist reinvention of PAS*, Abingdon: Routledge.

Nagata, J. (1984) *The reflowering of Malaysian Islam: modern religious radicals and their roots*, Vancouver: University of British Columbia Press.

Nawab, M. (2018) *Hizbut Tahrir Indonesia and political Islam: identity, ideology and religio-political mobilization*, London and New York, NY: Routledge.

Olcott, M. B. (2007) *Roots of radical Islam in Central Asia*, Washington, DC: Carnegie Endowment for International Peace, available at www.carnegieendowment.org/files/cp_77_olcott_roots_final.pdf.

Stewart, A. B. (2016) *Chinese Muslims and the global Ummah Islamic revival and ethnic identity among the Hui of Qinghai Province*, London: Routledge.

7   Islam as Resistance

Letter from President James Earl, Jr. (Jimmy) Carter of the United States of America to President of Pakistan Mohammad Zia ul-Haq, April 30, 1980.[1]

Dear Mr. President: Thank you for your letter following the visit of Dr. Brzezinski and Mr. Christopher. I welcome the personal attention you have given US–Pakistan relations, and I hope that strengthened cooperation between our two nations will help to show the Soviet Union how seriously we view their ruthless and unprovoked aggression in Afghanistan.

I was deeply impressed by the reports of my emissaries of your country's determination to counter the Soviet challenge. Your leadership at the Islamic Foreign Ministers' Conference in January was vital in putting the Islamic world on record condemning the Soviet seizure of a neighboring Muslim country. I hope that Pakistan will exercise equally firm leadership at the Islamic Foreign Ministers' Conference in May to demonstrate that the Islamic world remains united in its condemnation of Soviet actions.

The struggle of the Afghan people against the Soviet occupation forces is one of the most stirring events of our time. I attach the greatest importance to this struggle and know that you share my admiration for the Mujahidin. Not only does their bravery deserve recognition, their ability to continue their resistance brings home the cost of aggression to the Soviets every day. Such resistance, therefore, is in the interest both of the Islamic world and of the democratic Western countries.

Crown Prince of the Kingdom of Saudi Arabia, speaking to Afghan Refugees in Pakistan, May 1984, in *Time*, June 11, 1984.[2]

Your struggle is a jihad [holy war] because you have taken up arms in defense of Islam. We will continue to assist you as we did in the past. We will always remain on your side.

The Mirror of Jehad, 2nd series, 1.1–2 (1986).[3]

If Afghans become victorious in their struggle, Inshaullah [*sic*], it will be a start of the revival of Islam, a corner-stone of the next Khilafat Ilahia, led by Afghans.

Jimmy Carter's invocation of the "greatness" of the Islamic resistance to the Soviet invasion of Afghanistan was rooted in his need to keep the perilous balance of the Cold War in place. For many of the Afghan

Source 7.1

"Islam's Heroes," by Hanif (October 28, 2008)

Nothing is known of "Hanif" beside the fact that he was part of the Taliban community in Afghanistan in the early 2000s. His poetry was not unique, as many poems – inspired by the long Afghan (and Persian) tradition of oral recitation – have been published and collected since the 1980s. This poem has been selected because of its being harnessed on the consciousness of the Afghan mujahidin's status in the eyes of Muslims worldwide, and the historical memory of both anti-British and anti-Soviet resistance.[4]

> Whoever has received the blow of an Afghan sword to his
>   head,
> Never resisted or escaped from the battlefield.
> His brave sword is clear to the entire world,
> So much so that the red infidels ran from his homeland.
> This is the soil of Islam; it has well-trained heroes;
> This is why they would have beaten the enemy on any ground.
> This homeland has reared and trained religion's heroes,
> Each one placed in the crib of zeal by their mothers.
> The entire Muslim world is proud of their *mujahedeen*
> Because they have brought shame to the name of Communism
>   around the world.
> You erased Lenin's communist system from the world;
> It was scattered in such a way that the whole universe laughs at
>   them.
> Look at history, which each Afghan has in the background:
> The English are a great example of those who have been
>   pushed out.
> Afghans made sacrifices for their honour;
> They made a revolution; each traitor is shaken by them.
> Nations are amazed by Afghans,
> Since they have beaten a power like Bush.
> Afghan sons don't have any parallel, O Ahmad Yar!
> Stop complimenting them, they are victorious in every field.

fighters, whose military efforts had been validated as a religious endeavor by the Muslim community, their struggle was aimed at establishing a new Caliphate, or Islamic state.

The term *mujahidin* – the individuals engaged in *jihad* – thus entered Western colloquial language to denote Afghan "freedom-fighters" who were resisting the Soviet invasion of 1979 (a CIA officer had pointed to the importance of using these terms and avoiding any references to "insurgents" in a 1980 memo).[5] At the same time, Muslims worldwide looked to Afghanistan as a site for their global struggles, as for the first time in centuries the *umma* had come together to defend Islam, with Afghanistan described as "a revolutionary university for all other Islamic upheavals in the Muslim world."[6] Prominent Islamist ideologues and foreign fighters made it their home, developing their own theories and ideas of *jihad* based on the daily experience of the anti-Soviet battlefield.

But the legacy of this *jihad* did not end with the Soviet withdrawal, as for decades to come Afghanistan and the *mujahidin* would be reimagined and reconstituted as sites of Islamist popular culture and identity formation. *Jihadi* paraphernalia are commonly found the world over, from stickers to T-shirts that in their iconography and text more or less subtly reference al-Qa'eda and martyrdom. Similarly, *jihadi*s themselves have expressed their aesthetic and artistic sense in songs and poems, often exalting the qualities of the Afghan fighters who "erased Lenin's communist system from the world" (see Source 7.1).

A third perspective on *jihad* was brought center-stage in the post-9/11 context, when the Western public discourse came to associate *jihad* with so-called Islamic terrorism and violent attacks on American and European targets. Reminiscent of dynamics that dominated colonial politics in the nineteenth century, the new millennium has seen governments in the West and across Asia understanding all forms of resistance led by Muslims as religiously driven, labeling it as *jihad*, and therefore condemning it as a terrorist enterprise.

★★★

Alas, not all things in life are easy;
Even man struggles to be human.[7]

Momin, if you have any respect for faith,
Jihad means battle: so go there now;
Be fair, more than God you love that life
Which you used to sacrifice for idols![8]

With these poems, two South Asian intellectuals of the early nineteenth century expressed their (diverging) understanding of "effort," or *jihad*. Whereas Hakim Momin Khan Momin (1801–1852) unabatedly asserted the term's meaning as physical armed battle, the Urdu poet Mirza Asadullah Khan Ghalib (1797–1869) identified the primary struggle as "liv[ing] up to the ethical standards of true humanity."[9]

Source 7.2

The Struggle for Gender Justice, by amina wadud (1999, 2006)

The following excerpts are from the seminal Islamic feminist author amina wadud (further discussed in Chapter 8), and have been selected to show a different (but some would say not much less engaged) understanding and political deployment of the concept of "jihad" as struggle.

"Preface," from *Qur'an and Woman: Rereading the Sacred Text from a Woman's Perspective* (1999).

In the battle for gender parity, those who stand guard at the gateposts of Muslim status quo have sometimes reacted vehemently against claims for justice. The trenches are deep and the fighting often unfair, but the motivation for my entry into the struggle is nonnegotiable. One of the special merits of Islam as *din*, or, way of life, is that establishing and re-establishing orthodoxy set an agenda for Islamic praxis. One cannot stand on the sidelines in the face of injustice and still be recognized as fully Muslim, fully *khalifah*. I have accepted the responsibility and continue in the struggle.

"Conclusion: The Final Reason for Fighting the Gender Jihad," from *Inside the Gender Jihad* (2006).

Ultimately, I want to live and to share the experience of life with all who care to put down the weapons of *jihad*, and take up the tools of wholesome reconstruction. I have lived inside the gender *jihad* long enough to know that I had to take it up. It was my only means to survive. Now, I want to see and bring about the end of the necessity for *jihad*. The only reason I have been engaged in this *jihad*, the struggle for gender justice, is because that justice and full human dignity granted to us by Allah has been ignored or abused. The history of nearly exclusive male and androcentric Islamic interpretation and codification has not nearly recognized the importance of women's contributions from their specific experience of being female and fully human with the intellectual capacity to contribute to a holistic understanding of what it means to have a relationship with both the divine and other humans, while they have consistently shown the spiritual fortitude to live as Muslims despite lack of recognition. The spaces for women to demonstrate both their self-identification as female and their full humanity are not reserved for only those whom elite male scholars and laypersons have already manipulated in mind and body, but belong to all women who have endeavored to sustain their roles as women and Muslims despite silence, separation, violence, and invisibility. Still, too few women are recognized for their capacity to lead by example, not by asserting power over, but by representing power with, all others.

In fact, the term *jihad* embodies a vast array of meanings within the semantic field of "striving, making an effort, exerting oneself" (see Source 7.2). These efforts may be pursued through the tongue, the pen, or the sword, depending on the circumstances, and may be directed toward converting a non-Muslim, redirecting a lapsed believer to the right path, being "a better Muslim" oneself, or fending off an attack. Traditionally this latter form of "striving" – aligned with the much more common understanding of *jihad* as "holy war" – has been called "the lesser *jihad*" vis-à-vis "the greater *jihad*" against inner forces.

In the second half of the 1980s, the renowned Central Asian scholar Muhammadjan Hindustani (1892–1989, see Chapters 5 and 6) engaged in a fierce debate with a younger generation of Islamists, whom he saw as having "deviated" from Hanafi *fiqh*, embracing instead the thought of Ibn Taymiyah and what he called "wahhabism":

Do you know how many parts the jihad for the faith consists of? If one part is the jihad against unbelievers on the field of battle, then another is to cleanse oneself of evil thoughts and deliver oneself from ignorance. The Lord Prophet of Allah called this second part *jihad-i akbar,* the greatest jihad. I, praise be to Allah, have also waged the "jihad of the tongue," and for this have been deprived of my freedom many times. And I have also imparted [religious] knowledge to so many people, delivering them from ignorance and turning them away from evil behavior.[10]

Groups of Muslims have deployed Islam as a discourse of resistance – to internal and external challenges alike – in the social, spiritual, and political spheres, from the pre-colonial through the post-colonial periods. If from the late seventeenth through the end of the nineteenth centuries the focus was on efforts to reaffirm "orthodoxy" in the face of what were perceived to be rampant "deviations" (or "innovations," *bid'a*) (see the end of Chapter 2 and Chapter 3), from the last quarter of the nineteenth century onward we have seen much opposition to the European presence, as some Muslims argued for the need for a co-religionist as their political leader; but we have also seen how other Muslims recognized the legitimacy of European rule without denying their own religious identity (Chapter 4). With the transition to the post-colonial, the interplay of Islam and Western modernity was no longer an exclusively Muslim/non-Muslim affair, as secularism had been embraced by Muslim leaders as well (Chapter 5); "Islamic resistance," or broader efforts to reaffirm Islam *vis-à-vis* non-Islamic frameworks, was increasingly an insider dynamic (Chapter 6).

The year 1979, and more specifically the Soviet invasion of Afghanistan, opened up a new front and site for resistance to outside forces. Against the background of the Cold War, Afghanistan was to become the battlefield for the neo-imperialist competition between the Soviet and

---

Box 7.1   Afghanistan

Because of its strategic position at the heart of Central Asia, bordering Persia, British India, and the Russian/Soviet Empire, Afghanistan has been the target of international diplomacy since the late 1800s. As with Meiji Japan and Chakri Siam (Thailand), "independence" had been possible because of the country's leaders' readiness to negotiate and "modernize" according to Western parameters. Taking advantage of Britain's and Russia's desires to exert indirect control – going through the motions of what has come to be called "The Great Game" – King Amanullah embraced a program of Western-inspired reforms that was set to pave the way for later efforts toward women's emancipation, a modern education, freedom of the press, and secularization of the law. Yet, Western-style reforms were not seen by all as progress, and after a decade of such transformative policies, King Amanullah was forced to abdicate in favor of Bacha-yi Saqqao (lit. "the son of the water carrier"). A Tajik from the Shamali valley, north of Kabul, Bacha-yi Saqqao had rallied the support of the Naqshbandi, *shari'a*-minded, traditional *'ulama*. The reign of Bacha-yi Saqqao advanced an anti-Western, *shari'a*-based mode of governance, but its roots were in traditional networks of authority: he had been crowned king (as Habibullah Kalakani, r. January–October, 1929) by a Sufi representative of both the Naqshbandi *tariqa* and the Deobandi school. But a lack of tribal support led to his dethronement after less than a year. Under the more conventional rule of King Muhammad Nadir Shah (r. 1929–1933), "modernization" reforms were soon after resumed: Kabul University was established as early as 1931, opening its doors to the first cohort of students in 1932, and allowing women to join since the 1940s.

---

the Western blocks, creating, through the decades, multiple vectors of resistance from Muslims worldwide.

This chapter takes as its point of departure the Soviet invasion of Afghanistan, the emergence of an image (projected on the global stage) of the Afghan resistance as the archetype of twentieth-century *jihad* warfare, and the internationalization of this *jihad*; notably, the latter phenomenon took place both as Muslim and non-Muslim foreigners came to participate in the anti-Soviet effort and as discourses pertaining to, and actors involved in, the Afghan resistance spread over the world. This endeavor is advanced in order to shine light on how and why acts of physical resistance to established authorities pursued by Muslims in the twenty-first century have been framed as religious (i.e. as *jihad* in its most reductive meaning), sometimes by the *mujahidin* themselves, but more so by outsiders (Muslims and non-Muslims; fighters, governments, and observers), either as a way to discredit their grievances or as an outright expression of anti-Muslim racism. To this effect, the second part of the chapter analyses three other geographical areas which have been labeled as *jihadi* hotspots in the twenty-first century: Southeast Asia (with a focus on Thailand, the Philippines, and Indonesia), Kashmir in the Indian subcontinent, and Xinjiang in the People's Republic of China.

Jihad in Afghanistan: Between Local Dynamics and Global Tensions

On Christmas Eve 1979 Russian Soviet tanks entered Afghan territory, and within days Kabul had fallen under their control. Before the end of the year a new government had been formed under the leadership of the Marxist Babrak Karmal (1929–1996), who would remain as the official head of the state of Afghanistan until 1986. Although Marxism-Communism had been an important player in Afghan politics in the 1960s and 1970s, this was largely an urban phenomenon, and one that was pitted against the emerging Islamist movement. In the tribal areas the Soviet invasion and their takeover sparked a fierce resistance, which soon took shape as an Islamic struggle against "infidel" and "atheist" invaders and became a primary field for the expression, on the battlefield, of the Islamic revival of the 1960s and 1970s.

Beginning in the 1960s, much of the young Afghan Islamist intelligentsia had emerged from urban universities, as the modernization of education – which brought theological instruction within the fold of Western-style universities – did not prevent, but actually facilitated, the politicization of Islam. The first wave of Islamist movements had surfaced in the late 1950s and early 1960s from among the professors of the Faculty of Theology at Kabul University (mostly alumni of Cairo's al-Azhar) and the graduates of the government-sponsored *madrasas*. As a group interested in reviving Islamic culture on campus, the Afghan Jamiyyat-i Islam (JI, Islamic Society, inspired by Pakistan's Jama'at-e Islami) focused on spiritual growth and the establishment of a mass movement, mostly distributing translations of the works by Sayyid Qutb and Mawdudi until 1972.

The Islamic Society was against anything Western and un-Islamic, i.e. Zionism, communism, the monarchy, tribalism, and the traditional clergy; yet, besides university students, it also found support among several Naqshbandi *pir* who had been trained in the Deobandi *madrasas*, such as those of the Shamali valley. At the same time as Communism infiltrated the army and the government, the Society won the student elections on the Kabul campus and began a *da'wa* campaign in the countryside; by now the Islamist movement was split between those who envisioned a popular uprising (represented by the young members of the Jamiyyat, led by the engineer Hekmatyar; b. 1949), and those who advocated for a long-term infiltration of the state (under the leadership of the al-Azhar graduate Rabbani; 1940–2011). In the aftermath to the 1975 communist coup, the movement polarized further: Rabbani sought to unify the Muslim opposition, whereas Hekmatyar established the Hizb-i Islami as a "radical" Islamist political party (1976). The leaders of both factions had by then escaped the communist repression, going into exile in neighboring Pakistan.

There, both Rabbani and Hekmatyar were able to channel the local support of Bhutto's socialist People's Party (see Chapter 6). But because of the concomitant transformation of Pakistan's JI, Hekmatyar's Hizb-i Islami was the party that eventually received the most support from Pakistan (and thus from Saudi Arabia).

Because of the interweaving of transnational threads, the narrative about the Afghan *jihad* is often framed as one cast in the power of transnational Islamist-*jihadi* networks, in which Saudi financial support and Wahhabi indoctrination, Pakistani ideological and military backing, and the influx of foreign Muslim fighters were the key elements that led to the radicalization of Afghanistan and the defeat of the Soviets. These three elements cannot – and should not – be discounted, as within the broader picture of the Cold War the Soviet invasion of Afghanistan turned the Afghan Islamists into the United States' best allies. As stated in a US National Security Council memorandum from April 1980:

How to Operate. There are 53 Afghan refugee camps along the Pakistan border. We should have at least three agents in each of those camps; ostensibly for refugee relief purposes, but principally to ensure that the *Mujahidin* are getting the weapons they need. A similar effort should be made in eastern Iran …

The Public Line. We could do the above without changing our public line (i.e., we do not comment about matters of this kind) in the slightest. The Soviets have already accused us repeatedly of supplying the rebel forces and have, in fact, used this as their justification for invading Afghanistan. They and their Afghans will make the same amount of noise, which will have roughly the same propaganda effect, whether we are supplying the *Mujahidin* effectively or ineffectively. I vote for supplying them effectively. How the world turns may ultimately depend on our ability to do so.[11]

Saudi Arabia, Pakistan, and the United States provided weapons, ammunition, and monetary funds to finance their anti-communist *jihad*, but this was not without potential problems:

Some argued that Zia cannot politically afford an overt program. The Saudis will also protest abandoning the covert mode. Finally, for the US to take the public lead, the effect would be to "de-Islamicize" the program. It was also argued that the present support programs might be jeopardized.[12]

It is important, then, to consider the impact of Afghanistan's own circumstances on these developments as well as the impact of the Afghan *jihad* on Islamic struggles worldwide, especially in the post-Soviet era. At the onset of the Soviet invasion, Afghanistan's society was fragmented and badly organized, reflecting deep-seated fractures within its national population. Not only were the religiously minded opposed to, and by, middle-class royalists embedded in tribal politics and by the hyper-nationalist officers who resented the idea of being led by Soviets; the recently-emerged Islamists, the traditional *'ulama*, and the *tariqa* members, all operated separately from each other, organized in mutually exclusive networks. As the months passed, the Islamic factions were to take control of the movement, sometimes in a coordinated fashion, but often as a constellation of groups.

The Taliban

Afghanistan's urban centers experienced the emergence of an Islamist movement among its educated youth beginning in the 1950s and 1960s as a reaction to, and a product of, modernization and Westernization; in the meantime, the rural areas had been dominated by Sufism, traditional *'ulama*, and tribalism. The beginning of the anti-Soviet resistance created a third context, that of refugee camps, which combined the reality of rural Afghanistan with the influence of Deobandi puritanism, Pakistani politics, and Saudi-sponsored Arab *jihadi*s, ultimately leading to the emergence of the so-called Taliban as an Afghan Islamic militia.

As the anti-Soviet resistance movement advanced through the country, many non-combatants escaped the cities and contested territories to find refuge on the Afghan-Pakistani border. Among them, about three million[13] were able to cross the border into Pakistan, while unknown numbers of Afghans were accommodated in refugee camps. Some camps were official and sponsored by international aid agencies, others were informal conglomerations of people. Alongside temporary housing and other infrastructure, the camps also offered educational institutions, *madrasa*s. Literally "places of study," *madrasa*s on the Afghan-Pakistani border soon had a reputation for being breeding pools for extremism and jihadism.

These border *madrasa*s had popped up in the 1980s as part of Zia ul-Haqq's Islamization policies, which had already sponsored the opening of similar schools across the country (Pakistan went from 900 registered *madrasa*s in 1971 to 8,000 in 1988),[14] run largely by Pakistani Deobandi teachers who belonged to the Jamiat Ulema-i Islam. The JUI, established in 1947, was a party which from the beginning had embraced a utilitarian approach to political alliance-building, siding with the Muslim League to join the call for the establishment of Pakistan (see Chapter 5), and distancing itself from the "original" stand of Deoband's Dar-ul-'Ulum, which was apolitical. Despite (or maybe because of) the Afghan state's invitation to Dar-ul-'Ulum teachers to help with the modernization reforms of the 1930s, India's Deobandi *ulama* were unable to make a dent in 1980s Afghan society, whereas the Pakistani JUI exerted a great impact.

Several of these *madrasa*s located along the Afghan-Pakistani border were led by *ulama* whose religious-intellectual outlook was characterized by Deobandi restrictive social norms, deep concern for ritual orthopraxy, and a narrow understanding of *shari'a*. This approach was integrated with the Pashtunwali tribal code and Wahhabi beliefs, the latter having been brought to the table by these teachers' interaction with "Arab volunteers" who had come to Afghanistan to fight the Soviets.

The influx of "Arabs" – largely Wahhabi or Salafi *jihadis* – influenced the Deobandi of Pakistan, effecting change in their schools and thus giving birth to a new generation of students (hence the epithet Taliban, from the Persian and Pashtu *talib*, meaning student) whose outlook reflected the multiple influences that Afghanistan as a whole was absorbing in the 1980s. Conversely, these "Arabs" were themselves influenced by their experience abroad, not just by the practice of *jihad*, which would in later years deeply affect the religious, social, and political landscape of Saudi Arabia itself, but also by South Asian scholarly traditions, most notably the school of Deoband itself, and the Ahl-e-Hadith.

The *madrasa* most emblematic of this phenomenon was the Dar-ul-'Ulum Haqqania, in Akhora Khattak (North-West Frontier Province). The school, which was completely free of charge, attracted pupils from Pakistan, Afghanistan, and the Soviet Republics of Tajikistan, Uzbekistan, and Kazakhstan; scores of its graduates became leaders in the Taliban movement and subsequent government; the school's network provided thousands of fighters; and its own founder, Samiul Haq (b. 1937), was a close advisor of "Mullah" Mohammad Omar (1960–2013), who claimed the title of *amir-ul-mu'minin* and thus reaching closest to being a Caliph since the institution's abolition in 1924.

But what enabled a group of students, largely concerned with outward expressions of piety and with maintaining a morally ordered microcosmos within the walls of their schools, to become militants and – more astoundingly – to take control and run a country? Their Deobandi background allowed them to "embrace the political culture of their time and place ... seeking allies wherever they could find them,"[15] a strategy which translated into their ability to attract the support of Pakistan (which saw them as the only stabilizing force in the country), the United States (which needed to secure a route for the transport of Central Asian oil while also limiting the Soviet sphere of influence), and the Arabs led by Abdallah 'Azzam (1941–1989) and Osama bin Laden (1957–2011) (who had an ideological stake in the conflict, as discussed below).

Pulling in the various resources that found their way to Kandahar, the Taliban were able to project their *madrasa*-centric reality of religious orthopraxy, gender segregation, *shari'a* compliance, and corporal punishment onto the macro-cosmos of Afghanistan, or whichever part of that territory they controlled at any given time.

Internationalizing Afghanistan

The internationalization of the Afghan *jihad* followed a binary dynamic: as the anti-Soviet resistance was framed as a cause that was compelling for all Muslims, Muslims were attracted to fight in Afghanistan, from the Philippines to Africa, and everywhere in between, including Europe and the US. Further breaking down these intersecting responses generates important insight into how flows of people and ideological framings fomented the internationalization of the Afghan resistance as well as the Islamization of other struggles pursued by Muslims worldwide at that time.

Not only were Pakistani Deobandis teaching young Afghan refugees how to practice their own form of "correct Islam" by enforcing rigid gender segregation and eradicating local rituals, but scores of Arabs also began to flow into Afghanistan to join in the resistance. In the immediate aftermath to the invasion the numbers had been small ("only a few tens" before 1987),[16] but in the second half of the 1980s there is evidence of hundreds of foreign men reaching Pakistan to go on to Afghanistan.[17] The uptake in the numbers of "Arab Afghans" was the direct result of the work of Abdallah 'Azzam, a Palestinian member of the Jordanian Muslim Brotherhood. Following the suggestion of a brother-in-law of Sayyid Qutb, 'Azzam had traveled to Islamabad in 1981, and had shortly after emerged as the most influential ideologue and most successful recruiter for the Afghan *jihad*, providing the theoretical scaffolding for the anti-Soviet resistance to be presented as an individual duty for all Muslims.

'Azzam's scholarly credentials rested on a double track that gave him much clout with Muslims of different backgrounds. He had earned a Ph.D. in *shari'a* from al-Azhar in Cairo, and after fleeing Jordan because of his Muslim Brotherhood involvement, he established himself as a teacher at King Abdul Aziz University in Jeddah, Saudi Arabia. While there, his undivided commitment to the liberation of Palestine became overshadowed by the realization that freeing Afghanistan was a fundamental first step in that direction: "not because Afghanistan is more important than Palestine, not at all, Palestine is the foremost Islamic problem," but because "The Islamists have been the first to take control of the battles in Afghanistan ... while in Palestine the leadership has been appropriated by a variety of people, of them sincere Muslims, communists, nationalists and modernist Muslims. Together they have hoisted the banner of a secular state."[18]

In theological terms, his reasoning was similar to that of Muhammad 'Abduh's a century earlier and al-Qursawi's in the eighteenth century (see Chapter 3). In 1984 'Azzam argued that the Soviet invasion of Afghanistan was – as an infidel encroachment on a Muslim country – an indication of the *umma*'s weakened sense of piety, and thus participation in this struggle was an individual duty (*fard-ul-'ayni*). Regaining control of Afghanistan was to create a base from which to launch a global *jihad* to establish Islamic rule over "Palestine, the Philippines, Kashmir, Lebanon, Chad, Eritrea, etc."[19]

Logistically, 'Azzam positioned himself as a receiver of Saudi donations for the support of Afghan refugees in Pakistan, promoted their cause abroad, and trained Arab fighters who wanted to join the *jihad*. In 1984 'Azzam opened the Services Bureau (Maktam al-Khidamat) in Peshawar (Pakistan) in order to achieve those goals without having to deal with the unstable *mujahidin* factions or with the disengaged Muslim Brotherhood that opposed 'Azzam's plans to recruit West Asian Arab fighters for the *jihad* in Afghanistan. It was at this juncture that Osama bin Laden entered the scene.

Born in 1957 to a wealthy and well-connected Hadrami family in Saudi Arabia, bin Laden had enjoyed a "royal" education. Upon finishing high school, he enrolled briefly in the faculty of Engineering at Abdul Aziz University in 1976, but his interests steered him toward Islamic Studies. It is not clear whether it was in Jeddah or Peshawar – where he traveled to in 1979 – that he first crossed paths with Abdallah 'Azzam. What is certain, however, is that after this encounter he became involved in raising funds for the Afghan *mujahidin*, and he settled in Peshawar. After a first trip to Afghanistan in 1982, bin Laden joined forces with 'Azzam, and it was together that they opened the Services Bureau in Peshawar. By 1986 bin Laden, 'Azzam, and Ayman al-Zawahiri (an Egyptian medical doctor and militant activist who had joined the cause in 1986; b. 1951) had become the international face of the Afghan resistance.

Since then, the Services Bureau facilitated the arrival and training of foreign fighters, able to provide financial and logistical help thanks to the direct support of Saudi citizens and the tacit support of the United States. Within two years, they were able to set up training camps, and after two more years the first chatter emerged about al-Qa'eda ("the rule" or "the database") as a list of weapons-trained and battle-ready foreign Muslims (often called "Arab Afghans") stationed in Afghanistan.

This international *jihadi* contingent (some Salafis, others Wahhabis) inserted itself as a third party between the "traditional" *mujahidin* faction (led by Ahmad Shah Massoud, 1953–2001) and the Taliban, eventually joining forces with the latter. Despite their separate genealogies and frameworks, most of the Arab Afghans were sent to support the Taliban: this alliance was sealed when several of them were in the Taliban ranks and files during the battle for Kabul against Massoud's *mujahidin* faction. This union resulted partly from the fact that Arab Afghans were unimpressed by the tribal fragmentation of the Afghan *mujahidin* resistance, and thus did not want to fight with them. But partly this was also because of an ideological alignment between Saudi Salafis and Wahhabis on the one hand and the Afghan Deobandi (now "Taliban") *jihadis*.

Upon the Soviet withdrawal precipitated by the USSR's own crumbling under internal pressures for reform in 1989, the balance of power remained perilous, with the Taliban and Massoud's factions in control of different parts of the country. And as the domestic narrative of the withdrawal was framed as the victory of the militant Muslim resistance, new energy was added to the Islamist enterprise. Confident after this "victory" and tired of tribal politics, al-Qa'eda solidified its alliance with the Taliban while at the same time moving (at least temporarily) its center of activities outside Afghanistan. Al-Qa'eda had deep roots in the Afghan experience, but it also had strong connections with the wider Muslim world. This combination, alongside Abdallah 'Azzam's death, which allowed al-Zawahiri's more militant and less ideological approach to take over, led to the group's undergoing major changes in the 1990s.

Bin Laden returned to Saudi Arabia just months before the Iraqi invasion of Kuwait and, finding himself back in the royal entourage, he presented al-Qa'eda as an Islamic army ready to help repel Saddam Hussain's Iraqi invasion of Kuwait (which led to the eruption of the so-called First Gulf War). Upon the King's refusal – and his acceptance of American troops instead – bin Laden turned into a sharp critic of the Saudi monarchy; so much so that in 1992 he was pressured to leave the country. Bin Laden thus moved first to Sudan, which at the time was experiencing an Islamic rebellion; after four years, though, US and Saudi lobbying proved successful and he was expelled; he then relocated to Afghanistan, where he gained the tutelage and protection of the Taliban regime.

These experiences caused a shift in bin Laden's approach and opened a new phase in the activities of al-Qa'eda. Throughout the 1990s bin Laden's main target was the United States and its allies, most notably Saudi Arabia, seen as the enabler of the *kafir* occupation of the Holy Land. Operations claimed by al-Qa'eda were pursued around the world, including a first attack on the World Trade Center in New York City in 1993, the 1998 bombing of two US embassies in East Africa, attacks in Madrid (2004) and London (2005), and several incidents in Saudi Arabia (2003–2005). As al-Zawahiri's militantism held sway, and a new front of inter-ethnic and inter-religious strife was opened up by the collapse of Tito's communist regime in Yugoslavia, starting in 1992 Arab Afghans flooded the Balkans to defend Bosnian Muslims. *Jihadi* inter-nationalism was (and still is, in the era of ISIS) both a marker of belonging to a global community of believers and a rejection of boundaries largely imposed by imperial powers in the early twentieth century (see Source 7.3).

'Azzam's life was cut short by a roadside bomb in 1989, but his idea of the Afghan *jihad* as a stepping-stone toward freeing other Muslim lands was becoming reality. And despite of (or maybe because of) bin Laden's recurrent relocations, al-Qa'eda was now able to maintain a dual identity, straddling the local and the global: on the one hand they were supporters, enablers, and protégées of the Taliban; on the other, they called for a *jihad* against America and exported fighters worldwide. Bin Laden remained in Afghanistan until the American invasion that followed the September 11, 2001, attacks on the World Trade Center in New York City and the Pentagon in DC. After that, he lived along the border with Pakistan, claiming nominal leadership of al-Qa'eda until his assassination in Abbottabad (Pakistan) in May 2011.

The Impact of the Afghan Jihad *Outside of Afghanistan*

A few days after the death of Osama bin Laden, the head of the Hamas government in the Gaza Strip (in the occupied Palestinian Territories), called bin Laden "one of the Lions of Islam."[20] The previous year, Mahmoud al-Ramahi, secretary-general of the Palestinian Parliament and Hamas leader, recalled that "The Islamic Revolution in Iran ... and the mujahedeen of Afghanistan showed the people that with the resistance and the revolution maybe we can change our life."[21]

Palestinian resistance to the establishment of an Israeli state had displayed a religious tinge only in its earliest days, in the 1930s. In the

Source 7.3

The Blaze of Truth, by Ahlam al-Nasr (a.k.a. "The Poetess of the Islamic State") (2014)

Known as the "the Poetess of the Islamic State," Ahlam al-Nasr writes poetry in classical Arabic meters for the members of the so-called Islamic State (or ISIS, ISIL, Da'esh); her work is widely circulated in militant networks and is performed on YouTube. In this poem, Ahlam al-Nasr points at the irrelevance of ethnicity, language, and national belonging in the face of belonging to the Muslim umma as she openly rejects the very idea of the nation-state. [22]

> My homeland is the land of truth,
> the sons of Islam are my brothers.
> I do not love the Arab of the South
> any more than the Arab of the North.
> My brother in India, you are my brother,
> and so are you, my brother in the Balkans.
> In Ahwaz [southern Iran] and Aqsa [Jerusalem],
> in Arabia and Chechnya.
> If Palestine cries out,
> or if Afghanistan calls out,
> If Kosovo is wronged,
> or Assam or Pattani is wronged,
> My heart stretches out to them,
> longing to help those in need.
> There is no difference among them,
> this is the teaching of Islam.
> We are all one body,
> this is our happy creed.
> We differ by language and color,
> but we share the very same vein.

intervening decades, pragmatism, Arabism, socialism, and secular ideologies had taken over. It was the Iranian Revolution and the *jihad* in Afghanistan that re-ignited the Islamist discourse, thus completing a cycle of mutual influence; it should be recalled that 'Azzam's theory of *jihad* had been tailored for the Afghan experience but had its genesis in the history and condition of Palestine. He had bemoaned Soviet (communist and atheist) involvement in the Palestinian defense against Israel and Yasser Arafat's (1929–2004) choice of secularism as a middle ground for all factions. The political movement, led by Yasser Arafat, was committed to secularism, and the Muslim Brotherhood – despite its activist origins – had been exclusively involved in social welfare and educational programs for decades. But the lead-up to the Palestinian *intifada* ("uprising," which erupted in December 1987) had been informed by a growing sense that Islam needed to be part of the resistance and liberation process.

In the 1980s an Islamist activist discourse had begun to seep through the Muslim Brotherhood cadres, from both the top ('Azzam himself was originally a Muslim Brother) and the bottom (as university students were increasingly radicalized in their vision). First a break-out group reconstituted itself under the name "Islamic Jihad" (previously "Islamic Vanguard") as a direct act of protest against the Muslim Brotherhood's apolitical stance; and then, through a process of covert transformation during which the organization began to train some selected cells, the Brotherhood itself adopted a stronger militant stance under the leadership of Shaykh Ahmad Yasin (1937–2004). In early 1988 Hamas emerged publicly as the "strong arm" of the Muslim Brotherhood; in open rivalry with Arafat's Palestinian Liberation Organization (PLO) and in line with 'Azzam's *Defense of the Muslims Lands*, the charter published in August 1988 declared that "There will be no solution to the Palestinian problem except through jihad. All these international initiatives, proposals and conferences are perfectly futile and a waste of time."[23] Hamas' influence in Islamizing the Palestinian resistance would continue through the 1990s and 2000s: a decade after the first *intifada*, in fact, Shaykh Yasin and a handful of Hamas militants traveled to Pakistan for religious training. One of them was then recruited for further military training in an al-Qa'eda camp, eventually establishing a direct link that connected 'Azzam's geographical locales, his ideological goals, and extant organizational structures.

In line with 'Azzam was Shaykh ibn Baz (1910–1999), the *mufti* of Saudi Arabia (1993–1999), who issued a *fatwa* inciting Saudis' participation in the Afghan *jihad*: "We thank God who is generous. He allows us to issue a *fatwa* stating that one should perform *jihad* in Afghanistan against the enemies of religion. Muslims from all over the world came to help, asking for reward and for heaven. *Jihad* was confirmed in its global Islamic image."[24] Bin Baz's confirmation of 'Azzam's *fatwa* was a clear political move to confer a stronger aura of religious legitimacy to the Saudi state which, since its last territorial annexations in 1932, had had to run on a thin theoretical discourse of *jihad* and Wahhabi propagation. As Madawi al-Rasheed argues, "redirecting this zeal abroad would be both a confirmation of Saudi religious credentials and a way to absorb local discontent and contestation."[25] The issuing of the *fatwa* allowed the Saudi state to put a positive spin on the effective expulsion of *jihadi*-minded citizens, de facto eliminating the risks of in-country rebellions. And it was against this backdrop that bin Laden's initiatives were supported. Although the recruitment of Saudi jihadists had initially been slow, by mid-1987 "Saudi jihadism had effectively become a social movement,"[26] and the flow continued for a few years after the Soviet withdrawal.

Supporting jihadism abroad and hoping for it to not impact domestic developments proved to be a short-sighted strategy: we have seen how bin Laden eventually took a confrontational stand against the Saudi state, and how prompt the state was in expelling him, eventually revoking his citizenship. He was not an outlier. Saudis in Afghanistan acquired new awareness of what an Islamic society should be, and like bin Laden, many of them returned "home" dissatisfied with the royal leadership. Whereas in previous decades dissent had only been articulated at the discursive level (Islamist literature had circulated widely in Saudi Arabia), participating in the *jihad* in Afghanistan had provided Saudi veterans with a lived experience of militant Islamism. Despite the state's attempt to control this engagement by supporting its ideological and logistical infrastructures, participating in the Afghan *jihad* enabled religiously concerned young Saudis to see through the smoke screen of piety and legitimacy created by the monarchy in its decades of rule. And the sporadic but persistent terrorist attacks on local targets in Saudi Arabia is a constant reminder to the ruling elite that some Saudis – mostly those with an Afghan pedigree – are no longer accepting of the Saudi-Wahhabi compromise, and instead are demanding change through a Salafi-Jihadi paradigm.

Framing Resistance as *Jihad*

The Afghan experience was important in multiple ways. For Muslims, it created a first international platform for Islamist militantism; it spearheaded the development of a religious-intellectual discourse to support *jihadi* activism; it created ripples at "the center" of the Muslim world; and it offered a training ground for subsequent activism. 'Azzam himself had stated that Afghanistan was just the first step toward reclaiming other Muslim lands under non-Muslim rule. As the Balkans became a clear receptacle for Arab Afghans, smaller yet visible contingents of veterans joined the resistance movements that emerged in Algeria, Somalia, the Philippines, Kashmir, Eritrea, Tajikistan, and Chechnya throughout the 1990s. The narrative until this point was of foreign "Afghans" traveling to these locations to support local struggles.

Interestingly, in the post 9/11 era and in the context of al-Qa'eda's prominence in the media, another narrative emerged, advanced by non-Muslims (observers and politicians) who found it advantageous to deploy the transnational dimension of the Afghan *jihad* to frame local resistance movements as "*jihadi*," terroristic, and anti-Western, regardless of the specific context or the stated motivations and goals of the militants. As pointed out by Sylvester Johnson, in post 9/11 United States, "Muslims were deemed public enemies by presumption," and religious ritual practice has been seen as a clear sign of extremism, with mosques and community centers constantly under surveillance.[27] But this was not a unique situation, in either time or space.

When the British came under attack in the 1857 Rebellion, Muslims – and their religion – were identified as the primary culprits. The British ignored the contrasting interpretations of *jihad* that existed at the time among various groups of South Asian Muslims, and came to equate the Great Rebellion with *jihad*, favoring the most scripturalist of readings. They elided the multiple identities that existed within this broader body of Muslims, equating them to "Wahhabis," and therefore to *jihadi*s, meaning "rebellious and treasonous" subjects. Hence, Ilyse Morgenstein Fuerst argues, "the production of jihad as the preeminent identifier of Islam [was] possible because of the minoritization and racialization of Muslims" in the Subcontinent.[28]

Muslims across Asia are similarly experiencing both the "constant state of fear of ongoing surveillance and infiltration" identified by Johnson[29] and their racialization as threatening minorities, as politics, Islam, and ethno-religious identity have intersected in various ways. What follows is an exploration of what role (if any) Islamic ideology played in selected contexts of Muslim rebellion, as they unfolded in Asia during the late twentieth and twenty-first centuries. In Southeast Asia, we look at Indonesia, the Southern Philippines, and Southern Thailand; in South Asia, we focus on Kashmir; and in East Asia, we turn our attention to China's westernmost province, Xinjiang. Wanting to understand how the framework of *jihad* has been deployed by internal actors and external observers, sometimes as an honorific, at other times as a pejorative characterization of activism, this section maintains a dual focus: on the histories, hopes, and grievances of these groups, and on external narratives and discourses as they took shape in the post-9/11 era.

Indonesia

One year, one month, and one day after the attacks on the World Trade Center in New York City and the Pentagon in Washington, DC, a bomb exploded in a night club on the island of Bali, in Indonesia. There were 202 fatalities, mostly Australian tourists, plus scores of uncounted

Indonesians who worked in and around the club. The attack was shortly afterwards pigeonholed as the first large-scale exploit of a Southeast Asian terrorist group associated with al-Qa'eda.

Imam Samudera, one of the masterminds of the Bali attack, was eventually executed by the Indonesian government in 2004. In the meantime, he was extremely prolific during his time in prison, writing extensively on the responsibilities of the United States and other Western countries for killing Muslims worldwide, as well as the necessity for Muslims to respond, specifically focusing on the efforts of al-Qa'eda in that direction, in Afghanistan and beyond. Samudera, then, claimed a personal connection to al-Qa'eda and, by proxy, what had come to be labeled the Jemaah Islamiyah group.

The name "Jemaah Islamiyah" had begun to appear in court documents in the 1980s to refer to an (alleged) new organization, supposedly aiming to establish communities ruled according to Islamic law across Southeast Asia. In the words of a policy report, however, "at the end of 1979, it remained unclear whether *Jemaah Islamiyah* was a construct of the [Indonesian] government, a revival of Darul Islam [see Chapter 5], an amorphous gathering of like-minded Muslims, or a structured organization." In the mid-1980s, Indonesian activists exiled to Malaysia used the Jemaah Islamiyah label to recruit Indonesians to join the *jihad* in Afghanistan but there was "little hard evidence that *Jemaah Islamiyah* was in fact an organization with an identifiable leadership." In 2001 and 2002 the Singaporean and Malaysian governments were able to arrest several men on suspicion of belonging to the JI, now an organization that authorities claimed was linked to al-Qa'eda.[30]

However, there is another side to this story. In the 1980s and 1990s, Imam Samudera had been active in West Java in the ranks of the revived Darul Islam movement, and it was from this local connection that his fellow Acong – who actually died in the Bali suicide attack – drew his motives (see also Source 7.4):

I am a child of DI/NII [Darul Islam/Negara Islam Indonesia] who is ready to sacrifice myself for Islam. Remember, o mujahidin of Malingping, how our imam, SM Kartosuwiryo built and upheld and proclaimed the independence of the Islamic State of Indonesia with the blood and lives of martyrs, not by relaxing and fooling around the way we do today. If you are serious about seeing the glory of the buried Islamic State of Indonesia rise again, shed your blood so that you won't be ashamed to face Allah, you who acknowledge yourselves to be children of DI/NII.[31]

The Indonesian government had labeled the Darul Islam as "separatist" and "anti-national" in the 1950s and 1960s; through the 1980s

Source 7.4

The Last Testament of Iqbal alias Arnasan alias Acong (2002)

This text is the last testament left behind by Acong, the West Javanese man who pursued the suicide attack on the Sari Club in Kuta, Bali in 2002. It is important here to notice that all references are to West Java (the village of Malimping specifically) and to the local struggle for an Islamic state led by S. M. Kartosuwiryo in the late colonial and early post-colonial periods.[32]

Bismillah arrahman arrahim,

To: Bah Otong, Haji Ndih, Pak Jafar, Pak Boo, Pak Ook, Saparudin, Didin, Dayat, Asmar, Usup, Pak Jamal, Eji, Ojak, Komandan Jali, Undang, Mukhsin, Ajob, Bisri, Udin, Kyai Udin, Ipit, Kaka, and friends in Gunung Batu

To all my brothers in Malingping [Sundanese spelling of Malimping], I ask your forgiveness because I have frequently caused you problems. My message to Didi and Dayat – don't joke around too much and humiliate yourselves; I fear that Allah will humiliate you even more. To Eji, please teach your wife to fully follow Islamic teachings, not just go half way. I beg your forgiveness and hope Eji isn't offended, because in fact I feel sorry for you, because later on the judgement day, Eji is going to be asked about this, so do a good job of teaching your wife.

In particular for my friends in Malingping, I ask your prayers because today there is lots of work to be done, and prayer that my martyrdom may be an inspiration to all mujahidin. Today I say: that I am a child of DI/NII [Darul Islam/Negara Islam Indonesia] who is ready to sacrifice myself for Islam. Remember, o mujahidin of Malingping, how our imam, SM Kartosuwiryo built and upheld and proclaimed the independence of the Islamic State of Indonesia with the blood and lives of martyrs, not by relaxing and fooling around the way we do today. If you are serious about seeing the glory of the buried Islamic State of Indonesia rise again, shed your blood so that you won't be ashamed to face Allah, you who acknowledge yourselves to be children of DI/NII [note: this isn't just figurative – most of this group had fathers who were in DI].

My brothers, for whoever once felt himself a commander of DI, raise up the spirits of your troops, don't lie around doing nothing. Get ready to make the Crusader forces tremble. Shoulder to shoulder, the mujahidin of Malingping will go forward to raise the spirit of jihad. God willing others of us will be ready as we were before.

For Jali, Usup, Jamal, Bisri, Naseh, Didin, Hahi Sarip. Ojak, Endang, Yudi, Aan, Dayat, Asman, Musih and others in Gunung Batu, take this issue and discuss it among yourselves, because we will all be called to account on the judgement day.

This is my last testament, please convey it to other ikhwan.

I am,

Acong

In the land of jihad

Allahu Akbar, Allahu Akbar, Allahu Akbar

and 1990s, some international observers highlighted its "home-grown" dimension, isolating the influence of veterans from the Afghan *jihad* as lone-wolves. But in the aftermath of 9/11 and George H. W. Bush's (1924–2018) launch of the so-called War on Terror, the grievances of Indonesia's Islamists and those of other groups across Asia came to be connected to groups at the global level. Similarly, insurgencies and rebellions led by Muslims, but not primarily religiously motivated, were now referred to as "Islamist" and "jihadist," with alleged support from abroad; in most cases, analysts and governments ignored these groups' own visions or histories.

Besides the sensationalism of advancing claims of a global transnational terrorist network under the oversight of al-Qa'eda, which had much capital in the early 2000s, this approach allowed affected governments to receive US military and intelligence support in eradicating groups that had been active on their national soil for a long time, challenging their sovereignty. As articulated in Robinson's writings on Kashmir (see below), *jihad* "has become an object of public culture on a global scale and a concept that mobilizes political and military interventions in the name of multiple (and divergent) ethical goals."[33]

Southern Philippines

The arrival of the Spaniards in the Philippines in the sixteenth century interrupted the connection between the southern part of this archipelago – the Sulu and Mindanao areas – and the rest of maritime Southeast Asia, at a time when Islam was becoming more established. During the first hundred years of the Spanish era, not only was the ongoing gradual process of Islamization halted, but this was substituted by repeated Spanish attempts at gaining military and political control of the Sulu-Mindanao region, and possibly to Christianize it. Between the mid-seventeenth and mid-nineteenth centuries, then, Muslim rulers retaliated with northward expeditions, aimed largely at taking slaves. Retaliations aside, the Spaniards were eventually able to take control of the Muslim areas in the late 1800s, shortly before the American takeover.

Whereas the Spanish had not envisaged imposing any direct control over the region, only expressing the desire to transform the socioreligious outlook of the south, the Americans led protracted efforts to quash all challenges to their authority while explaining that hostilities were due to political reasons, not a clash of cultures. The campaigns spanned from 1902 to 1912, with the loss of many Muslim lives.

By 1915, American officials in the south started to be replaced with (northerner, Hispanized) Filipino officials, initiating the process of what they called national integration.[34]

Since the American takeover of 1898 – and especially in the 1930s and 1940s – Catholics from the north had migrated south, purchasing or confiscating land with the consent of the state. Further supported by the post-colonial state, Christian Filipinos had control over most economic resources in the south. By the 1960s, local Muslims were poorer than the "immigrant" Christians, discriminated against, and generally alienated in their own land. The killing of twenty-eight Muslim Philippine Army recruits in 1968 led to the formation of the Mindanao Independence Movement as a group envisioning the separation of "Bangsa Moro" ("Muslim homeland") from the Philippine republic. Transformed into the Moro National Liberation Front (MNLF) in 1972, Mindanao's separatists remained inspired by a secular leftist ideology that followed socio-economic concerns and attempted self-defense from President Marcos' predatory state. The combination of a Muslim identity with a leftist ideology helped the Moros find support among the Arab nations, and Muhammar Ghaddafi of Libya emerged as a primary champion of their cause; he is said to have provided militants with training and weapons, and he brokered the 1976 peace agreement which granted the Moros a first degree of regional autonomy.

A decade later, in 1981, a faction of the MNLF embraced Islam as their primary ideology, forming the Moro Islamic National Front. Its leader, Hashim Selamat, had graduated from al-Azhar, and on his own account his thought was influenced by al-Banna, Qutb, and Mawdudi. After a few years of confrontation with the secular movement and the republican army, the MILF declared a *jihad* for the establishment of the Bangsamoro as an Islamic state. Its openly Islamist and militant outlook functioned as a magnet for several veterans of the Afghan *jihad*, and it appears that in the 1990s the Moro Islamic Liberation Front also forged direct connections with al-Qa'eda by receiving military training and accepting financial support through bin Laden's brother-in-law, who administered an Islamic charity in Manila.

Yet, it is the combination of nationalism and Islamism that characterized the Moro Islamic Liberation Front, not jihadism or Islamism alone. In fact, the shockwaves of the 9/11 events brought Mindanao's insurgents closer to a peace deal with the government, rather than deeper into the trenches of *jihad*. Although this does not exclude the involvement of individuals with transnational networks, Moro Islamic Liberation Front leaders rejected publicly all suggestions of al-Qa'eda affiliation, pan-Islamism, and terrorism in general, emphasizing instead the group's exclusive commitment to a resolution of the Bangsamoro crisis as an ethnic and territorial problem.

Southern Thailand

The insurgency in Southern Thailand similarly finds its roots in European intervention. In the nineteenth century, Britain ceded the semi-independent northern provinces of Malaya to Siam, effectively making the Muslim Malays of "Greater Patani" a minority within a Tai Buddhist kingdom. By the early 1920s, Bangkok and Patani were already clashing, following the central government's attempt to erase local identity through educational reforms. In 1939, after the first of a long series of coups, the military government introduced new policies that forced minorities to assimilate; for Malay Muslims this meant being forced to abandon Muslim names, laws, and clothing. For the second time in twenty years, Malay rebellions were quashed. In the post-war era, Thailand built new civil bureaucratic infrastructures, creating an illusion of addressing Muslims' administrative needs; however, the geographical distance and ideological hierarchy between Bangkok and Patani nullified the potential outcome of any reform, fostering instead the desire for self-administration or incorporation into neighboring Malaysia.

Like the Christians in the Philippines, in the 1960s Buddhists were encouraged to relocate to the South of Thailand, further widening the socio-economic gap between ethnic groups and making the prosperity and development of Malaysian Malays even more compelling to their northern neighbors. In subsequent years the military launched special campaigns dedicated to destroying the separatist movement of Southern Thailand, resulting in over 300 deaths and a thousand arrests. In December 1975, the killing of five Patani youths sparked the largest anti-government demonstration ever in the region, reaching into Malaysia (and many more such incidents have occurred since).

Throughout that decade, Patani Malays had transitioned from relying on the charisma of traditional leaders and teachers to creating structured groups, such as the Patani National Liberation Front (BNPP, 1971), the National Revolutionary Front (BRN, 1960), and the Patani United Liberation Organization (PULO, 1968). As is evident from their names, these groups took ethnicity as their foremost marker of identity, focusing on their rejection of Bangkok's overbearing presence in a secular manner; but Islam and connections to West Asia were also important. The BRN had support from the Arab League, and the PULO – led by scholars trained in West and South Asia – began attending the World Muslim

League Conference in 1977. Islam came out into the open and to the fore in the 1980s, as the Patani National Liberation Front split and reconstituted itself into two groups, the United Mujahideen Front of Patani and the Islamic Liberation Front of Patani, stating their intention of advancing Islamist politics. A few years later, veterans of the Afghan *jihad* established the Patani Mujahideen Movement.

Patani Malay's struggle is more than just part of a global *jihad*. Not only have Patani militants eschewed foreign targets (despite the popularity of Thai beaches among Western tourists), and rejected offers of assistance from al-Qaeda and from the Jemaah Islamiyah; the region's history indicates that the militants' priorities are to defend their ethnolinguistic identity and obtain a degree of administrative power. At the same time, the so-called *jihadi* literature from the region clearly indicates that their struggle is nationalist and separatist in nature, pursuing "the liberation of our beloved country, one which is continuously under the occupation of heretic imperialists and their alliances."[35]

Kashmir

In December 2001, the Indian Parliament in Delhi was bombed. In 2006, commuter trains were attacked in Mumbai. In 2016, grenades were launched on Indian Army headquarters in Indian Kashmir. In February 2019, a car exploded, killing dozens of Indian paramilitaries stationed in Kashmir. All these attacks were claimed by groups that sought the liberation of Kashmir from Indian control in the name of its Islamic identity.

The territory of Kashmir has been contested for centuries. Many dynasties and regimes have tried to assert their authority over this land, located at the strategic point of intersection between India, Pakistan, and China, and largely populated by Muslims.

The princely state of Jammu and Kashmir had been the largest and most populous in British India, and at the time of partition of British South Asia its position was evidently complicated by its own demographic and socio-political reality. Although the population was predominantly Muslim – the region having been converted in the fourteenth century – the state had been ruled by a Hindu maharaja since the early nineteenth century, when the Sikh ruler of Punjab defeated the authority of the Afghan Durrani Empire (1750s to 1819) and granted the land in fief to a Dogra Hindu.

In the mid-1940s it became evident that the Maharaja wished to remain independent, while the other two political entities were split along sectarian lines: the National Conference, allied with Congress, advocated for joining (Hindu) India while the Muslim Conference called for joining Pakistan. Pressured to choose sides, and increasingly concerned that Pakistan might invade Kashmir, the Maharaja eventually pledged allegiance to India in exchange for military support to repel Pakistani actions.

One of the conditions of partition was popular consultation in the form of a free and impartial plebiscite or referendum. The population of Jammu and Kashmir, however, was not given a chance to participate in elections, not even after the involvement of the United Nations. Pakistan eventually took a stake in the situation and claimed control over part of the territory. Following multiple confrontations, Kashmiri territory was divided in two parts along the so-called Line of Control, at the end of Pakistan's 1971 civil war.

Whereas a militant movement had existed since at least the 1960s – the Jammu and Kashmir Liberation Front (JKLF) had constituted itself to fight for an independent state in 1965 – it was only in the late 1980s that Islamic identities were politicized and mobilized. Local political exclusion had turned into alienation and combined itself with economic stagnation, growing unemployment, and increased emphasis on secularism. The mid-1980s thus saw an increase in anti-Hindu attacks across Kashmir, and the launching of an Islamist campaign by the Kashmiri Jama'at-e Islami, which led to severe riots across the territory. It was in this context that the influence of regional developments and the global revival (i.e. the Iranian Revolution, Afghanistan's anti-Soviet *jihad*, and the outward reach of Saudi Arabia) were further amplified, leading to the formation of multiple *jihadi* organizations which were active in what they called "Free Kashmir," launching attacks across the Line of Control into Indian territory and onto Hindu targets throughout the 1990s.[36]

Most prominent among these groups have been the Lashkar-e Toiba (LeT) and the Hizbul Mujahidin (HM). The Hizbul Mujahidin was founded in 1989 as the militant wing of the local branch of the Pakistani Jama'at-e Islam, which has been present in Kashmir since 1953; by virtue of this historical connection, its goal has been consistently framed as that of Kashmir's annexation to Pakistan. But a year later, in 1990, the LeT was created as the *jihadi* counterpart to the Ahl-e Hadith and Salafi *da'wa* organization Markaz Da'wa Irshad. Originally established by a number of Pakistanis plus the Palestinian Abdallah 'Azzam with the specific goal of training Pakistanis to fight in Afghanistan, the LeT later shifted its priorities to the liberation of Kashmir. LeT had an international outlook since the outset, and because of the high impact of its attacks – including the Mumbai and Indian Parliament attacks – this group has been able to dominate the discourse of the Kashmiri insurgency, characterizing it as an element of the global *jihadi* movement and al-Qa'eda's network.

For decades the Kashmiri problem had been approached and understood within the problematics of post-colonial South Asia, and the politics of partition specifically. Yet the post-1989 Islamization of the insurgency and the surfacing of *jihadi* connections linking Afghanistan, Pakistan, and Kashmir shifted the discourse, allowing the Indian government to point the finger at Pakistan and transnational Islamist groups for the insurgency, thus framing the current problem as "*jihadi*," "terrorist," and "global." As Mariam Abou Zahab concludes,

The *jihadi* movements have to some extent Islamised a nationalist struggle but, notwithstanding the presence of foreign delegates in the congregations and the rhetoric about the oppressed Muslims in every part of the world, the main objective of the LeT recruits waging the Kashmiri *jihad* is to complete the unachieved partition of 1947 and integrate Kashmir into Pakistan.[37]

Xinjiang

In April 1990, riots hit Baren, a town in Akto county (thirty miles from Kashgar), in the western area of Xinjiang. The confrontation started as a small-group conversation critical of the Chinese Communist Party's (CCP) policies marginalizing Uyghur ethnics, and developed into a mass protest calling for a *jihad* to expel the "infidel Han" out of the province; it ended with several casualties on both sides.[38]

As the clashes took place after a decade of Deng Xiaoping's Open Door policy, which among other things had also encouraged exchanges between Xinjiang and the Central Asian republics (see Chapter 6) and Pakistan, the Chinese media were able to portray the uprising as an organized scheme to advance a *jihadi*-Islamist agenda. Within this narrative, Afghan *mujahidin* and Uyghur exiles in Turkey were said to have maneuvered local youth into launching a *jihad*, in connection with the aspirations of the Taliban and the East Turkestan Republic.

But the open call for Islam in the Baren riots was a rare case in Xinjiang's long history of contestation with the Chinese authority, as the vast majority of disturbances that had dotted the decades between the 1960s and the 1990s were ethno-nationalist in nature and discourse. As Han Chinese migration into Xinjiang skyrocketed between the establishment of the People's Republic in 1949 and the 1980s (from 6 percent in 1949 to 40 percent in 1982), Uyghur unrest has been consistently driven by ethnic discrimination and socio-economic grievances. By the twentieth century, Uyghur identity had become coterminous with Islam, and celebrated national heroes were seen as "shrined saints" (such as the Qarakhanid Satuq Bughra Khan, see Source 3.1 and Figure 1.2); however, as religious belonging was subsumed into Uyghur ethnic identity through the PRC's "nationalities" system (similar to that of the Central Asian Soviet Republics), so their hagiographies have been re-written as secular narratives (sometimes novels) by the state, making "Islam" a facet of this prism of ethnic identity. In the 1990s, Uyghur resistance was "mostly seen [by the Chinese Communist Party] as ethno-nationalist 'separatism' fueled by pan-Turkic ideology."[39]

Yet, in later years the Chinese state has been adamant in framing Uyghur discontent as specifically and exclusively religious rather than ethno-nationalist (and especially so in the post-9/11 context, when the US started to seek allies in its "War on Terror"). Branding the Baren riots as connected to the Taliban and the East Turkestan Movement allowed for the reversal of the 1980s opening policies: school books were edited to erase all references to *jihad*, foreigners were no longer allowed to teach in the Urumqi Islamic seminar, and fewer students were allowed to study abroad.

Second, framing the unrest as an Islamic "holy war" (the subtext and implication being its connection with "terrorism") has allowed the Chinese state to repress Uyghur aspirations for independence more violently, and with the endorsement of the international community. A clear example of the latter case occurred in 2015. Between the end of 2014 and mid-2015, Xinjiang saw several ethnic clashes, involving civilians as well as the police and military. By July, hundreds of Uyghurs had escaped from Xinjiang, many traveling to Southeast Asia as they attempted to reach Turkey, a country that for decades has proven friendly to these exiles. However, as the situation in West Asia became more and more unstable under the expansion of the Islamic State of Iraq and Syria (ISIS), China was able to pressure Thailand into sending over 100 Uyghurs back to China, claiming – without evidence – that they were on their way to Turkey as a stepping-stone to reach Syria or Iraq to join the *jihadi* terrorist enterprise. "Since 2012," stated the China director of Human Rights Watch in 2015, "law enforcement forces have killed hundreds of Uighurs in what authorities claimed were counter-terrorism operations ... but whether those killed or convicted were actually responsible for the violence ... will remain unknown to the outside world."[40]

Third, assigning blame to the international Islamist-*jihadi* revival places the origins of the conflict outside the Chinese own state's sphere of responsibility; instead of the state needing to change its policies, it is the Uyghur who must be distanced from their Islamic identity and brought closer to "China." Starting in 2014, officials of the CCP have been dispatched to Xinjiang for a "home stay" program; during these visits, the officials ask questions about their hosts' family life and political views, teach them Mandarin, and sing the national anthem. In 2018 the government launched yet another initiative to thwart the spread of "terrorism, separatism and religious extremism" by detaining hundreds of thousands of Uyghurs in "political education" camps in which they "are required to praise the ruling Communist Party, sing revolutionary songs, learn to speak Mandarin, study the thought of Chinese leader Xi Jinping, and confess perceived transgressions such as praying at a mosque or traveling abroad."[41]

Conclusions

Jihad, a heavily loaded word in the post-9/11 discourse, has many layers in theological and historical terms. This chapter has shown how the anti-Soviet resistance to the invasion and occupation of Afghanistan in the 1980s turned this Central Asian country into the receptacle for religiously oriented ideologues and militants from all over the world. Building on the social and political transformations of the 1960s and 1970s, and the conflation of local self-determination, radicalization of refugees, absorption of foreign militants, the charisma of a Palestinian Muslim Brother, and the wealth of a well-connected Saudi man, all come together in shaping the Afghan *jihad* as a symbolic and imagined site of resistance to outside forces for the global *umma*.

As Afghanistan absorbed the input of foreign Muslims, it also released them again, and in the post-Soviet era trained *mujahidin* were to be found in a variety of locales. If in the 1980s *jihad* had carried a positive connotation of liberation, since the 9/11 attacks, labeling a movement as "jihadist" has become an enabler of unquestionable repression, a convenient way for governments to tackle unrest in Muslim areas, even where struggles had been taking place for decades without much connection to Islamist aspirations, as seen in the cases of the Southern Philippines, Indonesia, Southern Thailand, Kashmir, and Western China.

Further Reading

Abinales, P. N. (2010) *Orthodoxy and history in the Muslim-Mindanao narrative*, Quezon City, Philippines: Ateneo de Manila University Press.

Al-Rasheed, M. (2007) *Contesting the Saudi state: Islamic voices from a new generation*, Cambridge: Cambridge University Press.

Atwill, D. G. (2006) *The Chinese sultanate: Islam, ethnicity, and the Panthay rebellion in Southwest China, 1856–1873*, Stanford, CA: Stanford University Press.

Bovingdon, G. (2010) *The Uyghurs: strangers in their own land*, New York, NY: Columbia University Press.

DeBergh Robinson, C. (2013) *Body of victim, body of warrior: refugee families and the making of Kashmiri jihadists*, Berkeley, CA: University of California Press.

Federspiel, H. M. (1998) "Islam and Muslims in the southern territories of the Philippine Islands during the American colonial period (1898 to 1946)," *Journal of Southeast Asian Studies* 29(2): 340–356.

Hegghammer, T. (2010) *Jihad in Saudi Arabia: violence and pan-Islamism since 1979*, New York, NY: Cambridge University Press.

Hooker, V. M., and Fealy, G. (2007) *Voices of Islam in Southeast Asia: a contemporary sourcebook*, Singapore: Institute of Southeast Asian Studies.

Jalal, A. (2008) *Partisans of Allah: Jihad in South Asia*, Cambridge, MA: Harvard University Press.

Kepel, G., and Roberts, A. F. (2014) *Jihad: the trail of political Islam*, London: Tauris.

Kim, H. (2010) *Holy war in China: the Muslim rebellion and state in Chinese Central Asia, 1864–1877*, Stanford, CA: Stanford University Press.

Lawrence, B. B. (1999) *Defenders of god: the fundamentalist revolt against the modern age*, Columbia, SC: University of South Carolina Press.

McCargo, D. (2008) *Tearing apart the land: Islam and legitimacy in Southern Thailand*, Ithaca, NY: Cornell University Press.

Miller, F. (2015) *The audacious ascetic: what Osama bin Laden's sound archive reveals about Al-qa'ida*, Oxford: Oxford University Press.

Morgenstein Fuerst, I. R. (2017) *Indian Muslim minorities and the 1857 Rebellion: religion, rebels, and jihad*, London: I. B. Tauris.

Peters, R. (2016) *Jihad: a history in documents*, Princeton, NJ: Markus Wiener Publishing Inc.

Sidel, J. T. (2006) *Riots, pogroms, jihad: religious violence in Indonesia*, Ithaca, NY: Cornell University Press.

Thum, R. (2012) "Modular history: identity maintenance before Uyghur nationalism," *The Journal of Asian Studies* 71(3): 627–653.

Figure 8.1 Advertisement for "Malaysia Drink" in Turfan
(Xinjiang, China).
© Chiara Formichi

8   De-centering Islamic Authority

On the streets of Turfan, Xinjiang province, food stalls, restaurants, and groceries patronized by the local Uyghur population are assured to be *halal* ("permitted"), as this ethnic group has been entirely Muslim for at least a couple of centuries.[1] Establishments servicing the more recently immigrated communities of non-Muslim Han Chinese serve products containing pork and alcohol. In this multi-ethnic environment, where the local Uyghur majority has been superseded socially and politically by the smaller group of migrant Hans, and where national politics has dictated the segregation, suppression, and incarceration of Western China's Muslims, food has become a site of contestation in the public sphere.

If Uyghur and Hui communities have manufactured and sought *halal* products for their own consumption, more recently the government of the People's Republic of China (PRC) has regarded the *halal* market as a desirable niche in which to expand, as it is projected to grow to US $280 billion by 2030.[2] At the same time, however, social media platforms have been flooded with concerns over the halalization of China, and the central government in Beijing has forbidden the advertisement of *halal* products across Xinjiang as yet another measure to curb the supposedly rampant "Islamization" and "radicalization" of the Uyghur population.

In this clash of desires and policies, the illustrated advertisement for an energy drink (Figure 8.1) gives prominence to its being "Malaysian" (in English, Chinese, and Uyghur languages), as a proxy for its being *halal*. The can itself has no writing in Malay, but with descriptions in English and Arabic the packaging creates an assumption that the product is marketed for export to Arabophone, and likely more generally Muslim, markets. And yet, there is no visible sign of the *halal* logo on this advertisement.

Malaysia emerged in the 1990s as a leading player in the global market in the standardization of *halal* production, and its government's worldwide reputation for promoting Islamically compliant products, from food to banking and tourism, seems to have become enough of a trademark to reassure Muslim consumers that a Malaysian drink produced for the Muslim market would be *halal*, regardless of the (in)visibility of a logo.

This chapter revolves around the emergence of new sites of authority as the outcome of a very peculiar connection between upward mobility, consumption, state intervention, shifting gender norms, and concerns with piety, and illustrates them with cases of *halal* certification as well as modest fashion and feminist juridical interpretation of the scriptures.

The "sites" of authority here are not only innovative because they are the outcome of modern socio-political developments, but also because, through the deployment of new technologies, they have been elevated from "local" to "global" (or at least transnational), challenging discourses on religious authority that for centuries privileged the Arab "center" over Asian "peripheries," and ultimately positioning Southeast Asia's Muslims as authoritative "pathfinders."

Proliferating Religious Authority

Religious authority, meaning the sources and methods deployed to determine what is acceptable for, and conforming to, Islamic principles, has been largely constructed as grounded in the content of the Qur'an and *hadith*, in the acquisition of canonized knowledge (*'ilm*), the ability to apply an increasingly standardized set of methodological skills to interpret the texts (*ijtihad*), and the lineage (*silsila*) – either scholarly or genealogical – of its bearers. *'Ulama*, traditionally men (especially since the sixteenth century) and most often with connections to the Arab world, have thus held the reins of interpretation and have been looked to as the most reliable authority.[3] Yet, this chapter suggests that social, political, and technological transformations between the nineteenth and twenty-first centuries have led to re-definitions of religious authority across the Muslim *umma*.

In sixteenth-century Europe, "[p]rint lay at the heart of that great challenge to religious authority, the Protestant Reformation,"[4] as the possibility of owning a Bible transformed itself in the desire to read the text and to understand it independently. When printing was adapted to Arabic script in the early nineteenth century, it was poised to stimulate the same kind of transformation, in the Arabophone world as well as in other geographical areas where vernacular languages had come to use that script – from the Tamil *arwi* to Java's *pegon*, northern India's *urdu*, and many others. While Francis Robinson has argued that printed books "attack[ed] the very heart of Islamic systems for the transmission of knowledge," as authority had been granted through oral transmission of the Qur'an and exegetical texts, a process sometimes validated with a written certification (*ijiaza*) attesting a pupil's achievements under the personal guidance of a trustworthy teacher,[5] Asma Sayeed has pointed out that the availability of a written corpus of Islamic legal-religious thought allowed women from scholarly families to reclaim a place as '*alima*.[6]

In colonized nineteenth-century India, the printing of religious texts – one of the earliest books to be printed in the Urdu vernacular was the *Taqwiyyat al-Iman* (see Chapter 6) – ushered in a new phase characterized by "Islamic protestantism" (taken to mean an individual approach and meticulous application of the scriptures), a broader vision of the *umma*, a pan-Islamic sense of identity (enabled by easier travel and the circulation of transregional periodicals), and "the erosion of the authority of the [professional] ulama as interpreters of Islam."[7] At the turn of the twentieth century, printing, the telegraph, and the steam ship had revolutionized commercial and human interaction among Muslims, allowing, for example, the South Asian Khilafat movement to be a catalyst for conversations about the Ottoman crisis worldwide (as seen in Chapter 4).

Looking at contemporary developments, Anderson and Gonzales-Quijan have thus argued that "as the print revolution fostered new classes, styles and sites of Islamic interpretation complementing the 'ulama-based ones of mosque and madrasa, the Internet provides a similar site and body of technical practice in the contemporary public spheres of the Muslim-majority world."[8] The introduction of advanced technologies (from the Internet, which made religious scriptures and exegetical texts available globally and digitally, to accessible education and the creation of a virtual *umma*), combined with new social structures (especially the emergence of Muslim middle classes and the changing roles of women in social and professional spheres), a diversification of needs, priorities, and desires among Muslim communities ultimately enabled voices that have traditionally been marginalized – a marginalization induced by the positions they advanced, their interpretative path, their perceived status in traditional hierarchies, or their geographical location – to be heard beyond their immediate constituency.

Bearers of "religious authority" now hail from diverse socio-economic backgrounds and geographical contexts, having undertaken traditional and non-traditional educational careers alike, invoking canonical and non-conventional sources, and applying "new" interpretative methods. Breaking through many of the traditional boundaries, these new generations are "de-centering" – in terms of content, identity, methods, and location – previous understandings and practices of Islamic authority.

Individual "lay" Muslims preoccupied with leading a pious lifestyle in a "modern" (possibly non-Islamic) context came to air their own interpretative opinions alongside, and independent of, those of *madrasa*-trained *'ulama*, producing what Krämer and Schmidtke have defined as "a proliferation of religious knowledge, actors and normative statements of uncertain status."[9] The opinions of traditional male *'ulama* now compete for "authority" in the public sphere with those of non-specialists, or individuals who studied Islamic "sciences" in non-traditional institutions, such as secular universities. Some are non-religious professionals (doctors, economists, etc.) who have become recognized as religious authorities because of the emergence of a culture of professionalism;[10] others are intellectuals, political activists, or "new religious intellectuals"[11] whose knowledge is in many cases acquired in Western schools, their opinions grounded in the scriptures *plus* other sources and distributed through modern technologies for an audience of (Western-)educated urbanites.[12] Among them are the Doha-based Yusuf al-Qaradawi, the Javanese Aa Gym, the Egyptian Amr Khaled, the Indian Zakir Naik, the Canada-based Pakistani (woman) Farhat Hashmi, and many more "Muslim televangelists" whose opinions occupy the entire spectrum from "liberal" to "conservative," as no connection exists between any of those "de-centering" factors and religious orientation.[13]

What has become evident in the twenty-first century is the coexistence of multiple realities emergent from the combination of new intersections between local politics, the global economy, the socio-economic status of Muslims, consumerism, and the pervasive presence of technology.

Indonesia and Malaysia experienced similar paths to economic development, as Suharto's New Order (Indonesia, 1967–1998) and Mahathir Mohammad's New Economic Policy (Malaysia, 1970) pushed a powerful agenda of state-driven economic growth. Although each country had its own experiences and reactions, in both cases the sudden industrialization, urbanization, and loss of traditional family structures contributed significantly to the success of the *da'wa* movement as a social phenomenon and a tool of the state (see Chapter 6); this newly formed cohort of well-educated and gainfully employed Muslim men and women came to negotiate their identities between Islam, traditional values, national belonging, and aspirations to modernity as "mutually constitutive," rather than seeing them as opposing forces.[14]

These middle classes eventually emerged as "pious modern" consumers (interested in leading a trendy and *halal* lifestyle); and despite the fact that national projects of development pictured women as mothers and wives, their gainful employment fueled consumption. Women were becoming financially independent and felt increasingly emancipated; even though neither the state nor society recognized them as such, the advertising industry did, making women their primary audience. At the same time, "pious modern" women have also led efforts to rethink their own social standing within religious discourse, claiming authority in the interpretation of the scriptures. As David Kloos suggests, the very gendering of the *da'wa* movement, both in terms of knowledge-seeking and consumption, "created a demand for female religious authority."[15]

This chapter, then, proposes that Muslim Southeast Asia's combination and sequence of factors – ranging from authoritarian capitalist states that embraced a development-friendly approach to Islam, to local traditions that promoted the presence of women in the public sphere, alongside a commitment to their education – has allowed for the emergence of "religious authority" from the margins, in terms of geography, content, methods, and positionality, in Indonesia and Malaysia.

Halal Consumption

[3]You are forbidden to eat carrion; blood; pig's meat; any animal over which any name other than God's has been invoked; any animal strangled, or victim of a violent blow or a fall, or gored or savaged by a beast of prey, unless you still slaughter it [in the correct manner]; or anything sacrificed on idolatrous altars. You are also forbidden to allot shares [of meat] by drawing marked arrows – a heinous practice – today the disbelievers have lost all hope that you will give up your religion. Do not fear them: fear Me. Today I have perfected your religion for you, completed My blessing upon you, and chosen as your religion *islam* [total devotion to God]: but if any of you is forced by hunger to eat forbidden food, with no intention of doing wrong, then God is most forgiving and merciful.

[4]They ask you, Prophet, what is lawful for them. Say, "All good things are lawful for you." [This includes] what you have taught your birds and beasts of prey to catch, teaching them as God has taught you, so eat what they catch for you, but first pronounce God's name over it. Be mindful of God: He is swift to take account. [5]Today all good things have been made lawful for you. The food of the People of the Book is lawful for you as your food is lawful for them. So are chaste, believing, women as well as chaste women of the people who were given the Scripture before you, as long as you have given them their bride-gifts and married them, not taking them as lovers or secret mistresses. The deeds of anyone who rejects faith will come to nothing, and in the Hereafter he will be one of the losers. (*Sura* of The Feast, Q 5: 3–5)

The Qur'an deploys the categories of *haram* (forbidden) and *halal* (lawful, permissible) to delineate the boundaries of acceptable consumption and behavior. Some specific foods are forbidden, some are made exceptions for, and all others are allowed. This classification applies to more than just food (brides, for example, as cited above), and it is not necessarily unequivocal: intoxicants receive a fluctuating assessment, as wine is first "a delight" of heaven (Q 47:15) but in a later revelation "intoxicants and gambling" become "idolatrous practices … Satan's doing" (Q 5:90). Several aspects of *halal* determination are debated between schools of law; and between *halal* and *haram*, the category of *masbuh* (doubtful) further complicates matters, leaving it to the interpreters to make a determination.

Fast-forwarding to the latter part of the twentieth century, amidst the *da'wa* movement of the 1970s–1990s, concerns over the dichotomy between *halal* and *haram* became entangled with the embrace of outward displays of Islamic normativity and piety. The *da'wa* movement was prominent among recently urbanized Muslims; as it provided a support network able to substitute for the loss of the extended family, it was crucial to the re-drawing of boundaries in a more heterogenous environment, and it advocated for the reinstating of "proper" gender relations (see Chapter 6).

But in the twenty-first century it is the growing presence and availability of religiously compliant (*halal*) products that has driven the further Islamization of society:

The *halal/haram* binary informs and controls ideas and practices such as the wearing of gold and ornaments; wigs and hairpieces; statues; paintings; photographs; keeping dogs; cleanliness; industries and crafts; sexual appetite; spreading the secrets of conjugal life, and innumerable other areas.[16]

The desire (or requirement, or pressure) to lead a "*halal* life" has thus expanded into a process of "halalization."[17] No longer hinging on the mere need to bring Islam and devotion into everyday life by having access to *halal* food as defined by the Qur'an and subsequent exegesis, halalization points to the negotiations required to find the right balance between the consumeristic desires of the middle class (sometimes labeled as indicators of a Westernized modernity) and that which is acceptable and legitimate in Islam, as illustrated in this commercial:

If you are looking for *halal* chocolate and candy, look no further than these *halal* products. These luxurious and rich chocolates are a great choice for Muslims or someone looking to give the gift of Belgian chocolate to someone who is. Because these products are *halal*, you can feel at ease about the chocolate being appreciated by the recipient and enjoyed by all. Enjoy delicious GODIVA chocolate even if you have *halal* dietary restrictions. This chocolate and candy is *halal* and just as flavorful as all our products. This makes the *halal* chocolate we carry the perfect choice for practicing Muslims. Whether you want to enjoy them on your own or to give them as a present to someone in an Islamic household, GODIVA chocolate gifts are the perfect luxury chocolate choice.[18]

Shopping in a *halal* mall, like staying at a *halal* resort during the holidays, has come to be seen by many as crucial to creating an environment that fosters piety, as donning Islamic fashion is for several women a tool to be more self-aware, an inspiration to conform to an overall more Islamically appropriate behavior.

With the emergence of a large-enough Muslim middle class (in Malaysia, Indonesia, Turkey, and several other countries), consumers have exerted pressure to gain access to an Islamically compliant lifestyle, including *halal* restaurants, shopping experiences, and travel services. In addition to being a sign of piety, this "Islamic lifestyle" has become a characteristic of social status, economic wealth, aspiration to piety, and shrewd marketing, creating an economy (of products and advice) aimed at satisfying such desires, from clothing and personal accessories to home decor, entertainment, aesthetics, household maintenance, interpersonal relations, and general consumption.

Global expenditures in religious sub-markets reflect the impact of "pious consumption": the global *halal* food market is valued at about US$630 billion,[19] about as much as the Islamic fashion industry is estimated to be worth in 2020; by then, *halal* tourism is expected to reach US$220 billion, between 10 and 15 percent of the global market. Within this vast variety of realms, this section explores the emergence of two sub-sectors of the *halal* market, namely fashion and foodstuffs, investigating their connection to three factors in Southeast Asia: the *da'wa* movement of the 1970s–1990s, the emergence of a new middle class, and changing gender relations. As Johan Fischer suggests, food and dress are "the two object domains in which *halal*isation has been felt most forcefully."[20]

Regulating Halal *Food: From Malaysia to China*

Following the 1969 ethnic riots, Malaysia launched itself in a rapid process of state-driven development which encompassed industrialization, urbanization, and more widespread access to higher education. But these reforms led to multifarious socio-economic transformations that eventually intersected with the *da'wa* movement. One of the key actors was the Darul Arqam group, which had emerged as a reaction to the many (perceived) pitfalls of the rapid, state-driven, modernization effort, and thus propagandized the idea that a new balance could be achieved only by incorporating Islam into everyday life.

The scholarship of both Maila Stivens and Johan Fischer helps us to see that the trajectory from these reforms to *halal* consumption as "modernization" ultimately materialized itself as the development of suburban living, shopping malls, and restaurants: sites that came to be inhabited and patronized by the newly emerged Malay middle class. This new

Malay middle class defined itself as such on the grounds of upward social mobility and increased income, two aspects that were equally representative of the policies that enabled them (urbanization, access to higher education, and white-collar managerial occupations) and of the consumerist opportunities that they allowed.[21] The Darul Arqam fit squarely in this development pattern.

Darul Arqam's primary goal was, like that of other *da'wa* groups, to facilitate and guide the pious enhancement of Malay Muslims. However, in many ways Darul Arqam was different. Not only did its members embrace "Arab dress" (mostly meaning that women in the movement wore face-covering veils), but its "most distinctive feature [was] the cultivation of an economic organization based entirely on strict Islamic principles."[22] Anchored in the strong personality of its leader, Darul Arqam developed as a residential "gated" community where professionals and youth worked and lived together creating a fully Islamic environment. Whereas on the one hand they practiced *hijra* ("migration, separation"; see Box 6.2), Darul Arqam members were also deeply enmeshed in Malaysia's society and economy, as they sought *halal* self-sufficiency through independence from non-Muslims – generating their own electricity, growing their own produce, and processing basic foodstuffs – while also selling these products outside of their community, trading across the Malay Peninsula. The Darul Arqam group was eventually crushed by the Malaysian government, which labeled it a "deviant group" in 1994. The idea of a *halal* lifestyle and consumption was, however, not so marginal and "extreme."

After the Malaysian government responded to increased Islamization by marginalizing "sectarian" Islamist groups (such as Darul Arqam), it also pursued an agenda of "nationalization" (or cooptation) of Islam. According to Johan Fischer, "the increasing importance of *halal* discourses and practices is both a result of the increase in revivalism and an instrument of that resurgence," as the state's cooptation of sociopolitical aspects of Islam went hand in hand with its institutionalization and regulation of *halal*.[23] What is more, as *halal* regulation in-country became a key aspect of governance, the Malaysian state "developed the vision to become the world leader in *halal* production, trade and regulation."[24] In the 1990s, Malaysia already hosted the production of Japanese companies' *halal* foodstuffs, and in the mid-2010s, the general manager for Ajinomoto stated that "We will make Southeast Asia a base to tap the global halal market."[25]

While Indonesia, Thailand, and Singapore have all carved niches in the global *halal* market, Malaysia is the country that has emerged as its hub. The first step was to entrust the regulation and certification processes to a government agency; but whereas in the mid-1990s the Islamic Development Department of Malaysia (JAKIM) had no standardized method for vetting an industrial facility or product, in the 2010s Malaysia had a well-established *halal* assurance system that matched secular certification standards and withstood international scrutiny. In fact, Malaysia has become a global *halal* hub: not only were "*halal* industrial parks" established across the country, but JAKIM's certifications have also become recognized worldwide.

An additional important step in setting up Malaysia as a hub from where products can then be exported to West Asia and other Muslim countries (as in the case of US companies Kellogg and Hershey, for example),[26] was the development of "*halal* logistics." Projecting the past glories of sixteenth-century Malacca as a trading hub, in 2006 Malaysia's national shipping company launched the "Halal Express Service," a weekly cargo service ferrying *halal* beef from Australia and New Zealand to West Asia.[27] A little over a decade later, Malaysia's ports are holding conversations with Chinese and European port handlers.[28]

On May 14, 2018, a container ship filled with food, beverages, and body-care products inaugurated the "*Halal* Silk Route" with a voyage from western Malaysia's North Port in Port Klang (Selangor) to Weifang, Shandong province, in northeastern China. Its cargo was destined to reach China's Muslim provinces of Shaanxi, Ningxia, Gansu, Qinghai, and Xingjian, as "the first step towards linking the approximately 2.1 billion global Muslim population through the trade of *halal* products."[29] Most notably, besides providing the goods, Malaysia has also enabled Weifang to become the first Chinese port operator with *halal* certification from JAKIM, qualifying it as fit to retain the purity of the products.[30]

Malaysia's efforts to assert itself as a global *halal* hub met with China's interests in expanding its *halal* market. China has traditionally had a healthy local market for the production and consumption of *halal* foods, as its large Muslim population is complemented by non-Muslim Chinese who see *halal* food as more hygienic and cleaner than conventional foods (in Chinese, *halal* food is referred to as "clean and pure"). As the global consumption of *halal* increases, the Chinese government and business community have been keen on reaching beyond their domestic consumer base. But if "Made in China" is already a common brand in West Asia, where prayer beads, mats, and printed Qur'ans often carry the PRC mark – "most of the stuff over there [in Mecca and Medina] is made in China, apart from; [*sic*] dates and zam zam water," states a pilgrim on TripAdvisor – the food market remains limited.[31] The interest remains – "If we can tap into the market in Mecca, we would become trusted by Muslims all across the world, making it easier to enter other Muslim markets," stated the general manager of a Chinese *halal* company in 2016 – but this enterprise has encountered many obstacles.[32]

First of all, China's domestic *halal* consumption is estimated to be just over US$20 billion,[33] compared for example to ASEAN's *halal* market's projection of growth to US$280 billion by 2030,[34] making it by default a niche market. While some provinces have succeeded in keeping a share of their domestic markets and export their own *halal* products, numbers stay small: Ningxia province, for example, exports a little over a million US dollars-worth of *halal* food per year to Malaysia, the UAE, Qatar, and Egypt (out of 4.5 billion of total exports for the province).

Secondly, Chinese *halal* products have been implicated in several scandals, including findings of pork packaged as *halal* beef and other clear infringements of the *halal* dictum. The failure to gain consumer confidence has been further exacerbated by the fact that, as the government has attempted to seize this business opportunity by granting tax reductions and other benefits to companies claiming to fill this gap, many non-Muslims have entered the *halal* market. Not only are they seen as interlopers in a market once exclusively controlled by the Hui population, but there is also further debate over whether this affects the status of a product as *halal*. Concerns over mislabeling, mispackaging, and ultimately mishandling of *halal* products put an end to China's hopes of emerging as a global *halal* exporter, with major financial implications. In response, several groups advanced the idea of developing a nationwide certification system. Hong Kong has had its own certifying body for several decades (the Incorporated Trustees of the Islamic Community Fund); Taiwan's certification is managed by Indonesia's Islamic Council (MUI, since 2017). But Chinese netizens have most recently called for a boycott of *halal* products and food delivery "apps," voicing through social media a more general opposition to what has come to be referred to as "halalification" (*qing zhen fa hua*), and the government has been under strong pressure to limit – if not altogether ban – *halal* products.

As its political and legal contexts are making it hard to create the conditions for a standardized and reliable nationwide certification system, China has had to rely on imported goods and foreign certifying bodies. This is how Malaysia is emerging as the go-to source.

The Malaysian government has been promoting its *halal* products and certifying institutions in China for years. Not only does China account for 12 percent of consumption of Malaysia's total *halal* products (making China Malaysia's top *halal* export destination),[35] but Malaysia's Department of Islamic Development (JAKIM) has also become involved in lending its expertise, reinforcing this Southeast Asian country's aspiration to become a "global *halal* hub" – a goal set by the government as early as 2004, when Malaysia launched the first International *Halal* Showcase.

But why Malaysia and not the Saudi Arabia-based Muslim World League, which also issues certifications to Brazil and Japan, for example? It could be the advantage of proximity; of being an historically established trading partner of China; of hosting a large Chinese diaspora; or of being a multi-ethnic country which for decades has had to face the challenges of diverse dietary preferences and restrictions. But this is not about China's choice; rather, it is about Malaysia's policies and agendas, which have allowed it to be accepted by many other countries worldwide as a credible international *halal* certifier and regulator. Through the *"halal* drive" started in the early 2000s, the government sponsored the tightening-up of standardized certification and logistics, and the emergence of industrial parks to host local and foreign factories; Malaysia has been able to establish itself as a credible, reliable, and stable authority in the *halal* market. Far from being an exclusively logistical positioning, Malaysia is emerging as a new site of religious authority, determining the boundaries of what is Islamically "permissible and lawful" on a global scale.

Islamic Fashion: Indonesia Trending

With a mission to promote Indonesian culture, Dian Pelangi emphasizes its exceptional craftsmanship and use of traditional woven fabrics known as Tenun, tie dye fabrics, and batik, which makes it unique to the market. Starting from Melbourne Fashion Week in 2009, the brand has showcased its collection throughout the globe including the Middle East, Europe, and the US.[36]

In 2014 *The New York Times* described Dian Pelangi as "the unofficial poster girl for the introduction of Indonesian Islamic fashion to the world";[37] two years later she was invited to speak at New York University,[38] and in 2018 she made the *Forbes* Asia "30under30" list for "bringing modernity to the modest fashion market";[39] her batik and ikat fabrics were showcased at New York Fashion Week,[40] and eventually put on display at the de Young Museum in San Francisco.[41] At the close of 2018, Dian Pelangi had 5 million followers on Instagram and was selling her fashion worldwide.

In the early 2010s the collective Muslim clothing market was second only to that of the United States, with Turkey, Iran, and Indonesia as the biggest individual spenders. Malaysia and Thailand were seen as the leading Islamic fashion hubs alongside France. In 2017 Kuala Lumpur hosted the first Asia Islamic Fashion week under the slogan "Establishing Asia as a Global Center for Islamic Fashion," and the Indonesian government set itself the goal of emerging as a global Muslim fashion capital by 2020. Islamic fashion is gradually entering the mainstream on catwalks and in shop windows – from Dolce e Gabbana to Nike and Uniqlo – and Southeast Asia has a clear advantage, with its well-established manufacturing industry, creative human resources, and a large domestic consumer base.

Hoping to become the "Paris of the International Muslim vogue,"[42] Indonesia is projecting itself as a potential trendsetter; an endeavor confirmed by the success of Dian Pelangi (described above), Fatin Suhana (whose Instagram hashtag appears in Southeast Asia as well as Egypt, Nigeria, and the UAE),[43] and Irna Mutiara (whose clothes are purchased in France, Egypt, Dubai, Abu Dhabi, Malaysia, and Hong Kong).[44]

Islamic fashion (also referred to as "modest fashion," "pious fashion," or "Islamic clothing"), and more specifically Muslim women's fashion, is a highly visible display of piety, and one that is often pointed to as a site of gender inequality within Islam. Whereas it is a fact that governments (e.g. the Islamic Republic of Iran, Taliban-controlled areas of Afghanistan), societies (e.g. Malaysia, Afghanistan), and family members often apply pressure on young women to conform to certain expectations of modest clothing, it also ought to be recognized that this is not the only reality. Motivations and contexts for "veiling" (a term broadly used to refer to the donning of a head covering as well as more generally loose, shape-hiding clothes) are often connected to either oppression or religious conservatism, but in fact they have varied greatly over time and space. One primary distinction between Southeast Asia and West Asia is that the popularization of the headscarf in the 1980s and 1990s in Indonesia and Malaysia should not be considered a "re-veiling," as may have been the case in Egypt or Algeria, but rather as a new phenomenon characteristic of a new social class (see Source 6.1). Until this time, head covering had been a practice largely limited to older women who had performed the pilgrimage to Mecca (see Chapter 4).

In 1980s and 1990s Java (Indonesia), for example, "veiling" was embraced by young, urban, middle-class university students who aimed to reject (not re-enact) the local past: "Islamic clothing [was] a departure from Javanese styles of clothing as well as the Western styles that ha[d] increasingly replaced them."[45] As Suzanne Brenner suggests, the shift to veiling was driven by personal and religious motivations as much as by socio-political reflections on the status of Indonesian society in the New Order period. As Suharto's reforms combined state-driven industrialization, urbanization, wider access to higher education, and economic growth with rampant corruption and nepotism, the new wave of wealth enriched the top layer of society increasing the gap, and at the same time fostering urban consumer culture. Amidst these changes, the now educated lower-middle and middle classes became disenchanted with Western models of "development," sensitive to issues of moral decline, and – thanks to the spread of TV and print media – aware of global Islamic movements.

The West Asian Islamic revival projected alternatives to both Western and Javanese socio-economic paradigms, but also "provide[d] an alternative set of options to the gender ideologies promoted by the state and the Indonesian mass media."[46] Islamic fashion in this period, then, was the outcome of a previous decision to be pious – a reaction to older generations' (perceived) devotional laxity, New Order consumerism, corrupt representations of femininity, and more general secularly defined pursuits of personal enrichment. And it came to be manifest through a clothing style antithetical to any local or contemporary ideals of fashion and femininity (see Box 6.3).

In the mid-to-late 1990s, as the New Order edifice began to fracture and make concessions to Muslim constituencies, donning the headscarf became less a sign of political protest, and accessories of Islamic piety were more commodified. In 1996 the Association of Indonesian Fashion Designers created a subdivision dedicated to Islamic clothing, encouraging the creation, production, and export of local designs.[47] By the late 1990s Islamic dress in Java "had come to feel more like an unsurprising consumer choice among an array of dress styles for young women."[48]

Whereas this has at times been taken as a sign that "veiling" says relatively little about the wearer's commitment to piety, a counter-approach to this reading of contemporary practices of Islamic clothing as trendy and fashionable has thought about embracing an outward sign of piety ("the veil") as a stimulus to behave more piously because of the expectations entailed by such display, thus forging a connection between aesthetics and ethics.[49] "Indonesian women have learned how to veil so that we do it more beautifully now ... those baggy pastel outfits were not attractive, no one wants to look at that. Today we know *jilbab* should be modest, modern, and beautiful."[50] The relationship between pious consumption and personal piety has, then, become more complex: consuming Islamic products remains an overt sign of religiosity, but it has also come to be an implicit sign of wealth and a means of becoming more pious in everyday life: as Carla Jones argues, leading a visibly Islamic lifestyle has contributed to "constructing virtue through, rather than outside of, consumption."[51]

This novel approach to Islamic clothing has turned "veiling" into "Islamic fashion," thus creating a dedicated market, industry, and subculture that hinges on aspirations to piety and modesty as much as to cosmopolitanism and style. The magazine *NooR*, established in 2006, branded itself as "the first cosmopolitan Muslim women's magazine in Indonesia ... With the *tagline* [English in the original] confident - intelligent - stylish, *NooR* urges Indonesian women to be closer, more loving, and more pious [fearful] for Allah."[52] *NooR* was just the first of many religiously inspired consumption-oriented magazines that have since appeared on the market. The emergence and popularity of *NooR* and the like can be seen as the convergence of three factors that have characterized the post-Suharto era: first, the exponential expansion of the media industry, fomented by the partial lifting of censorship; second, the rise of Islam's visibility in the public (social and political) sphere; third, the emergence of a wider segment of middle-class Muslims. As pointedly noted by Ariel Heryanto at the end of the 1990s, "gone are the old and rigid meanings of 'religion' and 'politics', as well as the clear boundaries that separate them from 'lifestyle.'"[53] In this "new" environment, Indonesia's popular culture scene – from TV soap operas to music, magazines, and fashion – came to be permeated with piety and a preferred site for the "new" middle class.

In the last quarter of the twentieth century, embracing a more overtly pious attitude, often marked by the donning of a "veil," had multiple signifiers, several of which were empowering from a gender perspective. As in Indonesia, in Malaysia, too, modest fashion provided urban middle-class Muslim women with a tool to reject the nationalist ideal of traditional feminine identity, as well as the too easily sexualized Westernized image of modern womanhood. What is more, the many magazines, books, and blogs that offer advice on how to dress "properly," apply make-up, be professional in the workplace, or interact with men outside the family have emerged as a women-led interpretative effort amidst an overwhelmingly male-directed context of religious authority. As Elizabeth Bucar concludes in her study of pious fashion in Yogyakarta (Java, Indonesia),

women's sartorial practices occur within a web of norms not always of their making. But women are also the necessary synthesizers of these norms when they decide whether and how to wear pious fashion. Choosing an outfit involves a process of discerning what moral values are associated with particular items or styles, as well as determining what presents an appropriate yet attractive image.[54]

Women's Religious Leadership and Authority

In March 2005, amina wadud led a mixed-gender Friday prayer in Manhattan, defying the generally understood prohibition on women leading men in prayer. An African American convert and a professor of Qur'anic studies, amina wadud has been at the forefront of Islamic feminism since the 1980s. Instead of following Western secular feminist approaches that condemn religion per se as a conservative force holding women back, her feminism is one which embraces Islam as an enabler for women's rights, a goal she has pursued by applying Fazlur Rahman's hermeneutical exegesis of the Qur'an to its discussion of women (see also Source 8.1).

Box 8.1 Islamic Female Authority

The foundations of Islamic knowledge were shaped by Muslim men and women alike, from Muhammad's wives (especially 'A'isha) to his contemporaries and subsequent generations of transmitters and scholars. In the first century of Islam, a large portion of the Companions of the Prophet were women (as attested by early biographical dictionaries), and they thus held the important role of *muhaddithat* ("transmitters of the sayings"), their numbers dropping first in the eleventh century, and eventually disappearing altogether in the sixteenth century (see Chapter 3). But the memory of 'A'isha leading the Muslim army at the battle of Badr never disappeared, and Zaynab's defiance of the 'Umayyad commander has remained a hallmark of Shi'i revolutionary imaginations. Hence women have dotted the history of Islam, present through the centuries – from Turkey to China – as Sufi teachers, community leaders, and political leaders.

The idea of Divine Love was developed by a woman, Rabi'a al-'Adawiyyah (d. 801), and women were known as *shaykha*s and patrons of Sufism from Egypt to Turkey, Iran, and India. As Annemarie Schimmel suggests,

In India, the lower Indus Valley and the Punjab are dotted with minor sanctuaries of women saints, either single individuals or whole groups (preferably 'Seven Chaste Ladies' or so) who are said to have performed some acts of unusual piety. Some are venerated for their chastity, some were blessed with performing miracles and others are noted for their healing properties.[55]

In early twentieth-century Iran, Nusrat Amin (1886–1983) was known as a Sufi, but left her mark as a scholar of *hadith* and *fiqh*. Her published works attracted the attention of other (male) Shi'i scholars, who often consulted with her, seen as a peer and equal.

Yet, in most contexts textual religious authority has been held by those who have been traditionally trained (i.e. *'ulama*), and as pointed out by Masooda Bano and Hilary Kalmbach, the formal spaces of mosque and *madrasa* have traditionally excluded women, limiting the development and impact of their voices as authoritative in the scholarly realm until the second half of the twentieth century, when Muslim women obtained better access to higher religious education and professionalization worldwide.[56]

While "the West" was busy advancing an agenda of women's rights exclusively couched in the secular human rights' discourse – for which any impingement of religion over political, legal, or social dynamics translated into the oppression of women by men – Muslim women such as Fatima Mernissi, Leila Ahmed, Asma Barlas, and amina wadud, to name a few, were hard at work to bring back to the surface the "spirit" of the Qur'an: if in the seventh century Muhammad had spoken against the killing of baby girls, mandated that wives and daughters be eligible for inheritance, and asserted men and women's equality in front of God, this dramatic shift away from pre-Islamic Arabian traditions – alongside the characterization of Allah as a "just" God – ought to be interpreted as a sign of Islam's embedded quest for gender equality (see Chapter 1 for the transformation of women's roles during the Abbasid period).

On the other hand, it ought to be noted that the women mentioned above have all been based in the West (either Europe or the United States), potentially confirming Juliane Hammer's suggestion that whereas women worldwide could have carved a niche for themselves in the contemporary vacuum of authority described above, "those identified as new religious intellectuals have been predominantly male." But drawing from the example of amina wadud's 2005 prayer, Hammer posits that "It is in the North American context that some women have risen to the ranks of prominent Muslim intellectuals," pointing to North America's broader (although still limited) economic, social, and political opportunities for women, and to a minority context that "has privileged secular laws and the privatization of religious practices." Nonetheless, Hammer herself identifies a crucial problem, namely established (male) community leaders and scholars who criticize these women for "lack[ing] the training necessary to reinterpret Islamic laws."[57]

Taking an Asian perspective on this situation, a superficial excursus of Muslim societies where women have in the past enjoyed high socioreligious status would confirm the demoralizing reality that women have not been able to fill the vacuum: Muslim women in China and the Maldives have had "women mosques" for centuries, yet there has been no "next step" allowing female leadership in mixed congregations, and the status quo is also often contested. In Central Asia, women such as the *otines* held social and political high positions since before the Russian conquest and the Revolution, yet after independence from the Soviet Union their religious positioning has become unremarkable. From the early 1990s, Ladakhian Muslim women have been sent to Deobandi schools specifically to return as leaders of their congregations, but again, this has been a "women for women" effort. In the Indian subcontinent, women Sufi "saints" attract large crowds to their shrines, but their influence has not gone beyond claims to miracle-making.[58]

That being said, it is also worth bringing into the picture the fact that a milestone in Western Islamic feminism, wadud's own *Qur'an and Woman*, was first published in 1992 in Kuala Lumpur while she was teaching at the International Islamic University of Malaysia; from there, she would later visit Indonesia.[59] In both countries, wadud engaged in long-term conversations and organizational partnerships, equally contributing to and benefiting from a context where Muslim women's voices were increasingly heard and accepted as authoritative.

This section explores how Malaysia and Indonesia have been at the forefront of the movement to assert women's voices in the realm of religious authority in contemporary times. The analysis of Sisters in Islam (Malaysia) and the Indonesia Conference of Female Ulama (Kongres Ulama Perumpuan Indonesia, or KUPI) focuses on the relationship between these movements and their country's socio-political contexts (as illustrated above), the historically deep importance of women's religious education, and the relevance of kinship networks; the other side of this discourse on women as bearers of religious authority is inevitably the question of what impact their individual paths toward Islamic feminism are making globally in the field of textual interpretation. As suggested by Rachel Rinaldo, these women "have developed a pious critical agency that draws on both Islamic and feminist discourses to promote women's rights"[60] through interpretations of religious texts that emphasize different historical and cultural contexts.

Malaysia

Changes in the position of women in society had evidently not been part of the transformations envisioned by the New Economic Policy and New Education Policy of the 1970s; the policies focused on the "new Malay" as a male modern citizen, the breadwinner for the "modern Asian family," flanked by a housewife who was made to play the role of supporter of this nationalist endeavor. Yet, the achievement of "modernization" in tandem with the *da'wa* movement led to (at least) three developments crucial to women. First, because "being middle class" came to be performed through consumer culture,[61] the advertisement and media industries saw women as their primary targets, bringing them center-stage and portraying consumption as feminine. As Maila Stivens highlights, women became key images of affluent middle-class consumption.[62] Within this optic, gender dynamics and the role of religion in regulating social interactions became key.

"Women feature[d] strongly in many of the cultural productions of affluent middle classness and achievement,"[63] either as successful professionals or as consumers. Amidst this variety of images of women, ranging from embodiment of traditional Malay values to Westernized styles and Islamic fashion, glossy magazines propagating the new middle-class lifestyle were clearly concerned with protecting women's modesty, making sure that representations of "modern women" were not compromised by ideas of promiscuity and sexualization. While images of the new Malay man incurred no moral dangers, "the femininity of a new woman slides more easily into moral ambiguity. It is clouded with the eroticization of the commodity inherent in neomodern/post-modern consumption."[64] In this context, while Malay men were featured sporting Western-style clothing, Malay women "are constructed as bearers of a recreated nationality/nationalism and or Islamic piety in their everyday dress."[65]

Second, as Sylva Frisk has argued,[66] Malay women's involvement in the *da'wa* movement and Islamic study groups, their appropriation of knowledge and spaces that would generally be exclusive male domains, and their performing of collective religious rituals, has "creat[ed] a space for [women's] religious agency in public,"[67] and thus for their advancing claims to religious authority as preachers, teachers, and leaders of religious organizations.

Third, Malaysia's peculiar socio-political and legal context of the 1980s and 1990s propelled the emergence of a strand of feminism inspired by Islam and driven by the desire to uncover the egalitarian spirit of the Qur'an worldwide:

As Muslims living in a country where Islam is a source of law and public policy and practice how can we not engage with religion when it is used to discriminate and oppress us? How can we just ignore it and leave it to the religious authorities and the Islamists to define what Islam is and what it's not? ... Sisters in Islam had always been a group that bridged the gap between Islam and human rights. We didn't see any contradictions. We saw the possibility of engaging with religion to push for change.[68]

When civil society begun to self-organize in 1980s Malaysia, Sisters in Islam (SIS) was able to emerge as a bridge between purely secular, "Westernized," rights-based NGOs located in the country's major urban centers with international connections, and local Islamic NGOs that, while interested in a human rights' agenda, operated within a Malay sphere and discourse. SIS thus emerged as a strong, motivated, and empowered religious feminist organization.

When amina wadud reached Kuala Lumpur in 1989, a group of Malaysian women had already been discussing the issue of women's status under religious family law. Inspired by local debates on the acceptability of polygamy, her attendance at a workshop held by the international network of Women Living under Muslim Law (WLUML), and the activism of Muslim women in Pakistan, in 1988 Zainah Anwar had created a group interested in promoting women's rights within the framework of Islam. A few years later the group was formalized as an advocacy NGO, co-founded by Zainah Anwar, amina wadud, and five other Malaysian women.

The founding members of SIS came from peculiar backgrounds and began their activism under specific circumstances. Their parents were models of how Islamic piety and modernity were not in contradiction with each other: they spoke English and were civil employees during the late colonial era but believed in Malay nationalism; as young women they were allowed to wear miniskirts but were also required to participate in religious festivals. They grew up in Penang or Kuala Lumpur, their family friends were influential politicians and technocrats, and they often spent time studying abroad. Even though "women's groups acted independently of the political lobby of male-dominated structures,"[69] their activism cannot be separated from their belonging to a well-educated, productively employed, internationally minded, and politically connected "old" middle class.

Their "elite" status and their connection to those "male-dominated structures" created a favorable environment for the feminist agenda. But as important has been the fact that SIS's agenda also fit with Malaysia's modernization-*cum*-islamization vision led by Mahathir Mohammad in the 1990s (discussed in Chapter 6), allowing it to flourish and prosper. Even if in more recent years SIS has come under attack by the Islamist party PAS, the group has retained the endorsement of the "moderate" political establishment, as proven by Marina Mahathir's involvement in the organization (and its offshoot movement Musawah, discussed below).

Hence, the *da'wa* movement created the conditions for the formation of SIS as an impactful NGO advancing women's equality in a religious framework, attracting support and input from Muslim women worldwide. Obtaining local political endorsement and support, SIS maintained a stability in their activities that allowed it first to become an established and recognized presence nationally, and later to reach outside its borders to create a global network.

Recently this group has been able to rise to international prominence as, arguably, the most impactful advocacy group for women's rights in the Muslim world, by spearheading – with the support of the Indonesian Kamala Chandrakirana and many other Muslim women and men worldwide – the creation of Musawah in 2007–2009. It was the realization that "the divide [between Islam and human rights] didn't exist in Southeast Asia, but was very much present in the Arab world and in South Asia"[70] that pushed Zainah Anwar and other women to create "a global movement to bring together activists and scholars to shape a new dominant discourse that reconciles Islam with human rights."[71]

After half a decade of conversations and workshops with members of this worldwide network of Muslim feminist scholars and activists, in 2007 SIS – in collaboration with the Iranian legal anthropologist and activist Ziba Mir-Hosseini and the Singapore-based human rights lawyer Jana Rumminger – called for a meeting in Istanbul. Two years later, a gathering held in Kuala Lumpur and attended by over 250 participants from more than forty countries launched Musawah (Arabic for "equality") as "a global movement for equality and justice in Muslim families."[72] Aiming to "link scholarship with activism to bring new perspectives on Islamic teaching, with the objective of inserting women's voices and concerns into the production of religious knowledge and legal reform in Muslim contexts,"[73] Musawah works together with international Muslim legal experts with the multiple goals of reforming legal interpretations on the position of women *vis-à-vis* men, affirming the role of human agency and interpretation in the exegesis of the scriptures, and challenging the historical domination of male interpreters "claiming [women's] authority to speak on Islamic law and to participate in the construction of meaning ... at an international level" and going beyond "women's issues."[74]

Starting from a small NGO in Kuala Lumpur in the late 1980s, the trajectory of SIS led to the creation of Musawah as a movement specifically rooted in the Malaysian experience and dedicated to reaching out to other Muslim-majority countries to fill the knowledge gap "on understanding Islam from a rights' framework."[75] In Zainah Anwar's own words,

For me and Sisters in Islam ... Musawah was in some ways a vindication of a long and difficult struggle to find liberation within my faith and to translate into collective action my utter belief in a just God. This is the last frontier in the feminist movement, to break the theological stranglehold of the patriarchs that prevents Muslim women from enjoying equal rights.[76]

Source 8.1

"Feminist Islam," Interview with Zainah Anwar, Radio National, Australia Broadcasting Corporation (August 3, 2003)

The Malaysian Zainah Anwar was among the founding members of the advocacy NGO Sisters in Islam in 1989 as a group aimed at promoting feminist interpretations of Islamic scriptures. In this interview with the Australian Broadcasting Corporation, Zainah Anwar points at the legacy of patriarchal societies on textual exegesis and where the need for a contextualist exegesis comes from.[77]

ZAINAH ANWAR: I don't accept that interpretation of the Qur'anic verse [that the testimony of one man is equal to that of two women]. The problem that we have is that so many of these verses in the Qur'an are interpreted in isolation, literal interpretation of the verse, because we need to understand that the Qur'an was revealed within a social historical context. And we need to link that with the objective of the revelation. Now that verse on witnesses, was within a context to ensure that justice is done at a time when women were not so much in public life, when women were not involved in business transactions. In fact it was very much on business transactions, on contracts, witnesses to contracts, and the verse actually says the second woman is to ensure that no mistake is made, the other is to assist that man witness, not one man equals two women. But unfortunately in a very patriarchal society, that verse has been interpreted to mean one male witness equals the two female witnesses. So a lot of the problems that we have today with regard to women's rights in Islam has to do more with interpretations of the Qur'an, a process that has been dominated by men, within the context of very patriarchal societies. So now of course in the twenty-first century and the twentieth century in the past thirty to forty years, where within the context of the women's movement, of widespread education, women are getting educated, women are out there in public life, earning money, being in top positions, all these interpretations, gender- biased interpretations are being questioned. And so this is a challenge that is posed by the women's movement in particular, and human rights movements, to the religious authority. How do you make religion relevant to the lives of women today, who are independent, who are strong, who are opinionated and will not accept an inferior status in life? …

[T]here is a difference between what is revealed by God – and that is the words in the Qur'an, there are exact verses in the Qur'an that comes from God, that's revealed from God – and what is human understanding of the word of God. In understanding what is the word of God, there is the human agency, the human intervention. So the minute the process of reading the Qur'an and what you say as a result of reading the Qur'an, and what you understand as a result of reading the Qur'an, the process of human agency, of human understanding and human intervention, has come in and interacted with the revealed word. So this is the point we

Source 8.1   *(cont.)*

are making, that all these laws that are codified, all these pronouncements and fatwahs that are made in the name of God, in the name of Islam, are human understanding of God's word, and because they are human understanding of God's revealed message, therefore it can be challenged, it can be changed, given the context of changing times and circumstances. So we need to make, and this is a big problem that we have as well in the Muslim world, that there is a difference between what is the revealed word and what is human understanding of the revealed word ...

[T]his is the struggle I think for many Muslim women, because religion has meaning to us, and when you have religions [*sic*] authorities who interpret religion in a way that has no meaning and no relevance to your life, that's where you as a believer, then want to claim that right, to reclaim your religion ... we want to go back to that revolutionary spirit, if you follow that trajectory of Islam being the first religion to give women, to recognise women's individual rights as a human being, as an independent human being, that right now Muslim women and Islam should be the most liberating religion for women. But unfortunately that is not so because like all religions and within patriarchal societies, it is men who have dominated the religious authorities, it is the men who have interpreted the religions text for us, in a way that reflected their privileged status in life. So this is the struggle now.

Indonesia

The Indonesian government has celebrated the constructive role of women in society since independence, and women there have had access to family planning and higher education since the 1960s; but their role was by and large confined to the sphere of home-making and "mothering," even though Indonesian women had traditionally occupied a space in the public realm (from politics to the market). But since the late 1990s, with the advent of the reformation era, Indonesian Muslim women have become more active in promoting Islamic feminism, challenging previous failed efforts to promote their roles in Indonesia's major Islamic organizations. More importantly, these trends have intertwined with ongoing transformations within the largest Islamic organization, Nahdlatul Ulama, which since the late 1980s has embraced a commitment to a "socially relevant" religious jurisprudence. In this broader context, women active in the organization were able to "mov[e] toward a gender ideology that is compatible with the demands of modern life and firmly rooted in the traditionalist Islamic teachings" not in isolation, but together with their male colleagues. As Nelly van Doorn-Harder concluded in the early 2000s, "the winds of change in the *pesantren* [Indonesia's rural religious schools] cannot be halted."[78] A decade later, women emerging from the traditionalist environment of the *pesantren* shifted their agenda toward promoting and asserting women's religious-legal authority.

Earmarking Southeast Asia as a hotspot for the assertion of female religious authority and Muslim women's rights within a religious framework, in April 2017 a group of Indonesian religious scholars, academic researchers, and activists hosted the Indonesia Conference of Female Ulama (KUPI, Kongres Ulama Perumpuan Indonesia). The conference took place in a *pesantren* in West Java, and while the initiative was led by two of Indonesia's most well-known Islamic feminist organizations (Nahdlatul Ulama-affiliated Rahima and Fahmina) attracting women from many Muslim-majority countries (including Saudi Arabia, Pakistan, Sudan, and Kenya), it also received the endorsement of Indonesia's Ministry of Religious Affairs. These four factors are the key to understanding how varied the experience of Islamic feminism can be, and how a commitment to advancing a platform for female interpreters of Islamic law can emerge in diverse contexts.

The most visible organizer behind KUPI was Rahima, a Jakarta-based NGO established in 2001. Rahima can be described as an urban, internationally connected, middle-class organization founded by a group of Muslim women with a history of political activism in Jakarta and Yogyakarta, cities where they gained degrees in women's studies from state (non-religious) universities and participated in the student-led (secular) anti-Suharto reform movement (*reformasi*), coming under the influence of socialism and other left-leaning ideologies.

But to think of KUPI as the brainchild of this intellectual milieu would be misleading. The founding members of Rahima were raised and educated in a traditional Islamic setting, their background rooted in the rural environment of Nahdlatul Ulama *pesantren*, or, in a few instances, in small cities' government Islamic schools. Another key actor behind KUPI was Fahmina, an organization established by women *pesantren* alumna in the early 2000s with the goal of promoting an approach to Islam concerned with gender justice.

As Sally White and Maria Ulfah Anshor argue,

these organizations address their activism, not just to the state, but also to their own Islamic communities, seeking to change gender attitudes at both an intellectual and grassroots level by challenging traditional interpretations of Islamic teachings on gender, and by training men and women to be 'gender sensitive' in their actions and ideals.[79]

This might appear to be in stark contrast with the Kuala Lumpur-based SIS (and their global offshoot Musawah), who were described as the outcome of an elitist, urban, Western-oriented network; but in fact the leaders of Java's *pesantrens* (*kiyai*) have traditionally been representatives of influential families, with direct kinship relations to the bureaucracy and government as well as often claiming connections (spiritual or genealogical) to the prophet Muhammad; *kiyai*s and their offspring would have studied in regional urban centers if not abroad (in West or South Asia) before returning to the helms of their schools, holding control over their surrounding territory and exercising political influence.

Several of Rahima's and Fahmina's core members (and KUPI's) are, then, representative of a complex social milieu that has its roots in the highest echelons of Indonesia's rural society. They might sport a variety of styles, but all female Rahima and Fahmina members wear headscarves (unlike SIS's leaders). Some may have gone to non-religious universities, but most attended Islamic institutions, with quite a few specializing in Islamic theology or legal interpretation.

It is this multifaceted identity that has allowed a group of rural, traditionally educated, female students witnessing the political shifts of the post-1998 era to seamlessly merge religious activism with gender politics. Hence, the group envisioned its goal as one "not only [to] strengthen the position of women within Islamic societies (based on equality and justice), but to also assist in laying the foundations for the creation of a public democracy within Indonesian society."[80] KUPI and Musawah are, then, not so different; they both advocate for a contextualized approach to the interpretation of the scriptures (something that in Indonesia will resonate more among "traditional" *'ulama*) and lead the convergence of Islamic politics, democracy, and social justice; they also reflect a variation of what the middle class can look like in Asia, spanning the urban/rural divide.

Whereas both KUPI and SIS were able to garner support from some portions of the government, KUPI's grounding in the local framework of Java's *pesantrens* allows it to be heard domestically, while Sisters in Islam has faced much criticism. Malaysian government officials have objected to the organization's opinions because of its members' lack of traditional training in Islamic studies, limited knowledge of Arabic (if any), and limited expertise in the scriptures. What is more, in Malaysia it is the government that upholds ultimate authority on religious matters as the Department of Islamic Development (JAKIM) acts as a central body determining "correct" Islamic interpretation and behavior, invested with the power to draw the line between acceptability and deviance (as shown in the case of *halal* certification).

The fact that KUPI received official endorsement from the Indonesian Ministry of Religious Affairs has thus had two main consequences. On the one hand, this sent a strong message to the rising Islamist voices that in the late 2010s had been gaining increasing strength and attention. On the other hand, it provided "official" support for the assertion of the authority of women as interpreters of the scriptures and issuers of *fatawa*, as the conference collectively released legal opinions condemning violence against women, child marriage, and the destruction of the environment as *haram* practices.

Grounded in the scholarly and *fiqhi* tradition of Nahdlatul Ulama, Rahima and Fahmina activists approach the scriptures as a manifestation of the spirit of Islam which requires contextualization in time and place. It is through this methodology, largely embraced and encouraged by Indonesian *'ulama* in general, that KUPI activists are thus committed to what Rinaldo has described as a "pious critical agency." Aimed at supporting women's rights and equality through the contextual interpretation of the scriptures, Rahima and Fahmina have staff members dedicated to original interpretations, with their opinions regularly published in the organization's own journal but also in mainstream newspapers. They have a few female scholars producing alternative legal interpretations, and more are in the making as the organization regularly runs training programs in this direction. Yet, they also have among their numbers several male scholars, as the reality remains that opinions advanced by men carry more legitimacy and are more likely to rally wider support.

Conclusions

The "new technologies" of the late nineteenth century brought the "core" closer to the "peripheries" of Islam, allowing Asia's reformist and Khilafat movements to exert their influence well beyond their immediate audiences, but also challenging traditional modes of religious authority. Similarly, in the early twenty-first century, Asia is once again an interconnected space of Islamized interactions. And new technologies of communication are both strengthening the "global *umma*" and offering new ways to think about – and practice – religious authority. In this context, physical geography becomes irrelevant to discourses of hierarchy and authenticity.

Technology alone would not account for this, however, as it is ultimately only an enabler of transformations induced by socio-economic changes. This chapter has thus argued that in the twenty-first century it is Southeast Asia – and more specifically Indonesia and Malaysia – that has risen to prominence with the emergence of a vibrant middle class interested in self-identifying with pious consumption. As Fischer concluded that "these new middle-class Malays are modern individuals and groups acutely aware of practicing middle classness through Islam, consumption and legitimate taste,"[81] so Rinaldo suggested that "as Islamic piety has become a marker of distinction among the middle classes, these activists have come to embody distinctive ways of being pious and middle class,"[82] unwilling to compromise their cultural and religious values by embracing wholesale Western secular expressions.

Concluding this exploration of the interconnectedness of Islam and Asia's histories, then, this chapter brought us to reflect on how 1,400 years after Muhammad received the first revelation in Mecca, the perceived "syncretic" and "peripheral" Southeast Asia can be regarded as breeding grounds for new interpretative paths, leading to the emergence of Indonesia and Malaysia as global players in the definition of what is to be deemed "Islamic."

Further Reading

Abu-Lughod, L. (2015) *Do Muslim women need saving?* Cambridge, MA: Harvard University Press.

Ahmed-Ghosh, H. (2016) *Asian Muslim women*, New York, NY: State University of New York Press.

Ali, K. (2016) *Sexual ethics and Islam: feminist reflections on Qur'an, Hadith, and jurisprudence*, Oxford: Oneworld.

Andaya, B. W. (2006) *The flaming womb: repositioning women in early modern Southeast Asia*, Honolulu, HI: University of Hawai'i Press.

Armanios, F., and Ergene, B. A. (2018) *Halal food: a history*, New York, NY: Oxford University Press.

Bano, M., and Kalmbach, H. (2012) *Women, leadership, and mosques: changes in contemporary Islamic authority*, Leiden: Brill.

Barendregt, B. (2012) "Sonic discourses on Muslim Malay modernity: the Arqam sound," *Contemporary Islam* 6(3): 315–340.

Brenner, S. (1996) "Reconstructing self and society: Javanese Muslim women and "the veil," *American Ethnologist* 23: 673–697.

Bucar, E. M. (2017) *Pious fashion: how Muslim women dress*, Cambridge, MA: Harvard University Press.

Cesaro, M. C. (2000) "Consuming identities: food and resistance among the Uyghur in contemporary Xinjiang," *Inner Asia* 2(2): 225–238.

Doorn-Harder, P. V. (2006) *Women shaping Islam: Indonesian women reading the Qur'an*, Urbana, IL: University of Illinois Press.

Fischer, J. (2008) *Proper Islamic consumption: shopping among the Malays in modern Malaysia*, Copenhagen: NIAS.

Frisk, S. (2004) *Submitting to God: women's Islamization in urban Malaysia*, Gothenburg: Gothenburg University, Department of Social Anthropology.

Gillette, M. B. (2000) *Between Mecca and Beijing: modernization and consumption among urban Chinese Muslims*, Stanford, CA: Stanford University Press.

Hammer, J. (2012) *American Muslim women, religious authority, and activism: more than a prayer*, Austin, TX: University of Texas Press.

Heath, J. (2008) *The veil: women writers on its history, lore, and politics*, Los Angeles, CA: University of California Press.

Heryanto, A. (2014) *Identity and pleasure: the politics of Indonesian screen culture*, Singapore: NUS Press.

Jaschok, M., and Shui, J. (2015) *The history of women's mosques in Chinese Islam*, London: Routledge.

Jones, C. (2007) "Fashion and faith in urban Indonesia," *Fashion Theory* 11(2–3): 211–231.

Kloos, D., and Künkler, M. (2016) "Studying female Islamic authority: from top-down to bottom-up modes of certification," *Asian Studies Review* 40(4): 479–490.

Kueny, K. (2001) *The rhetoric of sobriety: wine in early Islam*, New York, NY: State University of New York Press.

Marranci, G. (2012). "Defensive or offensive dining? *Halal* dining practices among Malay Muslim Singaporeans and their effects on integration," *Australian Journal of Anthropology* 23(1): 84–100.

Rinaldo, R. (2013) *Mobilizing piety: Islam and feminism in Indonesia*, Oxford: Oxford University Press.

Robinson, K. (2010) *Gender, Islam and democracy in Indonesia*, London: Routledge.

Rudnyckyj, D. (2013) "From Wall Street to 'Halal' Street: Malaysia and the globalization of Islamic finance," *The Journal of Asian Studies* 72(4): 831–848.

Sen, K., and Stivens, M. (1998) *Gender and power in affluent Asia*, London: Routledge.

Sloane-White, P. (2017) *Corporate Islam: Sharia and the modern workplace*, Cambridge: Cambridge University Press.

wadud, a. (2005) *Qur'an and women: rereading the sacred text from a woman's perspective*, Samia Adnan.

Weintraub, A. N. (2011) *Islam and popular culture in Indonesia and Malaysia*, London: Routledge.

In 2006 the National Gallery of Australia and the Art Gallery of South Australia curated an exhibition titled *Crescent Moon: Islamic Art & Civilisation in Southeast Asia*. This had the explicit aim of "documenting the astonishingly diverse heritage of Islamic art in Southeast Asia," as it displayed Arabic calligraphy decorating architectural panels, ritual fans, sacred daggers, royal banners, Chinese ceramics, and talismanic cloths; ceremonial textiles worn during Islamic rites of passage; and a Qur'an box and several religious manuscripts. But the exhibit also included musical instruments, face masks, and shadow puppets that indexed the region's Hindu past while being used for entertainment at Islamized courts.[1]

Visiting the Islamic Art Museum of Malaysia in Kuala Lumpur, or the recently renovated galleries of the Asian Civilization Museum in Singapore, visitors are intrigued by the juxtaposition of Islamic artifacts from all over the world; in Singapore a Burmese lacquered Qur'an chest is displayed alongside a classic calligraphic jug from Kashan (Persia), a Talismanic prayer scroll from Ottoman Turkey, an Indian *kendi* water vessel inscribed with the word "Allah," and a blue-and-white Chinese ceramic plate with the Islamic profession of faith (*shahada*) painted in Arabic calligraphy, as discussed at the beginning of this book.

Within the scope of this book, none of the above appears out of place, but *The New York Times* published the view that "the show [*Crescent Moon*] was probably more a cultural experience than an artistic one, an effort perhaps to help the audience connect with Southeast Asia ... [because] Islamic art should feature calligraphy in Arabic form, with geometric and arabesque patterns."[2] And it should be noted that these comments, aired by a curator at the Metropolitan Museum in New York City, are actually much more representative of mainstream views of what constitutes Islamic art than what was exhibited by *Crescent Moon*.

The Louvre's galleries of Islamic Art offer an impressive array of ceramics, wooden panels, and glasses from North Africa, West Asia, and Persia,[3] as do the Victoria & Albert Museum in London, the Benaki

Museum in Athens, and the Museum of Islamic Art in Doha. Similarly, the collection of Islamic art at the Metropolitan Museum in New York City captivates its visitors with beautiful artifacts from Persia and Iraq, a Moroccan courtyard, and Indo-Persian miniatures from the Mughal court. But while the Indian subcontinent makes an occasional if fleeting appearance, China and Southeast Asia are conspicuous by their absence. Passing through the Ancient Near East rooms, one then arrives at the galleries of Asian Art, "one of the largest and the most comprehensive [collections] in the West."[4] There India, China, and Southeast Asia are most characteristically represented by statues of Shiva, Vishnu, and Buddha, miniature pagodas, lacquers, and Chinese calligraphic scrolls.

Today more than half of the world's Muslim population resides east of Persia (contemporary Iran), from Central Asia (i.e. Kazakhstan, Kyrgyzstan, Tajikistan, Turkmenistan, and Uzbekistan) eastward. These territories were referred to by the Romans as Transoxiana and by the Arabs as *ma wara' an-nahr*, translated as "that which is across the river," both Latin and Arabic names referred to the same river – the Oxus or Amu Darya – which runs west of Samarkand. On the eastern side of this imagined line of demarcation Islam is the majority religion of a dozen countries, and it has historically significant minority populations across most of the region.[5]

Far from being an exclusively demographic reality, Islam's presence across Asia – the outcome of those various trajectories of Muslim mobility for military, study, and trade purposes, investigated in Chapters 1 and 3 – created a deep-seated sense of belonging to a common culture and to a community of faith, the *umma*. However, it would be a mistake to interpret Muslim awareness of being a *communitas* as a universally deployable political tool. The Ottoman Caliph failed to rally Muslims' support in its anti-European efforts in 1914, as nationalist aspirations eventually trumped pan-Islamic propaganda (Chapter 4), and attempts to bring Islam into the societies and government apparatuses of newly established nation-states between the 1940s and 1960s also largely took place within national boundaries (Chapter 5). And yet, this sense of community resurfaced in the 1960s to 1990s, as local movements for the reconfiguration of Islamic piety intersected with, and adopted from, "exogenous" groups (Chapter 6). The interfacing of local and transnational dynamics peaked with the experience of Afghanistan's anti-Soviet resistance, when Muslims from the world over turned to "the heart of Asia," some to watch, others to effect its fate as a battleground for Islam (Chapter 7).

And yet, Western scholarship (and its public face, museums) present "Asia" and "Islam" as two separate and almost necessarily mutually exclusive labels, perpetuating an approach that for well over a century has seen the history of Islam as exclusively lodged within the history of West Asia (usually referred to as the Middle East) and North Africa, and of "Islam in Asia" as a derivative reality. This understanding describes the subject as the result of Muslims' expansion from an Arab center of authenticity into Asia, where pre-Abrahamic non-monotheistic traditions absorbed Islam, by adapting and transforming themselves *and* Islam into a syncretic hybrid, their only succor being the reformist movements that emerged in West Asia at the turn of the twentieth century.

Clifford Geertz – "the single most influential cultural anthropologist in the United States" in the latter part of the twentieth century[6] – evocatively captured this attitude in *The Religion of Java*, considered to be "the first significant anthropological study focusing explicitly on Islam":[7]

Islam came to Indonesia from India, brought by merchants. Its Mid-Eastern sense for the external conditions of life having been blunted and turned inward by Indian mysticism, it provided but a minimal contrast to the mélange of Hinduism, Buddhism and animism which had held the Indonesians enthralled for almost fifteen centuries … Indonesian Islam, cut off from its centers of orthodoxy at Mecca and Cairo, vegetated, another meandering tropical growth on an already overcrowded religious landscape. Buddhist mystic practices got Arabic names, Hindu radjas suffered a change of title to become Moslem Sultans, and the common people called some of their wood spirits djinns; but little else changed. Toward the middle of the nineteenth century the isolation of Indonesian Islam from its Mid-Eastern fountainhead began to break down … came Arab traders … and transmit their fine sense for orthodoxy to the local merchants.[8]

Concluding that "It is very hard for a Javanese to be a 'real Moslem,'"[9] Geertz was exemplifying the fault line between what had been constructed as two separate objects of study: Southeast Asia and Islam. Geertz perpetuated the approach which had emerged under Dutch colonialism for thinking about Java (then the most written-about site) as "Hindu-Buddhist."

In the 1860s these ideas were already expressed by Protestant missionaries stationed in Java. While one reported that "what one understands by Javanism … is not its own doctrine, its own system, but the unnatural union of the old [forms of] worship with the Indian and Arabic religion and philosophy,"[10] another, just a few years later, argued:

The religion of present-day Java is the product of Buddhism, Brahmanism, Shivaism, Mohammedanism, etc., not processed and brought together into a whole, but all mixed together and wonderfully confused. The Javanese world has not adopted religion out of conviction; as it cannot be said, either, that the Javanese people are a Mohammedan people in a straightforward sense as we say that the Dutch, English, etc., are Christian nations.[11]

But it was not only missionaries who took this approach. The Dutch scholar J. C. van Leur had graduated in Indology, a common course of study for colonial officers who were to serve in the East Indies (Indonesia), as in the 1940s "Southeast Asia" was still considered a cultural offshoot of India.[12] In his thesis, van Leur coined the longest-surviving image of Islam in Java: that of a "thin, easily flaking glaze" over an ever-strong substratum of Hindu-Buddhist tradition.[13]

The Muslims of Asia (as those of Africa, in fact)[14] became preferred "sites" for research that followed anthropology's fascination with Redfield's "Little Tradition" paradigm, emphasizing the perception that historically Islam had had a limited impact on Asia. Conversely, Asia's cultures, histories, and political regimes were consistently analyzed as outcomes of "indigenous" influences. Whether because of the influence of local political, historical, or religious dynamics, Islamic ritual practices across Asia were marked as heterodox, characterized as diverging from a perceived Arabo-Persian Islamic "norm."[15] Islam had, after all, emerged in the Arabian Peninsula, grounded in the Qur'an as God's revelation, delivered to Muhammad, in the Arabic language.

Since the 1990s some scholars have questioned this thinking. Some have argued in favor of approaching Islam in South and Southeast Asia as "authentic,"[16] while others have acknowledged the continuities between pre-Islamic and Islamic orders in West Asia.[17] Concurrently, anthropologists have elaborated on the Saidian critique to investigate relationships between Islam's particularism and universalism: some embracing a post-modernist or anti-essentialist take (i.e. the existence of plural *islam*s), and others analyzing Islam as a discursive tradition.[18] These latter re-conceptualizations have, however, remained marginal and disengaged from the study of Islam in Asia; and the handful of works attempting to reframe this specific subfield have not been successful in facilitating a wider intersected study of Asia's history and Islamic Studies on a broader plane.

Marshall Hodgson's *The Venture of Islam*, which appeared posthumously in the 1970s, is a rare example, offering an innovative approach to teaching the traditional "Islamic Civilization" sequence, hinged on the idea of "Islamicate" cultures to reflect the broader impact exerted by Islam worldwide. Hodgson's interest in bringing "the peripheries" within the scope of Islamic Studies has remained niche, but ripples of it can be found in scholarship on South Asia. Bruce Lawrence, for example, has postulated that "to teach Islamicate civilization is to announce, then pursue a resilient and persistent Asian focus," as Islamic Studies "fails to reflect its subject, unless one highlights the worldview of millions of Asians, from Central to South to Southeast Asia."[19] A stimulating contribution comes from another South Asianist, Richard Eaton, who has proposed thinking of the history of Islam as a window on global history.[20]

Since then more efforts have been pursued to highlight networks and the contribution of Asia's Muslims on global formations of Islam; however, multi-focal publications have tended to be limited to multi-authored volumes.[21] Even more problematic has been, in recent years, the proliferation of global terrorism literature, which boomed in the early 2000s.[22] As discussed in Chapter 7, the consequences of 9/11 reached far beyond the United States and military engagements; not only did "Islamic terrorism" become a useful tool for governments interested in curbing Muslim dissent, but it also infiltrated scholarly analyses of these movements.

Alongside scholarly and intellectual approaches rests the impact of knowledge institutionalization. The study of Islam reached North America in the 1800s, after centuries of life in Europe. There, this field had taken shape at the intersection of Theology and Oriental Studies as an offshoot of Biblical philological interests in the Semitic languages (primarily Hebrew, and only secondarily Arabic). Such a text-centered approach set up Syria and Egypt as privileged sources for the study of Islam. By the mid-twentieth century, this focus on the "heartlands" of Islamic written sources had become institutionalized, in the United States, through Federal funding schemes and the establishment of region-based National Research Centers. While European universities remained harnessed to a philological approach to the study of "Oriental" cultures, Cold War politics and the US government effort in "ensur[ing] trained expertise of sufficient quality and quantity to meet US national security needs"[23] subsumed "Islamic Studies" under the purview of "Near and Middle Eastern Studies." These developments marginalized the study of Islam as a non-Arab religious tradition, leaving behind long-lasting consequences: sixty years later Islamic Studies' "focus on the (greater) Middle East [still] persists in most academic institutions."[24]

Parallel biases are as evident when analyzing the genealogy of other Area Studies programs and the historiography of "Asia." The history of the region has mostly engaged the imperial and colonial eras and their institutional lenses. When addressed, the study of religion shadowed missionary interests and was limited to the "indigenous" traditions, i.e. Hinduism, Buddhism, and Confucianism. As recently argued by Michael Laffan, Dutch colonials talked of the East Indies (later to become Indonesia) as "Christianizable" and saw them primarily as "a domain for the study of its *Indic* heritage."[25] The Tropenmuseum's

Indies collection in Amsterdam is an effective reminder, as "collectors and museum staff were mainly interested in the colony's traditional cultures and the pre-Islamic Indo-Javanese heritage, which was considered more representative of the real Indonesia."[26] Once again, little has changed. Islam's socio-political influence has been largely diminished in narratives of Asia's history, rarely recognized as defining of local cultures, or of a comparable essential quality to Islam in the Arab lands.[27]

There is no questioning of the Arab roots of Islam, but dominant discourses in Western scholarship have reinforced this Arab-centric paradigm marginalizing the possible alternative narratives enabled by Islam's theological claims to universalism and its historical spread. The Moroccan jurist Ibn Battuta (1304–1377 or 1369) had left North Africa to perform the *hajj* pilgrimage to Mecca, but inspired by a desire to visit unknown lands, ended up traveling through Asia and back over a period of more than twenty years. During these years he observed, wrote about, and often joined the communities of Muslims he encountered, scattered between Tangier and Quanzhou:

In every Chinese city there is a quarter for Muslims in which they live by themselves, and in which they have mosques both for the Friday services and for other religious purposes. The Muslims are honoured and respected ... On the day that I reached Zaytun [Quanzhou] I saw there the amir who had come to India as an envoy with the present [to the sultan] ... I received visits from the qadi of the Muslims, the shaykh al-Islam, and the principal merchants.[28]

Ibn Battuta consistently acknowledged the presence of Islamic infrastructures for travelers, merchants, and settlers, and a reciprocal recognition of belonging to the Islamic *umma* among these communities. Muslims traveled along networks of mobility, recognizing their shared religious values, conceding differences, and generally without passing value judgments on the ways that Islam was practiced in other places. His account, for example, does not dwell upon the architectural style of China's mosques, even though we know that these buildings differed in form from their counterparts in West Asia and North Africa, most likely resembling pagodas. In the eyes of this *qadi*, form was not seen as a hindrance to holding correct religious belief (orthodoxy) and performing rituals (orthopraxy).

But as singled out here, many Western scholars harnessed their observations on Islam as a religious practice to idealized formalities. Ideals of Islamic orthopraxy and orthodoxy have been ever more strongly perceived as Arab since the Wahhabi-Saudi "revolution" in the 1920s. The early mosques of Java and Aceh, scattered on the northern coast and dated at around the mid-sixteenth century, are often described as reminiscent of Bali's Hindu temples, with features typical of pre-Islamic architecture. These structural characteristics, as well as their decorative ornaments, were deployed for almost a century to argue for a Hindu-ized form of Islam, the persistent presence of a "less authentic" form of Islam. But more recent scholarship has invoked a process of reconciliation between local and Islamic forms of religious devotion and identities, focusing on how Islamic practices, spaces, and doctrines have been consistently renegotiated, creating multiple instances of "contextual orthodoxy" (Chapter 2).

This book has, then, sought to make an intervention in the way that "Islam in Asia" has been dealt with in both the fields of Asian Studies and Islamic Studies, marginalized as either inconsequential or derivative. Taking inspiration from innovative approaches to cultural encounters and "translations," and applying these insights to the field at large, I have rejected the master narrative of Islam in Asia as "syncretic" or "foreign," offering instead a reading of Asia's history as intrinsically interconnected with the history of Islam, and vice versa. Writing a narrative of the intersections between Islam and Asia's history is a direct challenge to a constructed view of Islam and Asia as two separate objects of study.

In *Islam: The View from the Edge*, Richard W. Bulliet complemented the traditional Arab-focused approach to Islamic history "maintain[ing] that Iran played a unique and crucial role in the origination and diffusion of institutions [of religious authority] that eventually contributed to the centripetal tendency of later Islamic civilization." Taking on the idea that "[t]he edge in Islamic history exists wherever people make the decision to cross a social boundary and join the Muslim community,"[29] this book has pushed further East, moving the "edge" from Bulliet's eleventh-century Iran to Central Asia, the Indian subcontinent, China, and Southeast Asia.

Dislodging the assumption that because the historical roots of Islam are located in Arabia, then "Arab" or "Wahhabi" Islam should be a golden standard of purity and authenticity, this book has brought to light the multi-directional influences on Islamic practices and interpretations at the "center" as well as the "peripheries." The lives and religious-intellectual approaches of the individuals discussed in Chapter 3 illustrate how the impetus toward purification had come from scholars representative of both "mystical" and "juridical" strains of thought, and how such inspiration had initially emerged as a concern in continental Asia, not in Arabia. Centuries later Southeast Asia is emerging as a global site of religious authority, whether one thinks in terms of *halal* certification, modest fashion, or women's leadership in scriptural exegesis (Chapter 8). Along this trajectory of *longue durée*, in which Asia has become an interconnected space of Islamic interactions with multiple (or no) centers and peripheries, Muslims from all corners of this territorial expanse have been contributing to discourses on, and constructions of, Islamic orthodoxy and orthopraxy.

Glossary

'adat	local customs and one of the sources of Islamic jurisprudence
'alim, f. *'alima,* pl. *'ulama*	scholar of Islamic knowledge
'ibadat	ritual devotional practices that establish a vertical relationship between humans and God
'ilm	knowledge, science
'ilmu'l-hadith	field of study of the *hadith*, the traditions of the Prophet
'umra	minor pilgrimage to Mecca performed any time of year but not during the month of Dhul-Hijja
'urf	local customs and one of the sources of Islamic jurisprudence
adhan	call to prayer
ahong, f. *nu ahong*	community leader among China's Muslims
ansar	Muhammad's helpers and supporters at the time of the *hijra* from Mecca to Medina (622)
baraka	blessing bestowed by God (possibly through the intercession of a "saint")
begum	South Asian Persianate honorary title for women
bid'a	(evil) innovation, derogatory term to identify practices deemed un-Islamic
da'wa	"call" or "invitation," usually meant as an effort to deepen Muslims' commitment to their faith
dhikr	"remembrance," usually referring to devotional practices that foster remembrance of God

dhimmi	protected minority
faqih, f. *faqiha*, pl. *fuqaha*	scholars of Islamic jurisprudence (*fiqh*)
fatwa, pl. *fatawa*	legal opinion, non-binding, issued by a *mufti*/*muftiyya*
ghazi	fighter on the road of God
ghulam	slave soldier
hadith, pl. *ahadith*	the collected traditions, or sayings, of the Prophet
hafiz	a Muslim who has memorized the Qur'an
hajj	pilgrimage to Mecca performed during the month of Dhul-Hijja, the fifth pillar of Islam
hajji, f. *hajja*	Muslim who has performed the pilgrimage to Mecca during the month of Dhul-Hijja (*hajj*)
halal	"permissible" to Muslims
halaqa	religious study circles
Han Kitab	seventeenth-century Islamic intellectual and literary tradition of China
haqiqa	(mystical) truth
haram	"forbidden" to Muslims; also, "sacred" and "sanctuary," as in *masjid al-haram*, the sacred mosque in Mecca
hijra	Muhammad's migration from Mecca to Medina in 622; in the twentieth century, has come to refer to strategies of isolation and non-cooperation with non-Islamic rule
hudud	crimes with penalties specifically listed in the Qur'an, considered infringements of God's "limits"
hujra	unregistered (hence illegal) study circles in Soviet Central Asia
ijaza	written certification attesting a pupil's achievement under a specific teacher
ijtihad	juridical interpretation, effort (same root as *jihad*)
Ikhwani	pertaining to the Ikhwan al-Muslims, the Muslim Brotherhood (established 1928 in Egypt)

imam	commonly refers to a "leader" of a congregation or community; in Shi'a Islam refers to the line of spiritual-*cum*-political leaders descending from the Prophet Muhammad through his daughter Fatima and her husband (Muhammad's cousin and son-in-law) 'Ali ibn Abu Talib (himself the first imam)
ishan	Sufi master (*shaykh*) in Central Asia
isnad	chain of transmission, of individuals' knowledge or *ahadith* text
jadidism	intellectual, social, political movement of reform in nineteenth and twentieth-century Central Asia
jahililiyya	pre-Islamic (era of) ignorance; in twentieth-century Islamist ideology becomes a reference to non-Islamic governance by Muslim rulers
jawi	a Muslim from Southeast Asia
jihad	"effort, endeavor"; usually classified as *jihad* of the pen (literary effort to propagate Islamic beliefs and knowledge), of the tongue (verbal effort to do the same), of the soul (inner struggle to be a better Muslim) or of the sword (armed struggle against unbelievers). These classifications are often also categorized as the "greater" *jihad* of the soul or the "lesser" *jihad* of armed struggle.
jilbab	headscarf usually covering shoulders and navel, in Indonesia
kafir, pl. *kuffar*	infidel, non-Muslim
kalam	Islamic theology
kampung	village, Malaysia and Indonesia
khalifa	"deputy," "representative"; can be the deputy of God (the Caliph as a spiritual guide of the *umma*), or the deputy of a Sufi master
khan	Mongol political leader; on some occasions, Islamized leaders of Central Asia
khanaqa	Sufi lodge

khatun	Mongol and Central Asian honorary title for women
khutba	sermon delivered at the Friday congregational prayer
kiyai	leader of Java's rural religious schools
kudung	a loose head covering in Indonesia and Malaysia
ma wara' an-nahr	"that which is beyond the river," meaning the lands beyond the Oxus/Amu Darya river
madhhab, **pl.** *madhahib*	school of legal thought
madrasa	school; in more recent years it has come to denote a religious school
Mahdi	the last (twelfth) imam who shall be in occultation until shortly before the day of judgment
mamluk	slave soldier
maslaha	greater good of society, one of the principles of *ijtihad*
mihrab	prayer niche in a mosque indicating the direction of Mecca (*qibla*)
minbar	pulpit in mosque
mu'amalat	guidance principles for relations among human beings
mufti, **f.** *muftiyya*	issuer of legal opinions (*fatawa*)
muhaddith, **f.** *muhadditha*	scholar; person knowledgeable in the *hadith*, the traditions of the Prophet
mujaddid	renewer
mujahidin	individuals engaged in *jihad* (plural, in English often used also as singular)
mujtahid	scholar engaged in the legal interpretation of the scriptures (who performs *ijtihad*)
nu junshi	female religious scholars
nu xue	women's religious school in China
otine	knowledgeable woman in Muslim Central Asia who also acted as a religious leader for local women

pasisir	north coast of Java
pesantren	rural religious schools, usually boarding schools, in Java (Indonesia)
purdah	seclusion, practice of gender segregation among Hindu and Muslim communities in South Asia
qadi	judge in an Islamic court of law
qibla	direction of prayer toward Mecca and the Ka'ba
qing zhen	pure and clean, meaning *halal* among Chinese Muslims communities
raja	royal title
salat	ritual prayer (second pillar of Islam)
sawm	fasting (third pillar of Islam)
sayyid, **pl.** *sada*	individuals acknowledged as genealogical descendants from the Prophet Muhammad
shahada	profession of faith "There is no God but God and Muhammad is his Prophet" (first pillar of Islam)
shaykh-ul-Islam	highest office for religious and legal advice in a Muslim state (e.g. Ottoman Empire, Aceh, et al.)
shaykh, **f.** *shaykha*	master of a Sufi order, or more generally a knowledgeable religious leader
shari'a	the "path" of Islamic law
shirk	"associationism," derogatory term to identify practices that "associate" any others to God; commonly translated as polytheism
silsila	chain of transmission of individuals' knowledge or *ahadith* text
sirat al-mustaqim	"the right path" established by the Islamic revelation, mentioned in the first chapter of the Qur'an (*sura al-fatiha*)
sultan	Muslim ruler holding political power (can be either male or female)
sunna	tradition of the Prophet; in legal terms indicates the combination of the Qur'an and *ahadith*
sura	chapter of the Qur'an

tafsir	scriptural exegesis, interpretation (a scholarly science as well as a literary genre)
tajdid	renewal
takfir	practice of labeling a self-claimed Muslim as non-Muslim
taliban	plural of *talib*, student in Persian and Pashto
taqlid	"imitation" of previous legal opinion (opposed to *ijtihad*)
tarbiya	education, usually meaning Islamic education
tariqa, **pl.** *turuq*	Sufi mystical order
tasawwuf	field of study of (and literature on) Sufi practices, approaches, and methods
tauhid	unity, core principle of Islam's monotheism
tughra	signature of the Ottoman Caliphs
umma	community of believers; in its the narrowest sense, the community of Muslims
usra	family, often equivalent to *halaqa* in the activist movement of the 1980s and 1990s
wahdat-ul-shuhud	"unity of presence/being" of a human (Sufi) with the divine world; often referred to as monism
wahdat-ul-wujud	oneness of vision indicating the unity of the phenomenal world (the world we experience as humans)
wali songo	the "nine saints" credited with the spread of Islam in Java and Southeast Asia more broadly
waqf	property bequeathed in Islamic philanthropy
zakat	annual charitable tax set at circa 2.5 percent of a Muslim's net worth (fourth pillar of Islam)
ziyara	"visit" to tombs of ancestors and shrines of important Muslim personalities (often, but not necessarily) Sufis

Notes

Introduction

1 R. Finlay (1998) "The pilgrim art: the culture of porcelain in world history," *Journal of World History* 9(2): 141–187, at 152–153.
2 *Sahih Bukhari, ahadith* nos. 5633 and 5634; *Sahih Muslim, ahadith* nos. 2067, 2065.
3 J. Chao (1911) *Chau Ju-kua: his work on the Chinese and Arab trade in the twelfth and thirteenth centuries, entitled Chu-fan-chï*, edited by F. R. Hirth and W. W. Rockhill, St. Petersburg: Imperial Academy of Sciences, pp. 138, 141. Chau Ju-kua's account, originally published in 1225 CE, brought together a vast array of information on trade during the Song dynasty (tenth to thirteenth centuries).
4 Finlay, "The pilgrim art," p. 156.
5 G. R. Tibbetts (1979) *A study of the Arabic texts containing material on South-East Asia*, Leiden: Brill. See also V. Minorsky (2012) "Abū Dulaf" in P. Bearman, Th. Bianquis, C. E. Bosworth, E. van Donzel, and W. P. Heinrichs (Eds.) *Encyclopaedia of Islam, Second Edition*, http://dx.doi.org/10.1163/1573-3912_islam_SIM_0177 [accessed January 17 2019].
6 F. B. Flood (2018) *Objects of translation: material culture and medieval "Hindu–Muslim" encounter*, Princeton, NJ: Princeton University Press.
7 *Tabaqat al-khawass*, Shihab al-Din Ahmad al-Sharji (1410–ca. 1487/8) quoted in R. M. Feener and M. F. Laffan (2005) "Sufi scents across the Indian Ocean: Yemeni hagiography and the earliest history of Southeast Asian Islam," *Archipel* 70: 185–208, pp. 186–187.
8 H. C. Snouck Hurgronje (2007) *Mekka in the latter part of the 19th century: daily life, customs and learning. The Moslims of the East-Indian-Archipelago*, Leiden: Brill, p. 203.

Chapter 1

1 M. ibn Al-Biruni and E. Sachau (1910) *Alberuni's India: an account of the religion, philosophy, literature, geography, chronology, astronomy, customs, laws*

and astrology of India about AD 1030 (an English ed.), London: K. Paul, Trench, Trübner & Co., Ltd.

2 From "Descriptions of Plates VIII and IX" in Captain Lockyer Willis Hart (1843) *The character and costumes of Afghanistan,* London: H. Graves.

3 F. B. Flood (2018) *Objects of translation: material culture and medieval "Hindu–Muslim" encounter,* Princeton, NJ: Princeton University Press, pp. 32, 189, 240–241.

4 R. W. Bulliet (1994) *Islam: the view from the edge,* New York, NY: Columbia University Press, p. 7.

5 Ibid., p. 8.

6 A. C. S. Peacock (Ed.) (2017) *Islamisation: comparative perspectives from history,* Edinburgh: Edinburgh University Press, p. 3.

7 L. Ahmed (1992) *Women and gender in Islam: historical roots of a modern debate.* New Haven, CT and London: Yale University Press, Chapter 4, quote on p. 87.

8 A. Schimmel (1980) *Islam in the Indian subcontinent,* Leiden: Brill, pp. 4–5.

9 D. A. DeWeese (2017) "Khwaja Ahmad Yasavi as an Islamising saint: rethinking the role of Sufis in the Islamisation of the Turks of Central Asia" in Peacock (Ed.) *Islamisation,* pp. 336–352.

10 Quote from Ibn Battuta, in F. Mernissi and M. J. Lakeland (2012) *The forgotten queens of Islam,* Minneapolis, MN: University of Minnesota Press.

11 M. Adamson Sijapati (2011) *Islamic revival in Nepal: religion and a new nation,* London: Routledge, pp. 18–24.

12 D. G. Atwill (2006) *The Chinese sultanate: Islam, ethnicity, and the Panthay Rebellion in southwest China, 1856–1873,* Stanford, CA: Stanford University Press, p. 6.

13 G. T. Hakias (2011) "The Muslim Queens of the Himalayas: princess exchange in Ladakh and Baltistan" in A. Akasoy, C. Burnett, and R. Yoeli-Tlalim (Eds.) *Islam and Tibet: Interactions along the musk routes,* Farnham, UK: Ashgate, p. 232.

14 A. Papas (2011) "So close to Samarkand, Lhasa: Sufi hagiographies, founder myths and sacred space in Tibetan Islam" in Akasoy, Burnett, and Yoeli-Tlalim (Eds.) *Islam and Tibet,* pp. 262–264, 278.

15 Hakias, Hanas "The Muslim Queens of the Himalayas," pp. 236–237.

16 Mernissi and Lakeland, *The forgotten queens of Islam,* p. 106.

17 B. D. Metcalf and T. R. Metcalf (2012) *A concise history of modern India,* Cambridge: Cambridge University Press, p. 6.

18 Mernissi and Lakeland, *The forgotten queens of Islam,* p. 103.

19 S. C. Levi and R. Sela (Eds.) (2009) *Islamic Central Asia: an anthology of historical sources,* Bloomington, IN: Indiana University Press, pp. 151–153.

20 M. Smith (2002) *Muslim women mystics: the life and work of Rabi'a and other women mystics in Islam,* Oxford: One World Publications, pp. 19, 21; al-Ghazali quoted on p. 167.

21 A. Schimmel and S. H. Ray (1997) *My soul is a woman: the feminine in Islam,* New York, NY: Continuum, quote on p. 34; see also p. 42 on initiation.

22 Atwill, *The Chinese sultanate,* p. 35.

23 J. N. Lipman (1997) *Familiar strangers: a history of Muslims in Northwest China*, Seattle, WA: University of Washington Press.

24 D. Leslie (1986) *Islam in traditional China: a short history to 1800*, Belconnen: Canberra College of Advanced Education.

25 S. Yunli (2014) "Islamic astronomy in the service of Yuan and Ming monarchs," *Suhayl: International Journal for the History of the Exact and Natural Sciences in Islamic Civilisation*, 13: 41–61.

26 B. van Dalen and M. Yano (1998) "Islamic astronomy in China: two new sources for the Huihui Li ('Islamic Calendar')," *Highlights of Astronomy* 11(2): 697–700.

27 M. Jaschok and J. Shui (2000) *The history of women's mosques in Chinese Islam: a mosque of their own*, Richmond, VA: Curzon, p. 83.

28 A. Wink (2002) *Al-Hind: the making of the Indo-Islamic world, Vol. 1*, Leiden: Brill, p. 64.

29 H. J. de Graaf and Th. F. Pigeaud (2009) "Chinese Muslims in Java" in T. Hellwig and E. Tagliacozzo (Eds.) *The Indonesia reader*, Durham, NC: Duke University Press, pp. 70–74 (selection).

30 A recent monograph on the Islamization of the southern coast of India is S. R. Prange (2018) *Monsoon Islam: trade and faith on the medieval Malabar Coast*, New York, NY: Cambridge University Press.

31 A. Reid (1995) *Southeast Asia in the age of commerce, 1450–1680*, New Haven, CT: Yale University Press.

32 C. Guillot, L. Kalus, and M. O. Scalliet (2008) *Les monuments funeraires et l'histoire du Sultanat de Pasai à Sumatra*, Paris: Association Archipel.

33 A. Johns (1955) "Aspects of Sufi thought in India and Indonesia in the first half of the 17th century," *Journal of the Malayan Branch of the Royal Asiatic Society* 28(1): 70–77, at 71.

34 R. Winstedt (1950) *The Malays: a cultural history*, p. 50, quoted in M. T. Osman (1985) "Islamization of the Malays" in A. Ibrahim, S. Siddique, and Y. Hussain (Eds.) *Readings on Islam in Southeast Asia*, Singapore: Institute of Southeast Asian Studies, p. 46.

35 A. C. Milner, "Islam and Malay kingship" in Ibrahim, Siddique, and Hussain (Eds.) *Readings on Islam in Southeast Asia*, p. 26.

36 R. M. Feener (2019) "Islam in Southeast Asia to c. 1800" in D. Ludden (Ed.) *Oxford Research Encyclopedia of Asian History*, Oxford: Oxford University Press.

37 A. Maxwell Hill (1998) *Merchants and migrants: ethnicity and trade among Yunnanese Chinese in Southeast Asia*, New Haven, CT: Yale University Press.

38 C. J. Baker and P. Phongpaichit (2017) *A history of Ayutthaya: Siam in the early modern world*, Cambridge: Cambridge University Press, pp. 127–129.

39 S. B. A. L. Khan (2017) *Sovereign women in a Muslim kingdom: the sultanahs of Aceh, 1641–1699*, Singapore: NUS Press, p. 178.

40 M. C. Ricklefs (2006) *Mystic synthesis in Java: a history of Islamization from the fourteenth to the early nineteenth centuries*, Norwalk, CT: EastBridge.

41 Ibn Battuta (1953) *Travels in Asia and Africa 1325–1354 [Tuḥfat an-nuẓẓār fī garā'ib al-amṣār wa-'aǧā'ib al-asfār]*, translated and selected by H. A. R. Gibb, London: Routledge.

42 Baba Shah Mahmud and S. Digby (2002) *Sufis and soldiers in Awrangzeb's Deccan: Malfúzát-i Naqshbandiyya*, New Delhi: Oxford University Press, pp. 70–71.
43 G. Casale (2010) *The Ottoman age of exploration*, Oxford: Oxford University Press, p. 59.

Chapter 2

1 J. Kreemer (1922) *Atjèh: Algemeen Samenvattend Overzicht van Land en Volk van Atjèh en Onderhoorigheden*, Leiden: Brill, Vol. I, pp. 236–237.
2 Ibid.
3 W. Bouwsema-Raap (2009) *The Great Mosque of Banda Aceh: its history, architecture and relationship to the development of Islam in Sumatra*, Bangkok, Thailand: White Lotus Press, pp. 56, 60–62.
4 Direct quote included in Kreemer, *Atjèh*, p. 237.
5 A. Reid (1995) *Witnesses to Sumatra: a travellers' anthology*, Oxford: Oxford University Press, pp. 4, 9.
6 H. C. Snouck Hurgronje, A. W. S. O'Sullivan, and R. J. Wilkinson (1906) *The Achehnese*, Leiden: Brill [Dutch original published in 1893–1894], p. 83.
7 D. Lombard (1967) *Le sultanat d'Atjéh au temps d'Iskandar Muda: 1607–1636*, Paris: EFEO, p. 46.
8 Snouck Hurgronje, O'Sullivan, and Wilkinson, *The Achehnese*, p. 280.
9 This is what Shahab Ahmed has referred to as "Muslim meaning-making" in S. Ahmed (2015) *What is Islam? The importance of being Islamic*, Princeton, NJ: Princeton University Press.
10 T. K. Stewart and C. W. Ernst (2003) "Syncretism" in P. J. Claus and M. A. Mills (Eds.) *South Asian folklore: an encyclopaedia*, New York, NY: Garland Publishing, pp. 586–588.
11 D. A. DeWeese (2007) *Islamization and native religion in the Golden Horde: Baba Tükles and conversion to Islam in historical and epic tradition*, quotes on pp. 5, 56, and 54.
12 M. C. Ricklefs (2006) *Mystic synthesis in Java: a history of Islamization from the fourteenth to the early nineteenth centuries*, Norwalk, CT: EastBridge.
13 F. B. Flood (2018) *Objects of translation: material culture and medieval Hindu–Muslim encounter*, Princeton, NJ: Princeton University Press.
14 T. K. Stewart (2001) "In search of equivalence: conceiving Muslim–Hindu encounter through translation theory," *History of Religions* 40(3): 260–287, quotes at 273.
15 Z. Ben-Dor Benite (2005) *The Dao of Muhammad: a cultural history of Muslims in late imperial China*, Cambridge, MA: Harvard University Asia Center.
16 R. Thum (2017) "Surviving in a society-centric world: comments on Engseng Ho's inter-Asian concepts for mobile societies," *Journal of Asian Studies* 76(4): 929–933, quotes at 4–5.
17 Stewart and Ernst, "Syncretism."
18 A. L. Holt (1923) "The Future of the North Arabian Desert," *The Geographical Journal* 62(4): 259–268, quoted in F. E. Peters (2017) *The Arabs and Arabia on the eve of Islam*, Abingdon: Routledge, p. 74.

19 F. E. Peters (1996) *The Hajj: the Muslim pilgrimage to Mecca and the holy places*, Princeton, NJ: Princeton University Press, Chapter 1.

20 M. Tong, "A brief history of the Qadiriyya in China (translated from the Chinese and introduced by Jonathan Lipman)," *Journal of the History of Sufism* 1–2: 547–576, at 565.

21 M.A. Diddamari, *Waqi'at-i Kashmir* (RPD), *no. 1843, f. 145a*, in M. I. Khan (1989) "The significance of the Dargah of Hazratbal" in C. W. Troll (Ed.) *Muslim Shrines in India*, New Delhi: Oxford University Press, p. 175.

22 Quoted from Pir Muhammad Amin, *Jalwa-i Muy-i Sharif*, p. 6, in Khan, "The Significance of the Dargah of Hazratbal," p. 177.

23 Quoted in B. D. Metcalf (2013) "The pilgrimage remembered: South Asian accounts of the "hajj" in D. F. Eickelman and J. P. Piscatori, *Muslim travellers: pilgimage, migration, and the religious imagination*, London: Routledge, p. 103 fn 13.

24 P. Van Doorn-Harder and K. De Jong (2006) "Pilgrimage to Tembayat: tradition and revival in Islamic mysticism" in I. M. Abu-Rabi' (Ed.) *The Blackwell companion to contemporary Islamic thought*, Malden, MA: Blackwell, pp. 492, 500.

25 Quoted in T. Zarcone (2012) "Pilgrimage to the 'second Meccas' and 'ka'bas' of Central Asia" in *Central Asian pilgrims: hajj routes and pious visits between Central Asia and the Hijaz*, Berlin: Schwarz, pp. 251–277, at p. 255.

26 In ibid., p. 257.

27 Ibid.

28 S. R. Arjana (2016) *Pilgrimage in Islam: traditional and Modern Practices*, London: Oneworld Publication, quote on p. 191.

29 K. A. C. Creswell and J. W. Allan (1989) *A short account of early Muslim architecture*, Aldershot: Scolar Press, pp. 46–68.

30 R. Hillenbrand (2004) *Islamic architecture: form, function and meaning*, New York, NY: Columbia University Press, pp. 129–130.

31 O. Grabar (1963) "The Islamic dome: some considerations," *Journal of the Society of Architectural Historians/Society of Architectural Historians* 22(4): 191–198.

32 Flood, *Objects of translation*, p. 240.

33 Ibid.

34 S. R. Prange (2018) *Monsoon Islam: trade and faith on the medieval Malabar Coast*, New York, NY: Cambridge University Press, Chapter 2, "The Mosque."

35 H. Njoto (2015) "On the origins of the Javanese mosque," *The Newsletter*, *IIAS* 72, p. 45.

36 E. Ho (2006) *The graves of Tarim: genealogy and mobility across the Indian Ocean*, Berkeley, CA: University of California Press, pp. 250–251.

37 J. T. McDaniel (2018) "Ethnicity and the galactic polity: ideas and actualities in the history of Bangkok," *Journal of Southeast Asian Studies* 49(1): 129–148.

38 N. S. Steinhardt (2015) *China's early mosques*, Edinburgh: Edinburgh University Press, p. 52.

39 Ibid., p. 69.

40 *Sahih al-Bukhari*, Volume 7, Book of Dress, *Hadith* 838.
41 H. Njoto (2018) "What was Islamic about Javanese art in the early Islamic period (15th-17th century)?" *NSC Highlights* 7: 2–3.
42 Flood, *Objects of translation*, p. 32.
43 Ibid.
44 Ibid., p. 173.
45 I. Schulze and W. Schulze (2010) "The standing caliph coins of al-Jazīra: some problems and suggestions," *The Numismatic Chronicle (1966–)* 170: 331–353.
46 C. Gruber (2014) "Images" in A. Walker and C. Fitzpatrick (Eds.) *Muhammad in history, thought, and culture: an encyclopedia of the Prophet of God*, Santa Barbara, CA: ABC-CLIO.
47 R. Hillenbrand (2002) "The arts of the book in Ilkhanid Iran" in L. Komaroff and S. Carboni (Eds.) *The legacy of Genghis Khan: courtly art and culture in western Asia, 12561353*, pp. 135–167.
48 R. Finlay (1998) "The pilgrim art: the culture of porcelain in world history," *Journal of World History* 9(2): 141–187, at 178. See also P. Morgan (1991) "New thoughts on old Hormuz: Chinese ceramics in the Hormuz region in the thirteenth and fourteenth centuries," *Iran* 29: 67–83, at 78.
49 Finlay, "The pilgrim art," 178.
50 V. Gonzales (2016) *Aesthetic Hybridity in Mughal Painting, 1526–1658*, London: Routledge, p. 151.
51 Snouck Hurgronje, O'Sullivan, and Wilkinson, *The Achehnese*, p. 280.
52 L. Ahmed (1992) *Women and gender in Islam: historical roots of a modern debate*, New Haven, CT: Yale University Press.
53 Ricklefs, *Mystic synthesis in Java*, p. 224.
54 In ibid., pp. 34, 36.
55 In ibid., pp. 48–49.
56 A. C. Milner (1981) "Islam and Malay kingship," *Journal of the Royal Asiatic Society of Great Britain & Ireland* 113(1): 46–70, at 48.
57 Ibid., p. 49.
58 A. Wink (2002) *al- Hind: the making of the Indo-Islamic world*, Vol. 1, Leiden: Brill, p. 18.
59 Milner, "Islam and Malay kingship," p. 52.
60 Ben-Dor Benite, *The Dao of Muhammad*, p. 119.
61 Ibid., p. 120.
62 Wang Daiyu, *Zhengjiao zhenquan* [A true interpretation of the orthodox teaching], 16. Quoted in J. N. Lipman (1997) *Familiar strangers: a history of Muslims in Northwest China*, Seattle, WA: University of Washington Press, p. 77.
63 Ibid., p. 83.
64 As translated and quoted in R. Tontini (2016) *Muslim Sanzijing: shifts and continuities in the definition of Islam in China*, Leiden: Brill, pp. 37–38.
65 Ibid., p. 37.
66 Words of the vice minister of the Board of War, written in 1710. Quoted in Lipman, *Familiar Strangers*, p. 82.
67 Tontini, *Muslim Sanzijing*, pp. 105–106.

Chapter 3

1 'Abd Allāh ibn As'ad Yāfi'ī (1919) *Kitāb Mir'āt al-jinān wa-'ibrat al-yaqẓān: fī ma'rifat mā yu'tabaru min ḥawādith al-zamān. Ḥaydarābād al-Dakkan: Maṭba'at Dā'irat al-Ma'ārif al-Niẓāmīyah.* Abd Allah b. As'ad al-Yafi'i (1298–1367) is quoted in R. M. Feener and M. F. Laffan, "Sufi scents across the Indian Ocean: Yemeni hagiography and the earliest history of Southeast Asian Islam," *Archipel* 70: 185–208, at p. 197.

2 Shihab al-Din Ahmad al-Sharji (1410–ca. 1487/8) *Tabaqat al-khawass,* quoted in Feener and Laffan, "Sufi scents across the Indian Ocean," pp. 186–187.

3 *Kitāb Mir'āt al-jinān Yāfi'ī,* quoted in Feener and Laffan, "Sufi scents across the Indian Ocean," p. 199.

4 Ibid., p. 201.

5 H. C. Snouck Hurgronje (2007) *Mekka in the latter part of the 19th century: daily life, customs and learning, the Moslims of the East-Indian-Archipelago,* Leiden: Brill, p. 203.

6 M. Kooriadathodi (2016) Cosmopolis of law: Islamic legal ideas and texts across the Indian Ocean and Eastern Mediterranean Worlds, Doctoral Dissertation, Leiden University. S. Reichmuth (1999) "Murtadā az-Zabīdī (d. 1791) in biographical and autobiographical accounts. Glimpses of Islamic scholarship in the 18th century," *Die Welt des Islams,* New Series 39 (1): 64–102.

7 In A. Sayeed (2013) *Women and the transmission of religious knowledge in Islam,* Cambridge: Cambridge University Press, p. 108.

8 Ibid., p. 135.

9 C. W. Ernst (2011) *Sufism: an introduction to the mystical tradition of Islam,* Boston, MA: Shambhala, pp. 2–3.

10 Quoted in Ernst, *Sufism: an introduction,* p. 12.

11 J. van Ess (1999) "Sufism and its opponents: reflections on topoi, tribulations, and transformations" in F. de Jong and B. Radtke (Eds.) *Islamic mysticism contested: thirteen centuries of controversies and polemics,* Leiden: Brill, pp. 22–44, quote on p. 31.

12 D. Le Gall (2003) "Forgotten Naqshbandīs and the Culture of Pre-Modern Sufi Brotherhoods," *Studia Islamica* 97: 87–119, quote at p. 92; see also p. 117.

13 Translation in J. Eden (2019) *Warrior Saints of the Silk Road: Legends of the Qarakhanids,* Leiden: Brill, p. 85–86.

14 Hazrat Maulana Shah Isma'il Shahid, "Taqwiyyat al-Iman" reproduced in B. D. Metcalf (2009) *Islam in South Asia in practice,* Princeton, NJ: Princeton University Press, pp. 201–211.

15 Sayeed, *Women and the transmission of religious knowledge,* p. 143.

16 J. Voll (1975) "Muḥammad Ḥayyā al-Sindī and Muḥammad ibn 'Abd al-Wahhāb: an analysis of an intellectual group in eighteenth-century Madīna," *Bulletin of the School of Oriental and African Studies* 38(1): 32–39.

17 First quote by Julian Boldrick, echoed in van Ess "Sufism and its opponents," p. 34. Second quote by B. D. Ingram (2018) *Revival from below: the Deoband movement and global Islam,* Oakland, CA: University of California Press, p. 14.

18 S. C. Levi and R. Sela (Eds.) (2009) *Islamic Central Asia: an anthology of historical sources*, Bloomington, IN: Indiana University Press, p. 234.

19 In theological terms, the oneness of "vision" indicated the unity of the phenomenal world (the world we experience as humans), thus in direct opposition (and refutation) to the unity (or oneness) that a Sufi might attain in the divine world ("Being"). Ibn al-'Arabi, among others, argued that through "the path" of spiritual ecstasy the Sufi could reach oneness with God (monism).

20 In A. Azra (2004) *The origins of Islamic reformism in Southeast Asia: networks of Malay-Indonesian and Middle Eastern 'Ulama' in the seventeenth and eighteenth centuries*, Crows Nest, NSW: Allen & Unwin in association with Asian Studies Association of Australia, p. 107.

21 S. Haj (2011) *Reconfiguring Islamic tradition: reform, rationality, and modernity*, Stanford, CA: Stanford University Press, pp. 16, 15.

22 B. D. Metcalf (2009) "India" in *The Oxford Encyclopedia of the Islamic World. Oxford Islamic Studies Online*, www.oxfordislamicstudies.com/article/opr/t236/e0361 (accessed December 31, 2018).

23 J. N. Lipman (1997) *Familiar strangers: a history of Muslims in Northwest China*, Seattle, WA: University of Washington Press, p. 89.

24 Ibid., p. 87.

25 Ibid., pp. 70–71.

26 M. Kemper and S. A. Dudoignon (1996) "Entre Boukhara et la Moyenne-Volga: 'Abd an-Nasîr al-Qûrsâwî (1776–1812) en conflit avec les oulémas traditionalistes," *Cahiers du monde russe: Russie, Empire Russe, Union Soviétique, États Indépendants* 37(1): 41–51, at pp. 41–42.

27 S. A. Dudoignon (1996) "La question scolaire à Boukhara et au Turkestan russe, du 'premier renouveau' à la soviétisation (fin du XVIIIe siècle–1937)," *Cahiers du monde russe: Russie, Empire Russe, Union Soviétique, États Indépendants* 37(1): 133–210, at pp. 141–143.

28 Kemper and Dudoignon, "Entre Boukhara et la Moyenne-Volga," 43–45.

29 D. A. DeWeese (2016) "It was a dark and stagnant night ('til the Jadids brought the light): clichés, biases, and false dichotomies in the intellectual history of Central Asia," *Journal of the Economic and Social History of the Orient* 59(1–2): 37–92.

30 F. R. Bradley (2016) *Forging Islamic power and place: the legacy of Shaykh Daud bin Abd Allah al-Fatani in Mecca and Southeast Asia*, Honolulu, HI: University of Hawai'i Press, pp. 82–83.

31 Ibid., pp. 67–78.

32 N. Green (2013) *Bombay Islam: the religious economy of the West Indian Ocean, 1840–1915*, New York, NY: Cambridge University Press, quote on p. 243.

33 Ingram, *Revival from below*, p. 3.

34 Risalat al-waridat Muhammad 'Abduh, quoted in E. Sirriyeh (1999) *Sufis and anti-Sufis: the defense, rethinking and rejection of Sufism in the modern world*, Richmond: Curzon, p. 91.

35 *Al-Manar wa'l-Azhar* Rashid Rida (Cairo 1934–1935), p. 147, quoted in Sirriyeh *Sufis and anti-Sufis*, p. 99.

36 A. Hourani (1962) *Arabic thought in the liberal age 1798–1939*, London: Oxford University Press, p. 222.

Chapter 4

1 F. Kerlogue (2004) *Batik: design, style & history*, London: Thames & Hudson. F. Kerlogue (1997) Batik cloths from Jambi, Sumatra, Doctoral Dissertation, University of Hull, Chapter 10: The calligraphy batik of Jambi.

2 C. Formichi (2015) "Indonesian readings of Turkish history, 1890s to 1940s" in A. C. S. Peacock and A. Teh Gallop (Eds.) *From Anatolia to Aceh: Ottomans, Turks, and Southeast Asia*, Oxford: Published for the British Academy by Oxford University Press, pp. 241–262.

3 C. Aydin (2017) *The idea of the Muslim world: a global intellectual history*, Cambridge, MA: Harvard University Press, p. 6 (and more).

4 The full text, with a digital image of the original in Ottoman Turkish language, is available from www.turkeyswar.com/documents/ (last accessed January 5, 2019).

5 Aydin, *The idea of the Muslim world*, both quotes on p. 98.

6 In K. H. Karpat (2001) *Politicization of Islam: reconstructing identity, state, faith and community in the late Ottoman state*, Oxford: Oxford University Press, p. 495 (quote not dated).

7 Aydin, *The idea of the Muslim world*, pp. 14–15.

8 M. N. Qureshi (1999) *Pan-Islam in British Indian politics: a study of the Khilafat Movement, 1918–1924*, Leiden: Brill, p. 19 (see his footnote 48 for further details).

9 In D. Rahbar (2006) *Selected essays by Sir Sayyid Ahmad Khan*, translated by J. W. Wilder, Lahore: Sang-e Meel Publications, pp. 69–73, 85–87.

10 S. A. Dudoignon, H, Komatsu, and Yasushi K. (2009) *Intellectuals in the modern Islamic world: transmission, transformation, communication*, London: Routledge. M. F. Laffan (2003) *Islamic nationhood and colonial Indonesia: the umma below the winds*, New York, NY: Routledge.

11 Laffan, *Islamic nationhood*, pp. 123–24.

12 Karpat, *The politicization of Islam*, p. 235 (Sulu) and p. 237 (Boxer)

13 J. M. Landau (1990) *The politics of Pan-Islam: ideology and organization*, Oxford: Clarendon Press, p. 101.

14 Abdurreshid Ibrahim in Landau, *The politics of Pan-Islam*, p. 153.

15 S. Saaler and C. W. A. Szpilman (Eds.) (2011) *Pan-Asianism: a documentary history, 1850–1920*, Lanham, MD: Rowman & Littlefield, pp. 166–168.

16 Tanaka Ippei (1925) "Islam and Greater Asianism," quoted in H. Kramer (2014) "Pan-Asianism's religious undercurrents: the reception of Islam and translation of the Qur'ān in twentieth-century Japan," *The Journal of Asian Studies*, 73(3): 619–640, at p. 624.

17 Kramer, "Pan-Asianism's religious undercurrents," p. 634.

18 T. Buzpinar (1996) "Opposition to the Ottoman Caliphate in the early years of Abdülhamid II: 1877–1882," *Die Welt des Islams* 36(1): 59–89, at p. 64.

19 Karpat, *The politicization of Islam*, p. 543.

20 G. Minault (1982) "Purdah politics: the role of Muslim women in Indian nationalism, 1911–1924" in H. Papanek and G. Minault (Eds.) *Separate world: studies of purdah in South Asia*, Delhi: Chanakya Publications, p. 248.

21 F. Robinson (2001) "The 'Ulama of Farangi Mahall and Islamic Culture," *ISIM Newsletter* (International Institute for the Study of Islam in the Modern World) 8, at p. 24.

22 Quoted in K. A. Deutsch (1998) Muslim women in colonial North India circa 1920–1947: politics, law and community identity. Doctoral Thesis, University of Cambridge, p. 99.

23 Quoted in Minault "Purdah politics," p. 254.

24 Ibid., p. 249.

25 Tan Malaka (1922) *Communism and Pan-Islamism*, www.marxists.org/archive/malaka/1922-Panislamism.htm.

26 C. Formichi (2010) "Pan-Islam and religious nationalism: the case of Karto-suwiryo and Negara Islam Indonesia," *Indonesia* 90: 125–146.

27 The Zawahiri Secret Report, in M. S. Kramer (1986) *Islam assembled: the advent of the Muslim congresses*, New York, NY: Columbia University Press, p. 110.

28 S. J. White (2004) Reformist Islam, gender and marriage in late colonial Dutch East Indies, 1900–1942, Doctoral Thesis, Australian National University, p. 73.

29 G. Fealy and V. Hooker (Eds.) (2006) *Voices of Islam in Southeast Asia*, Singapore: ISEAS, "Piagam Jakarta Preamble to Undang-undang Dasar Republik Indonesia 1945," pp. 209–10.

30 R. Pipes (1964) *The formation of the Soviet Union: communism and nationalism, 1917–1923*, Cambridge, MA: Harvard University Press, p. 191.

31 Ibid., p. 183.

32 S. Yilmaz (2007) "In pursuit of elusive glory: Enver Pasha's role in the Pan-Islamic and the Basmachi movement" in B. Tezcan, K. K. Barbir, and N. Itzkowitz (Eds.) *Identity and identity formation in the Ottoman world: a volume of essays in honor of Norman Itzkowitz*, Madison, WI: Center for Turkish Studies at the University of Wisconsin, pp. 185–202, at p. 198.

33 As reported in the British PRO FO 371/8075.

34 D. T. Northrop (2004) *Veiled empire: gender and power in Stalinist Central Asia*, Ithaca, NY: Cornell University Press, p. 77.

35 Ibid., p. 81.

36 Ibid., p. 80.

37 Ibid., p. 92.

38 M. Jaschok and J. Shui (2000) *The history of women's mosques in Chinese Islam: a mosque of their own*, Richmond: Curzon, p. 187.

39 A. Mango (2004) *Atatürk*, London: John Murray, p. 434.

40 Begum Mazharul Haq at the AIWC Third Conference on Education Reform (Patna, 1929) quoted in Deutsch, Muslim women in colonial North India, p. 108.

41 In White, Reformist Islam, p. 135.

42 *The Leader*, November 30, 1928, p. 10 quoted in Deutsch, Muslim women in colonial North India, p. 117.

43 White, Reformist Islam, p. 130.

44 P. van Doorn-Harder (2006) *Women shaping Islam: reading the Quran in Indonesia*, Urbana, IL: University of Illinois Press, p. 13.

45 Jaschok and Shui, *The history of women's mosques in Chinese Islam*, pp. 95–97, quote on p. 95.

46 Article published in *Soeara Aisjijah* in 1941, quoted in White, Reformist Islam, p. 138.

Chapter 5

1 E. Armstrong (2015) "Before Bandung: the anti-imperialist women's movement in Asia and the Women's International Democratic Federation," *Signs: Journal of Women in Culture and Society* 41(2): 305–331, quote at p. 305.

2 Quoted in Armstrong, "Before Bandung," p. 312.

3 C. Stolte (2019) "The People's Bandung: local anti-imperialists on an Afro-Asian stage," *Journal of World History* 30(1–2): 125–156, quote at p. 151.

4 K. A. Deutsch (1998) Muslim women in colonial North India circa 1920–1947: politics, law and community identity, Doctoral Thesis, University of Cambridge, pp. 233–34.

5 A. Jalal (1994) *The sole spokesman: Jinnah, the Muslim League, and the demand for Pakistan*, Cambridge and New York, NY: Cambridge University Press, p. 14.

6 Deutsch, Muslim women in colonial North India, p. 257.

7 Jalal, *The sole spokesman*, p. 42.

8 A. Jalal (2008) *Partisans of Allah: Jihad in South Asia*, Cambridge, MA: Harvard University Press, p. 18.

9 I use the double name Burma/Myanmar as a way of acknowledging the official name change of 1989 as well as pleas from ethnic minorities that this form of political window-dressing should not be accepted. Many activists and intellectuals have since argued that, despite the name change, the country remains the nation of the *Bar-Ma* (see further below in this chapter).

10 N. Northrop (2004) *Veiled empire: gender and power in Stalinist Central Asia*. Ithaca, NY: Cornell University Press, p. 22.

11 A. Endang Saifuddin (1997) *Piagam Jakarta 22 Juni 1945: Sebuah konsensus nasional tentang dasar negara Republik Indonesia 1945–1959*, 3rd ed., Jakarta: Gema Insani Press, p. 48, quoted in English in C. Formichi (2012) *Islam and the making of the nation*, Leiden: KITLV Press, p. 82.

12 "Overzicht en Ontwikkeling van de Toestand 8 April 1800 uur tot 15 April 1800 uur," Territorial ts. Tropencommandant West Java [1948], Ministerie van Defensie: Archieven Strijdkrachten in Nederlands-Indië, no. 2224, National Archieves of the Netherlands, Den Haag. "Rencana ketenteraan oemmat Islam" in Jogjakarta Documenten, 1946–1948 no. 218h, National Archives of the Indonesian Republic, Jakarta (ANRI).

13 "Dunia Masyumi" in Jogjakarta Documenten no. 218h, ANRI.

14 "Maklumat Negara Islam Indonesia no. 6," 20 Safar 1368 AH/21 December 1948 CE, in A. Chaidar (1999) *Pemikiran politik proklamator negara Islam Indonesia S. M. Kartosoewirjo: fakta dan data sejarah Darul Islam*, Jakarta: Darul Falah, pp. 556–557. See also Formichi, *Islam and the making of the nation*.

15 "Membesarkan berita D. I. untuk keuntungan politik," *Harian Berita*, 21 September 1949.

16 "Ichtisar gerakan DI/Kartosuwiryo," Kemeterian Dalam Negeri Yogyakarta, July 24, 1950, Kabinet Perdana Menteri no. 150, ANRI; "Statement

Masjumi tentang perisitiwa 'Darul Islam,'" Ketua Dewan Pimpinan Partai Masjumi Moh. Natsir, April 23, 1950, KabPerd no. 150, ANRI; "Sikap PSII terhadap penjelesaian soal Darul Islam," May 4, 1950, RIS no. 107, ANRI; "Soal Darul Islam dan pembersihan jang telah diadakan," Menteri Pertahanan RIS, May 8, 1950, Kabinet Perdana Menteri no. 150, ANRI.

17 P. van Doorn-Harder (2006) *Women shaping Islam: reading the Quran in Indonesia*, Urbana, IL: University of Illinois Press, p. 242.

18 Ibid., p. 219.

19 Ibid., p. 220.

20 *Address by Quaid-i-Azam Mohammad Ali Jinnah at Lahore Session of Muslim League, March, 1940* published by Ministry of Information and Broadcasting, Government of Pakistan, Islamabad (1983) Islamabad: Directorate of Films and Publishing, pp. 5–23. www.columbia.edu/itc/mealac/pritchett/00islam links/txt_jinnah_lahore_1940.html (accessed January 6, 2019).

21 D. Gilmartin (2009) "Muslim League appeals to the voters of Punjab for support of Pakistan" in B. D. Metcalf (Ed.) *Islam in South Asia in practice*, Princeton, NJ: Princeton University Press.

22 B. D. Metcalf and T. R. Metcalf (2012) *A concise history of modern India*, 3rd ed., Cambridge: Cambridge University Press, p. 215.

23 A. Khalid (2014) *Islam after communism: religion and politics in Central Asia*, Berkeley, CA: University of California Press, p. 83.

24 Ibid., p. 85 (emphasis in original).

25 Quoted in Y. Ro'i (2000) *Islam in the Soviet Union: from the Second World War to Gorbachev*, New York, NY: Columbia University Press, p. 288 fn 5.

26 State archive of the Federation (GARF) f.69991, o.3, d.47, ll. 113–14, quoted in Ro'i, *Islam in the Soviet Union*, p. 389.

27 Article by A. L. Troitskaya, quoted in H. Fathi (1997) "Otines: the unknown women clerics of Central Asian Islam," *Central Asian Survey* 16(1): 27–43, at p. 31.

28 November 6, 1953, quoted in E. Tasar (2017) *Soviet and Muslim: the institutionalization of Islam in Central Asia, 1943–1991*, Kettering: Oxford University Press, pp. 136–137.

29 Ibid., pp. 240–241.

30 Hindustani quoted in B. Babajanov and M. Kamilov "Muhammadjan Hindustani (1892–1989) and the beginning of the 'Great Schism' among the Muslims of Uzbekistan" in S. A. Dudoignon and K. Hisao (2009) *Islam in politics in Russia and central Asia: early eighteenth to late twentieth centuries*, London: Routledge, p. 216.

31 I. R. Morgenstein Fuerst (2017) *Indian Muslim minorities and the 1857 rebellion: religion, rebels, and jihad*, London: I. B. Tauris, p. 6.

32 Ibid., pp. 151, 153.

33 M. Ul-Haq (1972) *Islam in Secular India*, Simla: Indian Institute of Advanced Study, pp. 6, 8–9, 14–16, 19–21, 85–86, cited in "Islam in Secular India," *Oxford Islamic Studies Online*, www.oxfordislamicstudies.com/article/book/islam-9780195174304/islam-9780195174304-chapter-27 (accessed December 31, 2018).

34 M. D. Metcalf (2009) "India" in *The Oxford Encyclopedia of the Islamic World. Oxford Islamic Studies Online*, www.oxfordislamicstudies.com/article/opr/t236/ e0361 (accessed December 13, 2018).

35 Ibid.

36 Bureau of Democracy, Human Rights and Labor, *International Religious Freedom Report for 2017: India*, www.state.gov/j/drl/rls/irf/religiousfreedom/ index.htm?year=2017&dlid=281022 (accessed December 31, 2018).

37 (1875) *Report on the census of British Burma, taken in August 1872*, Rangoon: Government Press, pp. 15–16.

38 Ibid., p. 30.

39 (1881) *Report on the census of British Burma, taken on 17 February 1881. Accompanied by map*, Rangoon: Government Press, p. 38.

40 D. MacNeill (1883) *Report and gazetteer of Burma, Native and British: Part 2 Lower or British Burma*, Simla.

41 "Seventh meeting of the Commission," Deputations from the Burma Muslim Society, February 5, 1929." IOR, BL.

42 "Imperial Table XIII – Race. Part II – Race-groups by Religion and District" in S. G. Grantham (1923) *Census of India, 1921. Volume X. Burma Part I. Report*, Rangoon: Office of the Superintendent, Government Printing, Burma, pp. 192–197.

43 Central Intelligence Agency, "Burma" in *The World Factbook*, www.cia.gov/ library/publications/the-world-factbook/geos/bm.html#field-anchor-people- and-society-religions, last updated December 18, 2018: "religion estimate is based on the 2014 national census, including an estimate for the non- enumerated population of Rakhine State, which is assumed to mainly affiliate with the Islamic faith."

44 BBC News (2018) "Myanmar Rohingya," April 24, 2018, www.bbc.com/ news/world-asia-41566561 (accessed January 2, 2019).

45 www.doctorswithoutborders.org/rohingya-refugee-crisis?source=ADD190U 0U00&utm_source=AdWords&utm_medium=ppc&utm_campaign=Google Paid&utm_content=NonBrand&gclid=Cj0KCQiA37HhBRC8ARIsAPWoO 0ysADnK0BbgFAuU9eSL6DL8ltXvjTzNT5KDYLvTYm3gsvhzH3N3y2Q aAm32EALw_wcB.

46 United Nations, "Myanmar Military leaders must face genocide charges," UN report, August 27, 2018, https://news.un.org/en/story/2018/08/1017802 (accessed January 2, 2019).

47 The Arakan Project, (October 2017), map included at www.bbc.com/news/ world-asia-41566561 (accessed January 2, 2019).

48 Singapore Census of Population 2000.

49 "Maintenance of Religious Harmony Act (Chapter 167A), Original Enactment: Act 26 of 1990," http://statutes.agc.gov.sg/aol/search/display/view.w3p;page=0; query=DocId%3A77026343-e30d-40e2-a32e-b1f5d46c5bd7%20%20Status %3Ainforce%20Depth%3A0;rec=0 (accessed September 17, 2016).

50 M. N. Mohamed Osman (2018) "The secular and the religious in the management of Islam in Singapore," *Journal of Muslim Minority Affairs* 38(2): 246–262, at 249.

Chapter 6

1 W. Y. Ho (2015) "The emerging visibility of Islam through the powerless: Indonesian Muslim domestic helpers in Hong Kong," *Asian Anthropology*, 14(1): 79–90, quote at p. 85.

2 I. M. Lapidus (1997) "Islamic revival and modernity: the contemporary movements and the historical paradigms," *Journal of the Economic and Social History of the Orient* 40(4): 444–460, at p. 447.

3 Al-Banna quoted in S. Mahmood (2012) *Politics of piety: the Islamic revival and the feminist subject*, Princeton, NJ: Princeton University Press, p. 63.

4 Ibid., p. 69.

5 J. A. Nagata (1984) *The reflowering of Malaysian Islam: modern religious radicals and their roots*, Vancouver: University of British Columbia Press, p. 57.

6 Ibid., p. 74.

7 D. M. Müller (2014) *Islam, politics and youth in Malaysia: the pop-Islamist reinvention of PAS*, Abingdon: Routledge, p. 54.

8 A. Ong (1995) "State versus Islam: Malay families, women's bodies, and the body politic in Malaysia" in A. Ong and M. G. Peletz (Eds.) *Bewitching women, pious men*, Berkeley, CA: University of California Press, pp. 156–194, quote on p. 160.

9 S. Frisk (2009) *Submitting to God: women and Islam in urban Malaysia*, Seattle, WA: University of Washington Press, p. 15.

10 Ibid., pp. 91–92.

11 L. Abu-Lughod (2002) "Do Muslim women really need saving? Anthropological reflections on cultural relativism and its others," *American Anthropologist* 104(3): 783–790.

12 L. Ahmed (1992) *Women and gender in Islam: historical roots of a modern debate*, New Haven, CT: Yale University Press.

13 M. Lazreg (1994) *The eloquence of silence: Algerian women in question*, New York, NY: Routledge.

14 Abu-Lughod (2013) "Do Muslim women really need saving?"

15 Ibid.

16 M. B. Olcott (2007) *Roots of radical Islam in Central Asia*, Washington, DC: Carnegie Endowment for International Peace, p. 23.

17 A fascinating account of "Militant solidarity with the Arab peoples" is found in A. Vakhabov (1979) *Muslims in the USSR*, Moscow: Novosti Press Agency Publishing House.

18 E. Tasar (2017) *Soviet and Muslim: the institutionalization of Islam in Central Asia, 1943–1991*. Kettering: Oxford University Press, p. 356.

19 Hindustani, quoted in B. Babajanov and M. Kamilov (2009) "Muhammadjan Hindustani (1892–1989) and the beginning of the 'Great Schism' among the Muslims of Uzbekistan" in S. A. Dudoignon and K. Hisao (Eds.) *Islam in politics in Russia and central Asia: early eighteenth to late twentieth centuries*, London: Routledge, p. 200.

20 Article 110 of "The Draft Constitution of the Khilafah State," *Hizb ut-Tahrir*, 2011, www.hizb.org.uk/wp-content/uploads/2011/02/Draft-Constitution.pdf.

21 Sanya Sagnaeva, quoted in Farangis Najibullah, "Central Asia: Hizb ut-Tahrir gains support from women," *RadioFreeEurope RadioLiberty*, www.rferl.org/a/1077570.html.
22 E. Karagiannis (2011) *Political Islam in Central Asia: the challenge of Hizb ut-Tahrir*, London: Routledge, p. 72.
23 M. Jaschok and J. Shui (2000) *The history of women's mosques in Chinese Islam: a mosque of their own*, Richmond, VA: Curzon, p. 154.
24 A. S. Jamjoon (1985) "Notes on a visit to Mainland China," *Journal Institute of Muslim Minority Affairs*, 6(1): 208–218, at p. 208.
25 Ibid., p. 216.
26 Ibid., p. 218.
27 Ibid., p. 208.
28 M. S. Erie (2017) *China and Islam: the prophet, the party, and law*. Cambridge: Cambridge University Press, p. 153. Here Erie is referring only to the Salafiya, but his insight on an "imagined connection" has, I think, a broader application.
29 M. A. Mudzhar (1993) *Fatwa-fatwa Majelis Ulama Indonesia: sebuah studi tentang permikiran hukum Islam di Indonesia 1975-1988*, Jakarta: INIS, pp. 114–126. Atho Mudzhar is professor of Islamic law and currently head of the Office of Research and Development in the Department of Religion.
30 Billah (1989) "Gerakan Kelompok Islam di Yogyakarta" in A. Aziz, I. Tholkhah, and Soetarman (Eds.) *Gerakan Islam kontemporer di Indonesia*, Jakarta: Firdaus, p. 340.

Chapter 7

1 Included in Document no. 263 (2018) "Telegram from the Department of State to the Embassy in Pakistan," Washington, May 3, 1980. Quoted in D. Zierler (Ed.) *Foreign Relations of the United States, 1977–1980, Volume XII, Afghanistan*, Washington, DC: Government Printing Office.
2 Quoted in P. Iyer (1984) "Afghanistan: Caravans on Moonless Nights," *TIME Magazine*, June 11, p. 39.
3 M. E. Raoufi (1986) "Editorial: Year of 1978 as Challenge for Afghanistan Muslim People," *The Mirror of Jehad*, 2nd series, 1.1–2, p. 4, quoted in S. W. Fuchs (2017) "Glossy global leadership: unpacking the multilingual religious thought of the Jihad" in N. Green (Ed.) *Afghanistan's Islam: from conversion to the Taliban*, Oakland, CA: University of California Press, p. 195.
4 M. Rahmany, H. Stanikzai, A. S. van Linschoten, and F. Kuehn (Eds.) (2012) *Poetry of the Taliban*, London: Hurst & Co, p. 167.
5 "Mujahidin" in J. L. Esposito (Ed.) *The Oxford Dictionary of Islam*, *Oxford Islamic Studies Online*, www.oxfordislamicstudies.com/article/opr/t125/e1593 (accessed May 15, 2018). Document no. 324 "Paper Prepared in the Central Intelligence Agency" Washington, October 1, 1980, quoted in Zierler, *Foreign Relations of the United States*.
6 Fuchs, "Glossy global leadership," p. 198.

7 A. Jalal (2008) *Partisans of Allah: Jihad in South Asia*. Cambridge, MA: Harvard University Press, p. 4.

8 Ibid., p. 58.

9 Ibid., p. 4.

10 Hindustani, quoted in B. Babajanov and M. Kamilov (2009) "Muhammad-jan Hindustani (1892–1989) and the Beginning of the 'Great Schism' among the Muslims of Uzbekistan" in S. A. Dudoignon and K. Hisao (Eds.) *Islam in politics in Russia and central Asia: early eighteenth to late twentieth centuries*, London: Routledge, p. 214.

11 Document no. 258 "Memorandum from Marshall Brement of the National Security Council Staff to the President's Assistant for National Security Affairs (Brzezinski)," Washington, April 30, 1980. Quoted in Zierler, *Foreign Relations of the United States*.

12 Document no. 257 "Summary of Conclusions of a Special Coordination Committee Meeting," Washington, April 23, 1980. Quoted in Zierler, *Foreign Relations of the United States*.

13 N. H. Dupree (1988) "Demographic reporting on Afghan refugees in Pakistan," *Modern Asian Studies* 22(4): 845–865.

14 A. Rashid (2001) *Taliban: the story of the Afghan Warlords*, London: Pan Books, p. 89.

15 B. D. Metcalf (2002) "Traditionalist Islamic activism: Deoband, Tablighis, and Talibs," *ISIM Papers* 4, at p. 14.

16 T. Hegghammer (2010) *Jihad in Saudi Arabia: violence and pan-Islamism since 1979*, New York, NY: Cambridge University Press, p. 38.

17 Ibid., pp. 38–41.

18 A. Azzam (1984) *Defense of the Muslim Lands*, Chapter 2 (no page numbers).

19 Ibid.

20 S. Barṭal (2016) *Jihad in Palestine: political Islam and the Israeli-Palestine conflict*, London: Routledge, p. 26.

21 T. Dunning (2017) *Hamas, jihad and popular legitimacy: reinterpreting resistance in Palestine* [S.l.]: Routledge, p. 172.

22 T. Hegghammer (Ed.) (2017) *Jihadi culture: the art and social practices of militant Islamists*, Cambridge: Cambridge University Press, p. 33. See also R. Creswell and B. Haykel, "Battle lines: want to understand the jihadis? Read their poetry," *The New Yorker*, June 8 & 15, 2015 Issue, www.newyorker.com/magazine/2015/06/08/battle-lines-jihad-creswell-and-haykel.

23 G. Kepel (2014) *Jihad: the trail of political Islam*, London: I. B. Tauris, p. 156.

24 Quoted in M. Al-Rasheed (2007) *Contesting the Saudi state: Islamic voices from a new generation*, Cambridge: Cambridge University Press, p. 107.

25 Ibid., p. 106.

26 Hegghammer, *Jihad in Saudi Arabia*, p. 45.

27 S. A. Johnson (2015) *African American religions, 1500–2000: colonialism, democracy, and freedom*, Cambridge: Cambridge University Press, p. 385.

28 I. R. Morgenstein Fuerst (2017) *Indian Muslim minorities and the 1857 rebellion: religion, rebels, and jihad*, London: I. B. Tauris, p. 125.

29 Johnson, *African American religions, 1500–2000*, p. 388.

30 International Crisis Group (2002) "Al-Qaeda in Southeast Asia: the case of the Ngruki Network in Indonesia," Brussels, quotes on pp. 6 and 8.

31 Last Testament of Iqbal, alias Arnasan, alias Acong, October 2002. I am grateful to Ms. Sidney Jones for sharing this document.

32 Ibid.

33 C. Robinson DeBergh (2013) *Body of victim, body of warrior: refugee families and the making of Kashmiri jihadists*, Berkeley, CA: University of California Press, p. 5.

34 H. M. Federspiel (1998) "Islam and Muslims in the Southern Territories of the Philippine Islands during the American colonial period (1898 to 1946)," *Journal of Southeast Asian Studies* 29(2): 340–356.

35 *Berjihad di Patani* (2004?), in D. McCargo (2008) *Tearing apart the land: Islam and legitimacy in Southern Thailand*, Ithaca, NY: Cornell University Press.

36 Robinson de Bergh, *Body of victim, body of warrior*, Chapter 1.

37 M. Abou Zahab (2013) "Salafism in Pakistan: the Ahl-e Hadith movement" in Roel Meijer (Ed.) *Global salafism: Islam's new religious movement*, New York, NY: Oxford University Press, p. 141.

38 G. Bovingdon (2010) *The Uyghurs: strangers in their own land*, New York, NY: Columbia University Press, p. 66.

39 R. Thum (2018) "China's mass internment camps have no clear end in sight," *Foreign Policy*, August 22, 2018.

40 S. Richardson, in P. Popham, "As China joins the anti-Isis brigade, must we keep quiet about the Uighurs?" *The Independent*, November 20, 2015, www.independent.co.uk/news/world/asia/as-china-joins-the-anti-isis-brigade-must-we-keep-quiet-about-the-uighurs-a6742641.html.

41 S. Jiang, "Thousands of Uyghur Muslims detained in Chinese 'political education' camps," CNN, February 2, 2018, www.cnn.com/2018/02/02/asia/china-xinjiang-detention-camps-intl/index.html (accessed November 1, 2018).

Chapter 8

1 This chapter has particularly benefited from detailed input and feedback from David Kloos, and from sustained conversations with students participating in the Fall 2018 seminar "Performing Islam in Southeast Asia" at Cornell University. All mistakes remain mine.

2 H. Singh (2018) "Powering the Halal Silk Route," September 7, 2018, *The Malaysian Reserve*, https://themalaysianreserve.com/2018/09/07/powering-the-halal-silk-route/.

3 M. B. Hooker (2008) *Indonesian Syariah: defining a national school of Islamic law*, Singapore: Institute of Southeast Asian Studies, pp. 132–133.

4 F. Robinson (1993) "Technology and religious change: Islam and the impact of print," *Modern Asian Studies* 27(1): 229–251, at p. 232.

5 Ibid., p. 234.

6 A. Sayeed (2013) *Women and the transmission of religious knowledge in Islam*, Cambridge: Cambridge University Press.

7 Robinson, "Technology and religious change," p. 244.

8 J. W. Anderson and Y. Gonzales-Quijan (2004) "Technological mediation and the emergence of transnational Muslim publics" in A. Salvatore and D. F. Eickelman (Eds.) *Public Islam and the common good*, Leiden: Brill, at p. 54.

9 G. Krämer and S. Schmidtke (2006) "Introduction: religious authority and religious authorities in Muslim societies. A critical overview" in G. Krämer and S. Schmidtke (Eds.) *Speaking for Islam: religious authorities in Muslim societies*, Leiden: Brill, pp. 1–14.

10 D. Kloos (2019) "Experts beyond discourse: women, Islamic authority, and the performance of professionalism in Malaysia," *American Ethnologist* 46(2): 162–175, at p. 163.

11 Krämer and Schmidtke, "Introduction."

12 Ibid.

13 On al-Qaradawi see B. Gräf and J. Skovgaard-Petersen (2009) *Global Mufti: the phenomenon of Yūsuf al-Qaraḍāwī*, London: Hurst and Company. On Aa Gym, J. B. Hoesterey (2015) *Rebranding Islam: piety, prosperity, and a self-help guru*, Stanford, CA: Stanford University Press. On Farhat Hashmi, J. L. Esposito (2010) *The future of Islam*, New York, NY: Oxford University Press.

14 M. Stivens (2006) "'Family values' and Islamic revival: gender, rights and state moral projects in Malaysia," *Women's Studies International Forum* 29(4): 354–367, at p. 357; I expand Stivens' observation on Malaysia to Indonesia.

15 Kloos, "Experts beyond discourse," p. 166.

16 J. Fischer (2008) *Proper Islamic consumption: shopping among the Malays in modern Malaysia*, Copenhagen: NIAS Press, p. 29.

17 Ibid.

18 Ramadan Collection, Our most treasured halal chocolates tied with special ribbon for Ramadan, www.godiva.com/halal-chocolate-and-candy (accessed January 5, 2019).

19 Agriculture and Agri-Food Canada (2011) *Global Halal food market*, Ottawa, p. 11.

20 Fischer, *Proper Islamic consumption*, p. 78.

21 M. Stivens (1998) "Sex, gender and the making of the new Malay middle classes" in K. Sen and M. Stivens (Eds.) *Gender and power in affluent Asia*, London: Routledge, pp. 87–126; Stivens, "'Family values' and Islamic revival"; and Fischer, *Proper Islamic consumption*.

22 J. A. Nagata (1984) *The reflowering of Malaysian Islam: modern religious radicals and their roots*, Vancouver: University of British Columbia Press, p. 107.

23 J. Fischer (2016) "Manufacturing halal in Malaysia," *Contemporary Islam: Dynamics of Muslim Life* 10(1): 35–52, at pp. 38–39.

24 Ibid., p. 40.

25 Etsuhiro Takato quoted in A. Tomiyama and W. Yoshida (2014) "Southeast Asia becoming global hub for halal foods," *Nikkei Review*, February 22.

26 Ibid.

27 C. Power and I. Gatsiounis (2007) "Meeting the Halal Test," *Forbes*, April 6.

28 A. Ali (May 17, 2017) "Closing Remarks by YAB Dato Seri Mohamad Azmin Ali at the Halal Hub-to-Hub roundtable Meeting in collaboration with Wallonia Logistics at Liege, Belgium."

29 Datuk Azman Shah Mohd. Yusof, CEO of Northport (M) Bhd, quoted by H. Singh (2018) "Powering the halal Silk Route," *The Malaysian Reserve* September 7, https://themalaysianreserve.com/2018/09/07/powering-the-halal-silk-route/.

30 B. Y. Hui (May 16, 2018) "A bigger market share for Malaysia's halal products," *The Star Online*.

31 TripAdvisor thread, "Re: shopping tips," response by the_musafir, posted on February 6, 2015.

32 Zhang Hongyi, general manager of Jingyitai Halal Food Co., quoted by B. Allen-Ebrahimian, "China Wants to Feed the World's 1.6 Billion Muslims," *Foreign Policy*, May 2, 2016.

33 Singh, "Powering the Halal Silk Route."

34 Ibid.

35 MITI Weekly Bulletin, Volume 441, Jan–Jul 2017, p. 3.

36 http://dianpelangi.com/about-the-brand/.

37 Quoting *The Jakarta Post*, www.nytimes.com/2014/11/27/fashion/reading-between-the-seams-at-the-islamic-fashion-festival-in-malaysia.html.

38 https://steinhardt.nyu.edu/art/costume/archive_events/meeting_through_modesty; https://www.nytimes.com/2016/11/03/fashion/what-does-modest-fashion-mean.html.

39 www.forbes.com/profile/dian-pelangi/#40e08f7a32e6.

40 www.nytimes.com/2018/09/25/arts/design/de-young-museum-contemporary-muslim-fashions.html.

41 https://deyoung.famsf.org/exhibitions/contemporary-muslim-fashions.

42 E. Bucar (2017) *Pious fashion how Muslim women dress*, Cambridge, MA: Harvard University Press, p. 114, quoting at p. 112 Irna Mutiara, "one of the most prominent Indonesian designers of Islamic women's fashion."

43 L. Schmidt (2017) *Islamic modernities in Southeast Asia exploring Indonesian popular and visual culture*, London: Rowan and Littlefield, Chapter 6.

44 Bucar, *Pious fashion*, p. 113.

45 S. Brenner (1996) "Reconstructing self and society: Javanese Muslim women and 'the veil,'" *American Ethnologist* 23: 673–697, at p. 682.

46 Ibid., p. 678.

47 E. Amrullah (2008) "Indonesian Muslim fashion: styles and designs," *ISIM Newsletter* 22: 22–23.

48 C. Jones (2007) "Fashion and faith in urban Indonesia," *Fashion Theory*, 11(2–3): 211–231, at p. 221.

49 Bucar, *Pious fashion*, p. 82.

50 Arti, a twenty-one-year-old UGM student, quoted in Ibid., p. 81.

51 C. Jones (2010) "Materializing piety: gendered anxieties about faithful consumption in contemporary urban Indonesia," *American Ethnologist* 37(4): 617–637, at p. 618.

52 Statement of *NooR* magazine, www.noor-magazine.com/tentang-kami/ (translation by author).

53 A. Heryanto (1999) "Where communism never dies: violence, trauma and narration in the last Cold War capitalist authoritarian state," *International Journal of Cultural Studies* 2(2): 147–177, at p. 177.

54 Bucar, *Pious fashion*, p. 118.

55 A. Schimmel (1982) "Women in mystical Islam," *Women's Studies International Forum*: 145–151, quote at p. 149.

56 M. Bano and H. Kalmbach (2012) *Women, leadership and mosques: changes in contemporary Islamic authority*. Leiden: Brill.

57 J. Hammer (2012) *American Muslim women, religious authority, and activism: more than a prayer*. Austin, TX: University of Texas Press, quotes on pp. 103, 104, 114.

58 M. Jaschok and J. Shui (2000) *The history of women's mosques in Chinese Islam: a mosque of their own*, Richmond: Curzon; J.H. Fewkes (2009) "A 'women's space' at the Indian Ocean Crossroads: women's mosques in the Maldives" in N. Kara (Ed.) *Gender at the crossroads: multi-disciplinary perspectives*, Famagusta, North Cyprus: Eastern Mediterranean University Press, pp. 277–284; H. Fathi (1997) "Otines: the unknown women clerics of Central Asian Islam," *Central Asian Survey* 16(1): 27–43; J. H. Fewkes (2018) "Perspectives from the field: interviews with the alima of Ladakh," *Himalaya* 38(2): 90–99; and K. Pemberton (2010) *Women mystics and Sufi shrines in India*, Columbia, SC: University of South Carolina Press.

59 A. Kull (2015) "At the forefront of a post-patriarchal Islamic education: female teachers in Indonesia" in H. Ahmed-Ghosh (Ed.) *Asian Muslim women: globalization and local realities*, Albany, NY: SUNY Press, p. 165.

60 R. Rinaldo (2013) *Mobilizing piety: Islam and feminism in Indonesia*, New York, NY: Oxford University Press, p. 65.

61 Fischer, *Proper Islamic consumption*, p. 61.

62 Stivens, "Sex, gender and the making of the new Malay middle classes," pp. 108–109.

63 Ibid., p. 93.

64 Ibid., p. 94

65 Ibid., p. 110.

66 S. Frisk (2009) *Submitting to God: women and Islam in urban Malaysia*, Seattle, WA: University of Washington Press, p. 158.

67 Ibid.

68 "Musawah Milestones," *Vision*, September 2017, p. 9.

69 A. Basarudin (2016) *Humanizing the sacred Sisters in Islam and the struggle for gender justice in Malaysia*, Seattle, WA: University of Washington Press, p. 153.

70 "Musawah Milestones," p. 9.

71 Ibid., p. 3.

72 Zainah Anwar (2015) in Z. Mir-Hosseini, M. al-Sharmani, and J. Rumminger (Ed.) *Men in Charge?* London: Oneworld, p. xi.

73 Ibid.

74 Zainah Anwar in Segran "The Rise of the Islamic Feminists," *The Nation*, December 4, 2013.

75 "Musawah Milestones," p. 9.

76 Zainah Anwar, "Bearer of Change," *The New York Times*, March 5, 2009

77 www.abc.net.au/radionational/programs/archived/nationalinterest/feminist-islam/3375734 (accessed January 5, 2019).

78 P. van Doorn-Harder (2006) *Women shaping Islam: reading the Quran in Indonesia*, Urbana, IL: University of Illinois Press, pp. 200–201.

79 S. White and M. U. Anshor (2008) "Islam and gender in contemporary Indonesia: public discourses on duties, rights and morality" in G. Fealy and S. White (Eds.) *Expressing Islam: Religious Life and Politics in Indonesia*, Singapore: ISEAS, pp. 137–158, at p. 139.
80 Rinaldo, *Mobilizing piety*, p. 76.
81 Fischer, *Proper Islamic consumption*, p. 65.
82 Rinaldo, *Mobilizing piety*, p. 62.

Chapter 9

1 J. Bennett (2006) *Crescent moon: Islamic art and civilisation in Southeast Asia*, Seattle, WA: University of Washington Press, quote on p. 5. See also http://nga.gov.au/crescentmoon/index.cfm (last accessed November 15, 2018). Some of the material presented in this chapter also appeared in C. Formichi (2016) "Islamic Studies or Asian Studies? Islam in Southeast Asia," *Muslim World* 106(4): 696–718.
2 J. Perlez, "Southeast Asia, too, is on map of Islamic art." quoting the associate curator of Islamic Art at the Metropolitan Museum of Art in New York www.nytimes.com/2006/03/16/arts/design/16isla.html?_r=0.
3 The Louvre's new wing on Islamic Arts appears to hold "18,000 treasures from an area stretching from Europe to India," also excluding Southeast Asia, www.france24.com/en/20120922-france-paris-louvre-museum-unveils-new-islamic-art-wing-culture-peace/.
4 www.metmuseum.org/about-the-met/curatorial-departments/asian-art.
5 Pew Research Center, "Religious composition by Country, 2010–2050," April 2, 2015 www.pewforum.org/2015/04/02/religious-projection-table/2010/percent/Asia-Pacific/ (accessed November 7, 2018). According to a Pew Forum report, in 2010, Asia (excluding the greater Middle East region) hosted 52 percent of the world's Muslim population, while only 20 percent resided in the MENA region.
6 C. Geertz, R. A. Shweder and B. Good (2005) *Clifford Geertz by his colleagues*, Chicago, IL: University of Chicago Press, p. 1.
7 R. Launay in O. Anjum (2007) "Islam as a discursive tradition: Talal Asad and his interlocutors," *Comparative Studies of South Asia, Africa and the Middle East* 27(3): 656–672, at p. 657.
8 C. Geertz (1960) *The Religion of Java*, Glencoe, IL: Free Press, pp. 160, 124–125.
9 Ibid., p. 160.
10 S.E. Harthoorn (1860) "De zending op Java en meer bepaald die van Malang" [The mission on Java and more specifically the one of Malang], *Mededeelingen van wege het Nederlandsche Zendelinggenootschap* 4: 105–137, quote at p. 111 (my own translation).
11 C. Poensen (1865) "Een en ander over den godsdienstigen toestand van den Javaan" [Some things about the religious condition of the Javanese], *Mededeelingen van wege het Nederlandsche Zendelinggenootschap* 9: 161–204, quote at p. 178 (my own translation).
12 See R. Heine-Geldern (1956[1942]) *Conceptions of state and kingship in Southeast Asia*, Ithaca, NY: Southeast Asia Program, Cornell University, p. 11.

13 J. C. van Leur, ([1941]1983) "The world of Southeast Asia, 1500–1650" in *Indonesian Trade and Society: Essays in Asian Social and Economic History*, Dordrecht: Foris Publications Holland, p. 169.

14 For an overview see A. M. Masquelier (2009) *Women and Islamic revival in a West African town*, Urbana, IL: Indiana University Press.

15 This was under the influence of Redfield's paradigm: R. Redfield (1956) *Peasant society and culture: an anthropological approach to civilization*, Chicago, IL: University of Chicago Press.

16 In the regional field of Islam in South Asia, paramount in bringing South Asia within the purview of Islamic Studies, directly addressing colonial constructions of Sufism and "Indian Islam" as syncretic and spurious has been the scholarship of A. Schimmel (1980) *Islam in the Indian subcontinent*, Leiden: Brill; B. D. Metcalf (1982) *Islamic revival in British India: Deoband, 1860–1900*, Princeton, NJ: Princeton University Press; K. P. Ewing (1988) *Shari'at and ambiguity in South Asian Islam*, Delhi: Oxford University Press; K. P. Ewing (1997) *Arguing sainthood: modernity, psychoanalysis and Islam*, Durham, NC: Duke University Press; and C. W. Ernst and B. B. Lawrence (2002) *Sufi martyrs of love: the Chishti Order in South Asia and beyond*, New York, NY: Palgrave. In the field of Southeast Asia, defining scholarship has been produced by A. H. Johns (1975) "Islam in Southeast Asia: reflections and new directions," *Indonesia* 19:33–56; M. C. Ricklefs (1978) "Six centuries of Islamization in Java" in N. Levtzion (Ed.) *Conversion to Islam*, New York, NY: Holmes & Meier; W. R. Roff (1971) *Islam as an agent of modernization: an episode in Kelantan history* Singapore: ISEAS; A. Reid (1967) "Nineteenth century pan-Islam in Indonesia and Malaysia," *The Journal of Asian Studies* 26(2): 267–283; A. C. Milner (1983) "Islam and the Muslim state" in M. B. Hooker (Ed.) *Islam in South-East Asia*, Leiden: Brill, pp. 23–49; J. R. Bowen (1988) "The transformation of an Indonesian property system: adat, Islam, and social change in the Gayo highlands," *American Ethnologist* 15(2): 274–293; M. B. Hooker (1972) *Adat laws in modern Malaya: land tenure, traditional government and religion*, Kuala Lumpur: Oxford University Press; M. B. Hooker (Ed.) (1983) *Islam in South-East Asia*, Leiden: Brill; M. R. Woodward (1989) *Islam in Java: normative piety and mysticism in the sultanate of Yogyakarta*, Tucson: University of Arizona; R. M. Feener and M. F. Laffan (2005) "Sufi scents across the Indian Ocean: Yemeni hagiography and the earliest history of Southeast Asian Islam," *Archipel* 70: 185–208; N. Florida (1995) *Writing the past, inscribing the future: history as prophecy in colonial Java*, Durham: Duke University Press; L. J. Sears (1996) *Shadows of empire: colonial discourse and Javanese tales*, Durham, NC: Duke University Press; R. Ricci (2011) *Islam translated: literature, conversion, and the Arabic cosmopolis of South and Southeast Asia*, Chicago, IL: University of Chicago Press; and E. Tagliacozzo (2009) *Southeast Asia and the Middle East: Islam, movement, and the longue durée*, Stanford, CA: Stanford University Press. For a detailed discussion see C. Formichi (2016) "Islamic Studies or Asian Studies? Islam in Southeast Asia," *Muslim World* 106(4): 696–718.

17 On Islamic ritual, see F. E. Peters (1994) *The hajj: the Muslim pilgrimage to Mecca and the holy places*, Princeton, NJ: Princeton University Press; and S. D. Goitein (2004) "Ramadan, the Muslim month of fasting" in

G. R. Hawting (Ed.) *The Development of Islamic Ritual*, Burlington, VT: Ashgate, pp. 151–171. For an overview of incorporation of Sasanian, Persian, Hellenic, and Byzantine customs and socio-political frames of reference, see R.M. Eaton (1990) *Islamic history as global history*, Washington, DC: American Historical Association.

18 For an overview of these approaches, see S. McLoughlin (2007) "Islam(s) in context: orientalism and the anthropology of Muslim societies and cultures," *Journal of Beliefs & Values* 28(3): 273–296.

19 B. Lawrence (2002) "Islamicate civilization: the view from Asia" in B. M. Wheeler (Ed.) *Teaching Islam*, Oxford: Oxford University Press, p. 63.

20 Eaton, *Islamic history as global history*.

21 E.g. J. L. Esposito, J. O. Voll, and O. Bakar (2008) *Asian Islam in the 21st century*, Oxford: Oxford University Press; J. Gedacht and R. M. Feener (2018) *Challenging cosmopolitanism: coercion, mobility and displacement in Islamic Asia*, Edinburgh: Edinburgh University Press; R. M. Feener and T. Sevea (2009) *Islamic connections: Muslim societies in South and Southeast Asia*, Singapore: Institute of Southeast Asian Studies; and M. Cooke and B. B. Lawrence (2005) *Muslim networks: from medieval scholars to modern feminists*, Chapel Hill, NC: University of North Carolina Press.

22 Most prolific have been Rohan Gunaratna and Arabinda Acharya, among others.

23 "National Defense Education Act of 1958," Committee on Education and Labor, Conference Report submitted by Graham Arthur Barden, August 21, 1958.

24 Formichi, "Islamic Studies or Asian Studies?" p. 717. It also marginalized the study of Islam within the religious studies paradigm, emphasizing political sciences and anthropology; only one paper presented at the American Academy of Religion in 1973 addressed Islam. For the trajectory of Islamic Studies within the broader Study of Religion, see C. W. Ernst (1998) "The Study of Religion and the Study of Islam," paper presented at the *Integrating Islamic Studies in Liberal Arts Curricula* conference, University of Washington.

25 M. F. Laffan, *The makings of Indonesian Islam: orientalism and the narration of a Sufi past*, Princeton, NJ: Princeton University Press, p. 128.

26 M. Shatanawi (2014) *Islam at the Tropenmuseum*. Arnhem: L. M. Publishers, p. 31.

27 E.g. D. F. Eickelman (1982) "The study of Islam in local contexts," *Contributions to Asian Studies* 17: 1–16.

28 Ibn Battuta and H. A. R. Gibb (1953) *Travels in Asia and Africa 1325–1354* [*Tuḥfat an-nuẓẓār fī garā'ib al-amṣār wa-'aǧā'ib al-asfār*], transl. and selected by H.A.R. Gibb. A longer excerpt of Ibn Battuta's travels to China is included in Chapter 1.

29 R. W. Bulliet (1994) *Islam: the view from the edge*, New York, NY: Columbia University Press, p. 9.

Index

New Approaches to Asian History